Microsoft 365 Security and Compliance for Administrators

A definitive guide to planning, implementing, and maintaining Microsoft 365 security posture

Sasha Kranjac

Omar Kudović

Microsoft 365 Security and Compliance for Administrators

Group Product Manager: Pavan Ramchandani
Publishing Product Manager: Prachi Sawant
Book Project Manager: Ashwin Dinesh Kharwa
Senior Editor: Sujata Tripathi
Technical Editor: Irfa Ansari
Copy Editor: Safis Editing
Indexer: Hemangini Bari
Production Designer: Ponraj Dhandapani
DevRel Marketing Coordinator: Marylou De Mello

First published: March 2024

Production reference: 1140324

Published by Packt Publishing Ltd.
Grosvenor House
11 St Paul's Square
Birmingham
B3 1RB, UK

ISBN 978-1-83763-837-6

www.packtpub.com

To my loving family. None of this would be possible and nothing would make sense without your love and support. Love you all.

– Sasha Kranjac

To my beloved wife and cherished daughter, my deepest gratitude for your support on this incredible journey. Thank you for all your support and long live Rockabilly. HZ87 forever!

– Omar Kudović

Contributors

About the authors

Sasha Kranjac is the CEO of Kloudatech and the CEO of Kranjac Consulting and Training. As a Microsoft Partner, an AWS Partner, and a CompTIA Authorized Delivery Partner, his companies specialize in IT training and consulting, cloud security architecture and engineering, civil engineering, and CAD design.

Sasha is a Microsoft Regional Director, Microsoft MVP in two categories (Security and Azure), a Microsoft Certified Trainer, MCT Regional Lead, Certified EC-Council Instructor, CompTIA Instructor, a frequent speaker at various international conferences, user groups, and events, and book author.

I want to thank my loving family for riding the roller-coaster of life together. You are the ones who give the ride meaning; it is because of you that the ride makes sense, and it is because of you the ride is fun.

Omar Kudović is a senior system engineer at SYS Company d.o.o., Sarajevo. With over 15 years immersed in the dynamic field of IT, his expertise has been focused on cloud solutions (Microsoft 365 and Azure) and security and compliance. Over the past decade, he has dedicated efforts to seamlessly integrating cloud services and application solutions within the complex landscape of business enterprises, specifically emphasizing security and compliance, endpoint protection, audio, video, voice, and messaging. During the last 12 years, Omar has been awarded the Microsoft MVP award for the Office365 Apps and Services category. He is also a regular speaker at international IT conferences, user groups, and events. On a more personal note, he finds enjoyment in the world of Hi-Fi audiophiles, rockabilly music and culture, and fine wine.

About the reviewers

Rahul Singh is a seasoned IT professional and Chief Teaching Officer at SV9 Academy, which is a Microsoft Learning Partner. Rahul has 18 years of experience in the IT field, as of 2024, and holds numerous certifications in the Microsoft technological stack. In addition, Rahul has also been an MCT since 2020. He is deeply passionate about technology and demystifying complex technical architectures using various pedagogies and a systems-based learning mechanism, making learning an enjoyable and enriching experience.

With the ever-changing technical world, testing and reviewing technical content can be a very daunting task, requiring perseverance and patience. I would like to take this opportunity to thank my lovely parents, who I have been blessed with by the Divine, as, without their support, I would not have been able to be a part of this amazing project from Packt.

Mustafa Toroman is a technology professional and the Chief Technology Officer at **run.events**, a company that provides a platform for organizing and managing events. He has over 20 years of experience in the IT industry and has held various technical and leadership positions in companies around the world. He has a deep understanding of software development, cloud computing, and IT infrastructure management. Mustafa is a Microsoft MVP, a frequent speaker at technology conferences and events, and also a community leader organizing meetups and events. He is also a published author and has written several books on Microsoft technologies and cloud computing.

Steve Miles, aka *SMiles*, is CTO at Westcoast Cloud, part of a multi-billion turnover IT distributor based in the UK and Ireland. Steve holds 25+ Microsoft certifications, one of which is **Microsoft 365 Certified: Administrator Expert**, he is also a Microsoft MVP (Most Valuable Professional), MCT (Microsoft Certified Trainer), as well as an Alibaba Cloud MVP. With 25+ years of technology experience, and a previous military career in engineering, signals and communications. Amongst other books, Steve is the author of *Windows 11 for Enterprise Administrators*.

He is also a petrolhead and can also be found tinkering on cars when he is not writing.

This is my contribution to the worldwide technical learning community, and I would like to thank all of you who are investing your valuable time in committing to reading this book and learning these skills.

Rio Hindle is a Cloud Security Microsoft MVP with 5 years of experience in this field and 8 years of experience in information technology. He also has certifications for Microsoft services in Microsoft 365, Azure, and Cybersecurity. He has delivered training on various solution areas to many organizations, from beginner to advanced-level courses. He has worked in different areas of the industry, including end user, reseller channels, and vendor spaces, with global networks, data and app security vendors, and hardware distribution. He has held roles such as cloud practice lead, service desk manager, and head of technical services. He now works for a top muti-cloud distributor in the UK and Ireland in a cloud and hybrid technology leadership role.

Thanks to Steve Miles for your valuable guidance and support. Also, a big thanks to my current employer for giving me this opportunity.

Table of Contents

Part 2: Microsoft 365 Security

3

4

5

Getting Started with Microsoft Purview 165

6

Microsoft Defender for Cloud Apps 211

7

Microsoft Defender Vulnerability Management 253

8

Microsoft Defender for Identity 279

Part 3: Microsoft 365 Governance and Compliance

9

10

11

Preface

Microsoft 365 is a complex, comprehensive, ever-evolving, and expanding suite, or collection of products, covering broad aspects of cloud computing, work, communication, and collaboration. In summary, it is huge, and it is always changing. You know what they say about cloud and cloud-related products – the only constant thing is change! Microsoft 365 and its related products and features are not an exception to this *rule* or saying. We wanted to include in the book everything that has anything to do with security and compliance in Microsoft 365, and we were very enthusiastic, motivated, and thrilled. However, it was easier to say and wish than to make it happen. There was – and still is – simply too much to include, too many features, products, capabilities, and so many things to mention, introduce and explain.

We tried to focus our time and energy on addressing all changes, ultimately deciding to bring you the most valuable and useful security and governance knowledge from our day-to-day, real-life, hands-on working experience with Microsoft 365. Compromises were made in what to include and what to leave out of the book, and we hope it will help you to sharpen your skills and become a better Microsoft 365 security and governance administrator, specialist, or user.

Who this book is for

This book is for security engineers, technical engineers, consultants, solution and cloud architects, systems administrators, security professionals, security analysts, IT professionals, system architects and SecOps teams working with Microsoft 365 security solutions, and Microsoft 365 security and compliance professionals, all looking to improve their security and compliance posture in Microsoft 365. Individuals, businesses, enterprises, and organizations of various sizes and industries face increasingly hostile cyber-threat environments and complex compliance landscapes.

What this book covers

Chapter 1, Getting Started with Microsoft 365 Security and Compliance, introduces what Microsoft 365 is, what it can do, and what it offers. You will also learn about plans, licensing, and how Microsoft 365 helps you comply with various regulations and standards.

Chapter 2, The Role of Microsoft Entra ID in Microsoft 365 Security, covers Microsoft Entra ID's plans and features, roles and groups, and Entra ID protection.

Chapter 3, Microsoft Defender for Office 365, discusses Microsoft Defender for Office 365 and how it protects email and collaboration content.

Chapter 4, Microsoft Defender for Endpoint, presents vast endpoint protection capabilities, essential features, and configuration steps.

Chapter 5, Getting Started with Microsoft Purview, familiarizes you with Microsoft Purview configuration, data classification, data search, and Data Loss Prevention features.

Chapter 6, Microsoft Defender for Cloud Apps, presents cloud apps protection capabilities with Microsoft 365, configuration, Oauth apps and files management, governance, and policies in Defender for Cloud Apps.

Chapter 7, Microsoft Defender Vulnerability Management, explains vulnerability management features in Microsoft and what to do when an inventory has weaknesses, analyzes recommendations, and looks at how to remediate vulnerabilities.

Chapter 8, Microsoft Defender for Identity, introduces on-premises identity protection capabilities, and the configuration and management of Defender for Identity.

Chapter 9, Microsoft Purview Insider Risk Management, discusses insider risk management, information barriers, and communication compliance.

Chapter 10, Microsoft Purview Information Protection, explores information protection, labeling, classification capabilities, as well as configuration steps.

Chapter 11, Understanding the Lifecycle of Auditing and Records, explains auditing and records life cycle management in Microsoft 365, including data retention, archiving, e-discovery, and data holds.

To get the most out of this book

To get started with the book, you should have access to a Microsoft 365 subscription and the products mentioned in the book. Any subscription will work, as long as you have access to the licensed products or features – a trial subscription or a commercial subscription.

You should have some basic, fundamental knowledge of Microsoft 365 generally, and fundamental knowledge of security and compliance principles. Additionally, some fundamental knowledge of relevant Microsoft 365 security and compliance services and products is desirable and beneficial, but not required.

Software/hardware covered in the book	Operating system requirements
Microsoft 365	Windows, macOS, or Linux

Microsoft published a full comparison (PDF) document of Microsoft 365 plans and features on this page: `https://www.microsoft.com/en/microsoft-365/enterprise/e5`. Consult the information available online and in the full comparison document to find out more about products and licenses. More information about products and licenses is available in *Chapter 1, Getting Started with Microsoft 365 Security and Compliance.*

Conventions used

There are a number of text conventions used throughout this book.

`Code in text`: Indicates code words in text, database table names, folder names, filenames, file extensions, pathnames, dummy URLs, user input, and Twitter handles. Here is an example:

```
IdentityLogonEvents

| where TimeGenerated >= ago (7d)

| where UserPrincipalName == "user name@domain"
```

Bold: Indicates a new term, an important word, or words that you see on screen. For instance, words in menus or dialog boxes appear in **bold**. Here is an example: "In the Microsoft 365 Defender portal, select **Permissions**, then **Settings**, followed by **Microsoft 365 Defender**. Select **Permissions and roles** to view the available options."

> **Tips or important notes**
> Appear like this.

Get in touch

Feedback from our readers is always welcome.

General feedback: If you have questions about any aspect of this book, email us at `customercare@packtpub.com` and mention the book title in the subject of your message.

Errata: Although we have taken every care to ensure the accuracy of our content, mistakes do happen. If you have found a mistake in this book, we would be grateful if you would report this to us. Please visit `www.packtpub.com/support/errata` and fill in the form.

Piracy: If you come across any illegal copies of our works in any form on the internet, we would be grateful if you would provide us with the location address or website name. Please contact us at `copyright@packt.com` with a link to the material.

If you are interested in becoming an author: If there is a topic that you have expertise in and you are interested in either writing or contributing to a book, please visit `authors.packtpub.com`.

Share Your Thoughts

Once you've read *Microsoft 365 Security and Compliance for Administrators*, we'd love to hear your thoughts! Scan the QR code below to go straight to the Amazon review page for this book and share your feedback.

`https://packt.link/r/1837638373`

Your review is important to us and the tech community and will help us make sure we're delivering excellent quality content.

Download a free PDF copy of this book

Thanks for purchasing this book!

Do you like to read on the go but are unable to carry your print books everywhere?

Is your eBook purchase not compatible with the device of your choice?

Don't worry, now with every Packt book you get a DRM-free PDF version of that book at no cost.

Read anywhere, any place, on any device. Search, copy, and paste code from your favorite technical books directly into your application.

The perks don't stop there, you can get exclusive access to discounts, newsletters, and great free content in your inbox daily

Follow these simple steps to get the benefits:

1. Scan the QR code or visit the link below

`https://packt.link/free-ebook/9781837638376`

2. Submit your proof of purchase
3. That's it! We'll send your free PDF and other benefits to your email directly

Part 1:
Introduction to Microsoft 365

In this part, we introduce you to Microsoft 365, explaining what it can do, and what it offers. You will learn about currently available plans in Microsoft 365, licensing, and how Microsoft 365 helps you comply with various regulations and standards. Furthermore, we will cover Microsoft Entra ID plans and features, its roles and groups, as well as Entra ID protection.

This part includes the following chapters:

- *Chapter 1, Getting Started with Microsoft 365 Security and Compliance*
- *Chapter 2, The Role of Microsoft Entra ID in Microsoft 365 Security*

1

Getting Started with Microsoft 365 Security and Compliance

Microsoft 365 is a subscription-based service from Microsoft that provides users with a suite of applications and services for productivity, collaboration, and communication, helping businesses and individuals work more efficiently. It includes popular software such as Microsoft Word, Excel, PowerPoint, and Outlook, as well as cloud-based services such as OneDrive and SharePoint.

In this chapter, we are going to cover the following main topics:

- Introduction to Microsoft 365 offers, plans, and licenses
- Introduction to Microsoft 365 security
- Introduction to Microsoft 365 compliance

In this chapter, readers will learn what Microsoft 365 is and its capabilities and products, plans, and offers. Additionally, you will learn about Microsoft 365 security, Microsoft 365 Defender, and related security products. Finally, we will conclude this chapter by introducing Microsoft 365's comprehensive compliance features.

Technical requirements

Microsoft 365 is a subscription-based service and, to try and experience the functionality of each product and service, a user must have an appropriate license. It does not matter whether a user has a trial license, or they have a "regular" or paid license – as long as they have a license assigned, they can enjoy the proper product.

Introduction to Microsoft 365 offers, plans, and licenses

More than a decade ago, Microsoft introduced Office 365, a **software as a service** (**SaaS**) offering, as a natural evolution from the very popular business productivity suite. The suite, or the bundle, consisted of core productivity desktop-based applications such as Outlook, Word, Excel, PowerPoint, OneNote, and Access, including server-based services such as SharePoint, Exchange, and Skype for Business.

It became obvious that productivity encompasses and needs more than just productivity tools. That led to a logical move by Microsoft to include more essential products and services and bring together Windows and **Enterprise Mobility + Security** (**EM+S**) to form Microsoft 365.

Microsoft 365 is a name for Microsoft's cloud-based service, that is, a collection of cloud-based services with common denominators including enhanced user productivity, efficient collaboration, and communication, while keeping data and devices secure wherever they are, whether that be in the office, at home, or on the go.

One of the main benefits of Microsoft 365 is that it allows users to access their files and applications from anywhere on any device. This is made possible through the integration of cloud-based services such as OneDrive, which allows users to store and share files online. This means that users can access their files from a desktop computer, laptop, tablet, or smartphone, as long as they have an internet connection.

Another benefit of Microsoft 365 is the ability to collaborate and communicate with others in real-time. Applications such as SharePoint and Teams allow users to share and co-author documents, as well as participate in virtual meetings and chat with their colleagues. This makes it easy for teams to work together, regardless of their physical location.

In addition to the productivity and collaboration features, Microsoft 365 also includes security and compliance tools to help protect users' data and ensure compliance with regulatory requirements. For example, it uses machine learning and behavioral analysis to detect and block malicious emails, links, and files, and can also help to identify and respond to security threats in near real-time. Among many features that Microsoft 365 offers is **Data Loss Prevention** (**DLP**), which helps to prevent sensitive data from being shared or leaked. DLP is just one of the numerous Microsoft 365 security features; we will take a closer look and learn more about them later in the book.

In terms of compliance, Microsoft 365 includes several features to help organizations meet regulatory requirements. For example, it includes eDiscovery, which allows administrators to search for and export data from email, SharePoint, and Teams to comply with legal and regulatory requests. Additionally, it also includes retention and archiving capabilities, which allow organizations to retain and archive data for compliance purposes.

In general, Microsoft 365 is a comprehensive solution for businesses and individuals looking to increase their productivity, collaboration, and communication while also ensuring the security of their data. With its range of applications and services, it provides users with everything they need to work effectively, whether they are in the office or working remotely.

As a subscription-based service, Microsoft 365 offers subscription plans and bundles tailored for personal use, small businesses, enterprises, schools, educational and governmental users, and more.

While classic Office applications such as Word, Excel, Outlook, and PowerPoint are available as a one-time purchase via Office Home & Business 2021 or Office Home & Student 2021, these do not include some popular capabilities and products such as cloud storage or Microsoft Teams.

Microsoft 365 plans and components

There are four fundamental Microsoft 365 plans groups, each containing two or more Microsoft 365 plans:

- **Microsoft 365 For Home plans**: These include the following plans:
  - Microsoft 365 Family
  - Microsoft 365 Personal
  - Office Home & Business 2021
  - Office Home & Home 2021
- **Microsoft 365 For Small and Medium Businesses plans**: These include the following plans:
  - Microsoft 365 Business Basic
  - Microsoft 365 Business Standard
  - Microsoft 365 Business Premium
  - Microsoft 365 Apps for Business
- **Microsoft 365 For Enterprise plans**: These include the following plans:
  - Microsoft 365 E3
  - Microsoft 365 E5
  - Microsoft 365 Apps for Enterprise
- **Microsoft 365 For Frontline Workers plans**: These include the following plans:
  - Microsoft 365 F1
  - Microsoft 365 F3
  - Microsoft 365 F5

Other Microsoft 365 and Office 365 offers include plans specifically suited for governments, education (academic institutions), nonprofit organizations, the US government, and 21Vianet-operated areas (China).

Microsoft 365 is comprised of three components, and each component has its own tier, such as E3, F3, or A3, with different capabilities included:

- **Office 365**: This includes a cloud-based suite of productivity applications and services, information protection capabilities such as message encryption, rights management, and data loss prevention for files and email messages; compliance capabilities such as mailbox litigation hold and eDiscovery; and data analytics with powerful visualization
- **Windows Enterprise**: This includes advanced features aimed and designed specifically for larger organizations and enterprises, such as operating system deployment and update control, device and application management capabilities, universal print, **Microsoft Defender for Endpoint**, and advanced protection against security threats
- **EM+S**: This is a mobility management and security platform that includes advanced identity and access management, endpoint management, information protection capabilities, and advanced identity-related security enhancements

Microsoft 365 comprises many products and features, such as the web, mobile, and desktop versions of Word, Excel, PowerPoint, and Outlook, advanced security, tools to create personalized documents, cyber threat protection, and access and data control features. Depending on organizational size, Microsoft has gathered and included a variety of products in different product packages, or plans, and we will introduce the most important and most prevalent ones.

> **Products and features**
>
> While products included in Microsoft 365 plans have many features, we have put an emphasis on security and compliance capabilities. That means we deliberately have not included tables and descriptions of all features, with the intention of preserving readability, decluttering the book content, and focusing on security and compliance-related products.

Microsoft 365 for small and medium-sized businesses

Microsoft 365 Business plans are specifically adapted to the needs of small and medium businesses, for up to 300 users. If your organization has a need to license more than 300 users, you need to consider using Microsoft 365 Enterprise licenses.

The following table shows you the security and compliance capabilities and features of Microsoft 365 user subscription suites for small and medium-sized businesses:

Microsoft 365 Suites for Small and Medium-Sized Businesses			
	Basic	**Standard**	**Premium**
Threat Protection			
Microsoft Defender for Business			•
Microsoft Defender Exploit Guard			•
Microsoft Defender Credential Guard			•
BitLocker and BitLocker To Go			•
Windows Information Protection			•
Microsoft Defender for Office 365 Plan 1			•
Identity and Access Management			
Microsoft Entra ID 1			•
User provisioning			•
Cloud user self-service password change	•	•	•
Cloud user self-service password reset		•	•
Hybrid user self-service password change/reset with on-premises write-back			•
Conditional Access			•
On-premises Active Directory sync for single sign-on (SSO)			•
Windows Hello for Business			•
Cloud Access Security Broker			
Microsoft Defender for Cloud Apps Discovery			•
Information Protection			
Azure Information Protection			Plan 1
Manual, default, and mandatory sensitivity labeling in Office 365			•
Manual labeling with the AIP app and plugin			•
Data Loss Prevention (DLP) for emails and files			•
Basic Message Encryption			•
Data Lifecycle Management			
Manual retention labels			•
Basic org-wide or location-wide retention policies			•
Teams message retention policies	•	•	•

Microsoft 365 Suites for Small and Medium-Sized Businesses			
	Basic	**Standard**	**Premium**
eDiscovery and Auditing			
Content Search	•	•	•
Litigation Hold			•
Audit (Standard)	•	•	•
Security and Compliance			
Microsoft 365 Information Protection and Governance	+1	+1	+
Microsoft 365 E5 Insider Risk Management	+	+	+
Microsoft 365 E5 eDiscovery and Audit	+	+	+
Microsoft Defender for Business	+	+	•
Microsoft Defender for Business servers add-ons for Microsoft Defender for Business	+5	+5	+5
Microsoft Defender for Identity	+	+	+
Microsoft Defender for Office 365 Plan 1	+	+	•
Microsoft Defender for Office 365 Plan 2	+	+	+
Microsoft Defender for Cloud Apps	+	+	+
App governance add-on for Microsoft Defender for Cloud Apps	+2	+2	+2
Microsoft Defender for Endpoint Plan 1	+	+	+
Microsoft Defender for Endpoint Plan 2	+	+	+
Premium Assessments add-on for Compliance Manager3	+	+	+
Microsoft Entra ID 1	+	+	•
Microsoft Entra ID 2	+	+	+
Microsoft Intune Plan 1	+	+	•
Microsoft Intune Plan 2	+4	+4	+
Microsoft Intune Suite	+4	+4	+
Microsoft Intune Remote Help	+4	+4	+
Microsoft Purview Data Loss Prevention (for email and files)	+	+	•
Exchange Archiving	+	+	•

Table 1.1 – Microsoft 365 Suites for small and medium-sized businesses

For the current list of features in Microsoft 365 Business plans, see the following page: `https://www.microsoft.com/en/microsoft-365/business/compare-all-microsoft-365-business-products-d?market=af`

Here is what the different symbols in the table mean:

- • = Included in the plan.
- + = Can be added to the plan.
- [1] Requires EMS E3 or Azure Information Protection Plan 1 standalone.
- [2] Requires **Microsoft Defender for Cloud Apps**.
- [3] Available assessment details, which can be found at `https://learn.microsoft.com/en-us/microsoft-365/compliance/compliance-manager-templates-list?view=o365-worldwide#premium-templates` and `https://learn.microsoft.com/en-us/office365/servicedescriptions/microsoft-365-service-descriptions/microsoft-365-tenantlevel-services-licensing-guidance/microsoft-365-security-compliance-licensing-guidance#compliance-manager`.
- [4] Requires Microsoft Intune Plan 1.
- [5] Requires Microsoft Defender for Business or Microsoft 365 Business Premium. The maximum quantity/seat cap is 60 licenses per customer.

Microsoft 365 for Enterprise plans represent a suite of products bundled and tailored specifically for the enterprise market, with some unique capabilities relevant to organizations with a larger employee base.

Microsoft 365 for enterprise

Microsoft 365 for Enterprise suites contain solutions and products designed for and targeted primarily at large organizations, although small businesses or medium-sized businesses can take advantage of these more advanced security, compliance, and productivity solutions as well.

Local and productivity services include content and productivity applications such as Microsoft 365 Apps for Enterprise with enterprise deployment and update options, Exchange Online, SharePoint Online, Skype for Business, Microsoft Teams, and Yammer, including simplified and advanced deployment, management, and servicing options such as Windows Enterprise deployment with an upgrade in place and Autopilot, plus auto-enrollment of Windows PCs and devices.

Security options comprise possibilities that span operating systems, device management, and advanced security services and include identity and access management, information protection, threat protection, and security management products and features such as Microsoft Defender for Office 365, SharePoint and Exchange Online access policies, **Azure Information Protection** (**AIP**), Microsoft 365 DLP policies, Microsoft Defender for Endpoint, Windows Hello for Business, **Windows Information Protection** (**WIP**), Microsoft Intune, device-based Conditional Access policies, Microsoft Entra ID **Privileged Identity Management** (**PIM**), **Advanced Threat Analytics** (**ATA**), **Microsoft Defender for Identity**, and Microsoft Cloud App Security Azure Multi-Factor Authentication.

> **Note**
>
> Microsoft stopped developing WIP from July 2022. WIP will still work on the Windows versions that support it, but it will not get any new features or updates. Future Windows versions will not have WIP. Microsoft suggests that you use **Microsoft Purview Information Protection** and **Microsoft Purview Data Loss Prevention** for your data protection needs. Purview makes it easier to set up and offers more advanced capabilities.

When customers and information technology professionals think about Microsoft 365 Enterprise plans, they usually refer to two major plans:

- Microsoft 365 E3
- Microsoft 365 E5

Though there are, of course, more than two Microsoft 365 plans, some that even Microsoft sometimes likes to classify as plans with Enterprise-like features:

- Microsoft 365 F1
- Microsoft 365 F3
- Microsoft 365 F5

For Microsoft 365 Enterprise plans customers, several add-ons are available:

- Identity & Threat Protection
- Information Protection & Governance
- Compliance
- Insider Risk Management
- eDiscovery & Audit
- Security

Companies who want to bring their security posture to a higher level can decide to invest in EM+S suites, which include advanced identity and access management, endpoint management, and information protection products.

Conveniently, the following tables compare Microsoft 365 E3, E5, E5 Security, and E5 Compliance plans along with EM+S E3 and E5 plans and show their characteristics.

The following table shows the comprehensive information protection, data loss prevention, and threat protection capabilities in Microsoft 365, including a list of numerous products carrying the Microsoft Defender name:

	Microsoft 365				Enterprise Mobility + Security	
	E3	E5	E5 Security[1]	E5 Compliance[1]	E3	E5
Information Protection						
Azure Information Protection Plan 1	•				•	
Azure Information Protection Plan 2		•		•		•
Manual, default, and mandatory sensitivity labeling in Microsoft 365 apps	•	•			•	•
Automatic sensitivity labeling in Microsoft 365 apps		•		•		•
Manual labeling with the AIP app and plugin	•	•			•	•
Automatic labeling in the AIP plugin		•		•		•
Default sensitivity labels for SharePoint document libraries		•		•		
Automatic sensitivity labels in Exchange, SharePoint, and OneDrive		•		•		
Sensitivity labels based on machine learning/trainable classifiers/exact data match		•		•		
Sensitivity labels for containers in Microsoft 365	•	•				
Basic message encryption	•	•			•2	•2
Advanced message encryption		•		•		•2
Customer Key		•		•		
Personal Data Encryption	•	•				
Data Loss Prevention (DLP)						
DLP for emails and files	•	•				
DLP for Teams chat		•		•		
Endpoint DLP		•		•		
Threat Protection						
Microsoft Defender Antimalware	•	•				
Microsoft Defender Firewall	•	•				
Microsoft Defender Exploit Guard	•	•				
Microsoft Defender Credential Guard	•	•				

	Microsoft 365				Enterprise Mobility + Security	
	E3	E5	E5 Security1	E5 Compliance1	E3	E5
BitLocker and BitLocker To Go	•	•				
Microsoft Defender for Endpoint Plan 1	•	•				
Microsoft Defender for Endpoint Plan 2		•	•			
Microsoft Defender for Identity		•	•			•
Microsoft Defender for Office 365 Plan 2		•	•			
Microsoft Defender Application Guard for Edge	•	•				
Microsoft Defender Application Guard for Office		•	•			
Safe Documents		•	•			
Cloud Access Security Broker						
Microsoft Defender for Cloud Apps Discovery	•	•			•	•
Microsoft Defender for Cloud Apps		•	•	•		•
Office 365 Cloud App Security			•	•		•

Table 1.2 – Microsoft 365 plans Information Protection, DLP and Threat Protection features

This table shows the broad identity and access management, as well as endpoint and application management, capabilities available in Microsoft 365 suites:

	Microsoft 365				**Enterprise Mobility + Security**	
	E3	**E5**	**E5 Security1**	**E5 Compliance1**	**E3**	**E5**
Identity and Access Management						
Microsoft Entra ID P1	•				•	
Microsoft Entra ID P2		•	•			•
User provisioning	•	•	•		•	•
Cloud user self-service password change	•	•	•		•	•

	Microsoft 365				Enterprise Mobility + Security	
	E3	E5	E5 Security1	E5 Compliance1	E3	E5
Cloud user self-service password reset	•	•	•		•	•
Hybrid user self-service password change/reset with on-premises write-back	•	•	•		•	•
Advanced security reports	•	•	•		•	•
Multifactor authentication	•	•	•		•	•
Conditional Access	•	•	•		•	•
Risk-based Conditional Access/Identity Protection		•	•			•
PIM		•	•			•
Access reviews		•	•			•
Entitlement management		•	•			•
Microsoft 365 Groups	•	•				
On-premises Active Directory sync for SSO	•	•			•	•
DirectAccess supported	•	•				
Windows Hello for Business	•	•				
Microsoft ATA	•	•			•	•
Endpoint and Application Management						
Microsoft Intune Plan 1	•	•			•	•
Mobile Device Management	•	•			•	•
Mobile Application Management	•	•			•	•
Windows Autopilot	•	•			•[3]	•[3]
Group Policy support	•	•				
Cloud Policy service for Microsoft 365	•	•				
Shared computer activation for Microsoft 365 apps	•	•				
Endpoint analytics	•	•			•	•
Cortana management	•	•				

Table 1.3 – Microsoft 365 plans IAM, and Endpoint and Application Management features

Thorough insider risk management, governance, and records management, together with discovery and auditing features in Microsoft 365 are listed in the following table:

	Microsoft 365				Enterprise Mobility + Security	
	E3	E5	E5 Security1	E5 Compliance1	E3	E5
Data Lifecycle Management						
Manual retention labels	•	•			•	•
Basic org-wide or location-wide retention labels	•	•				
Rule-based automatic retention policies		•				
Machine learning-based retention		•				
Teams message retention policies	•	•				
Records management		•				
eDiscovery and Auditing						
Content search	•	•				
eDiscovery (Standard) (including Hold and Export)	•	•				
Litigation hold	•	•				
eDiscovery (Premium)		•				
Audit (Standard)	•	•				
Audit (Premium)		•				
Insider Risk Management						
Microsoft Purview Insider Risk Management		•				
Communication Compliance		•				
Information Barriers		•				
Customer Lockbox		•				
Privileged access management		•				

Table 1.4 – Microsoft 365 plans DLM, eDiscovery, and IRM features

Here is what the different symbols in the table mean:

- • = Included in the plan
- [1] - Requires Microsoft 365 E3 (or Office 365 E3 and EM+S E3)
- [2] - Does not include an Exchange email service
- [3] – Does not include a Windows license

Along with product and feature placement into suites and plans, it is important to know that if you have already purchased a plan license, there is a possibility to acquire a license for a product or a feature as a separate license. That way, flexible options exist to tailor and adjust licensing options and product licensing tightly to your company's requirements and needs. Additionally, licensing is available as a monthly subscription, as well as a yearly commitment, enabling you to save additional costs.

Microsoft 365 add-ons

Microsoft 365 plans include additional options as add-ons, where this table displays add-on subscriptions for E3 and E5 plans:

Microsoft 365 Add-On Subscriptions		
	E3	E5
Microsoft 365 E5 Security	+	•
Microsoft 365 E5 Compliance	+	•
Microsoft 365 E5 Information Protection and Governance	+	•
Microsoft 365 E5 Insider Risk Management	+	•
Forensic evidence add-on for Insider Risk Management	N/A	•
Microsoft 365 E5 eDiscovery and Audit	+	•
Microsoft Defender for Identity	+	•
Microsoft Defender for Office 365 Plan 1	+	•
Microsoft Defender for Office 365 Plan 2	+	•
Microsoft Defender for Cloud Apps	+	•
App governance add-on for Microsoft Defender for Cloud Apps	+1	+
Microsoft Defender for Endpoint Plan 1	•	•
Microsoft Defender for Endpoint Plan 2	+	•
Microsoft Defender Vulnerability Management	+2	+
Premium Assessments add-on for Compliance Manager3	+	+
Priva Privacy Risk Management	+	+
Priva Subject Rights Requests	+	+
Compliance Program for Microsoft Cloud	+	+

Microsoft 365 Add-On Subscriptions		
	E3	E5
Microsoft Purview Data Loss Prevention (for email and files)	•	•
Exchange Archiving	•	•
Microsoft Entra ID P1	•	•
Microsoft Entra ID P2	+	•
Microsoft Intune Plan 1	•	•
Microsoft Intune Plan 2	+	+
Microsoft Intune Suite	+	+
Microsoft Intune Remote Help	+	+
10-year audit log retention	N/A	+

Table 1.5 – Add ons for Microsoft 365 E3 and E5 plans

Here is what the different symbols in the table mean:

- • = Included in the plan
- + = Can be added to the plan
- **N/A** = Not available for the plan
- [1] - Requires Microsoft Defender for Cloud Apps
- [2] - Requires Microsoft Defender for Endpoint Plan 2
- [3] - Available assessment details are available at `https://learn.microsoft.com/en-us/microsoft-365/compliance/compliance-manager-templates-list?view=o365-worldwide#premium-templates` and `https://learn.microsoft.com/en-us/office365/servicedescriptions/microsoft-365-service-descriptions/microsoft-365-tenantlevel-services-licensing-guidance/microsoft-365-security-compliance-licensing-guidance#compliance-manager`

Microsoft has provided flexible licensing options and plans tailored to a variety of business, academic, and not-for-profit users, as well as individual licensing options. However, you should always check the current plans, products, features, characteristics, and prices whenever considering purchasing licenses for plans and products.

Microsoft 365 and Office 365 service descriptions

For an up-to-date and very detailed overview of Microsoft 365 and Office 365 service descriptions, please visit the official Microsoft page at `https://learn.microsoft.com/en-us/office365/servicedescriptions/office-365-service-descriptions-technet-library`.

Microsoft 365 licensing

Microsoft 365 is licensed on a **User Subscription License** (USL) principle, where each user that accesses Microsoft 365 services and/or software requires a license or a USL. If you meet the prerequisites for a plan, you can use any combination of Microsoft 365 plans.

Licensing Program is the name of a channel through which you can purchase Microsoft 365 licenses, and there are several Licensing Programs where you can obtain a license. One way is through Microsoft **Volume Licensing** (VL) where several options are available for commercial customers:

- **Enterprise Agreement** (EA)
- **Enterprise Agreement Subscription** (EAS)
- **Microsoft Products and Services Agreement** (MPSA): This is for commercial and government customers

Additional channels, for customers with cloud-only deployments, Microsoft 365 is also available via the following services:

- **Cloud Solution Provider** (CSP) program
- **Microsoft Online Subscription Program** (MOSP/Web Direct)

Microsoft 365 F1/F3 and E3/E5 are available through the Enterprise Enrollment or Enterprise Subscription Enrollment as a full user subscription license. Microsoft 365 E3/E5 is also available as an add-on license, or a "From SA" USL. (SA stands for Software Assurance)

Here is the comparison table for different licensing options:

License	Who the license is for	Can be ordered
Microsoft 365 Full USL	New Enterprise Agreement/Enterprise Agreement subscription customers Existing Enterprise Agreement/Enterprise Agreement subscription customers who are in one of two positions: Customers who are not currently licensed Customers who want to license net new users	Mid-term Anniversary Renewal

Microsoft 365 Add-on	Existing Enterprise Agreement/Enterprise Agreement subscription customers who are in one of the following positions: Customers who are currently paying for Licenses and Software Assurance (L+SA) Customers who want to license some or all existing users for the enterprise platform Customers who want to maintain on-premises use rights	Mid-term Anniversary Renewal
Microsoft 365 "From SA" US	Existing Enterprise Agreement/Enterprise Agreement subscription customers who are in one of the following positions: Customers who have fully paid licenses Customers who are currently paying for Software Assurance only Customers who want to license existing users	Anniversary Renewal (recommended)

Table 1.6 - Comparing different licensing options

Microsoft 365 users are entitled to on-premises rights to Productivity Servers and Office Professional Plus when purchasing through EA/EAS enrollment, but not when purchasing through Microsoft Customer Agreement or Web Direct, on the following terms:

- While it is not a license entitlement, users have a right to install and use server and client software for the duration of the subscription; that is, they have the rights to access any licensed on-premises servers.
- Users have the rights to install the server software on on-premises servers. Downgrade rights are included.
- Rights to install Exchange Server, SharePoint Server, Skype for Business Server.
- On-premises rights do not include Software Assurance benefits and are not license rights.

The Productivity Server right includes the following features:

- Unlimited server installs
- Access rights are granted exclusively to Microsoft 365 Enterprise users
- Customer-dedicated hardware server deployments only

- No rights to deploy in multi-tenant cloud scenarios

Office Professional Plus includes the following features:

- One copy for local installation per duration of Microsoft 365 subscription
- The rights to Full User Subscription License (FUSL) users, up to a 1:1 ratio of "From SA" USLs purchased Downgrade rights are included for Office Professional Plus software
- No rights to deploy clients on servers with RDS

> **Note**
>
> Microsoft 365 E3 and E5 USL license a user for access to Windows Server but do not include a license for the Windows Server product itself.

After reviewing licensing and product options for a variety of Microsoft 365 plans, products, and features, we are now ready to explore products in Microsoft 365 related to security, protection, and governance.

Introduction to Microsoft 365 security

Microsoft 365 is a comprehensive service, spanning diverse productivity, collaboration, and communication spheres, along with wide identities, devices, and data areas that need equally comprehensive and diverse protection against malicious actors and increasingly sophisticated attacks. Obviously, such a service that spans vast endpoints, identity, and application areas cannot be protected by one product, but by using multiple specialized products and solutions.

Moreover, all these products and components need to communicate and exchange information and signals to provide complete protection across all protected points.

Microsoft 365 Defender is an integrated enterprise protection collection of solutions and products that provides protection across all areas, assessing threat signals from multiple sources or products:

- Microsoft Defender for Office 365
- Microsoft Defender for Endpoint
- Microsoft Defender for Identity
- Microsoft Defender for Cloud Apps
- Microsoft Defender Vulnerability Management
- Microsoft Entra ID Protection
- Microsoft Data Loss Prevention
- Application Governance

Most Microsoft 365 security products and features have their place under one roof – the Microsoft 365 Defender portal, available at `https://security.microsoft.com`. Of course, there are many places that other security-related products can call their home, but lately, this is becoming a go-to place for managing and overseeing security from one unified roof. For example, Microsoft Defender for Cloud Apps is undergoing a transition from its dedicated home portal to a unified Microsoft 365 Defender portal. Other products have their dedicated portals, such as the Entra family of products, for example. The following figure is a screenshot of the Microsoft 365 Defender portal, showing some of the dashboards and menu options available:

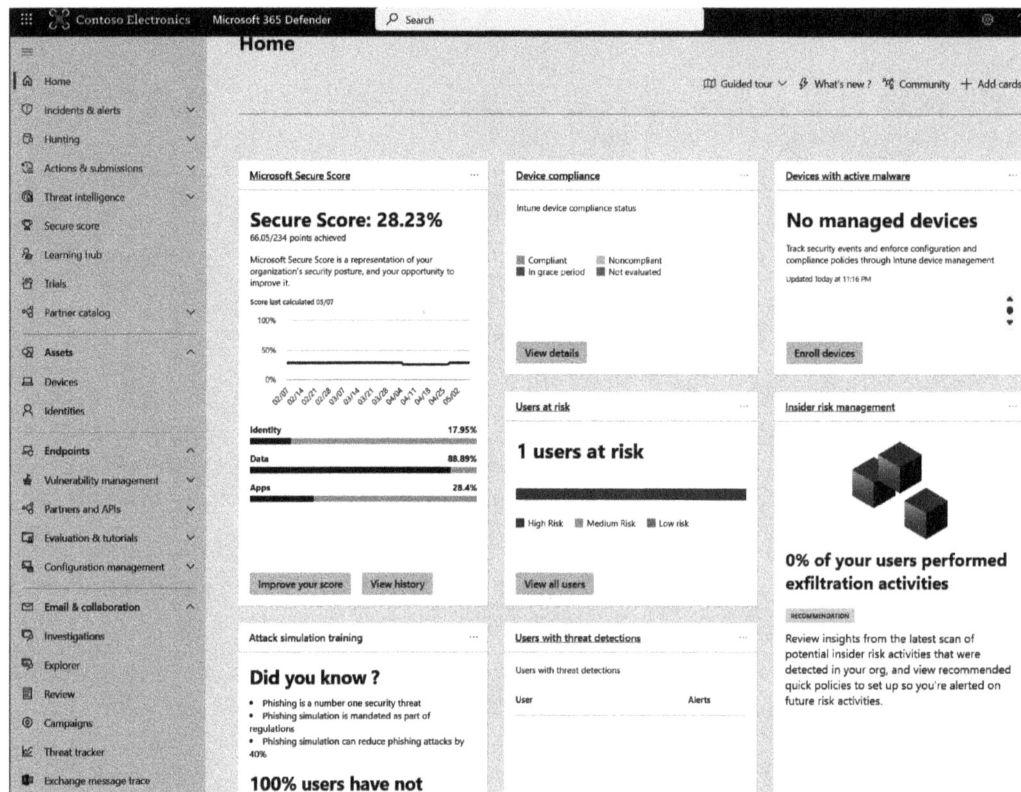

Figure 1.1 – Microsoft 365 Defender Portal

Microsoft Defender for Office 365 provides protection to email messages, links (URLs), and attachments across collaboration tools such as Teams, Outlook, and SharePoint. Some important protection features include the following:

- Threat protection policies involve defining policies that establish a suitable level of protection for your organization.

- Reports can be accessed to monitor the performance of Microsoft Defender for Office 365 in real time
- Utilize advanced tools to investigate, comprehend, simulate, and proactively prevent threats, enhancing your threat investigation and response capabilities
- Efficiently save time and resources by employing **automated investigation and response** (**AIR**) capabilities to investigate and mitigate threats

Microsoft Defender for Office 365 has two plans, where Microsoft Defender for Office 365 Plan 1 includes the following features:

- **Safe Attachments**: This checks email attachments and provides protection against malicious content
- **Safe Links**: This proactively scans for malicious links in messages and documents, allowing safe links, but blocking malicious links
- **Safe Attachments for SharePoint, OneDrive, and Microsoft Teams**: This identifies and blocks malicious files in team sites and document libraries
- **Anti-phishing protection**: This detects and protects user impersonation attempts
- **Real-time detections**: This monitoring capability includes a real-time report that allows you to identify, analyze, and prioritize threats

Including all essential protection features in Plan 1, Microsoft Defender for Office 365 Plan 2 introduces more protection tools:

- **Threat Trackers**: This provides cybersecurity intelligence issues that allow you to take proactive, timely countermeasures before threats occur.
- **Threat Explorer**: A real-time report that allows users to identify and analyze recent threats.
- **AIR**: This enables users to initiate automated investigation processes in response to existing, recognized threats. By automating specific investigation tasks, security operations teams can enhance their efficiency and effectiveness. Remedial actions, such as deleting malicious email messages, can be completed upon approval from a security operations team.
- **Attack simulation training**: Enables the execution of authentic attack scenarios within your organization to identify vulnerabilities. These simulations assess the effectiveness of your security policies and practices while also providing training opportunities for security professionals.
- **Advanced hunting:** This proactively hunts for threats using a **Kusto Query Language** (**KQL**)-based threat hunting tool.
- **Microsoft 365 Defender integration:** This efficiently detects, examines, and responds to incidents and alerts.

Microsoft Defender for Endpoint provides an endpoint platform for threat protection, detection, prevention, protection, automated investigation, and response. Microsoft Defender for Endpoint P1 Plan includes the following features:

- Unified security tools and centralized management
- Next-generation antimalware
- Attack surface reduction rules
- Device control (such as USB)
- Endpoint firewall
- Network protection
- Web control / category-based URL blocking
- Device-based Conditional Access
- Controlled folder access
- APIs, SIEM connector, custom threat intelligence
- Application control

Microsoft Defender for Endpoint P2 Plan contains all capabilities in Plan 1, including these features:

- Endpoint detection and response
- Automated investigation and remediation
- Threat and vulnerability management
- Threat intelligence (threat analytics)
- Sandbox (deep analysis)
- Microsoft Defender Experts

Microsoft Defender for Identity protects on-premises identities using cloud-based intelligence. It monitors and analyzes user behavior and activities to create a baseline for a user, and identifies suspicious identity-related activities, which helps prevent attacks.

Microsoft Defender for Cloud Apps is a **cloud access security broker** (**CASB**), a SasS cloud application protection solution that performs cloud app discovery, discovers and controls the use of shadow IT, protects against anomalous behavior across cloud apps, and assesses cloud apps' compliance.

Microsoft Defender Vulnerability Management is a solution to identify, assess, remediate, and track vulnerabilities across critical assets, through three main ways:

- **Continuous asset discovery and monitoring**: This includes the following features:
  - Security baselines assessment
  - Visibility into software and vulnerabilities
  - Network share assessment
  - Authenticated scan for Windows
  - Threat analytics and event timelines
  - Browser extensions assessment
  - Digital certificates assessment
  - Hardware and firmware assessment
- **Risk-based intelligent prioritization**: This emphasizes the following points:
  - Focus on emerging threats
  - Pinpoints active breaches
  - Protects high-value assets
- **Remediation and tracking**: This consists of the following actions:
  - Remediation requests sent to IT
  - Block vulnerable applications
  - Alternate mitigations
  - Real-time remediation status

Microsoft Entra ID Protection examines and assesses trillions of signals gathered daily with Microsoft Entra ID, Microsoft accounts, and from Xbox, to detect and remediate identity-based risks, ultimately securing access through policy enforcement.

Application Governance is a Defender for Cloud Apps governance add-on feature that enables you to get visibility into how OAuth-enabled applications and their users handle sensitive data in Microsoft 365.

We have briefly described the main Microsoft 365 security features and products, mainly the ones that we will talk about more deeply and thoroughly in the next chapters. Now is the time to briefly look at Microsoft 365 compliance products and capabilities, primarily the ones that we will discuss in this book.

Introduction to Microsoft 365 compliance

Microsoft provides a range of robust compliance and data governance solutions to assist organizations in effectively handling risks, safeguarding, governing sensitive data, and meeting regulatory obligations.

Microsoft 365 has thorough compliance and data governance solutions to protect valuable data across multiple clouds, applications, and endpoints while being able to detect and address significant risks within small and medium businesses and large enterprises. With these tools, compliance professionals are able to examine and address legal obligations using pertinent data, as well as evaluate compliance and address regulatory requirements.

The Microsoft Purview compliance portal is a central place for all compliance tools and organizational needs. It is available to users with one of the following roles: **Global Administrator**, **Compliance Administrator**, and **Compliance Data Administrator**:

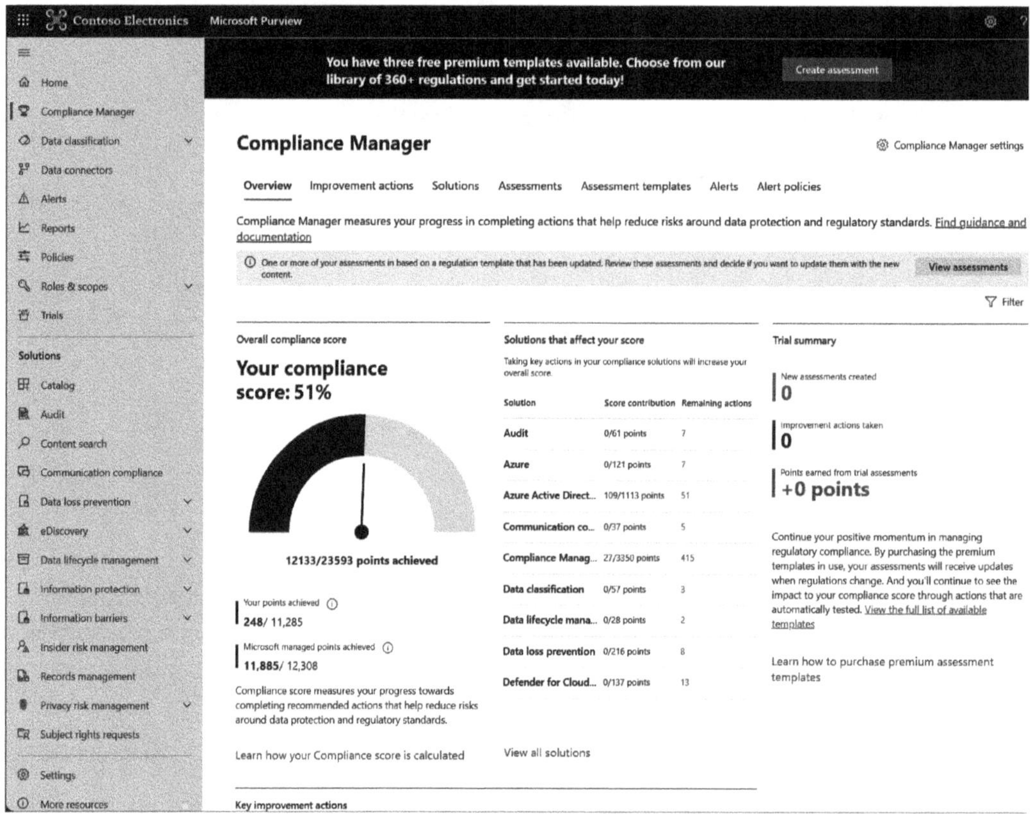

Figure 1.2 – Microsoft Purview compliance portal

Microsoft Purview is now the common prefix for Microsoft 365 compliance and risk management solutions, for protecting and governing sensitive data and addressing regulatory standards requirements.

Microsoft Purview Data Loss Prevention is a solution that detects and prevents sensitive organizational data loss via DLP policies across multiple locations, using deep content analysis:

- Teams, Exchange, SharePoint, and OneDrive accounts and other Microsoft 365 services
- Office applications such as Word, Excel, and PowerPoint
- Windows 10, Windows 11, and macOS (three latest released versions) endpoints
- Non-Microsoft cloud apps
- On-premises file shares and on-premises SharePoint libraries
- Power BI

Microsoft Purview Information Protection is an all-inclusive solution that enables organizations to do the following things:

- Know their data or understand the data landscape, identify sensitive information types using trainable classifiers, custom regular expressions, or functions, and gain data classification information
- Protect organizational data by applying sensitivity labels automatically, encrypting data end email messages, applying access restrictions, and using Customer Key
- Prevent data loss through detecting risky behavior that is extended to endpoints and extend DLP monitoring on-premises and Teams
- Govern data via automatic actions

Microsoft Purview has numerous components and features used for governance and compliance. Here, we have introduced and described some of the most important parts:

- **Data Lifecycle Management** enables customers to retain content using event-based retention, for example, when employees are leaving the company, when their contract expires, or when the retention is tight to a product lifetime.
- **Message Encryption**: By utilizing **Advanced Message Encryption in Office 365**, customers can effectively fulfill compliance requirements that necessitate enhanced control over external recipients and their ability to access encrypted emails. This feature empowers users to regulate sensitive emails shared outside the organization through automated policies, while also providing the capability to track these activities via access logs in the encrypted message portal.
- **Communication Compliance: Microsoft Purview Communication Compliance** is a solution designed to mitigate communication risks originating from within your organization. It assists in identifying, capturing, and taking action on potentially inappropriate messages, enabling compliance personnel to proactively address any concerning communication incidents.
- **Customer Lockbox**: With Customer Lockbox, you retain full control over your content, as Microsoft is unable to access it for service operations without your explicit consent. It involves

you in the approval workflow utilized by Microsoft to guarantee that only authorized requests grant access to your content.

- **Microsoft Purview Audit**: The audit feature within Microsoft Purview offers organizations enhanced visibility into a wide range of audited activities across various Microsoft 365 services. The audit functionality allows for comprehensive monitoring and tracking of different types of activities within the organization.
- **Compliance Manager**: **Microsoft Purview Compliance Manager** is a component within the compliance portal of Microsoft Purview that assists in automating the evaluation and oversight of compliance throughout your multi-cloud environment, enabling you to efficiently assess and manage compliance requirements across multiple cloud platforms.
- **Customer Key**: This helps you meet regulatory or compliance obligations for controlling root keys and provides extra protection against accessing data by unauthorized parties.
- **Insider Risk Management**: **Microsoft Purview Insider Risk Management** is a compliance solution designed to mitigate internal risks by empowering you to identify, investigate, and take appropriate action against both malicious and unintentional activities occurring within your organization, aiding in proactively addressing potential threats originating from within the organization.
- **Information Barriers**: To establish necessary restrictions to prevent unauthorized or undesired interactions within your organization, Microsoft Purview **Information Barriers** (**IB**) is a compliance solution that provides the capability to limit bidirectional communication and collaboration between groups and individual users.
- **eDiscovery**: The eDiscovery feature presents a comprehensive workflow that covers the entire process of preserving, collecting, analyzing, reviewing, and exporting relevant content for internal and external investigations conducted by your organization. Furthermore, it provides legal teams with the ability to effectively manage the complete workflow for legal hold notifications and communication with custodians involved in a case.

Summary

This chapter covered Microsoft 365 offers, plans, and their component products, as well as licensing options for various components. Although anyone and any business can purchase any licenses available, it is important to know which plans and products are available on the market, and what is the most suitable and beneficial Microsoft 365 plan and add-on option for you, without breaking the bank and compromising on productivity or security capabilities. After introducing and describing Microsoft 365 security and compliance products, we are now ready to dive deeper into a fundamental part of any Microsoft-based cloud environment today – Microsoft Entra ID.

2

The Role of Microsoft Entra ID in Microsoft 365 Security

As organizations embrace cloud-based productivity solutions, the need for robust **identity and access management** (**IAM**) becomes increasingly important. Microsoft 365, a comprehensive suite of productivity tools, leverages **Microsoft Entra ID** to provide a secure and efficient IAM framework. Microsoft Entra ID plays a vital role in managing user identities, enforcing access controls, and ensuring the integrity of data within the Microsoft 365 ecosystem.

Microsoft Entra ID is Microsoft's cloud-based IAM service; or, in short, IAM establishes the basis for the identification of Microsoft's public cloud services. Microsoft Entra ID encompasses a wide range of objects and related services, and it is a rather complex and wide topic; it deserves a whole book for itself alone. In this chapter, we will focus on the Microsoft Entra ID functionalities and features that are more tightly connected to, or more directly connected to, Microsoft 365 security and compliance features.

In this chapter, we are going to cover the following main topics:

- Microsoft Entra ID plans and features
- Microsoft Entra ID roles and groups
- Microsoft Entra ID Protection

In this chapter, readers will understand and learn about Microsoft Entra ID's role in Microsoft 365 security, get acquainted with the importance of Microsoft Entra ID Protection and Microsoft Entra ID **Privileged Identity Management** (**PIM**), as well as learn about guest accounts and Microsoft Entra ID Conditional Access as pillars of Microsoft 365 security.

Technical requirements

Microsoft 365 is a subscription-based service and to try and experience the functionality of each product and service, a user must have an appropriate license. It does not matter whether a user has a trial license, a "regular," or a paid license – if they have a license assigned, they can enjoy the full scope of the licensed product, its benefits, and functionalities.

Microsoft Entra ID plans and features

Microsoft Entra ID is available in five editions:

- **Microsoft Entra ID Free**: This edition provides the basic but still very important IAM functionality to several online services such as Azure, Intune, Power Platform, Dynamics 365, and Microsoft 365.
- **Office 365**: This edition is like Microsoft Entra ID Free, but it includes some additional functionalities on top of Microsoft Entra ID Free, such as a customizable sign-in page, self-service sign-in activity and reporting, and features available and included with Office 365 E1, E3, E5, F1, and F3 subscriptions.
- **Microsoft Entra ID P1**: This is available for purchase for Azure and Office 365 subscribers and is included with Office E3 and Enterprise Mobility + Security E3 plans.
- **Microsoft Entra ID P2**: This is available for purchase for Azure and Office 365 subscribers and is included with Office E5 and Enterprise Mobility + Security E5 plans.
- **Microsoft Entra ID Governance**: You can use Microsoft Entra ID Governance if you have Microsoft Entra ID P1 or P2. Microsoft Entra ID Governance lets you boost productivity by giving users the right access to the right resources at the right time, without manual delays, enhances security by minimizing the risk of access misuse and making smart access decisions based on machine learning, and simplifies the approval process for common resource access requests, so you can focus on the exceptions and insights from AI.

The following table lists the Microsoft Entra ID plans and features in a convenient format that allows you to compare their main features. Please keep in mind that while features and capabilities are subject to change, some of the Microsoft Entra ID features have more detailed licensing requirements and availability, such as **multifactor authentication** (**MFA**). For example, MFA has additional capabilities whose availability depends on the Microsoft Entra ID plan, and other Microsoft Entra ID features might have similar characteristics, so planning for Microsoft Entra ID features must be more detailed than what this table and the product landing pages provide:

Microsoft Entra ID Plans and Features				
	Microsoft Entra ID Free	Office 365	Microsoft Entra ID P1	Microsoft Entra ID P2
Authentication, single sign-on, and MFA				
Cloud authentication (pass-through authentication, password hash synchronization)	Yes	Yes	Yes	Yes
Federated authentication (Active Directory Federation Services or federation with other identity providers)	Yes	Yes	Yes	Yes
Single sign-on (SSO) unlimited	Yes	Yes	Yes	Yes
MFA	Yes	Yes	Yes	Yes
Passwordless (Windows Hello for Business, Microsoft Authenticator, FIDO2 security key integrations	Yes	Yes	Yes	Yes
Service-level agreement	N/A	N/A	Yes	Yes
Customizable user sign-in page	N/A	Yes	Yes	Yes
Application access				
SaaS apps with modern authentication (Microsoft Entra ID application gallery apps, SAML, and OAuth 2.0)	Yes	Yes	Yes	Yes
Group assignment to applications	N/A	N/A	Yes	Yes
Cloud app discovery (Microsoft Defender for Cloud Apps)	N/A	N/A	Yes	Yes
Application proxy for on-premises, header-based, and integrated Windows authentication	N/A	N/A	Yes	Yes

Secure hybrid access partnerships (Kerberos, NTLM, LDAP, RDP, and SSH authentication)	Yes	Yes	Yes	Yes
Authorization and Conditional Access				
Role-based access control (RBAC)	Yes	Yes	Yes	Yes
Conditional Access	N/A	N/A	Yes	Yes
SharePoint limited access	N/A	N/A	Yes	Yes
Session lifetime management	N/A	N/A	Yes	Yes
Identity protection (risky sign-ins, risky users, risk-based Conditional Access)	N/A	N/A	N/A	Yes
Custom security attributes	N/A	N/A	Yes	Yes
Administration and hybrid identity				
User and group management	Yes	Yes	Yes	Yes
Advanced group management (dynamic groups, naming policies, expiration, default classification)	N/A	N/A	Yes	Yes
Directory synchronization—Microsoft Entra ID Connect (sync and cloud sync)	Yes	Yes	Yes	Yes
Microsoft Entra ID Connect Health reporting	N/A	N/A	Yes	Yes
Delegated administration – built-in roles	Yes	Yes	Yes	Yes
Global password protection and management – cloud-only users	Yes	Yes	Yes	Yes
Global password protection and management – custom banned passwords, users synchronized from on-premises Active Directory	N/A	N/A	Yes	Yes

Microsoft Identity Manager user client access license (CAL)	N/A	N/A	Yes	Yes
Cross-tenant user synchronization	N/A	N/A	Yes	Yes
End user self-service				
Application launch portal (My Apps)	Yes	Yes	Yes	Yes
User application collections in My Apps	Yes	Yes	Yes	Yes
Self-service account management portal (My Account)	Yes	Yes	Yes	Yes
Self-service password change for cloud users	Yes	Yes	Yes	Yes
Self-service password reset/change/unlock with on-premises write-back	N/A	N/A	Yes	Yes
Self-service sign-in activity search and reporting	N/A	Yes	Yes	Yes
Self-service group management (My Groups)	N/A	N/A	Yes	Yes
Self-service entitlement management (My Access)	N/A	N/A	N/A	Yes
Identity governance				
Automated user provisioning to apps	Yes	Yes	Yes	Yes
Automated group provisioning to apps	N/A	N/A	Yes	Yes
HR-driven provisioning	N/A	N/A	Yes	Yes
Terms of use attestation	N/A	N/A	Yes	Yes

Access certifications and reviews	N/A	N/A	N/A	Yes
Entitlements management	N/A	N/A	N/A	Yes
PIM, just in time access	N/A	N/A	N/A	Yes
Event logging and reporting				
Basic security and usage reports	Yes	Yes	Yes	Yes
Advanced security and usage reports	N/A	N/A	Yes	Yes
Identity Protection: vulnerabilities and risky accounts	N/A	N/A	N/A	Yes
Identity Protection: risk events investigation, SIEM connectivity	N/A	N/A	N/A	Yes
Frontline workers				
SMS sign-in	N/A	N/A	Yes	Yes
Shared device sign-out	N/A	N/A	Yes	Yes
Delegated user management portal (My Staff)	N/A	N/A	Yes	Yes

Table 2.1 – Microsoft Entra ID plans and features

Another important factor in choosing the right Microsoft Entra ID plan, and an important factor in planning for almost any service in this cloud world, is the **Service Level Agreement** (**SLA**) for Microsoft Online Services. Naturally, it is in businesses' interests to know what availability they can count on, but laws and regulations have, or should have, significant influence on planning decisions.

The SLA for Microsoft Entra ID Basic and Microsoft Entra ID Premium defines *Downtime* as "*any period of time when users are unable to log in to the Microsoft Entra ID service, or Microsoft Entra ID fails to successfully emit the authentication and authorization tokens required for users to log into applications connected to the service.*" Additionally, "User Minutes" is defined as "*the sum of the number of users who attempted to access the service during each minute of the month.*"

Based on that, the Monthly Uptime Percentage is calculated using the following formula:

$$\frac{User\ Minutes\ -Downtime}{User\ Minutes} x\ 100$$

Downtime is measured in User Minutes; that is, for each month, Downtime is the sum of the number of users with unresolved failures at any minute of the month.

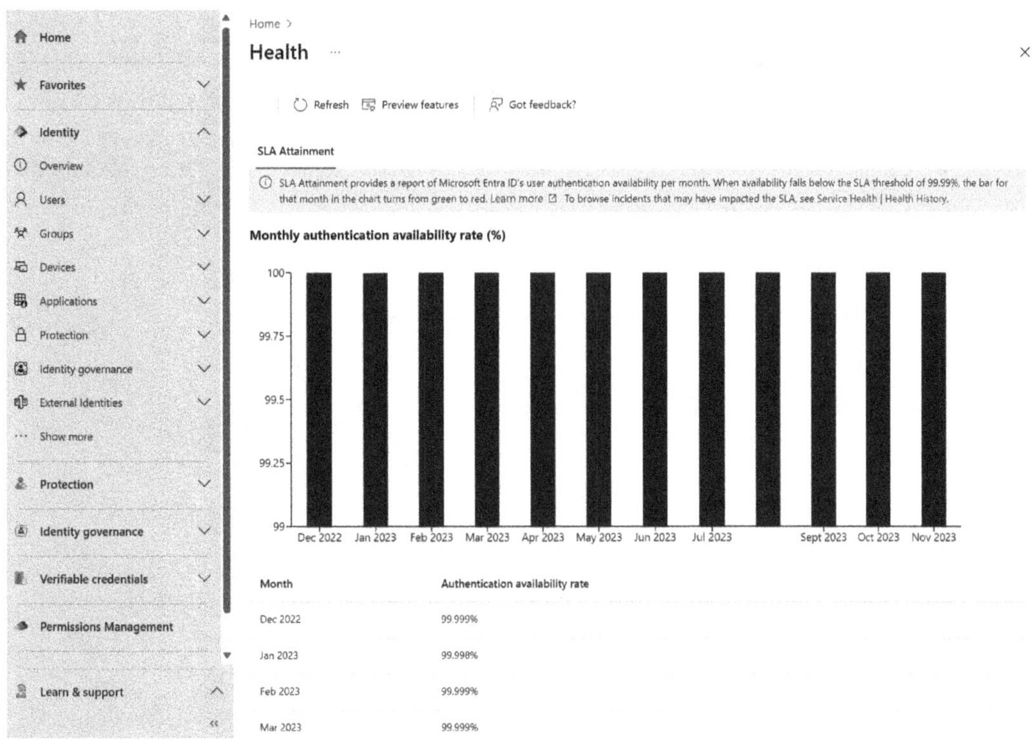

Figure 2.1 – Microsoft Entra ID health status

The Microsoft Entra ID health status is graphically and numerically displayed in the Microsoft Entra ID admin center. To display the health status, visit `https:/entra.microsoft.com`, and under the **Monitoring & Health** section select **Health (Preview)**.

Finally, what is the SLA for Microsoft Entra ID? The Microsoft Entra ID Premium editions guarantee a 99.99% SLA. When the monthly uptime percentage is less than 99.99%, service credits apply. For a detailed explanation of Microsoft SLA for Online Services, please consult the official documentation, found at the link in the following note.

> **Note**
>
> This information is based on the SLA for Microsoft Online Services, June 1, 2023, available at `https://go.microsoft.com/fwlink/p/?linkid=626920`.
>
> Microsoft Entra ID Free, as a free service, does not have an SLA.

Microsoft Entra ID roles and groups

As Microsoft Entra ID is the identity provider for Microsoft services it is used to define roles not only for Microsoft 365 but for other cloud products and services as well. Some services, such as the following, have their specific roles and role assignments stored in their respective, different **role-based access control** (**RBAC**) systems:

- Microsoft Entra ID
- Microsoft 365 and Microsoft 365 Defender family of services
- Microsoft Intune
- Microsoft Exchange
- Compliance
- Cost management

What does this mean? From an administrative point of view, it means that you still have a very granular control mechanism available, but to control access to a resource, you have different categories and different service portals where you can perform these administrative tasks, but not a unified portal to do that. It also means that separate RBAC systems will control different resource categories.

The following diagram illustrates the connection between Microsoft Entra ID and Microsoft 365 roles, or Microsoft Entra ID roles, and between Microsoft Entra ID and Azure roles, or more popular and known RBAC roles:

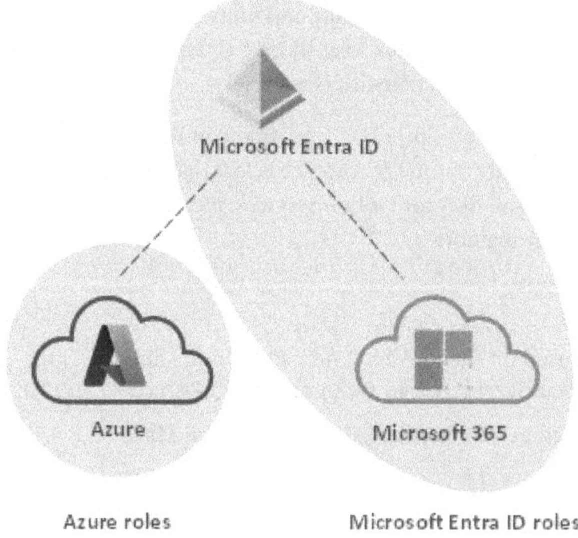

Figure 2.2 – Microsoft Entra ID roles and Azure roles in Microsoft Entra ID

Depending on where Microsoft Entra ID built-in roles can be used, we can identify three types of roles:

- **Microsoft Entra ID-specific roles**: These, as the name implies, define permissions to manage resources inside Microsoft Entra ID exclusively, such as User Administrator and Groups Administrator.
- **Service-specific roles**: These are roles used to define permissions to manage a specific service and its features, such as Exchange Administrator or SharePoint Administrator.
- **Cross-service roles**: These are certain roles that span the boundaries of a service and are used in more than one service, often in multiple services. Some well-known examples of such roles are Global Administrator, Security Administrator, or Compliance Administrator.

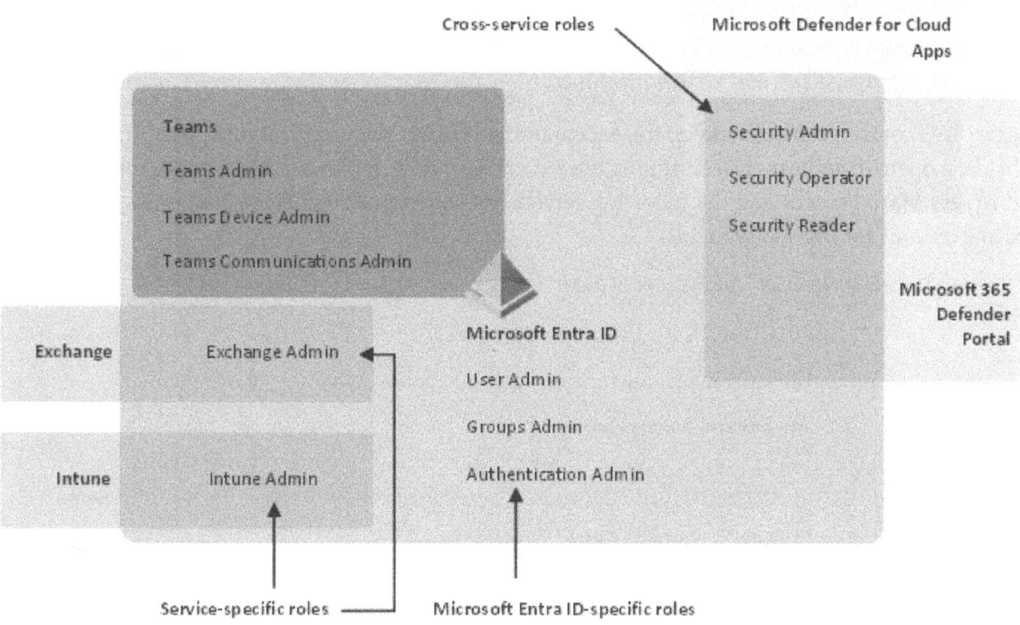

Figure 2.3 – Roles in Microsoft Entra ID and their relation

Microsoft Entra ID currently supports the following three roles:

- Azure roles, or Azure RBAC roles
- Microsoft Entra ID roles
- Classic roles

Although very similar, each of these three roles has its distinct characteristics and usage, described in the following paragraphs in more detail.

Azure roles, or Azure RBAC roles

Azure roles, or RBAC roles, are the default way to control access to resources in Azure today. A significant leap forward in capabilities from the now almost obsolete Service Manager model is built on Azure Resource Manager, the deployment and management service for Azure. While Azure RBAC supports many built-in roles, its three fundamental roles, **Owner**, **Contributor**, and **Reader**, apply to all types of resources. The fourth, the **User Access Administrator** role, although a fundamental role as well, manages user access to only Azure resources.

The Owner role has full access to all resources and a user with an Owner role can delegate access to other users. The Contributor role is slightly less permissive than the Owner role, and users granted the Contributor role can't grant access to other users but have rights to create and manage all types of Azure resources. The third, the Reader role, applies to all resource types as well, but its permissions include read capabilities only. Every other built-in role allows management of specific Azure resources, such as blob storage, disks, and virtual machines.

Azure RBAC controls can be found on the **Access control (IAM)** blade in the Azure portal. This menu, or blade, if opened, is always placed among the top entries on the left menu. **IAM** stands for **Identity and Access Management** and the following screenshot shows one such blade containing different tabs and options for role assignments:

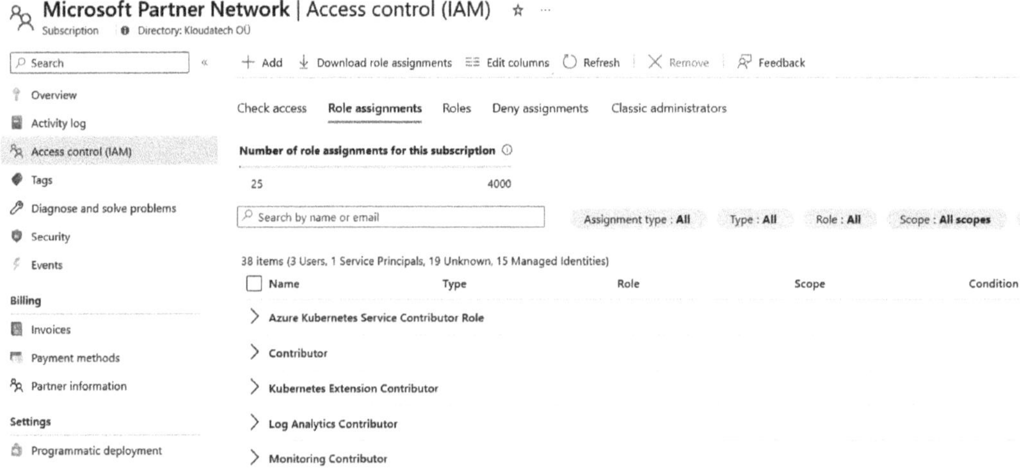

Figure 2.4 – Access control (IAM) blade in the Azure portal

After describing Azure RBAC, let's explore what Microsoft Entra ID roles are and how they differ from RBAC roles.

Microsoft Entra ID roles

To manage Microsoft Entra ID resources in a directory, or to grant access for privileged actions in Microsoft Entra ID, Microsoft Entra ID roles are used. Like the **Access control (IAM)** menu and blade options, options to assign Microsoft Entra ID roles look similar, containing Microsoft Entra ID-specific built-in roles as well as custom-built roles, but with fewer tabs, as seen in the following screenshot:

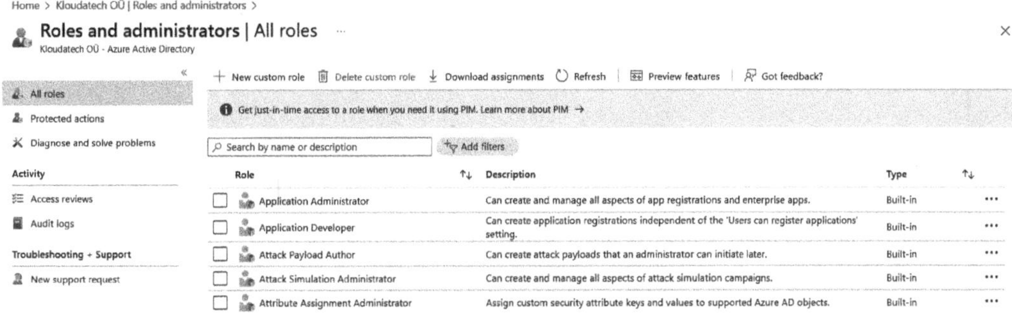

Figure 2.5 – Microsoft Entra ID roles blade

In a few words, Azure roles manage and control access to Azure resources, while Microsoft Entra ID roles manage access to Microsoft Entra ID resources. Generally, Microsoft Entra ID roles and Azure roles do not overlap, but if a user has a Global Administrator role – a role in Microsoft Entra ID – it can elevate its access to span and include access to all subscriptions and management groups for an individual tenant. This is specifically useful if you want to have access to all Azure subscriptions and management groups in an organization (or a tenant), grant a user access to a particular subscription or a management group, or eventually re-establish access to an Azure management group or a subscription.

This option is located in the Microsoft Entra ID tenant **Properties** blade, at the bottom, as shown in the following screenshot:

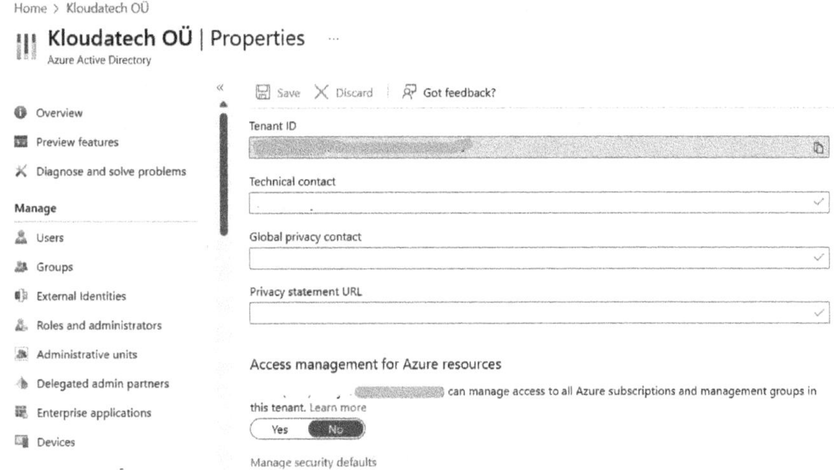

Figure 2.6 – Microsoft Entra ID tenant Properties blade, containing access management for Azure resources toggle button

After you set **Yes** and enable **Access management for Azure resources**, the Global Administrator will be granted the User Access Administrator role at a root scope and allow access to underlying resources. As a best security practice, ensure you remove this elevated access once you have made all required changes.

The relationship between non-elevated and elevated Azure subscription management status, or the enabled or disabled `Access management for Azure resources` option, is illustrated in the next diagram:

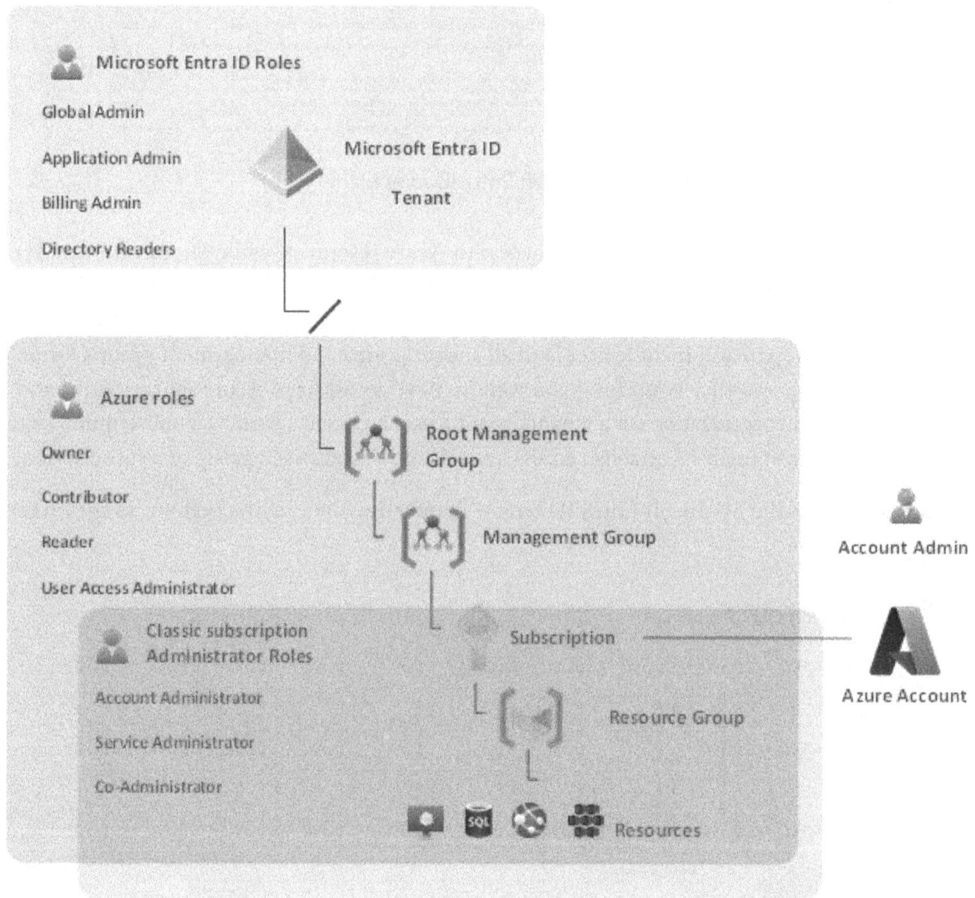

Figure 2.7 – Access management for Azure resources relation

The last and least-used role option these days is **Classic roles**, available for compatibility reasons, and available until it will be eventually phased out and retired.

Classic roles

Classic roles are roles defined by the Azure Service Manager (Classic) model, an early management model that will be retired soon. The three classic administrator roles are Account Administrator, Service Administrator, and Co-Administrator, where the first two administrator roles were automatically added as roles to the account used to sign up for the Azure service. Today only available as a legacy model, it is advised to abandon the classical management model and complete the transition to role-based access management before its retirement.

> **Note**
>
> Although Azure Role-Based Access and Microsoft Entra ID roles are significantly predominant, classic roles are still in use today: Co-Administrator, Account Administrator, and Service Administrator. The Cloud Services (classic) deployment model and these three classic roles and related classic resources will be retired on August 31st 2024.

Microsoft 365 roles in Microsoft Entra ID

Microsoft 365 offers a range of roles within Microsoft Entra ID that enable organizations to assign specific permissions and responsibilities to users.

Microsoft 365 includes a set of predefined administrator roles, accessible via the Microsoft 365 admin center (`https://admin.microsoft.com/`).

These roles govern access to Microsoft 365 services, data, and administrative features. Let's explore some key and most used Microsoft 365 roles and their significance in Microsoft Entra ID:

- **Global Administrator**: The Global Administrator role holds the highest level of administrative privileges within Microsoft Entra ID. Global Administrators have full control over Microsoft Entra ID, including the ability to manage user accounts, configure security settings, and assign other administrative roles. They play a crucial role in overseeing the overall security and management of the Microsoft 365 environment. The Global Administrator role can manage all aspects of Microsoft Entra ID and Microsoft services that use Microsoft Entra ID identities. Additional roles with *global* reach are described in the following list:
    - **Global Reader**: This can read everything that a Global Administrator can, but not update anything.
    - **Global Secure Access Admin**: This can create and manage all aspects of Microsoft Entra Internet Access and Microsoft Entra Private Access, including managing access to public and private endpoints.

- **User Administrator**: User Administrators are responsible for managing user accounts within Microsoft Entra ID. They can create, modify, and delete user accounts, reset passwords, assign licenses, and manage group memberships. User Administrators play a vital role in ensuring that user access is granted appropriately and aligned with organizational needs.
- **Exchange Administrator**: Exchange Administrators have specific responsibilities related to Microsoft Exchange Online, the email and calendar service within Microsoft 365. They manage mailboxes, configure email policies, set up distribution groups, and handle other Exchange-related tasks. Exchange Administrators help maintain a secure and efficient email communication system. In short, the Exchange Administrator can manage all aspects of the Exchange product. An important additional Exchange role is described in the following point:
    - **Exchange Recipient Admin**: This can create or update Exchange Online recipients within the Exchange Online organization
- **SharePoint Administrator**: SharePoint Administrators focus on managing SharePoint Online, the collaboration and document management platform within Microsoft 365. They oversee site creation, configure security settings, manage document libraries, and enforce governance policies. SharePoint Administrators enable efficient collaboration and ensure the protection of sensitive data within SharePoint Online.
- **Teams Administrator**: Teams Administrators are responsible for managing Microsoft Teams, the popular communication and collaboration platform. They handle tasks such as creating teams, managing channels, configuring policies, and ensuring proper integration with other Microsoft 365 services. Teams Administrators play a crucial role in fostering seamless teamwork and optimizing the utilization of Teams within an organization. While Teams Administrators can manage the whole Microsoft Teams service, there are other important Teams-related roles:
    - **Teams Communications Admin**: This role manages calling and meeting features within the Microsoft Teams service.
    - **Teams Communications Support Engineer**: This role troubleshoots communication issues within Teams using advanced tools.
    - **Teams Devices Admin**: This role performs management-related tasks on Teams-certified devices.
- **Security Administrator**: Security Administrators focus on implementing security measures and configuring security settings within Microsoft Entra ID and Microsoft 365. They manage security policies, conduct risk assessments, monitor security events, and respond to security incidents. Security Administrators contribute to strengthening the security posture of an organization's Microsoft 365 environment. Security Administrators can read security information and reports, and manage configuration in Microsoft Entra ID and Office 365. There are two significant security roles:
- **Security Operator**: This role can create and manage security events.

- **Security Reader**: This role can only read security information and reports in Microsoft Entra ID and Office 365.
- **Compliance Administrator**: Compliance Administrators have responsibilities related to data protection, governance, and regulatory compliance within Microsoft 365. They implement compliance policies, manage data retention, handle eDiscovery requests, and ensure adherence to relevant regulations. Compliance Administrators play a critical role in maintaining data privacy and meeting compliance requirements. The Compliance Administrator role can read and manage compliance configuration and reports in Microsoft Entra ID and Microsoft 365. The Compliance Data Administrator, on the other hand, can create and manage compliance content.

These roles are just a snapshot of the diverse set of administrative roles available within Microsoft Entra ID and Microsoft 365. Each role has specific responsibilities and permissions tailored to different aspects of the Microsoft 365 ecosystem. By assigning appropriate roles to users, organizations can ensure efficient management, secure access, and streamlined collaboration within their Microsoft 365 environment.

To put it briefly, Microsoft Entra ID provides a robust IAM framework for Microsoft 365 and the diverse range of roles within Microsoft Entra ID enables organizations to manage user identities, enforce access controls, and maintain the security and integrity of data. Leveraging the various Microsoft 365 roles available in Microsoft Entra ID allows organizations to align responsibilities with user roles, ensuring smooth operations and safeguarding critical resources. As organizations continue to embrace Microsoft 365, understanding and effectively utilizing these roles becomes essential for optimizing productivity and maintaining a secure digital workspace.

For a complete list of roles available, and their detailed descriptions, please consult `https://learn.microsoft.com/en-us/azure/active-directory/roles/permissions-reference`.

Besides Microsoft Entra ID built-in roles, which are also accessible from the **Microsoft Entra ID | Roles and administrators** blade in the Azure portal, the Microsoft 365 admin center allows you to access service-specific role definitions for Exchange, Intune, and Billing:

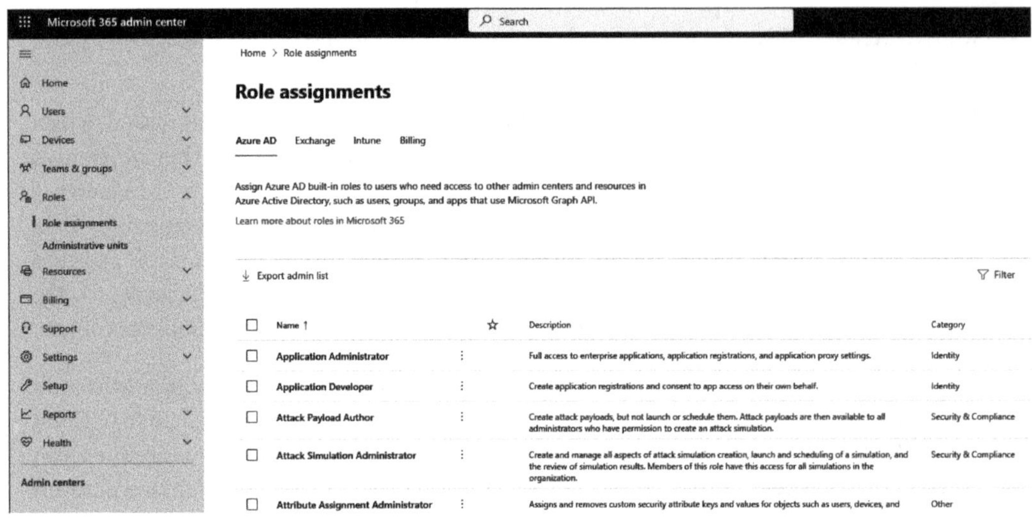

Figure 2.8 – Microsoft 365 admin center – role assignments

Additionally, role groups for compliance-related products and services are available on the Microsoft Purview portal, under the **Roles and Scopes** | **Permissions** menu. These role groups for Microsoft Purview solutions contain admin roles that enable users to perform tasks in the Microsoft Purview compliance portal, such as insider risk management, communication compliance, privacy management, and information protection.

Best practices for roles

What would be the best practices for roles? The first best practice for managing roles would be the principle of least privilege. It means that your users and administrators need to have just the permissions they need to do their job effectively, without giving them too restrictive permissions to perform their usual tasks and assignments or too wide permissions. Not only do you have to restrict a specific set of permissions that you assign to a role, but you also have to be very specific about the scope of the application of these permissions.

Microsoft recommends having up to five Global Administrator roles in your organization. Since Global Administrators can do everything – modify, create, and change configuration options and settings across the entire Microsoft 365 organization – you have to protect Global Administrators very strictly.

Nowadays, protecting identities and users with MFA shouldn't even be a discussion; it is a mandatory setting for security-conscious organizations. MFA should be turned on for all administrative accounts, including Global Administrator accounts. Numerous studies have shown that MFA can stop 99.9% of identity-based attacks. The best MFA is the one offering phishing-resistant strength; that is, one that includes methods that require an interaction between the authentication method and the sign-in surface, such as the hardware FIDO key, and the requirement to touch the key to successfully complete the authentication request.

On the other hand, not every Global Administrator account should have MFA protection enabled. The best practice is to have break-glass accounts that are assigned to the Global Administrator role that don't have MFA enabled or that don't have the same MFA method as your normal global administrative accounts enabled.

So, how do we ensure that global administrative accounts that don't have MFA enabled are adequately protected? The recommended best practice is to configure these accounts with a password as complex as possible, including numbers, lowercase and uppercase characters, and special characters. Then, the password should be split in two and stored in separate, protected places, where one person should not have access to both pieces of the Global Administrator password.

This practice goes back many decades in the past, when Windows Server, **Active Directory Domain Services** (**AD DS**), and Enterprise Administrator were introduced, and numerous companies have retained this practice as the best practice when storing and protecting sensitive administrative accounts credentials.

A part of the principle of least privilege is configuring administrative accounts with just-in-time access, achieved using Azure **Microsoft Entra ID Privileged Identity Management** (**Entra PIM**) to revoke access after the allowed time has expired. Additionally, Microsoft Entra ID PIM allows to receive notification when someone elevates or activates the role assignment, with additional approval capabilities.

Microsoft 365 groups

Groups are foundational, basic Microsoft Entra ID objects that enable membership services, operation actions, granting permission, access to resources, and more.

By default, any user can create Microsoft 365 groups and it generally sounds like a great collaboration feature that allows users to communicate and collaborate more effectively. From a security perspective, you should restrict who can create Microsoft 365 groups. Otherwise, the unreasonably high number of Microsoft 365 groups makes administration less efficient and less secure. As you limit group creation, all services that rely on that functionality will be affected, for example, SharePoint, Outlook, and Microsoft Teams. You should limit creating Microsoft 365 groups to a restricted group of users as a security best practice.

Microsoft 365 groups can have three roles:

- **Guests**: Guest members are users who belong to another organization, outside your organization
- **Members**: These are the regular users that belong to your organization, and they can access everything in the group except changing group settings
- **Owners**: Group owners have advanced group settings permissions such as delete, rename, and change capabilities

Only Group Administrators, User Administrators, or Global Administrators can create and manage groups. To manage groups, you can use **Active teams and groups** in **Microsoft 365 admin center**, as shown in the following screenshot:

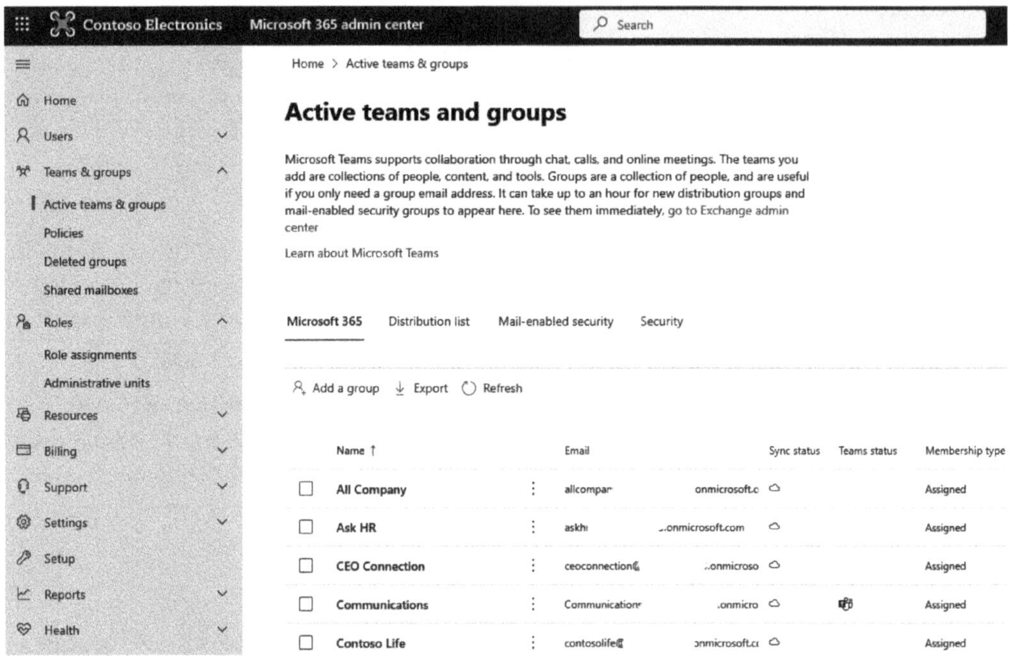

Figure 2.9 – Active teams and groups blade in Microsoft 365 admin center

From here, you can easily access Microsoft 365 groups, distribution lists or distribution-enabled groups, mail-enabled security groups, and security groups.

Another place where you can access group management capabilities is in the Azure portal, on Microsoft Entra ID blade, under **Groups**, as shown in the following screenshot:

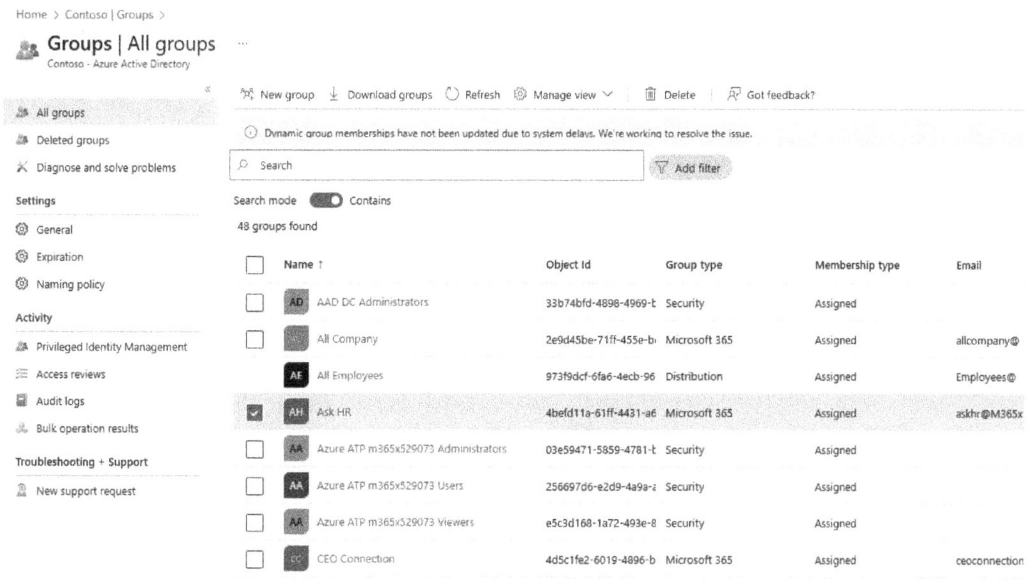

Figure 2.10 – All groups blade in the Azure portal

There are several Microsoft 365 group types, with the first two in the following list being the two most important group types:

- **Security group**: This is used to grant access or permission to resources. Security group membership can consist of users, other groups, service principals, and devices.
- **Microsoft 365 group**: This should be the default group for collaboration purposes and to give group members access to shared resources such as mailboxes, files, conversations, and calendars. These groups also have dynamic membership capabilities that allow their members to be assigned or removed automatically based on different attributes. This group type does not support group nesting; that is, it cannot contain groups or be a member of a group.
- **Distribution group**: This is a special group that has an email assigned, and as the name implies it is used to distribute or send emails to a group of people.
- **Mail-enabled security group**: This is a dual-purpose group; it is a mix of a security group and a distribution group where it can be used to give access to resources such as SharePoint and OneDrive and additionally provide emailing capabilities to its members. Membership of this group cannot be dynamic, and mail-enabled security groups cannot contain devices.
- **Dynamic distribution group**: This is the same group as the previously described distribution group but its membership can dynamically change.

- **Shared mailbox**: Shared mailboxes are typically used for collaboration and can receive external emails and include a calendar as well. This type is used when a group of people need access to the same mailbox.

There are three group membership types:

- **Assigned**: In this group membership, you can add specific users or people as members to the group from your own organization or, if enabled by the administrator, from outside your organization, and assign them the required permissions. The membership of the group does not change unless the administrator of the group performs membership changes.
- **Dynamic user**: This group membership can dynamically change based on members' attributes. You can use the rule builder or rule syntax to create a dynamic membership rule based on tens of available dynamic properties or attributes. The group members' attributes are constantly evaluated and if the users' attributes change and no longer meet the group membership requirements, their group membership is revoked, and the members are removed from the group. In the same way, if the users' attributes change so they meet the group membership requirement, users are granted group membership.
- **Dynamic device**: Similarly, the dynamic device group behaves like a dynamic user group except that the system looks for device attributes and their changes.

Moreover, the privacy setting of a group can be either public or private. If a group's privacy is set to **Public**, groups can be joined by everyone without getting approval from a group owner and therefore anyone can access the content from the group. Alternatively, the privacy of a group can be set to **Private** where only its members can access the group content. Group owners are the only ones that can add members to the group and a **Private** group is not open for everyone to join unless their membership is approved by a group owner.

Microsoft Entra ID Protection

While Microsoft Entra ID Protection is not categorized as a Microsoft 365 security feature, it is a security capability worthy of your attention and a bit of a deeper understanding.

The way we work and collaborate today has drastically changed compared to just a few years ago. Work has become increasingly digital and online; with the COVID-19 pandemic, enterprises adapted to a new reality by adopting new tools, and cloud computing has become a standard in almost every business and enterprise worldwide. Traditional perimeter-based security has changed, and the new reality is that identity has overtaken the new security perimeter and become the standard. It is imperative that we use solid products and policies that define efficient risk-based access controls.

In the past, internal networks defined security boundaries on closed systems, in on-premises systems, but today's reality is something completely different. Most workloads and data today are in the cloud, and we need adequate protection for identity-based attacks.

As Microsoft Entra ID is a Microsoft solution for IAM, Microsoft Entra ID Protection is a product that continuously evaluates a broad range of signals to help identify and detect risky identity-based behaviors such as impossible travel activity, leaked credentials, password spray attacks, anonymous IP address usage, and much more.

Figure 2.11 – Microsoft Entra ID Protection Overview blade

Microsoft Entra ID Protection maintains a comprehensive tracking system for all detected risks associated with an identity. It offers three essential reports to administrators, enabling them to delve into these risks and initiate appropriate actions:

- **Risk detections**: This report includes details of each identified risk as a separate entry, providing a comprehensive overview of the detected risks
- **Risky sign-ins**: Whenever one or more risk detections are flagged for a particular sign-in attempt, it is recorded as a risky sign-in and documented in this report

- **Risky users**: Users are marked as risky in this report if any of the following conditions are met:
  - The user has been associated with one or more risky sign-in attempts
  - One or more risk detections have been reported for the user

By utilizing these reports, administrators can thoroughly investigate potential security threats and implement necessary measures to ensure identity protection.

The risk in Microsoft Entra ID Protection is defined as any suspicious action that relates to user accounts in Microsoft Entra ID. There are two different types of risk detections: **real time** and **offline**, and these can be detected at the user and sign-in levels. Because Microsoft Entra ID Protection is available to Microsoft Entra ID P1 and Microsoft Entra ID P2 licensed users, specific detections are available to different customers.

The following table shows risk detections and their respective detection types and license availability to Microsoft Entra ID P2 licenses (Premium) and Microsoft Entra ID P1 and Microsoft Entra ID Free customers (Regular):

Risk detection	Detection type	Type
User risk definitions		
Atypical travel	Offline	Premium
Anomalous token	Offline	Premium
Token issuer anomaly	Offline	Premium
Suspicious browser	Offline	Premium
Unfamiliar sign-in properties	Real time	Premium
Malicious IP address	Offline	Premium
Suspicious inbox manipulation rules	Offline	Premium
Password spray	Offline	Premium
Impossible travel	Offline	Premium
New country	Offline	Premium
Activity from anonymous IP address	Offline	Premium
Suspicious inbox forwarding	Offline	Premium
Mass access to sensitive files	Offline	Premium
Verified threat actor IP	Real time	Premium
Additional risk detected	Real-time or offline	Regular

Anonymous IP address	Real time	Regular
Admin confirmed user compromised	Offline	Regular
Microsoft Entra ID threat intelligence	Real time or offline	Regular
User risk detections		
Possible attempt to access Primary Refresh Token (PRT)	Offline	Premium
Anomalous user activity	Offline	Premium
User reported suspicious activity	Offline	Premium
Additional risk detected	Real time or offline	Regular
Leaked credentials	Offline	Regular
Microsoft Entra ID threat intelligence	Offline	Regular

Table 2.2 – Microsoft Entra ID risk detection types

Microsoft Entra ID Protection provides robust identity protection from a variety of modern real-time and offline user-related risks, and while it is backed up and powered by cloud-based threat intelligence security capabilities, it helps protect one of the most vulnerable entities today – our Microsoft Entra ID digital identities.

Summary

In this chapter, we addressed an important part of any tenant's security – Microsoft Entra ID, its plans, features, and most notably, roles and groups, which are an essential and one of the foundational elements in organizational security posture. Not only are Microsoft 365 groups important, but so are Azure groups since choosing group types wisely and correctly assigning them to the right employees will significantly impact security in an organization.

The next chapter will focus on Microsoft Defender for Office 365, a product that protects email, specifically Exchange Online, against malicious attacks and threats such as malware or phishing messages.

Part 2: Microsoft 365 Security

In this second and the biggest part, we will cover Microsoft 365 Defender products responsible for the security of your cloud and on-premises assets and content. Specifically, we will cover Defender for Office 365 and its email and collaboration content protection capabilities; Defender for Endpoint with endpoint protection capabilities and Microsoft Purview configuration, data classification, data search, and data loss prevention features. Furthermore, we will explain the essential configuration of Defender for Cloud Apps as a SaaS and cloud apps protection product, OAuth apps and files management, governance, and policies; Microsoft Defender Vulnerability Management, a product whose task is to discover and remediate vulnerabilities in software across devices; and Microsoft Defender for Identity, a fantastic and powerful product designed to protect on-premises identities.

This part includes the following chapters:

- *Chapter 3, Microsoft Defender for Office 365*
- *Chapter 4, Microsoft Defender for Endpoint*
- *Chapter 5, Getting Started with Microsoft Purview*
- *Chapter 6, Microsoft Defender for Cloud Apps*
- *Chapter 7, Microsoft Defender Vulnerability Management*
- *Chapter 8, Microsoft Defender for Identity*

3

Microsoft Defender for Office 365

Nowadays, especially after the COVID-19 pandemic, companies are increasingly shifting their focus to protecting their systems, information, and data. This is important because companies have a lot of questions about the principles of *working from home*. And because of that, good planning for setting up protection and secure access to information from different remote locations is a big challenge.

Working from home can pose a risk to secure access to information, and it is important to point out that many employees do not have proper protection at home in terms of network security. All devices used to access information and send and receive emails are significant targets of attacks aiming to get hold of information. One of the biggest challenges that companies face is implementing sufficient protection for sending/receiving emails. In addition to protection against viruses, malware, and phishing, the training and proper education of employees is a very important part of the overall information protection system.

Microsoft Defender for Office 365 is a comprehensive product with the aim of protecting your email system (Exchange Online) against malware, viruses, and phishing attacks. Alongside the stated features in its Plan 1 and Plan 2 versions, Microsoft Defender for Office 365 offers the possibility of quality training for employees, intended to increase their knowledge of how to recognize emails and information which can cause damage to the company.

Microsoft Defender for Office 365 is a part of the Microsoft 365 Defender family, which, in addition to the aforementioned service, contains the following products, which will be discussed later in this book:

- Microsoft Entra ID Identity Protection
- Microsoft Defender for Identity
- Microsoft Defender for Cloud Apps (formerly CloudApp Security)
- Microsoft Defender for Endpoint
- Microsoft Identity Protection

- Microsoft Defender for Cloud
- Microsoft Defender Vulnerability Management
- Microsoft Data Loss Prevention
- App Governance (as a part of Microsoft Defender for Cloud Apps)

It is important to note that all the listed services can be added as add-ons to specific subscriptions, while some are an integral part of existing subscription packages. In this chapter, we will deal in detail with Microsoft Defender for Office 365. The product, as we touched upon before, can be added as an add-on to particular subscriptions and comes in two versions – Microsoft Defender for Office Plan 1 and Microsoft Defender for Office Plan 2.

Microsoft Defender for Office Plan 1 is an integral part of the following subscriptions:

- Microsoft 365 Business Premium (max 300 users)
- Microsoft 365 Enterprise E1
- Microsoft 365 Enterprise E3

Microsoft Defender for Office Plan 2 is an integral part of the following subscriptions:

- Microsoft 365 Enterprise E5
- Microsoft 365 F5 Security

Technical requirements

To access Microsoft Defender for Office 365, you need to have one of the previously mentioned licenses and administrator rights. It is enough to have Global Administrator rights to do any of the required configurations for the service. However, if you need to allocate access rights and activity permissions for the Microsoft Defender for Office 365 portal, then it is necessary to create a security group in Microsoft Entra ID and assign the following necessary administrator roles:

- Security Administrator
- Security Operator
- Security Reader
- Global Reader

> **Important note**
>
> Users with the specified administrator roles are also entitled to other Microsoft 365 Defender services, such as Microsoft Defender for Endpoint or Microsoft Defender for Cloud Apps.

Getting started with Microsoft Defender for Office 365

Not so long ago, if the organization was planning to set up an Exchange Server instance on-premises, they had to plan for setting up both a proxy server and the additional protections for proper filtering of mail traffic. What has not changed with the transition to Exchange Online is that you still require adequately set-up DNS records for authentication of your mail system. The following are the records that you do *still* need to upload to Exchange Online at the level of your tenant:

- MX records
- SPF records
- DKIM records
- DMARC records

Depending on which type of Microsoft Defender for Office 365 plan you have (Plan 1 or Plan 2), there are different options for configuring policies and rules.

Plan 1 has a lot of different options, which can be useful when setting up protection for your mail traffic. The basic settings of Exchange Online Protection, in most cases, are not sufficient to satisfy all requirements. The difference between Plan 1 and 2 is primarily reflected in the protection configuration options for policies and rules, especially in the **Threat policies** options.

The differences between Microsoft Defender for Office 365 Plan 1 and Plan 2 are as follows:

Microsoft Defender for Office 365 Plan 1	**Microsoft Defender for Office 365 Plan 2**
Real-time detection	Everything included in Plan 1 plus advanced threat policies
Safe Attachment	Advanced threat policies
Safe Links	Threat Trackers and Explorer
Anti-phishing, anti-malware, and anti-spam	Incident and alert investigation
Reporting	Attack simulation training
	Automated response

Table 3.1 – Microsoft Defender Plans

We will go through each of the aforementioned items in detail throughout the rest of this book, after which you will have a much clearer picture of the correct way to set up protections within Microsoft Defender for Office 365.

> **Important note**
>
> The correct implementation of protection for your mail system is a very important part of protecting the entire tenant from attempted attacks. Hence, it is important you draw up a plan that clearly outlines the direction in which you want to take your security system. It is important to keep in mind that every protection increase brings an increase in false-positive detections of inbound emails. This means that you will spend more time browsing the Quarantine folder. Of course, if the business requires you to have a very rigorous protection plan, then this option is not even questionable.

The first options that you need to configure on the Microsoft Defender for Office 365 side concern policies and rules. After activating the tenant and setting up the service using the licenses available to you, it is necessary to make changes to the basic policies found under the following items:

- **Threat policies**
- **Alert policy**
- **Manage advanced alerts**
- **Activity alerts**

The following screenshot illustrates where you can configure different threat policies in Microsoft Defender for Office 365:

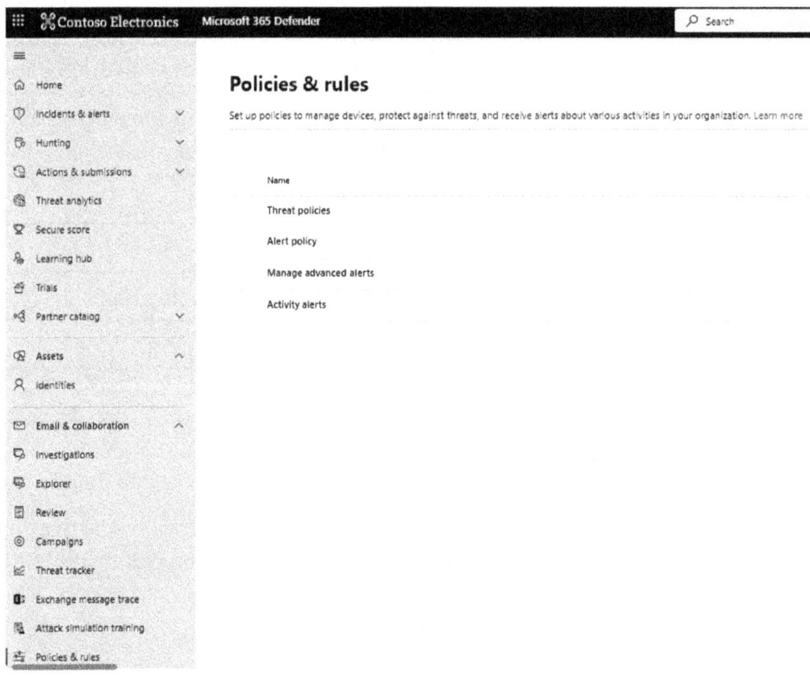

Figure 3.1 – Policies & rules

Most of this chapter will deal with the correct configuration of threat policies.

As we stated in the introduction, the successful configuration of each of the options here requires careful analysis in application and implementation. The biggest pitfall in the configuration of threat policies is that all rules and warnings can be set to the maximum level of protection. The big question is, what will you get as the result of such a configuration? Higher protection could lead to more demanding quarantine management in order to filter emails heading toward end users.

Clicking **Threat policies** shows the following options that you can configure:

- **Templated policies**:
  - **Preset security policies**
  - **Configuration analyser**
- **Policies**:
  - **Anti-phishing**
  - **Anti-spam**
  - **Anti-malware**
  - **Safe Attachment**
  - **Safe Links**
- **Rules**:
  - **Tenant Allow/Block Lists**
  - **Email authentication settings**
  - **Advanced delivery**
  - **Enhanced filtering**
  - **Quarantine policies**
- **Others**:
  - **Evaluation mode**

Whether to simply use template policies when configuring your defenses is one of the biggest questions. In smaller companies with fewer than 100 employees, templated policies are justified because the configuration is simpler. Nonetheless, a more granular configuration is recommended if you want to be able to clearly define all options for available Office 365 services.

Templated policies provide two effective solutions for enhanced protection: Present Security Policies and Configuration Analyzer. Within **Preset security policies**, three options are available, as illustrated in the following screenshot:

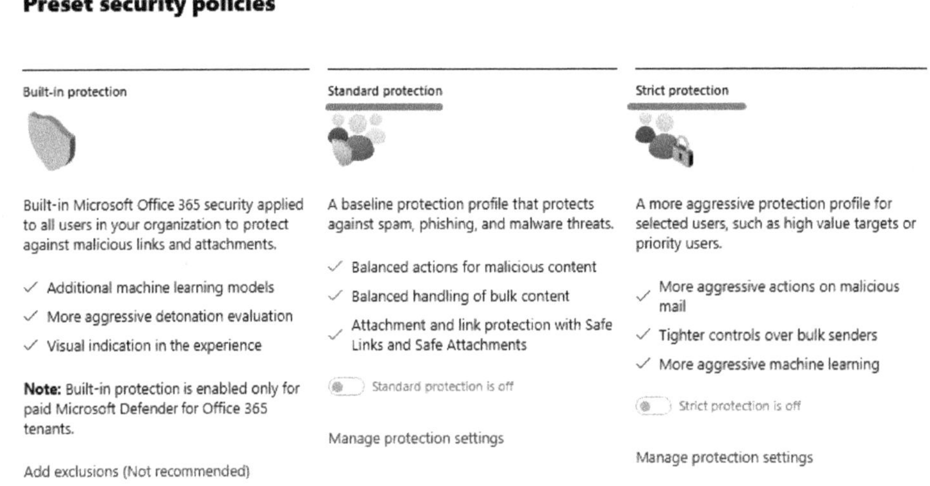

Figure 3.2 – Preset security policies

Let's go through these three options now.

The **Bulit-in protection** option is designed to provide a *good* protection configuration and is intended for organizations that do not want or do not have *greater* protection requirements. This option comes with an **Add exclusions** link, which allows the admin to optionally exclude users, groups, or domains from the Built-in protection functionality. It is precisely for this reason that this option is not recommended to be used.

The next two options offer a better level of preconfigured protection, but as we mentioned previously, a much wider range of options is available for configuration under **Policies**.

In the **Standard protection** option, you can apply protection to specific users, groups, and domains. This is configured as follows:

1. Log in as a Global Administrator on the tenant.
2. Open **Security Admin Center**.
3. Under the **Email & Collaboration** option, click **Policies**.
4. In the new window, click the **Threat policies** option.

5. In the new window, click the **Preset Security Policies** option (as shown in the following screenshot):

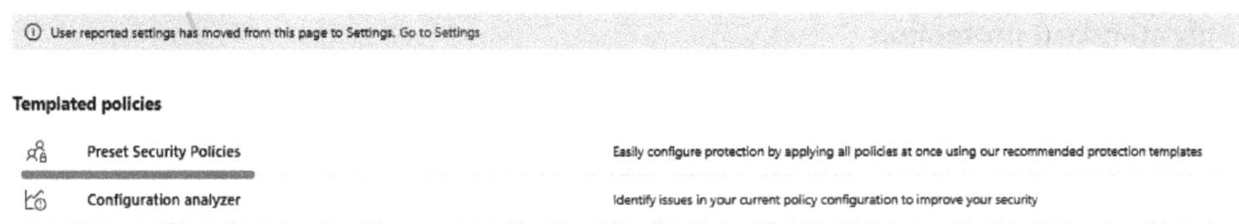

Figure 3.3 – Threat policies

The configuration of Standard protection and Strict protection is the same, the only difference is in the application of anti-phishing policy options, and stronger control over the application of policies (more on this later, when we review the anti-phishing configuration and settings). Of course, it should be noted that choosing Strict protection can lead to increased false-positive flagging of emails and greater control over the quarantine options. The following are the required steps to configure Standard protection:

1. Click **Manage protection settings**.
2. On the **Apply standard protection** screen, under **Apply Exchange Online Protection**, define who to apply the protection to, out of **All recipients** or **Specific recipients** (if you have a smaller number of users, you can use the **All recipients** option). This configuration includes pre-defined rules for anti-malware, anti-spam, and anti-spoofing configuration.

   If you want to exclude any recipients from this protection, please check the **Exclude these recipients** option:

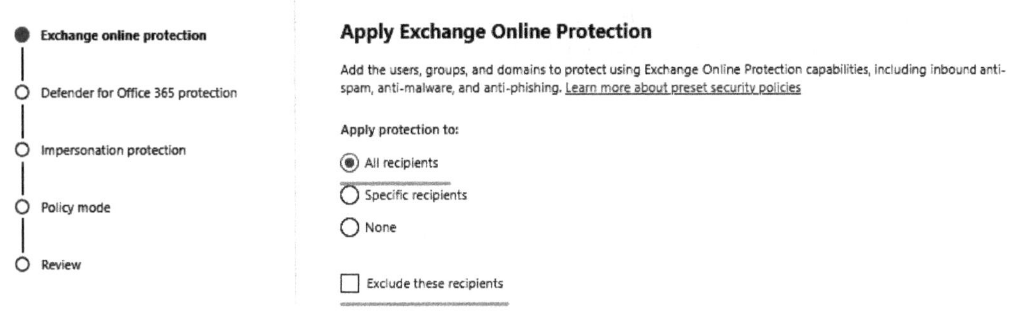

Figure 3.4 – Apply standard protection

3. On the **Apply Defender for Office 365 protection** screen, select one of the options to apply a set of pre-defined rules for the anti-phishing, Safe Attachment, and Safe Link functionalities. You can reuse your previous selection of users and groups to apply the policy to by simply clicking **Previously selected recipients**, or you can add only specific users or skip this configuration altogether.

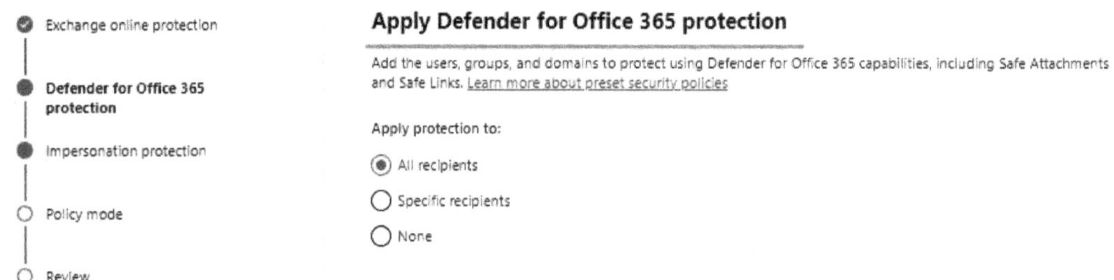

Figure 3.5 – Apply Defender for Office 365

4. Under **Impersonation protection**, configure additional protection for some specific users or domains if required. This protection will provide additional security checks for users' email addresses in similar domains. Impersonation protection offers an added layer of security by implementing further security check in instances where users receive emails from addresses on domains closely resembling their own. This means that if there are any email addresses that mimic those belonging to the users but are hosted on similar domains, the system will subject them to stronger security checks. By doing so, impersonation aims to mitigate the risk of impersonation-based attacks, where malicious actors attempt to deceive users by posing as legitimate senders from familiar domains. This proactive measure helps safeguard against potential threats originating from spoofed or fraudulent email addresses, enhancing overall email security for users and organizations alike. Bear in mind that the number of users that this additional protection can be applied to is limited to 350, and the number of domains to 50. We recommend adding users from C-level positions and other users who have greater access to sensitive information inside your organization.

Apply standard protection

Exchange online protection
Defender for Office 365 protection
Impersonation protection
Protected custom users (0/350)
Protected custom domains (0/50)
Trusted senders (0) and domains (0)
Policy mode
Review

Add email addresses to flag when impersonated by attackers

Add internal or external addresses of people who might be impersonated by attackers, such as top-level executives, board members, and other people in key roles. Messages detected with impersonated senders will be quarantined. Learn more about impersonation settings

Add a name
Add a valid email
Add
0 items
Search
Display name
Sender email address
No data available

Figure 3.6 – Add email addresses to flag for impersonation

5. Under **Add trusted email addresses and domains to not flag as an impersonation**, you can add domains that you know have alternative addresses that can be trusted. For example, `AnyName@something.com` could have an alternative email on another domain, such as `AnyName@somethingnew.com`. That domain, if fully trusted, can be added to bypass the previous rule.
6. On the **Policy mode** screen, choose when you want to activate the policy.
7. Under **Review and confirm your changes**, check how the policy will be applied and click **Finish**.

> **Important note**
>
> The same configuration steps are required if you want to configure Strict protection. The only difference between the two levels of protection is that Strict protection offers a higher level of anti-phishing protection.

Although the configuration we've just seen is quite good for protecting your tenant, you still have the option to set up more detailed protections for anti-phishing, anti-spam, anti-malware, Safe Attachment, and Safe Links functionalities. You can configure all these policies through access through the Microsoft 365 Defender portal under the **Threat policies** section. Under the **Policies** option, you will find all the aforementioned protection options, which you can configure according to your needs. If you decide to apply more detailed configurations (such as adding more flags, specific mail address, etc.) for the protection options, it would be desirable to have clearly defined policies and procedures on the protection of the mail system, in which you specify what and to what extent you want to protect your environment. This, of course, is not an obligation, but it is desirable to have such policies and procedures to standardize the process of configuration.

Each policy comes with default basic settings that cover all users of your tenancy. You can modify the policies according to your needs, but we recommend that you create your own policies and define the priority in which order the policies will be applied. In this way, you will be able to have more granular definitions of each policy.

Protecting assets with Microsoft Defender for Office 365

In today's fast-paced and interconnected world, keeping your sensitive information and digital treasures safe has become absolutely vital for organizations of all shapes and sizes. With remote work exploding in popularity and cyber threats becoming more and more sophisticated, making sure your organization's data and communications are secure has never been more critical. And in this ever-evolving landscape of digital dangers, Microsoft Defender for Office 365 steps up as a real superhero in the world of modern cybersecurity.

Think of Microsoft Defender for Office 365 as your trusty shield, specially designed to safeguard your organization's prized possessions within the Microsoft 365 universe. It's like having a high-tech security squad at your disposal, complete with cutting-edge threat-spotting skills, intelligent algorithms, and powerful protective features. This formidable defender stands tall, ready to ward off a wide range of cyber threats, from sneaky phishing attempts to malicious malware invasions and data breaches.

Whether you're running a small business or steering a massive enterprise ship, getting to know and making the most of what Microsoft Defender for Office 365 brings to the table is absolutely crucial in the ongoing battle to shield your digital assets from the ever-evolving world of cyber threats.

Quarantine policy

Microsoft 365 quarantine is a feature within the Microsoft 365 security suite that allows administrators to isolate and hold potentially malicious email messages in a quarantine area, rather than delivering them to the intended recipient's inbox. This allows the administrator to review the message and determine whether it is safe to deliver or it should be deleted. quarantine can also be used to hold spam and phishing messages.

But why configure this policy first? The simple answer to this question is that the quarantine policy is mostly used through the configuration of all other policies in Defender.

Open **Threat policies** and under **Rules**, you will find option to configure and define quarantine policies:

1. Click on **Quarantine policy**.
2. Two default policies are already created:
   - **DefaultFullAccessPolicy**
   - **AdminOnlyAccessPolicy**

3. Click on **Add custom policy** above **DefaultFullAccessPolicy** and **AdminOnlyAccessPolicy**:

Policies & rules > Threat policies > Quarantine policy

Quarantine policy

Use this page to configure how messages are handled by Office 365 Quarantine. You can also configure how end-users and admin users can view and manage quarantined messages. Learn more about quarantine policy

+ Add custom policy Refresh Export Global settings

	Policy name	Last updated
☐	DefaultFullAccessPolicy	
☐	AdminOnlyAccessPolicy	

Figure 3.7 – Add a custom quarantine policy

4. Provide a name for your quarantine policy (unfortunately, there is no option to add descriptions to custom policies).
5. Under **Recipient message access**, define the level of access to quarantines messages for users:
   - **Limited access** (users can see quarantined messages but cannot release message)
   - **Set specific access (Advanced)**
6. If you select **Set specific access (Advanced)**, you are given the options to configure your email release action preferences:
   - `Allow recipients to request a message to be released from quarantine`
   - `Allow recipients to release a message from quarantine`
7. Under **Select additional actions recipients can take on quarantined messages**, define which actions recipients can perform (such as **Delete**, **Preview**, and **Block sender**):

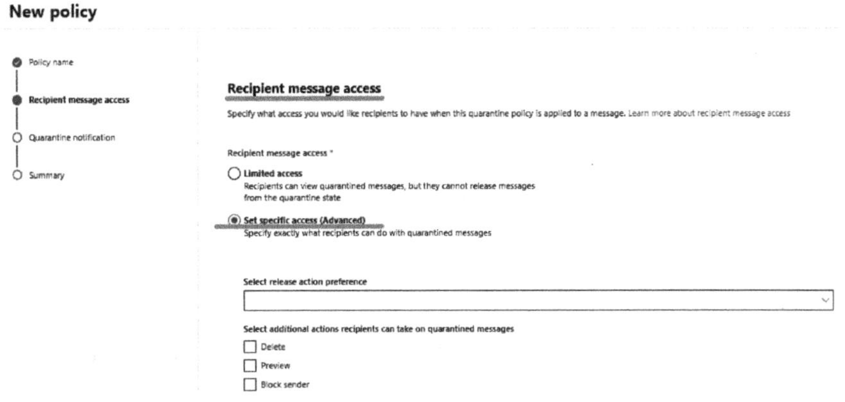

Figure 3.8 – Quarantine message access

8. Click **Next**.
9. Enable **Quarantine notification**.
10. Click **Next**.
11. Review your policy and click **Submit**.

Now you have a choice of three policies related to the quarantine policy. When creating any other option, you must define which quarantine policy will be used. Most companies decide to set `AdminOnlyAccessPolicy`, which prevents all other users from being able to interact at all with messages that are redirected to quarantine for further review.

Notifications about messages in quarantine can be adjusted by clicking on **Global settings** as is shown in the following screenshot:

Figure 3.9 – Quarantine global policy

Adjust the options as required and specify the frequency of notification emails about messages that are in quarantine. This is not a bad option to notify users that certain emails are in quarantine, which can significantly reduce the manual checking of incoming messages.

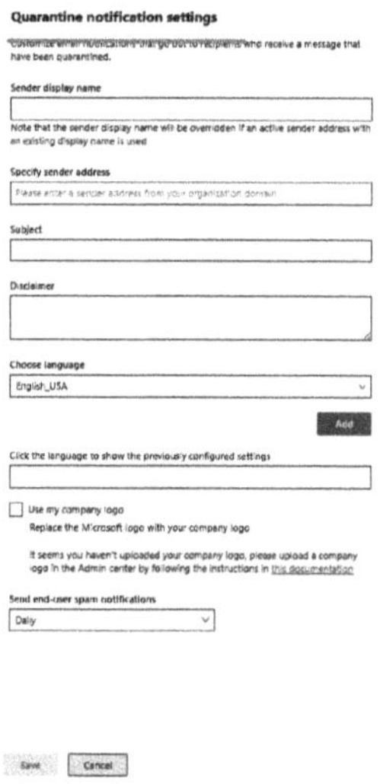

Figure 3.10 – Quarantine notification settings

After configuring the quarantine policy, a good practice is to check the current situation in your tenant by clicking on the **Evaluation mode** option. By clicking on the **Manage** option in the window that appears, you can check the current state of activity for all users or just one user, without any impact on production. This option can be very helpful before you start configuring the Anti-malware, Anti-phishing, Anti-spam, Safe Attachment, and Safe Links policies.

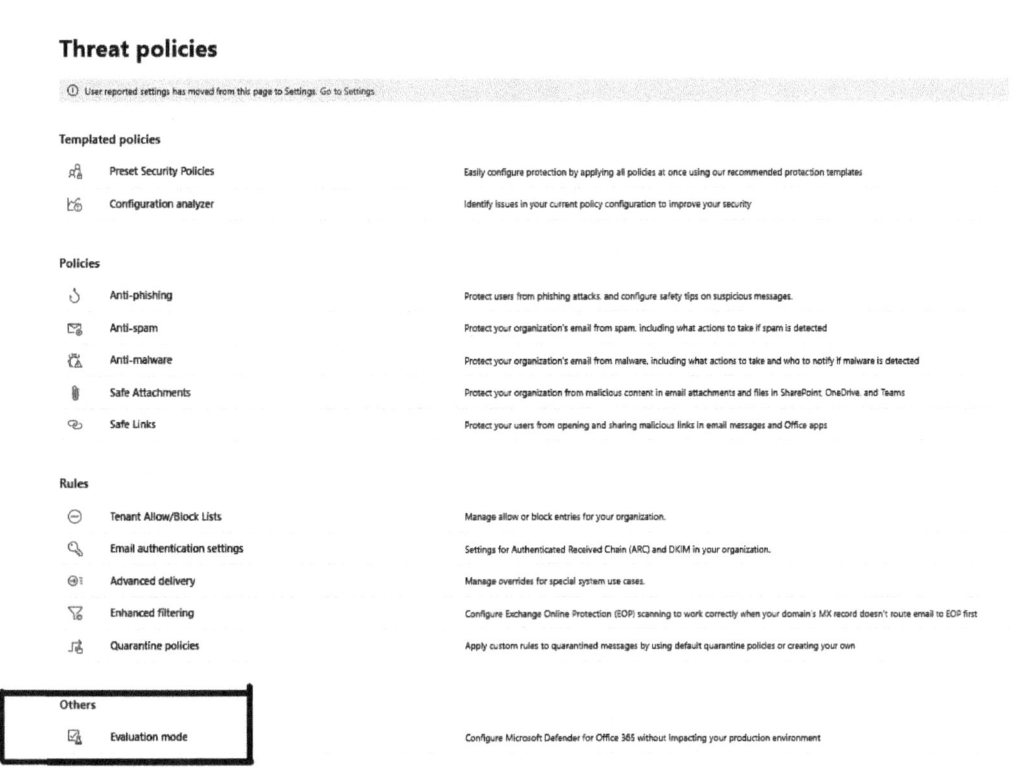

Figure 3.11 – Threat policies

Now that you're aware of the dangers of phishing attacks and how to recognize them, let's dive deeper into our anti-phishing policy to ensure the safety of your personal and company information.

Anti-phishing

The anti-phishing policy has a created default policy named **Office 365 Anti-Phishing Default (Default) policy** which covers all your tenancy users. To create a new anti-phishing policy according to your needs and requirements, go to **Policies & rules | Threat policies** and you will find options for configuring anti-phishing. Click on + **Create**:

1. In the new window that appears, provide a name for the new policy. In **Description**, it is useful to add a note about this new rule (this is optional, but can be a good idea if your organization has many different rules).

   Under **Users, groups, and domains**, specify the accounts, groups, or domains to which this policy will be applied. You can apply many rules to different users as well as groups or domains.

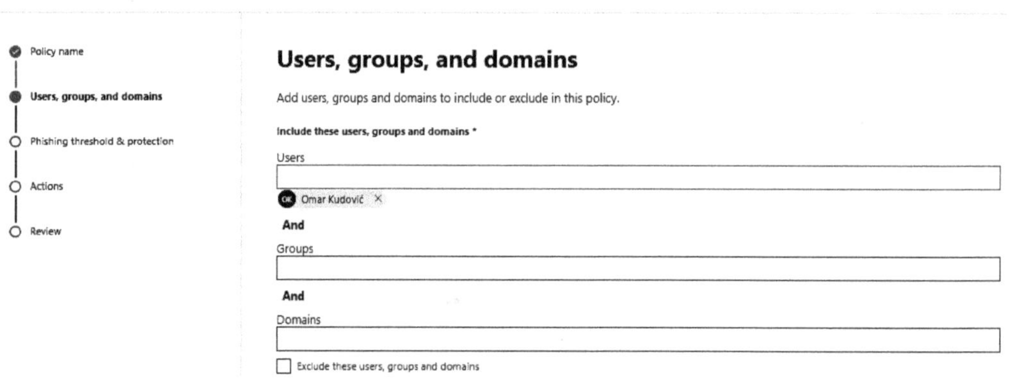

Figure 3.12 – Anti-phishing policy

2. Under **Phishing threshold & protection**, you can configure more granular options for the phishing email detection threshold. There are four steps:

   - **1 - Standard**
   - **2 - Aggressive**
   - **3 - More Aggressive**
   - **4 - Most Aggressive**

   Bear in mind that if you choose **4 - Most Aggressive** for **Phishing email threshold**, you can expect a higher volume of false-positive phishing detections and more frequent checking of the Quarantine folder as a result. Whatever you choose here can be changed at any time and applied to your users immediately:

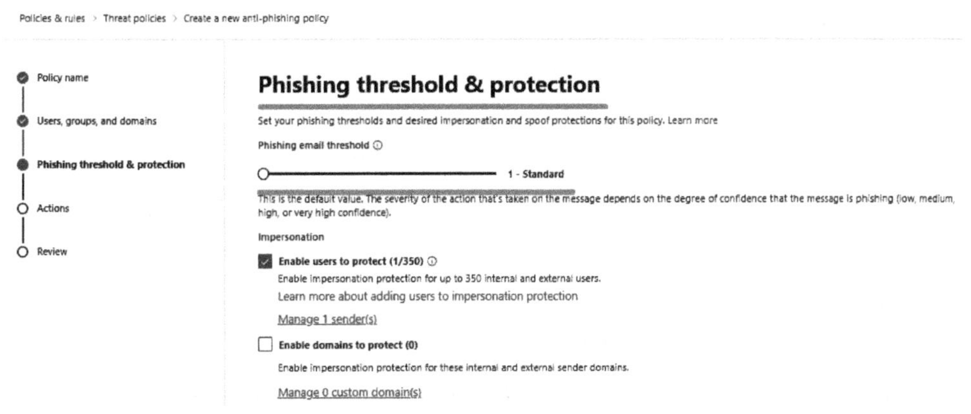

Figure 3.13 – Define anti-phishing threshold

3. Add users and domains if required to **Impersonation** and **Add trusted senders and domains**. The number of users that can be added here is limited to 350, and the number of domains to 50:

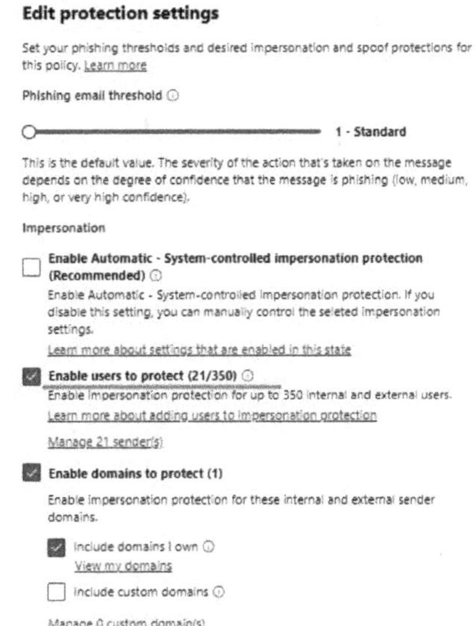

Figure 3.14 – Add additional protection to specific mail users

4. Leave the **Enable mailbox intelligence (Recommended)** check box marked.
5. Check the **Enable intelligence for impersonation protection (Recommended)** option. This option will provide additional protection to all your mailboxes added to the **Impersonation** screen.
6. For Spoof, leave the checkbox ON for **Enable spoof intelligence (Recommended)** ON

7. On the **Actions** screen, define what the system should do with mail detected as an impersonated user or spoof:

   - Recommend solution: quarantine the message (quarantine the message for a more comprehensive overview, ensuring a reduction in false-positive email messages.):

     - With this action, you benefit from extra safety. If the message is OK and the user confirms this, you can always add that address to a trusted mail sender.

   - Choose `Quarantine the message for "If the message is detected as a spoof-by-spoof intelligence"`

8. For **Quarantine policy**, choose one of the options, either **DefaultFullAccessPolicy** or **AdminOnlyAccessPolicy** (more about those two options was covered in the *Quarantine policy* section):

   - On **Safety tips & indicators**, leave the checked boxes as is and add a check to **Show first contact safety tip (Recommended)**. This option will add a textual notification to the top of the message when a user receives a message from a given sender for the first time:

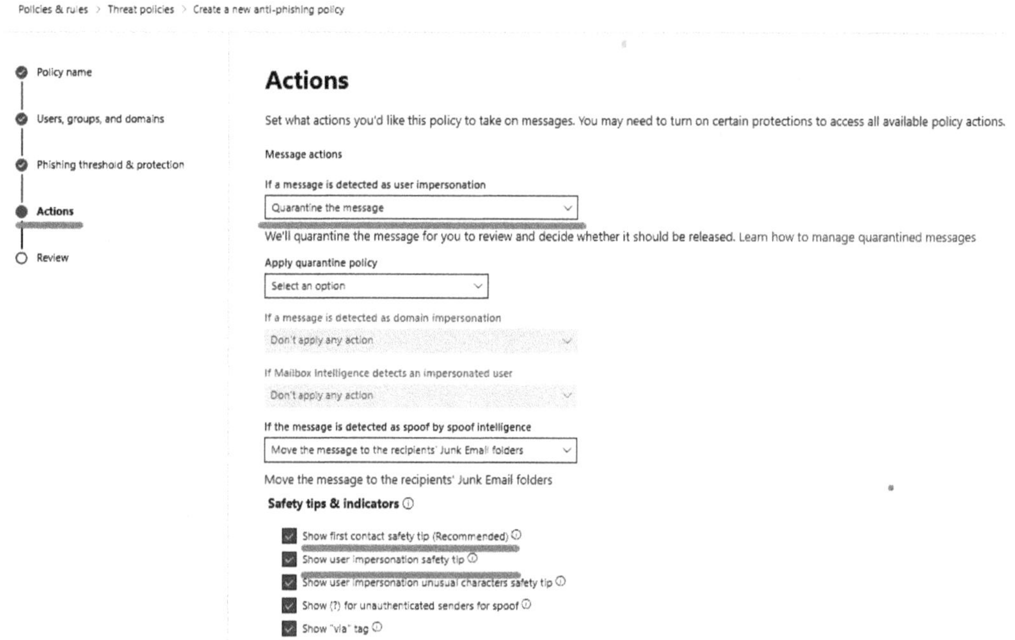

Figure 3.15 – Define the rules for anti-phishing actions

9. Review your policy and click **Submit**.

> **Note**
>
> The **Show first contact safety tip (Recommended)** option will work better if you create an Exchange Online rule to add a warning when your users get emails from outside the organization. The following is an example warning, along with the code to generate it:
>
> *[EXTERNAL CONTENT - USE WITH CAUTION!]*
>
> When creating your Exchange Online rule, paste the following into the **Apply a disclaimer to message** field:
>
> ```
> <div style='border:solid #9C6500 1.0pt;padding:2.0pt 2.0pt
> 2.0pt 2.0pt'><p class=MsoNormal style='line-height:12.0pt;backgr
> ound:#FFEB9C'></
> span> [EXTERNAL
> CONTENT - USE WITH CAUTION!]<o:p></o:p>
> ```

Anti-spam

The Microsoft 365 Defender for Office 365, anti-spam policy is a security feature in Microsoft 365 that helps protect users from spam and other unwanted email messages. It uses a combination of techniques such as signature-based detection, heuristics, and reputation analysis to identify and block spam messages. It also provides real-time protection and periodic scans to detect and remove spam messages that have already been delivered to a user's inbox. This feature is fully integrated with other security features in Microsoft 365, and can be used not only with **Exchange Online Protection** (**EOP**), but also with SharePoint Online and OneDrive for Business, providing comprehensive protection against spam and unwanted email messages.

The anti-spam policy allows administrators to set different levels of filtering for different types of email messages, such as bulk emails, phishing, and malicious emails. Administrators can also configure different actions to be taken when an email message is identified as spam, such as moving the message to the junk folder or quarantining the message.

It is included in several Microsoft 365 plans including Office 365 Enterprise E5, Office 365 A5, Office 365 E5, Microsoft 365 Business Premium, Microsoft 365 E5 Security, Microsoft 365 E5 Compliance, and Microsoft 365 E5 Information Protection and Governance.

The anti-spam policy settings contain three basic policies. All three basic policies have the Lowest priority (in the context of an Anti-Spam Policy for Microsoft 365, *lowest priority* typically indicates that created policies are considered the least urgent or important. This designation suggests that these policies will be handled with less immediate attention compared to emails categorized with higher priorities), and only basic settings are configured in them. For this reason, it is necessary to create new policies. The three basic policies are the following:

- Anti-spam inbound policy (Default)
- Connection filter policy (Default)

- Anti-spam outbound policy (Default)

Let's learn how to configure the Anti-spam inbound policy:

1. Click + **Create policy** and select the **Inbound** option:

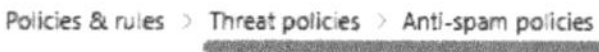

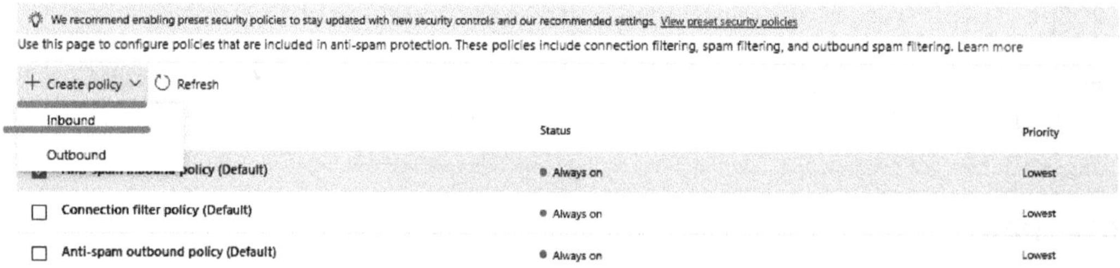

Figure 3.16 – Configure anti-spam policies

2. In the window screen text appears, **Name your policy**, define a name and add a description for your new policy.
3. Apply your created policy to the required users, groups, and domains. If you want to exclude some parties from this policy, check the **Exclude these users, groups, and domains** option.
4. Under **Bulk email threshold & spam properties**, leave **Bulk email threshold** on the default level (usually 7).
5. Under **Increase spam score**, you can configure the following options:
    - **Image links to remote websites**
    - **Numeric IP address in URL**
    - **URL redirect to other port**
    - **Links to .biz and .info websites**

To ensure compliance with Microsoft's policies and avoid any disruptions to your email service, it is recommended to review and adhere to the specific bulk email thresholds and guidelines provided by Microsoft for the email service you are using.

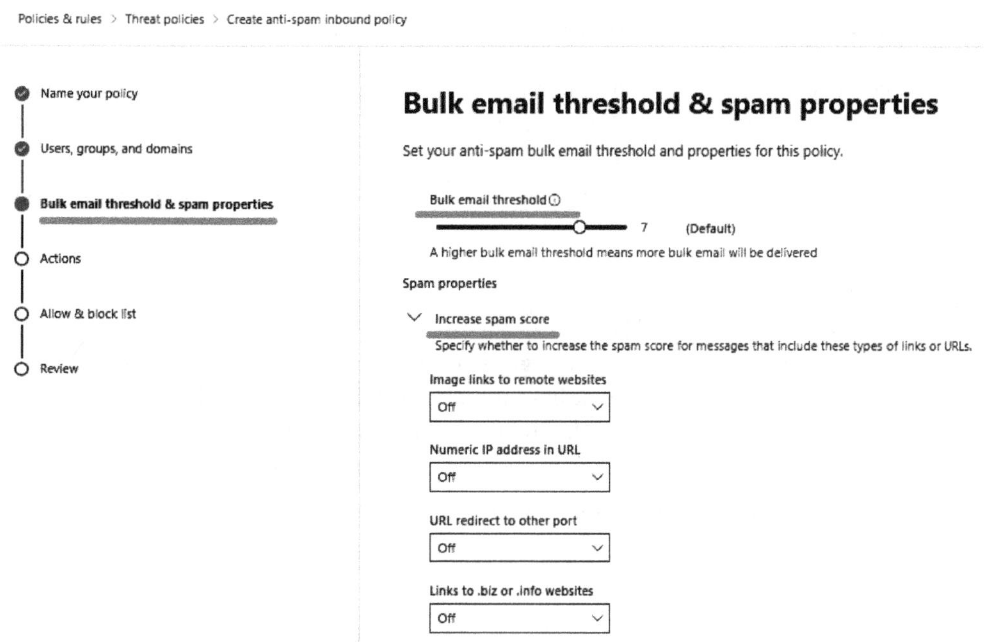

Figure 3.17 – Anti-spam email threshold properties

Under **Mark as spam**, you can configure several different options governing when to mark email messages as spam. From all the options available, we recommend enabling (i.e., setting to **On**) the following properties:

- Empty messages (who likes to get empty messages?)
- **SPF records**: hard fail (if sender's domain doesn't have properly configured SPF records, the email will be marked as spam)
- **Sender ID filtering**: hard fail (in combination with the SPF records hard fail option, this solution will increase your anti-spam protection). Sender ID filtering with the **hard fail** option in Anti-Spam policy within Exchange Online is a mechanism designed to enhance email security by verifying the authenticity of the sender's domain.
- **Backscatter** (also known as *Collateral Spam* or *Outscatter*, these are emails that usually act as a side effect of incoming Spam mail). Backscatter Anti-Spam solutions in Exchange Online are designed to address the issue of backscatter, which refers to the unwanted and misdirected **non-delivery reports** (**NDRs**) or bounce-back messages generated by email servers. These messages are typically a result of spam or phishing attacks that use forged sender addresses, causing the recipient server to generate NDRs to the unsuspecting, legitimate sender.
- **Contains specific language** (specify languages that you do not expect in incoming mail)

- **From these countries** (set countries from where you do not expect incoming mail to be sent)

Of course, take a good look at the other options as well, and if you find them to be useful in your environment, select and activate them. Once you're finished, you can set your policy to Test mode and check the results before activating it for your users, groups, or domains. To do this, under the **Test mode** option, set **Send BCC message** and add the email address of the administrators or others who will test this policy.

1. Click **Next**.
2. Under **Actions**, define what will be done with messages marked as spam. The recommendation is to set all actions to **Quarantine message**. With that, you can be sure that mail marked as spam is redirected, although of course in some cases, this will include legitimate messages (for example, as a result of bad SPF records – remember, there are quite a few domains around the world without correct SPF records).
3. Under **Safety tips** and **Zero-hour auto purge (ZAP)**, leave all options checked:

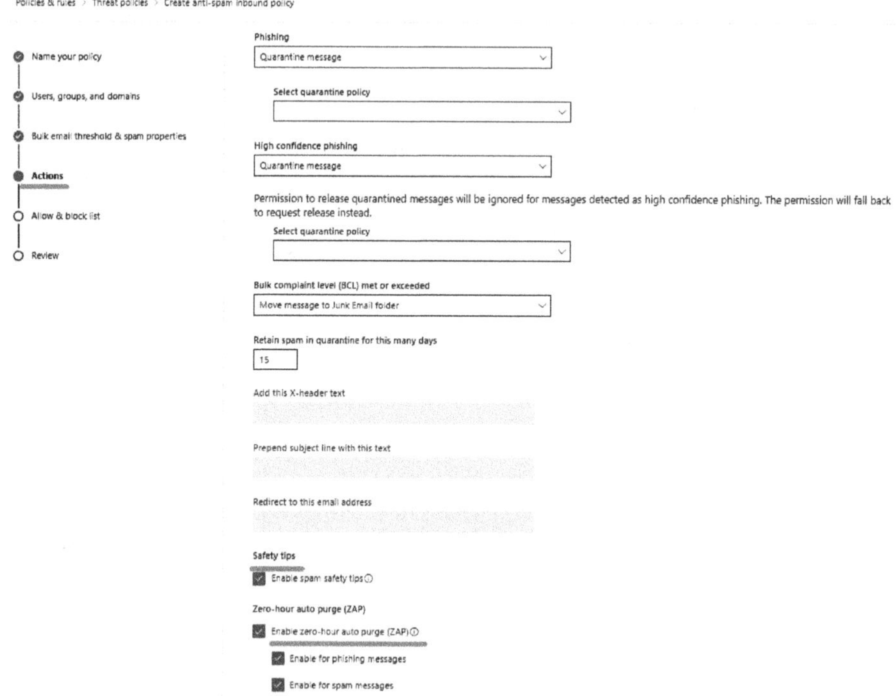

Figure 3.18 – Anti-spam action properties

4. Under **Allow & block list**, you can define allowed senders and domains and block specific senders and domains. Do not add your own domain to **Allowed domains** as spammers will try mostly to fake your domain.

5. Click **Next**, review your policy, and press **Create**.

After successfully configuring your anti-spam policy, let's dive into the next phase and explore the powerful options available for configuring your anti-malware policy.

Anti-malware

Microsoft 365's anti-malware policies are a security feature in Microsoft 365 that helps protect users from malware and other malicious content. It is designed to detect and block malware that is delivered through email, cloud storage, and other online services.

Anti-malware policies use a combination of different techniques including signature-based detection, heuristics, and behavioral analysis to identify and block malware. Besides this, the service also provides real-time protection and periodic scans to detect and remove malware that has already been downloaded to a device. The feature is fully integrated with other security features in Microsoft 365, such as **Exchange Online Protection** (**EOP**), SharePoint Online, and OneDrive for Business, providing comprehensive protection against malware. It also provides reporting and management capabilities to help administrators monitor the health of the environment, identify and respond to potential threats, and recover from malware incidents.

It is included in several Microsoft 365 plans including Office 365 Enterprise E5, Office 365 A5, Office 365 E5, Microsoft 365 Business Premium, Microsoft 365 E5 Security, Microsoft 365 E5 Compliance, and Microsoft 365 E5 Information Protection and Governance.

The specific steps to configure Microsoft 365 Anti-Malware will depend on the version of Microsoft 365 you are using and the subscription plan you have. However, in general, you will need to do the following:

1. Sign in to the Microsoft 365 admin center with your administrator account.
2. In the navigation panel, click on **Security & compliance**.
3. Select **Threat management**, then select **Policy**.
4. Select **Anti-malware**.

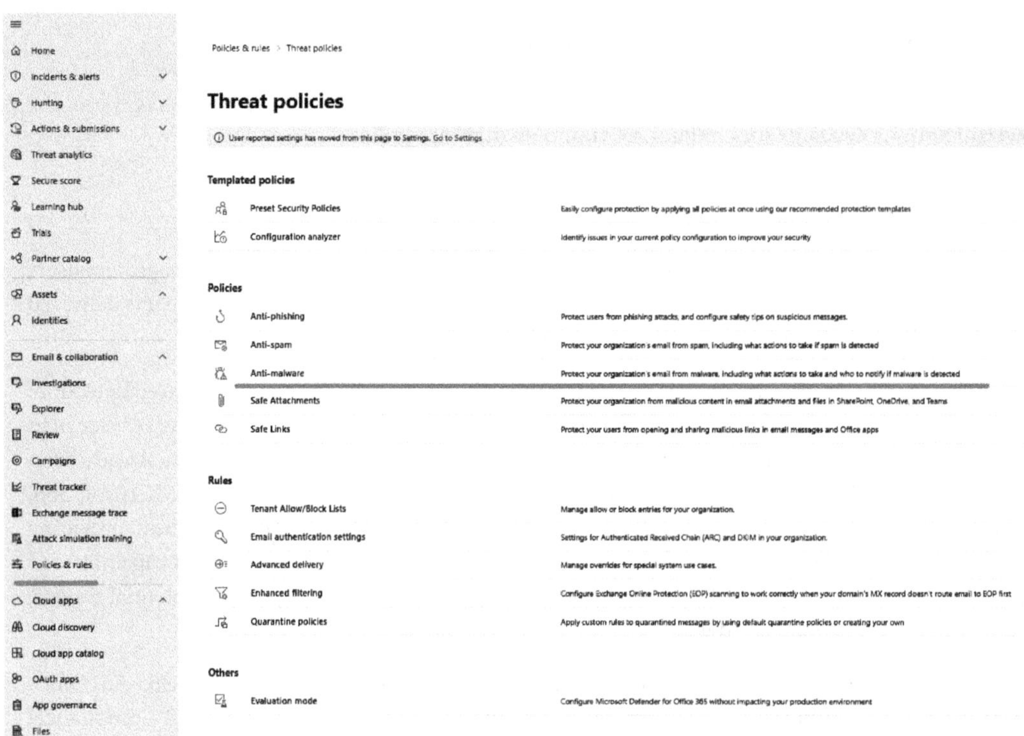

Figure 3.19 – Anti-malware policies

You can use the default policy or create a new one. Creating your own anti-malware policy allows you to define which settings you want to implement.

1. Define which users and groups the anti-malware policy will be applied to. If you don't want to distinguish between users and groups, simply add your domain address .
2. Under **Protection settings**, you can configure the anti-malware settings according to your organization's needs and policies:

   - Check **Enable the common attachments filter** (more than 50 different file types will be blocked by default) and add, if you want, your own file types.
   - Next, define what to do with messages where blocked file types are found:
     - **Reject with NDR**
     - **Send to Quarantine** (if you select this option, define which quarantine policy should be applied)

- Check the **Enable zero-hour auto purge for malware (Recommended)** option if you want to retroactively detect and delete messages containing malware that have already been delivered to users' mailboxes. (It is highly recommended to enable this.)
- Configure the notifications. A tip is to select both **Admin notifications** options to save time on checking quarantine. For a better overview, create a new folder in your mailbox and redirect detected messages there:

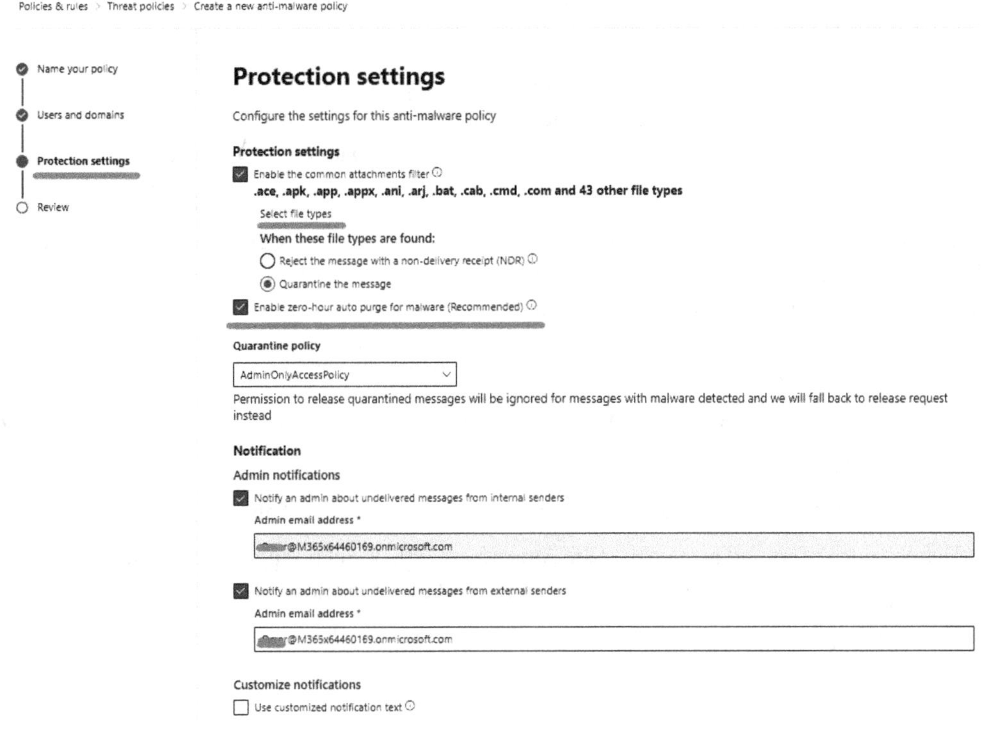

Figure 3.20 – Define protection settings

3. Once you are done and have reviewed your choices, click **Submit** to apply the changes.

Please be aware that the Microsoft 365 Anti-Malware policies are exclusively offered with specific subscription plans and may vary between Microsoft 365 Business and Enterprise Plans. Availability and features can differ based on the chosen subscription, so it's essential to review the details of your specific plan for accurate information on Anti-Malware policies. If you are using an on-premises Exchange server and have a hybrid deployment in your organization, you may need to configure Microsoft EOP to enable anti-malware protection. If you have a hybrid deployment and use a third-party proxy for email traffic, you can still configure the anti-malware options for users' mailboxes located on Exchange Online.

Safe Attachment

Microsoft 365 Safe Attachment is a security feature in Microsoft 365 that helps to protect users from malicious attachments in email messages. It works by analyzing attachments in email messages and identifying those that may contain malware or other malicious content. This service works together with anti-malware policies. If an attachment is identified as potentially dangerous, it is blocked and the user or administrator can be notified. The feature is fully integrated with other security features in Microsoft 365, such as EOP, SharePoint Online, and OneDrive for Business, providing comprehensive protection against malicious attachments.

Safe Attachment uses a combination of techniques such as signature-based detection, heuristics, and behavioral analysis to identify and block malicious attachments. It also provides real-time protection and periodic scans to detect and remove malicious attachments that have already been downloaded to a device.

Safe Attachment is included in several Microsoft 365 plans such as Office 365 Enterprise E5, Office 365 E5, Microsoft 365 Business Premium, Microsoft 365 E5 Security, Microsoft 365 E5 Compliance, and Microsoft 365 E5 Information Protection and Governance.

The following steps will help you to create a new Safe Attachment policy:

1. Click on the **Safe Attachment** button in the **Threat Policy** window.
2. Click **Create**.
3. In the window that appears, add a name and description for your Safe Attachment policy.
4. Define which users and groups the Safe Attachment policy will be applied to. If you don't want to distinguish between users and groups, simply add your domain address.
5. Under **Settings**, define what Safe Attachment should do when malware is detected in an attachment.

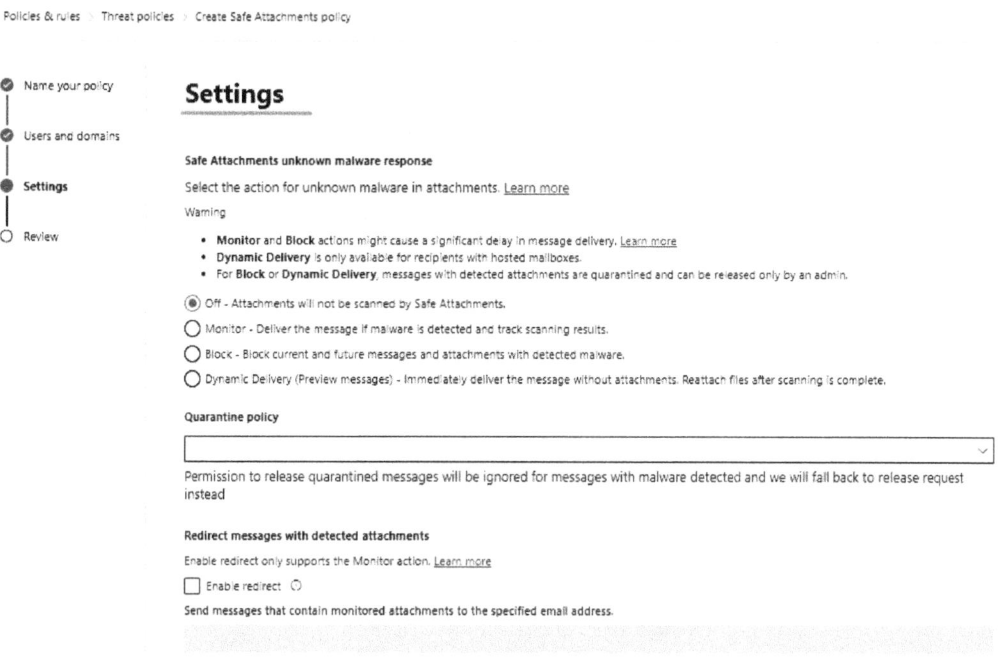

Figure 3.21 – Safe Attachments settings

- Before setting up your configurations, bear in mind that some actions defined in **Settings** can be done only by Administrators. Select one of the following actions:
  - Off: Attachment will not be scanned by Safe Attachment
  - Monitor: Deliver the message, if malware is detected and track scanning results
  - Block: Block current and future messages and attachments with detected malware
  - Dynamic Delivery: Immediately deliver the message without attachment. Reattach files after scanning is complete
- Choose your policy from the **Quarantine policy** dropdown.
- If you want, you can check the **Enable redirect** option to send messages with suspicious attachments to a specific mail address for further review. Note that this option will not work if you select the **Block** or **Replace** settings:

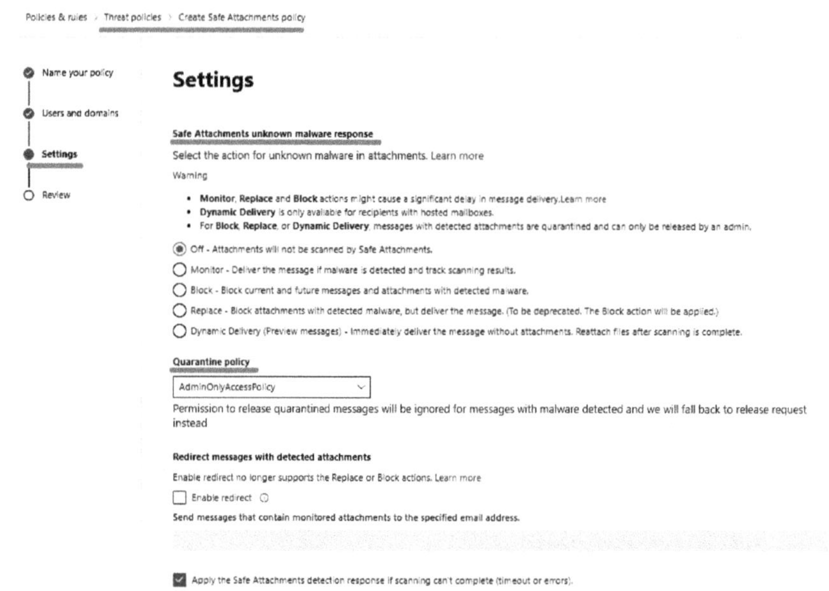

Figure 3.22 – Safe Attachment options

6. Once you are done with your configurations, click **Submit** to apply the changes.

Safe Links

The Safe Links feature in Microsoft Defender for Office 365 helps protect users from malicious links in email messages, instant messages, and other types of content. It works by analyzing links in email messages and other content and identifying those that may lead to malicious websites or other sources of malware. If a link is identified as potentially dangerous, it is blocked and the user is notified. When a user clicks on a link in an email message or other content, Safe Links checks the link against a database of known malicious websites and other sources of malware. If the link is determined to be safe, the user is allowed to access the website. If the link is determined to be potentially dangerous, the user is shown a warning and given the option to continue to the website or return to the original content.

Safe Links also provides real-time protection and periodic scans to detect and remove malicious links that have already been downloaded to a device. Reporting and management capabilities can also be configured to help administrators monitor the health of the environment and identify and respond to potential threats.

Much like Safe Attachment, Safe Links is included in several Microsoft 365 plans including Office 365 Enterprise E5, Office 365 A5, Office 365 E5, Microsoft 365 Business Premium, Microsoft 365 E5 Security, Microsoft 365 E5 Compliance, and Microsoft 365 E5 Information Protection and Governance.

Configuration of Safe Links is very easy.

1. On **Threat Policy**, click on **Safe Link**.
2. Click **Create**.
3. In the window that appears, add a name and description for your Safe Links policy.
4. Define the users and groups to which the Safe Links policy will be applied.
5. Under **URL & click protection settings**, leave the recommended options selected (check *Figure 3.22* below).

   A. Under **Do not rewrite the following URLs in email**, define which URLs should not be scanned by Safe Links.

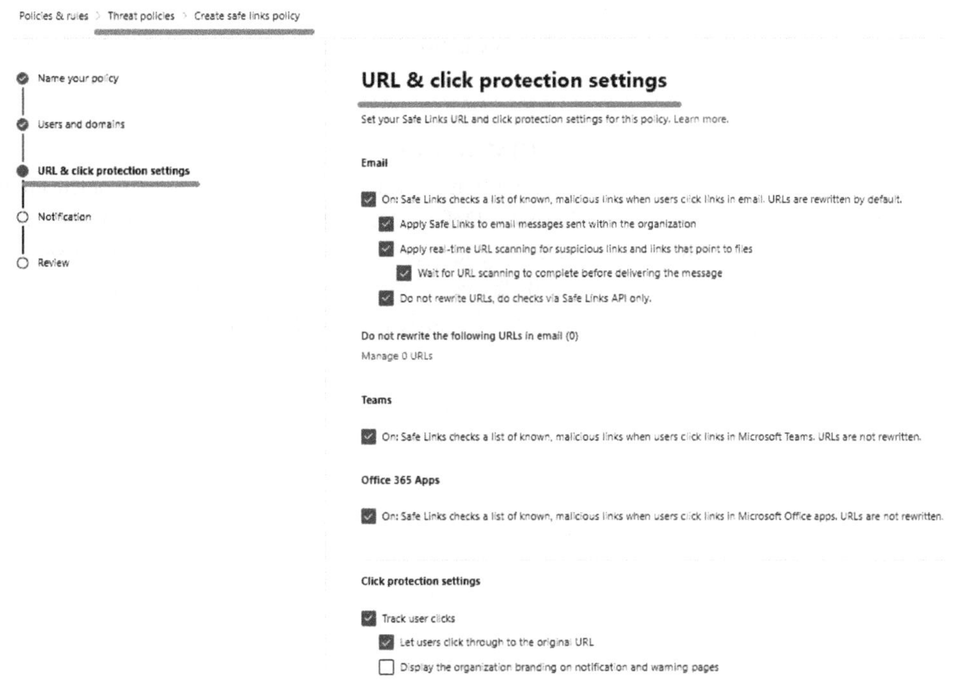

Figure 3.23 – Safe Links settings

6. Leave all other selected options at their defaults.
7. Once you are done reviewing your configuration, click **Submit** to apply the changes.

Rules

You have set up a lot of options to meet your requirements so far, but there are a few more options that can be useful for your security. In particular, the **Tenant Allow/Block** list configuration lets you easily and dynamically control incoming mail traffic and configure the settings for the following:

- Domains and addresses (block up to 20 domains in one rule and define the blocking time, from 30 days up to 90 days.)
- Spoofed senders (block by spoof type and define action)
- URLs (add up to 20 URLs per rule and define action)
- Files (block specific files)

You can simply configure DKIM records (**DKIM**, or **DomainKeys Identified Mail**, is an email authentication method that helps verify the authenticity of the sender and the integrity of the email message.) for your domain through the Microsoft Defender for Office 365 portal. Click on **Email authentication settings**, as shown in the following screenshot, and just follow a few steps and the system will configure important DKIM records for you. You will be required to add two CNAME records to your public DNS and after that, activate the DKIM authentication settings.

Figure 3.24 – Configure DKIM

Exchange Online **DomainKeys Identified Mail** (**DKIM**) is a feature in Exchange Online, part of Microsoft 365, that allows you to add an additional layer of authentication to your email messages. DKIM records use digital signatures to ensure that messages sent from your domain have not been modified during transit and that they were indeed sent from your domain. This helps to protect your domain from being used in phishing and email spoofing attacks. This service allows other mail servers to verify the authenticity of messages sent from your domain by checking the digital signature against the published public key. Bear in mind that besides DKIM records, you also need to have configured MX, SPF, and DMARC records and publish them on your DNS.

Figure 3.25 – Configure the email authentication settings

Attack simulation training

Attack simulation training is a security feature in Microsoft Defender for Office 365 that allows you to simulate phishing, spear-phishing, and ransomware attacks on your organization's users.

The goal of the training is to help educate and raise awareness among users about the different types of attacks they may encounter, as well as to test their ability to identify and respond to them. The training can be customized to fit the needs of your organization and can include simulated email messages, web pages, and social engineering techniques. Additionally, the service provides you with detailed reports on how users responded to the simulated attacks, which can be used to identify areas where additional training or security measures may be needed.

The Attack simulation training feature can be a useful tool for improving the security awareness and readiness of your organization's users. Simulating real-world attacks, it allows users to practice identifying and responding to potential threats, which can help to reduce the risk of a successful attack. Additionally, the training can help to identify areas where users may be particularly vulnerable to attack, allowing you to focus your security efforts where they are needed most.

However, it's important to note that this feature alone is not enough to protect your organization from cyberattacks. It should be used in conjunction with other security measures such as email filtering, firewalls, and anti-virus software. Also, it's essential to have a comprehensive security awareness program in place that includes regular training, testing, and communication with your users.

The Attack simulation training feature is available as part of the following Microsoft 365 plans:

- Microsoft 365 E5
- Microsoft 365 E5 Security
- Microsoft 365 A5
- Microsoft 365 A5 Security
- Microsoft 365 E5 Compliance
- Microsoft 365 A5 Compliance
- Microsoft 365 E5 Information Protection & Governance
- Microsoft 365 A5 Information Protection & Governance

It should be noted that some of these plans might require an additional license purchase.

To use Attack simulation training, you can use the Microsoft 365 Security Center. Here are the general steps you can follow:

1. Sign in to the **Microsoft 365 admin center** with your admin credentials.
2. Navigate to **Microsoft 365 Security Center**.
3. Click on **Attack simulation training** on the left side menu.

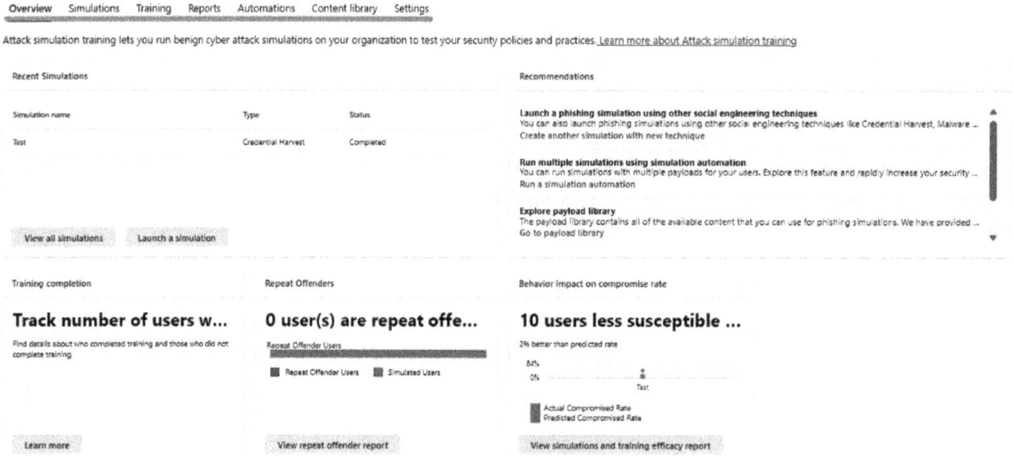

Figure 3.26 – Attack simulation training

4. Click on **Simulations** and select the **Launch a simulation** option:

Attack simulation training
Overview
Simulations
Automations
Content library
Settings
A list of all your simulations and their status.
Draft
0
Scheduled
0
In progress
0
Completed
0
Failed
0
Cancelled
0
+ Launch a simulation
Simulation Name
Type
Platform

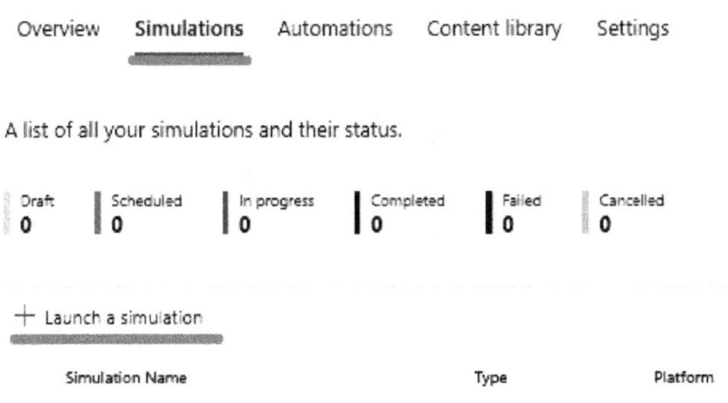

Figure 3.27 – Attack simulations overview

5. Select the attack simulation to be used:

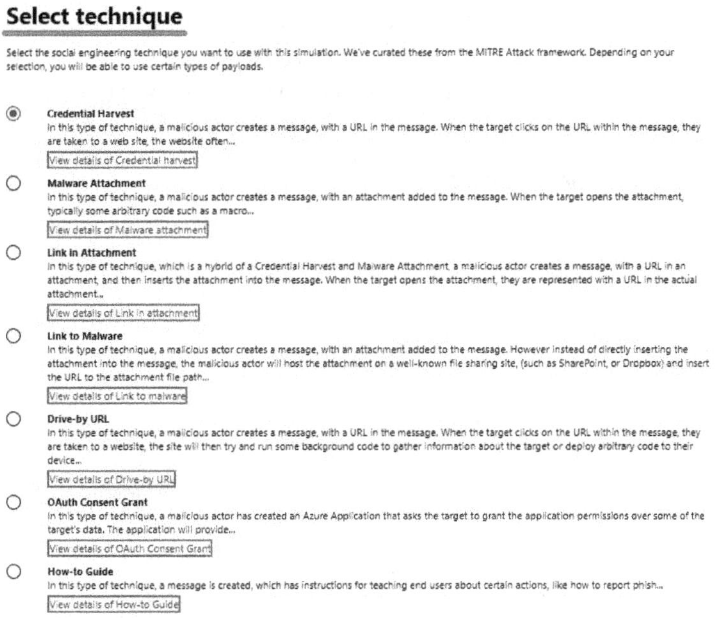

Select technique
Select the social engineering technique you want to use with this simulation. We've curated these from the MITRE Attack framework. Depending on your selection, you will be able to use certain types of payloads.
Credential Harvest
In this type of technique, a malicious actor creates a message, with a URL in the message. When the target clicks on the URL within the message, they are taken to a web site, the website often...
View details of Credential harvest
Malware Attachment
In this type of technique, a malicious actor creates a message, with an attachment added to the message. When the target opens the attachment, typically some arbitrary code such as a macro...
View details of Malware attachment
Link in Attachment
In this type of technique, which is a hybrid of a Credential Harvest and Malware Attachment, a malicious actor creates a message, with a URL in an attachment, and then inserts the attachment into the message. When the target opens the attachment, they are represented with a URL in the actual attachment...
View details of Link in attachment
Link to Malware
In this type of technique, a malicious actor creates a message, with an attachment added to the message. However instead of directly inserting the attachment into the message, the malicious actor will host the attachment on a well-known file sharing site, (such as SharePoint, or Dropbox) and insert the URL to the attachment file path...
View details of Link to malware
Drive-by URL
In this type of technique, a malicious actor creates a message, with a URL in the message. When the target clicks on the URL within the message, they are taken to a website, the site will then try and run some background code to gather information about the target or deploy arbitrary code to their device...
View details of Drive-by URL
OAuth Consent Grant
In this type of technique, a malicious actor has created an Azure Application that asks the target to grant the application permissions over some of the target's data. The application will provide...
View details of OAuth Consent Grant
How-to Guide
In this type of technique, a message is created, which has instructions for teaching end users about certain actions, like how to report phish...
View details of How-to Guide

Figure 3.28 – Select attack simulation technique

6. Under **Name Simulation**, write Simulation Name. Click **Next**.

7. Select the payload and login page. You can select a template or create your own payload. Your payload is sent to users and groups via email or Teams. A tip is to initially send it to yourself and check the payload.
8. Select the users you want to include in the simulation and the date range when the simulation will run. You can select specific users and groups or include all users (there is also the option to exclude specified users).

If your company has prepared security training for end-users, you can allocate this training and specify the deadline by which compromised users are required to complete it.

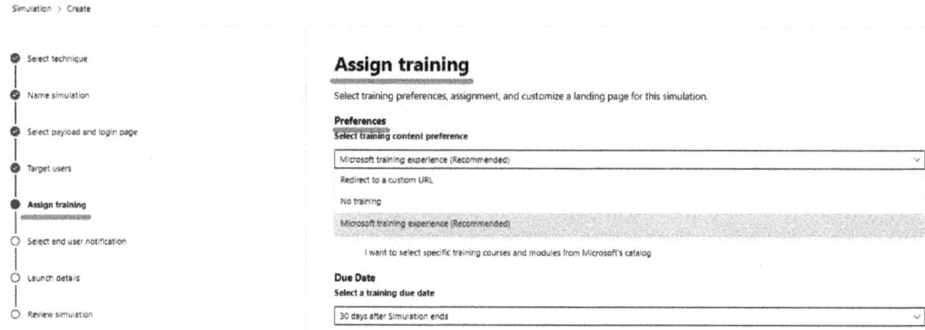

Figure 3.29 – Training assignment

1. Define notification and select recommended preference by Microsoft (you can customize your own notification as well):

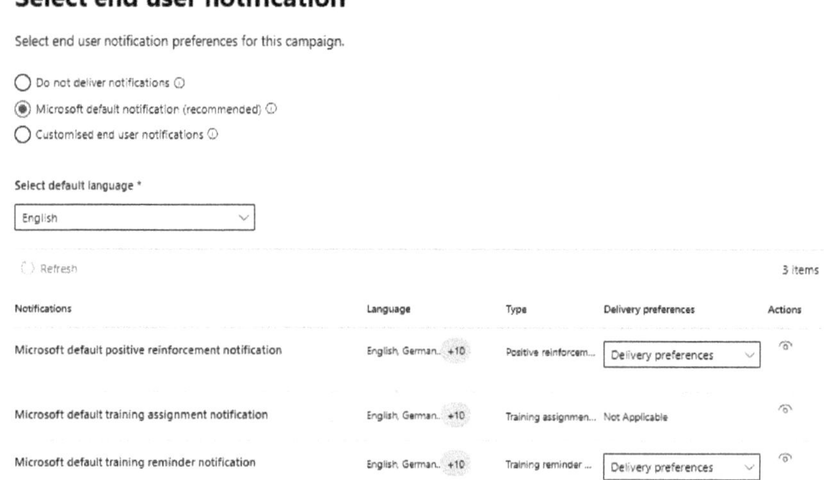

Figure 3.30 - End user notification

2. Review your simulation and click **Submit**.

Once the simulation is running, you will be able to see the results in the **Reports** section of the **Attack simulation training** portal. These reports will show you how many users received the simulation, how many clicked on it, and how many reported it as phishing. You can use this data to evaluate the effectiveness of the simulation and identify areas where additional training may be needed. It's also important to remember that the specifics of customizing the simulation may vary depending on the version of Microsoft 365 you are using.

Responding to alerts and mitigating threats

Threat Explorer is a feature in Microsoft Defender for Office 365 that provides an interactive interface to search and analyze threat intelligence data. It allows security administrators to quickly identify and investigate security threats, view threat information and trends, and take action to mitigate potential threats. Threat Explorer also provides insights into attacker behavior and helps to identify patterns and correlations in security events. This information can be used to fine-tune security policies, improve incident response procedures, and proactively detect and prevent future attacks. The following screenshot shows options and information available in the Threat Explorer portal. It is very useful for a daily or weekly overview of what is happening in your tenant:

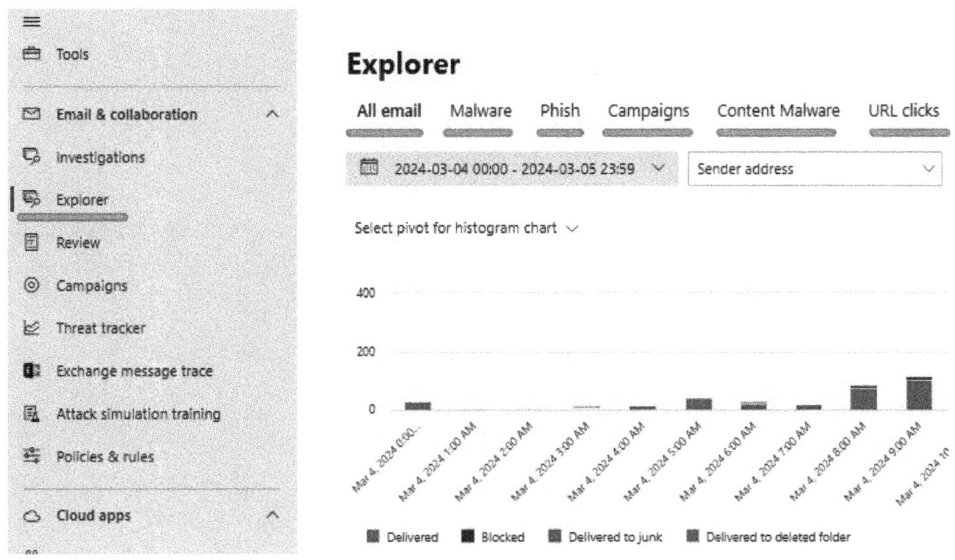

Figure 3.31 – The Threat Explorer portal

Also, keep in mind that it is important to check your own Secure Score from time to time. Microsoft Secure Score is a security analytics tool provided by Microsoft. It provides organizations with a comprehensive view of their security posture by evaluating their use of Microsoft security products and services. Secure Score provides a score based on an organization's security configuration, usage, and practices, and provides recommendations for how to improve their score and overall security posture. The tool evaluates a wide range of security aspects, including access controls, data protection, threat protection, and device security. Secure Score also provides insights into potential security risks and provides actionable recommendations to reduce these risks. Organizations can use the tool to track their progress over time and monitor changes in their security posture.

Microsoft Secure Score is an important tool for organizations that use Microsoft security products and services, as it provides a centralized view of their security posture, identifies areas for improvement, and provides actionable recommendations for reducing security risks. By using Secure Score, organizations can make informed decisions about their security strategy and ensure that their sensitive information and data are protected.

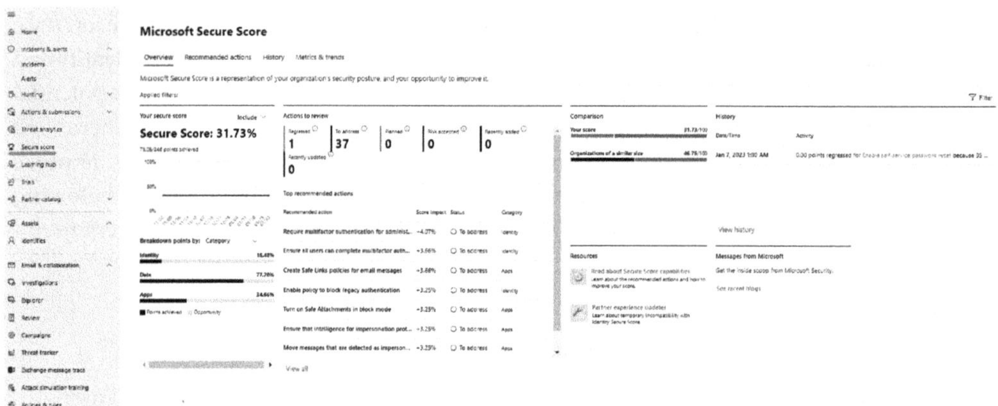

Figure 3.32 – Microsoft Secure Score

Use **Recommended actions** and check how you can improve your Secure Score. Inside **Recommended actions**, you can find different suggestions with clear explanations on their implementation and the impact on your Secure Score.

Microsoft Secure Score

Overview | Recommended actions | History | Metrics & trends

Actions you can take to improve your Microsoft Secure Score. Score updates may take up to 24 hours.

Rank	Recommended action	Score impact	Points achieved	Status	Regressed	Have license?	Category	Product	Last synced	Microsoft update	Notes
1	Require multifactor authentication for administrative roles	+4.07%	0/10	To address	No	Yes	Identity	Azure Active Directory	1/24/2023	None	None
2	Ensure all users can complete multifactor authentication	+3.66%	0/9	To address	No	Yes	Identity	Azure Active Directory	1/24/2023	None	None
3	Create Safe Links policies for email messages	+3.66%	0/9	To address	No	Yes	Apps	Defender for Office	1/30/2023	None	None
4	Enable policy to block legacy authentication	+3.25%	0/8	To address	No	Yes	Identity	Azure Active Directory	1/24/2023	None	None
5	Turn on Safe Attachments in block mode	+3.25%	0/8	To address	No	Yes	Apps	Defender for Office	1/30/2023	None	None
6	Ensure that intelligence for impersonation protection is enabled	+3.25%	0/8	To address	No	Yes	Apps	Defender for Office	1/30/2023	None	None
7	Move messages that are detected as impersonated users by mailbox intelligenc	+3.25%	0/8	To address	No	Yes	Apps	Defender for Office	1/30/2023	None	None
8	Enable impersonated domain protection	+3.25%	0/8	To address	No	Yes	Apps	Defender for Office	1/30/2023	None	None
9	Set the phishing email level threshold at 2 or higher	+3.25%	0/8	To address	No	Yes	Apps	Defender for Office	1/30/2023	None	None
10	Enable impersonated user protection	+3.25%	0/8	To address	No	Yes	Apps	Defender for Office	1/30/2023	None	None
11	Protect all users with a user risk policy	+2.85%	0/7	To address	No	Yes	Identity	Azure Active Directory	1/24/2023	None	None
12	Protect all users with a sign-in risk policy	+2.85%	0/7	To address	No	Yes	Identity	Azure Active Directory	1/24/2023	None	None
13	Quarantine messages that are detected from impersonated domains	+2.44%	0/6	To address	No	Yes	Apps	Defender for Office	1/30/2023	None	None
14	Quarantine messages that are detected from impersonated users	+2.44%	0/6	To address	No	Yes	Apps	Defender for Office	1/30/2023	None	None

Figure 3.33 – List of recommended actions to improve your Secure Score

Both Microsoft Threat Explorer and Secure Score play vital roles in the overall security strategy of an organization. While Threat Explorer focuses on threat detection and response, Secure Score provides a holistic view of an organization's security posture and helps identify areas for improvement. By leveraging these tools, organizations can gain better visibility into their security landscape, make informed decisions, and implement effective security measures to safeguard their digital assets and sensitive information. In conclusion, Microsoft Threat Explorer and Secure Score are two powerful tools offered by Microsoft that enhance the security posture of organizations and help protect against evolving cyber threats.

Summary

Microsoft Defender for Office 365 is a comprehensive security solution designed to protect against threats to an organization's Office 365 environment. It provides a multi-layered defense using a combination of machine learning, behavior analysis, and threat intelligence to detect and prevent attacks. This solution protects against a wide range of security threats such as phishing, malware, and ransomware attacks.

Microsoft Defender for Office 365 also includes threat protection for email, files, and links. It uses advanced filters and algorithms to identify suspicious content and can automatically take action to block or quarantine malicious messages, attachments, and links. The solution integrates with other Microsoft security products, such as Microsoft Entra ID, for a comprehensive defense across an organization's entire environment. In addition to protection against security threats, Microsoft Defender for Office 365 provides advanced reporting and management capabilities. It allows administrators to monitor and respond to security events in real time, as well as view detailed reports on the types of threats detected and prevented. The solution also provides regular updates to stay current with evolving security threats, ensuring that organizations are always protected against the latest threats.

Overall, Microsoft Defender for Office 365 is a powerful tool for protecting against the full range of security threats to an organization's Office 365 environment, providing advanced protection, reporting, and management capabilities to keep sensitive information and data safe. This helps to protect organizations from potential cyber-attacks, data breaches, and other security threats.

Given the increasing frequency and sophistication of cyberattacks, it is important for organizations to invest in a comprehensive security solution such as Microsoft Defender for Office 365 to protect their sensitive information and data.

In the next chapter, we are thrilled to introduce Microsoft Defender for Endpoint, a powerful solution designed to take your device protection and overall security to new heights. Microsoft Defender for Endpoint enables you to safeguard a variety of devices across your organization, including Windows, macOS, Linux, iOS, and Android. With its comprehensive endpoint protection features and advanced threat detection capabilities, you can proactively defend against sophisticated attacks, detect vulnerabilities, and respond swiftly to potential security incidents.

4

Microsoft Defender for Endpoint

Microsoft Defender for Endpoint is a Microsoft solution that provides protection for Windows, macOS, Android, and iPhone devices against various forms of malware, including viruses, spyware, and ransomware. It uses machine learning and behavioral analysis to detect and respond to threats in real-time. With its ease of use, scalability, and integration with Microsoft's security stack, Defender for Endpoint is a powerful tool for organizations looking to improve their endpoint security and protect against the latest threats.

This chapter will cover the following topics:

- Introducing Microsoft Defender for Endpoint
- Configuring Microsoft Defender for Endpoint
- An overview of the Microsoft Intune admin center
- Endpoint security in the Microsoft Intune admin center

Introducing Microsoft Defender for Endpoint

Defender for Endpoint integrates with the Microsoft 365 security stack and leverages the Microsoft cloud infrastructure to provide comprehensive, multi-layered security for endpoint devices. It uses behavioral sensors, cloud-based protection, and threat intelligence to detect and respond to advanced threats in a timely manner. In addition to its antivirus capabilities, Defender for Endpoint also includes features such as device control, firewall, and network protection. The solution also provides device management capabilities, allowing administrators to monitor and manage the security of all endpoint devices in their organization from a single console.

Microsoft Defender for Endpoint is important for several reasons:

- **Advanced threat protection**: Defender for Endpoint uses artificial intelligence and machine learning to detect and respond to threats in real-time. This helps organizations protect against the latest and most sophisticated threats, including zero-day attacks.
- **Multi-layered security**: Defender for Endpoint provides multi-layered security, including antivirus, device control, firewall, and network protection. This helps organizations ensure that their endpoint devices are protected against a wide range of threats.
- **Integration with Microsoft 365**: Defender for Endpoint integrates with the Microsoft 365 security stack, allowing organizations to use a single solution for their cybersecurity needs. This improves efficiency and reduces the risk of security gaps.
- **Cloud-based protection**: Defender for Endpoint uses cloud-based protection to leverage the latest threat intelligence and provide real-time protection. This helps organizations stay ahead of the latest threats and respond quickly to any security incidents.
- **Ease of use and scalability**: Defender for Endpoint is easy to use and scalable, making it ideal for organizations of all sizes. It provides a single console for monitoring and managing the security of all endpoint devices, reducing the complexity of endpoint security management.

Microsoft Defender for Endpoint offers several plans for organizations to choose from, including the following:

- **Microsoft Defender for Endpoint – E5**: This is the top-tier plan that includes all the security and productivity features of Microsoft Defender for Endpoint
- **Microsoft Defender for Endpoint – E3**: This is a mid-tier plan that includes the core features of Microsoft Defender for Endpoint
- **Microsoft Defender for Endpoint – Business**: This is a plan designed for small and medium-sized businesses that includes the essential features of Microsoft Defender for Endpoint

It's worth noting that Microsoft Defender for Endpoint is included as part of Microsoft 365 Enterprise and Microsoft 365 Business licenses, so organizations may not need to purchase a separate plan if they already have a Microsoft 365 license.

Microsoft Defender for Endpoint has the following capabilities:

- **Real-time protection**: Defender uses machine learning algorithms and threat intelligence to detect and prevent malicious activities on endpoints in real time. It blocks malicious files, network attacks, and scripts before they can cause harm.
- **Threat detection and response:** Defender uses a combination of signature-based detection and behavioral analysis to identify malicious activities. It also uses cloud-based security analytics and automated investigation to uncover and respond to threats.

- **Endpoint detection and response (EDR)**: Defender provides EDR capabilities that help security teams quickly detect, investigate, and respond to security incidents on endpoints.
- **Automated investigation and remediation**: Defender uses automated investigation and remediation processes to reduce the time and effort required to respond to security incidents. This includes the ability to automatically contain, isolate, and remove threats from infected devices.
- **Cloud security**: Defender leverages Microsoft's cloud infrastructure to provide fast, scalable, and up-to-date security protection. The security data generated by Defender is stored and analyzed in the cloud, allowing for a quick and effective response to threats.

In the ever-evolving landscape of cybersecurity, organizations require comprehensive tools to protect their endpoints and manage device configurations efficiently. Microsoft offers two powerful solutions that address these needs: Microsoft Defender for Endpoint and Intune. While both products are designed to enhance security and streamline device management, they serve different purposes and offer distinct features. In this chapter, we will explore the differences between Microsoft Defender for Endpoint and Intune, shedding light on their functionalities and benefits.

Microsoft Defender for Endpoint and Intune serve as integral components of an organization's cybersecurity and device management strategy. While Defender for Endpoint focuses on advanced threat detection and response, Intune provides comprehensive device management capabilities. By leveraging the strengths of both solutions, organizations can enhance their security posture, protect endpoints, and manage devices efficiently. Whether it's safeguarding against sophisticated threats or streamlining device configurations, Microsoft offers robust tools to address the diverse needs of modern businesses.

In summary, Microsoft Defender for Endpoint is a comprehensive solution that uses a combination of real-time protection, threat detection, response and remediation, cloud security, and machine learning algorithms to protect against advanced threats. Implementing Microsoft Defender for Endpoint is important for organizations to stay protected against the latest threats and ensure the security of their endpoint devices. In this chapter, we will see how both security solutions, Microsoft Defender for Endpoint and Intune, work.

Technical and license requirements

Microsoft Defender for Endpoint requires the following minimum administrative roles for managing the solution:

- **Global administrator**: To sign in and manage Microsoft Defender for Endpoint and related services
- **Security administrator**: To manage security policies and responses to threats
- **Device administrator**: To manage devices and device policies

It is important to note that these roles are the minimum required and the exact administrative roles required may vary depending on the specific needs and requirements of the organization.

Regarding supported browsers for Microsoft Defender for Endpoint, you can use either Microsoft Edge or Google Chrome. According to Microsoft's information site about Microsoft Defender for Endpoint, other browsers can be used, but only those two are supported fully.

Microsoft Defender for Endpoint is included in Enterprise plans or can be added to the tenant as a standalone plan. There are three options:

- Microsoft Defender for Endpoint Plan 1
- Microsoft Defender for Endpoint Plan 2
- Microsoft Defender for Business

Besides this, you can add a license for **Microsoft Defender Vulnerability Management** (**MDVM**). MDVM is a component of Microsoft Defender for Endpoint, a comprehensive endpoint security solution from Microsoft. It is designed to help organizations proactively identify, assess, and prioritize vulnerabilities on their endpoints and servers.

You can easily check your licenses for Microsoft Defender for Endpoint in **Settings**:

1. Click on **Settings** in the security portal.
2. Click on **Endpoints**.
3. Click on **Licenses**.

Figure 4.1 – Endpoint license

It uses a combination of threat intelligence and machine learning algorithms to detect and classify vulnerabilities and then provides actionable remediation guidance to help organizations mitigate these vulnerabilities. This includes identifying missing patches, configuration issues, and other security problems.

MDVM helps organizations stay ahead of potential attacks by continuously monitoring their environment and providing up-to-date information on the latest vulnerabilities and threats. It is an essential tool for organizations looking to improve their overall security posture and reduce the risk of a successful attack.

Microsoft Defender for Endpoint Plan 1 and Plan 2 are two different plans offered by Microsoft for its endpoint protection solution. The main differences between these two plans are as follows:

- **Features**: Microsoft Defender for Endpoint Plan 2 includes additional features such as vulnerability management, automated investigation and response, and threat and exploit protection, which are not available in Plan 1.
- **Price**: Microsoft Defender for Endpoint Plan 2 is more expensive than Plan 1, reflecting the additional features and capabilities it offers.
- **Scope of coverage**: Microsoft Defender for Endpoint Plan 2 protects a wider range of endpoints and devices, including servers, compared to Plan 1.
- **Management capabilities**: Microsoft Defender for Endpoint Plan 2 offers more advanced management capabilities, including centralized management and reporting, which makes it easier for organizations to manage their security posture and respond to threats.

In summary, Microsoft Defender for Endpoint Plan 1 is an entry-level solution suitable for smaller organizations or those who are looking for basic endpoint protection, while Plan 2 is a more advanced solution that offers a wider range of features and capabilities, making it a better choice for larger organizations or those looking for a more comprehensive security solution.

Important note

Microsoft Defender for Endpoint is an important security solution for businesses and organizations as it helps protect against various types of cyber threats and malware, including viruses, spyware, and ransomware, especially if you add Microsoft 365 Information Protection to your tenant and configure it to work together with Endpoint. If you are looking to protect your devices against cyber threats and integrate with other Microsoft security solutions with cost-effective views, Microsoft Defender for Endpoint is a perfect solution for you.

Configuring Microsoft Defender for Endpoint

The **Device Overview** portal in Microsoft Intune provides a comprehensive view of the security status of devices connected to an organization's network. The following are some of the key information and insights that you can see in the **Device Overview** portal:

- **Device count**: The **Device Overview** portal provides an overview of the number of devices that are connected to the network, including the number of devices that are protected by Microsoft Defender for Endpoint
- **Threats detected**: The portal displays the number of threats that have been detected and remediated on the network, including malware, ransomware, and other types of cyber threats:

- **Vulnerabilities**: The portal provides insight into the vulnerabilities on the network, including missing security updates, unpatched software, and other security weaknesses
- **Device health**: The portal displays the health of devices, including the operating system version, the status of security updates, and other relevant information
- **Alerts**: The portal provides an overview of the alerts generated by Microsoft Defender for Endpoint, including the type of alert, the time it was generated, and the device it was generated on
- **Threat trends**: The portal provides trend analysis and insights into the threats affecting the network, including the types of threats, the devices they are affecting, and the frequency of incidents
- **Compliance status**: The portal provides an overview of the compliance status of devices, including information on device configurations, software installations, and other relevant information

The **Device Overview** portal in the Microsoft Intune admin portal provides a single source of truth for organizations to understand the security status of their devices and take action to prevent threats and improve security:

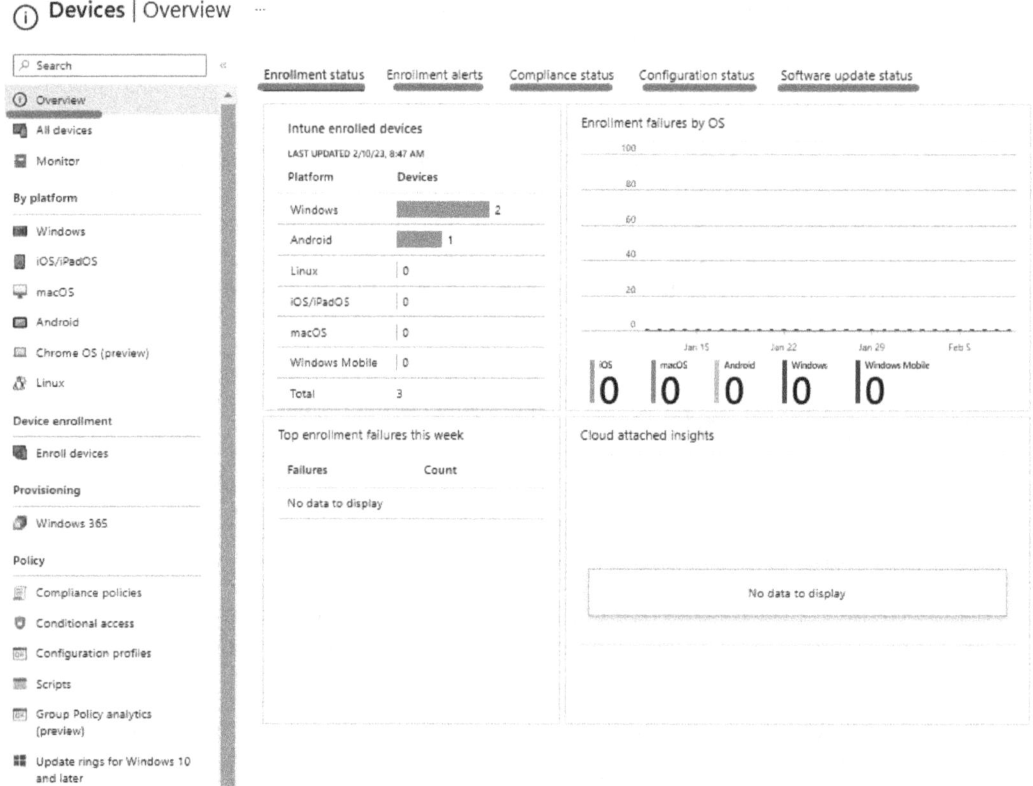

Figure 4.2 – Device overview

You can find the information about your Endpoint status under the following tabs:

- **Enrollment status**: Detailed information about Intune-enrolled devices
- **Enrollment alerts**: Predefined alerts about onboarded devices in Endpoint
- **Compliance status**: Compliance status for all enrolled devices in Endpoint
- **Configuration status**: All information about device configuration profile status
- **Software update status**: Information and graphics about device updates

Let's begin an adventure in the realm of Windows device onboarding. In this exploration, we will dive into the details of configuring and incorporating Windows devices, revealing the crucial components and steps needed to ensure a smooth onboarding experience.

Microsoft Defender Vulnerability Management dashboard

The MDVM dashboard is a comprehensive and powerful tool designed to assist organizations in identifying, assessing, and mitigating vulnerabilities within their IT infrastructure. As an integral component of the Microsoft Defender for Endpoint suite, the MDVM dashboard offers a centralized platform that enables security teams to efficiently manage and prioritize vulnerabilities, resulting in an improved overall security posture.

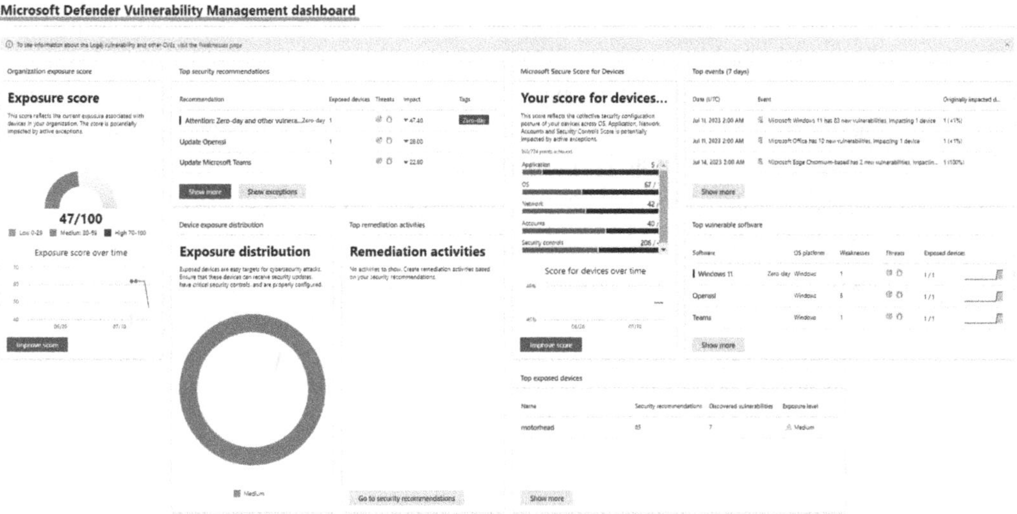

Figure 4.3 – Microsoft Defender Vulnerability Management dashboard

One of the key features of the MDVM dashboard is its ability to provide a holistic view of an organization's vulnerability landscape. It aggregates vulnerability data from various sources, such as vulnerability scanners, operating system updates, and third-party software, and presents it in a unified and intuitive interface. This consolidated view allows security professionals to gain a clear understanding of the vulnerabilities present across the organization, including their severity levels and potential impact on the network.

The MDVM dashboard employs advanced analytics and machine learning capabilities to prioritize vulnerabilities based on their risk levels. By analysing a range of factors such as exploit availability, vulnerability age, and asset criticality, the dashboard generates a risk score for each vulnerability. This risk-based approach enables security teams to focus their efforts on addressing the most critical vulnerabilities first, ensuring that limited resources are allocated efficiently.

Another significant aspect of the MDVM dashboard is its integration with other Microsoft security solutions. It seamlessly integrates with Microsoft Defender for Endpoint, Microsoft 365 Defender, and Azure Sentinel, enabling organizations to correlate vulnerability data with threat intelligence, endpoint protection, and security incident and event management. This integration allows security teams to gain deeper insights into the potential impact of vulnerabilities and respond to threats more effectively.

Furthermore, the MDVM dashboard offers robust reporting capabilities, enabling organizations to generate comprehensive vulnerability reports. These reports provide detailed information about the vulnerabilities detected, remediation status, and overall vulnerability trends. The reports can be customized based on specific requirements, making them suitable for various stakeholders, including executive management, compliance teams, and auditors. To enhance usability and ease of management, the MDVM dashboard provides flexible filtering and sorting options. Security teams can categorize vulnerabilities based on different criteria, such as severity, asset type, or remediation status. This flexibility enables the efficient tracking and prioritization of vulnerabilities, allowing organizations to streamline their remediation processes and reduce the time to mitigate critical issues.

Moreover, the MDVM dashboard supports automation and integration with third-party tools through APIs. This enables organizations to automate vulnerability assessment and remediation workflows, reducing manual efforts and enhancing overall efficiency. Additionally, the dashboard supports seamless integration with existing IT operations and ticketing systems, enabling security teams to seamlessly collaborate with IT teams and track the progress of vulnerability remediation activities.

In conclusion, the MDVM dashboard is a comprehensive and user-friendly solution that empowers organizations to effectively manage vulnerabilities within their IT infrastructure. With its centralized view, advanced analytics, integration with Microsoft security solutions, and customizable reporting capabilities, the MDVM dashboard provides security teams with the necessary tools to identify, prioritize, and remediate vulnerabilities efficiently. By leveraging this powerful tool, organizations can enhance their overall security posture and protect their critical assets from potential threats.

Microsoft Defender for Endpoint Device inventory

Microsoft Defender for Endpoint Device Inventory is a feature-rich component that provides organizations with a comprehensive view of the devices present in their environment. It collects and consolidates detailed information about devices, including hardware and software configurations, installed applications, network connectivity, and security-related data. This robust inventory enables security teams to effectively manage and secure their endpoints, identify potential risks, and respond to security incidents promptly. With its intuitive interface and real-time updates, Microsoft Defender for Endpoint Device Inventory empowers organizations to gain deep visibility into their endpoint landscape and make informed security decisions:

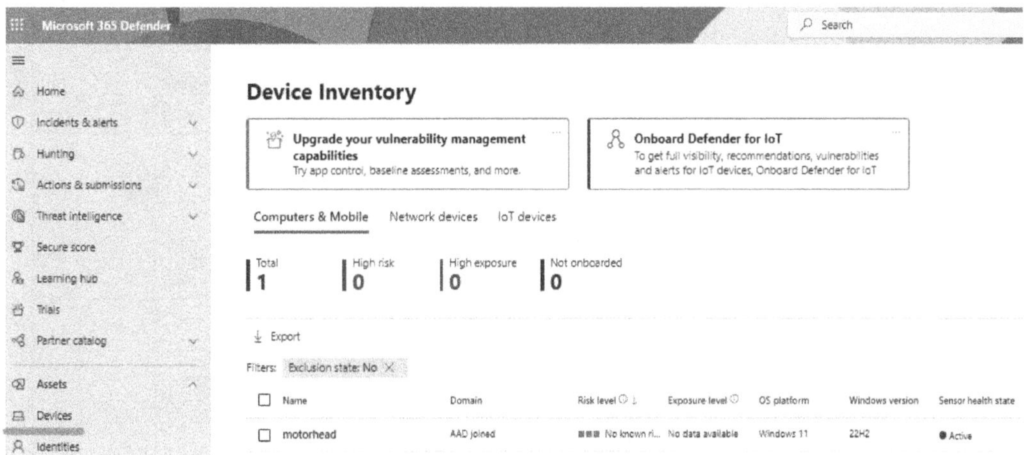

Figure 4.4 – Device inventory

One of the primary benefits of Microsoft Defender for Endpoint's device assets is their ability to provide real-time insights into device health and security posture. By continuously monitoring devices, they can detect and report any suspicious activities, malware infections, or potential breaches. This proactive approach enables organizations to identify and respond to security incidents promptly, minimizing the impact of potential threats and reducing the risk of data loss or compromise.

Windows devices

Let's start with onboarding Windows devices. We can divide this into two ways: onboarding on-premises Windows devices and onboarding Windows 365 devices. Supported Windows devices for Microsoft Defender for Endpoint are as follows:

Operating system	**Version**
Windows 7 SP1	• Enterprise • Pro (Both versions require an Extended Security Update license for support)
Windows 8.1	• Enterprise • Pro
Windows 10	• Enterprise • Enterprise IoT • Pro • Education • Pro Education
Windows 11	• Enterprise • Pro • Education • Pro Education
Windows Server	• Windows Server 2022 • Windows Server 2019 Core Edition • Windows Server 2019 • Windows Server 2016 • Windows Server 2012 R2 • Windows Server 2008 R2 SP1* *Version Server 2008 R2 SP1 and Windows Server 2012 R2 require the Extended Security Update license for support
Windows Virtual Desktop	
Windows 365	• Basic • Enterprise

Table 4.1 – Supported Windows devices

Enrolling a Windows device in Microsoft Defender for Endpoint means adding the device to the Microsoft Defender for Endpoint security solution. This process involves installing the Microsoft Defender for Endpoint client software on the device and registering it with the Microsoft Defender for Endpoint cloud service. Once enrolled, the device will be protected by Microsoft Defender for Endpoint's advanced threat protection capabilities, including real-time threat detection and remediation, data encryption, and device management. The device will also be subject to the security policies and configurations defined in the Microsoft Defender for Endpoint console.

Enrolling a Windows device in Microsoft Defender for Endpoint typically involves the following steps:

1. Download and install Microsoft Defender for Endpoint client software on the device.
2. Register the device with the Microsoft Defender for Endpoint cloud service by providing the necessary information, such as the device name, operating system version, and device group.
3. Assign the device to a security policy that defines the security configurations and settings to be applied to the device.
4. Monitor the device's security status and resolve any security incidents or vulnerabilities that are detected.

Enrolling Windows devices in Microsoft Defender for Endpoint is an important step in securing the devices and the data they contain. It helps organizations protect against cyber threats, secure sensitive data, meet regulatory compliance requirements, and ensure continuous protection for their endpoints:

1. Open the security portal as a Global Administrator.
2. Click on **Settings**.
3. Click on **Endpoints**.

Settings

Name	Description
Security center	General settings for the Microsoft 365 security center
Microsoft 365 Defender	General settings for Microsoft 365 Defender
Endpoints	General settings for endpoints
Email & collaboration	General settings for email & collaboration
Identities	General settings for identities
Device discovery	Select your device discovery mode and customize standard discovery settings
Cloud Apps	General settings for cloud apps

Figure 4.5 – Windows enrollment

4. From the new window, click on **Onboarding** under **Device management**:

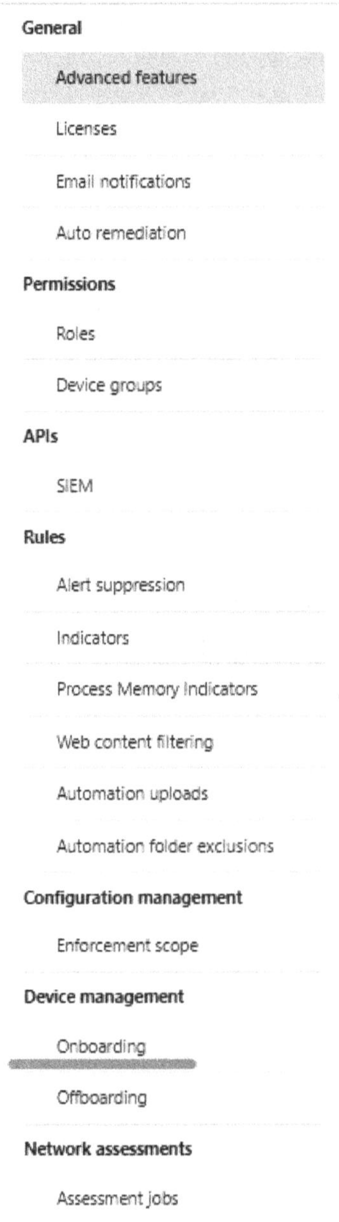

Figure 4.6 – Endpoint admin portal

5. Select the operating system to start the onboarding process.

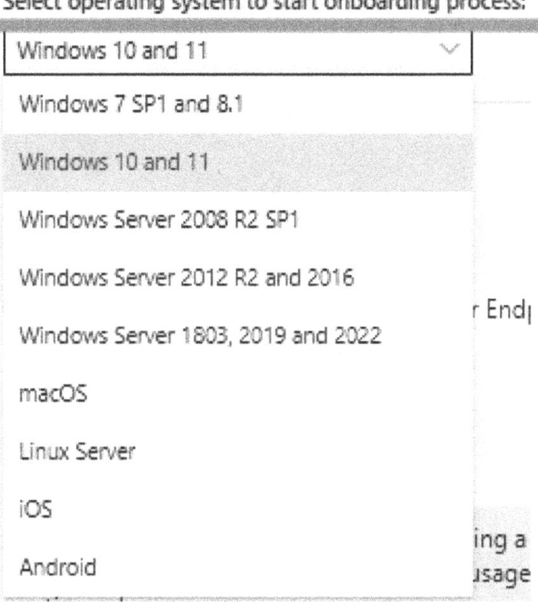

Figure 4.7 – Operating system for the onboarding process

6. Choose a deployment method.

   When onboarding a small number of devices onto Microsoft Defender for Endpoint, administrators have the flexibility to choose between two options: utilizing a local script or creating a group policy. These methods provide efficient ways to streamline the deployment process and ensure that the devices are protected by Microsoft Defender for Endpoint. The local script option allows administrators to run a script directly on each individual device. This approach is suitable for smaller-scale deployments as it involves manually executing the script on each machine. The local script contains the necessary configuration settings and commands to install and configure Microsoft Defender for Endpoint. Administrators can enjoy a smooth and customized onboarding experience for each device. On the other hand, the group policy option offers a centralized and automated approach for deploying Microsoft Defender for Endpoint. Administrators can create a group policy object within their Active Directory environment and configure the necessary settings for onboarding devices. When devices are connected to the network and join the domain, the group policy is automatically applied, initiating the installation and configuration of Microsoft Defender for Endpoint using Microsoft Intune, making it easier to manage and monitor the security of your devices from a centralized location. By using Microsoft Defender for Endpoint automatic enrollment, organizations can help protect their devices from the latest threats and ensure that their data is protected. You can create different security groups for the MDM and MAM scope and define URLs. All groups must be created on the Microsoft Entra ID level. This method is particularly advantageous for larger-scale deployments, as it eliminates the need for manual intervention on individual devices.

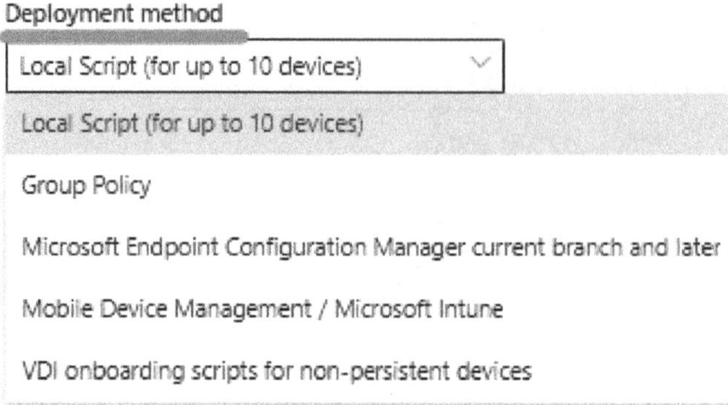

Figure 4.8 – Select deployment method

7. Run a detection test (copy and paste into Windows PowerShell and run the script).

```
powershell.exe -NoExit -ExecutionPolicy Bypass -WindowStyle Hidden $ErrorActionPreference= 'silentlycontinue';(New-Object
System.Net.WebClient).DownloadFile('http://127.0.0.1/1.exe', 'C:\\test-WDATP-test\\invoice.exe');Start-Process 'C:\\test-WDATP-
test\\invoice.exe'
```

Figure 4.9 – Run a detection test in PowerShell

To verify whether the onboarding device has been successfully added, follow these steps:

I. Navigate to the **Assets** section within Microsoft Defender for Endpoint.

II. Select the **Devices** tab.

III. Look for the onboarding device within the device list.

IV. Confirm that the device appears in the list, indicating a successful onboarding process.

By checking the **Assets** | **Device** section, administrators can ensure that the device has been properly added to Microsoft Defender for Endpoint and is now included in the overall device inventory. This step ensures that the onboarding process was completed successfully, allowing the organization to monitor and protect the device using the suite's comprehensive security features.

Configuring advanced features in Microsoft Defender for Endpoint

Configuring advanced features in Microsoft Defender for Endpoint allows organizations to customize and optimize their security settings. Here are the steps to configure advanced features in Microsoft Defender for Endpoint:

1. Access the Microsoft Defender security center portal using your administrator credentials.
2. Click on **Devices**.

3. Select **Windows Enrollment**.
4. Choose **Windows Hello for Business**.
5. Select the security group to which you will assign this enrollment method.
6. Choose **ENABLE** under **Configure Windows Hello for Business**.
7. Choose **Required for Use a Trusted Platform Module** (**TPM**).
8. Select a minimum PIN length (recommendation = 6).
9. Click **Save**.
10. Overall, **Microsoft Defender for Endpoint Windows Hello for Business** is a powerful security feature that helps organizations protect themselves. Navigate to the **Settings** section, usually located in the left-hand navigation menu, and select **Advanced features**.

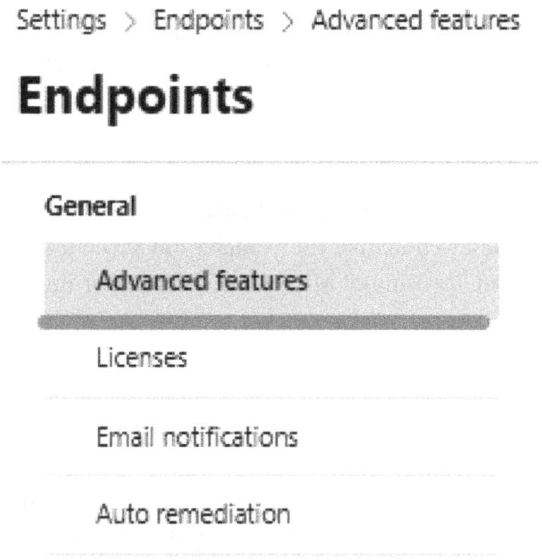

Settings > Endpoints > Advanced features

Endpoints

General

Advanced features

Licenses

Email notifications

Auto remediation

Figure 4.10 – Advanced features

11. Explore the available advanced features and settings, which may include the following options:

    A. **Threat and vulnerability management**: Configure advanced threat and vulnerability settings to detect and respond to potential risks effectively. This may include fine-tuning threat detection rules, managing exploit protection, and enabling **attack surface reduction** (**ASR**).

    B. **Automated investigation and response**: Enable and customize automated investigation and response capabilities to streamline incident response processes. Configure the actions to be taken when specific alerts are triggered, such as running remediation scripts or isolating affected devices.

C. **Endpoint detection and response**: Configure advanced EDR settings to enable deep visibility into endpoint activities and enhance threat hunting capabilities. This may include setting up detection exclusions, adjusting detection sensitivity, or enabling additional data collection options.

Figure 4.11 – Enable EDR in block mode

D. **Threat analytics and reports**: Customize threat analytics and reporting settings to generate detailed insights and reports on security incidents, threat trends, and the overall security posture. Adjust report generation schedules, define specific data to be included in reports, and set up alerts for specific events.

12. Review and adjust the settings according to your organization's security requirements and best practices. Ensure that the configurations align with your specific security policies and compliance obligations.
13. Save your settings and apply the changes.

Regularly review and update the advanced feature configurations as needed to adapt to evolving threats and security needs. It is important to note that the available advanced features and settings may vary based on the specific version and licensing of Microsoft Defender for Endpoint.

Security recommendations

Microsoft Defender for Endpoint Security recommendations is a powerful feature designed to provide organizations with actionable insights and guidance to improve their security posture. Leveraging advanced analytics and machine learning, it analyzes data from various sources, such as endpoint telemetry, threat intelligence, and industry best practices, to generate customized security recommendations. These recommendations cover a wide range of areas, including configuration settings, software updates, security policies, and threat remediation strategies. By following these recommendations, organizations can enhance their security defenses, reduce vulnerabilities, and proactively mitigate potential threats. Microsoft Defender for Endpoint Security recommendations serves as a valuable resource for security teams, empowering them to optimize their security strategies and protect their endpoints effectively.

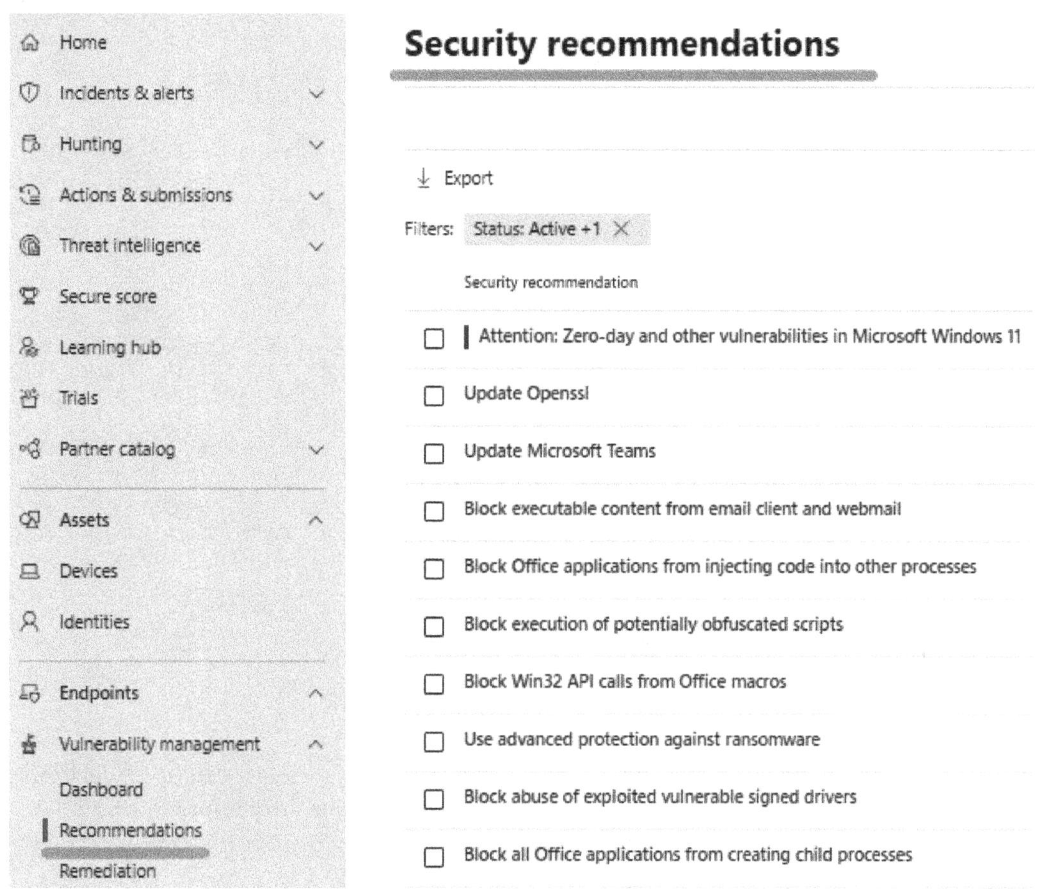

Figure 4.12 – Security recommendations

Microsoft Defender for Endpoint offers a range of robust features to address remediation, inventories, and weaknesses within an organization's endpoint environment. For remediation, it provides automated and guided response capabilities to help security teams swiftly respond to security incidents and mitigate threats. With built-in remediation actions, such as isolating compromised devices, terminating malicious processes, and quarantining files, organizations can quickly contain and neutralize potential risks.

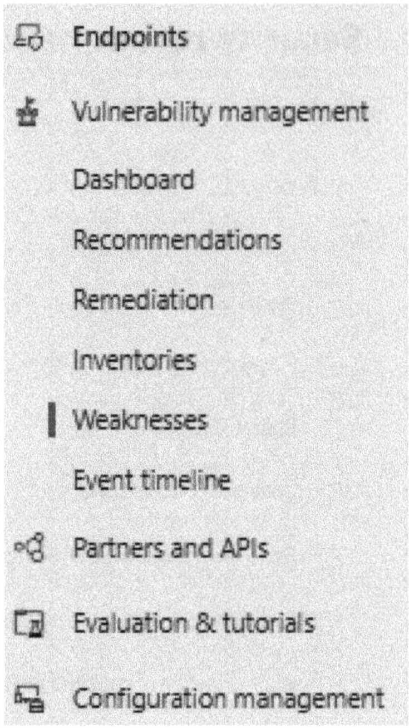

Figure 4.13 – Weaknesses portal

In terms of inventories, Microsoft Defender for Endpoint gathers comprehensive data about devices, including hardware, software, and configurations. This detailed inventory information allows organizations to maintain an accurate and up-to-date view of their endpoint ecosystem, facilitating effective asset management and vulnerability assessments.

Regarding weaknesses, Microsoft Defender for Endpoint offers vulnerability management capabilities. It scans and identifies vulnerabilities present on endpoints, prioritizes them based on risk factors, and provides recommendations for remediation. By leveraging these insights, security teams can proactively address weaknesses in their environment and strengthen their overall security posture.

The Microsoft Defender for Endpoint configuration management dashboard

The Microsoft Defender for Endpoint configuration management dashboard is an essential component of the Microsoft Defender for Endpoint suite, providing organizations with a centralized platform to manage and enforce security configurations across their endpoints. With its powerful features and intuitive interface, the configuration management dashboard empowers security teams to maintain a consistent and secure endpoint environment.

One of the key strengths of the configuration management dashboard is its ability to define and enforce security policies. Security teams can create customized policies based on industry best practices and organizational requirements. These policies encompass a wide range of settings, including firewall rules, antivirus configurations, device encryption, and application control. By defining these policies, organizations can ensure that all endpoints adhere to consistent security standards, reducing the risk of security breaches and unauthorized access:

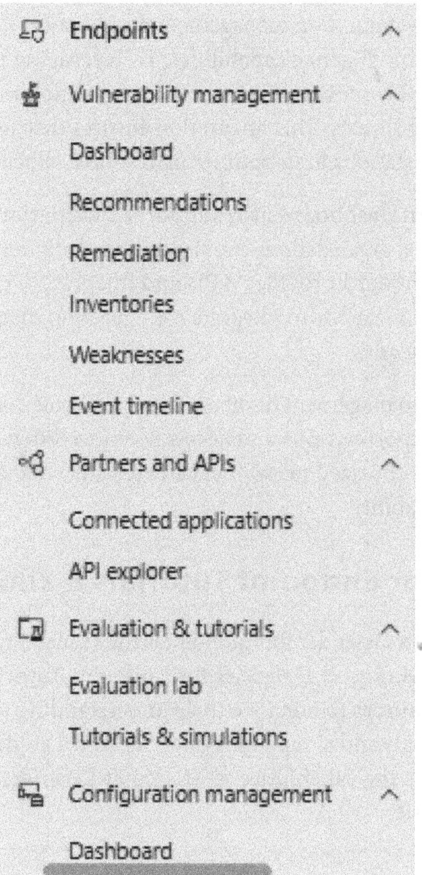

Figure 4.14 – Endpoint dashboard

The dashboard provides real-time visibility into the configuration status of devices. It offers comprehensive insights into the compliance levels of endpoints, highlighting any deviations from the defined security policies. This visibility allows security teams to quickly identify potential security gaps and take proactive measures to address them. Additionally, the dashboard offers granular reporting and analytics, enabling organizations to track and monitor the progress of configuration management efforts.

The configuration management dashboard includes powerful remediation capabilities. When a device is found to be non-compliant with the defined security policies, security teams can take remedial actions directly from the dashboard. These actions can include initiating remediation scripts, deploying security patches, or configuring settings remotely. By leveraging these remediation capabilities, organizations can swiftly bring non-compliant endpoints into alignment with their security policies, reducing the attack surface and improving overall security posture.

Another notable feature of the configuration management dashboard is its integration with Microsoft Defender for Endpoint's threat intelligence capabilities. By leveraging threat intelligence data, the dashboard can provide additional context and prioritize configuration management efforts based on the potential impact of emerging threats. This integration ensures that security teams are addressing the most critical security configurations first, optimizing resource allocation and incident response.

The configuration management dashboard also supports automation and orchestration. Using automation scripts and workflows, organizations can streamline configuration management processes, saving time and effort. The dashboard provides APIs and integration capabilities with existing IT management tools, allowing organizations to integrate configuration management with their existing IT workflows and systems seamlessly.

Furthermore, the configuration management dashboard supports role-based access control, enabling organizations to assign specific permissions and access levels to different security team members. This feature ensures that only authorized personnel can view and manage security configurations, enhancing security and accountability.

Microsoft Defender for Endpoint Tutorials & simulations

One of the best things in Microsoft Defender for Endpoint is the availability of tutorials and simulations for future onboarded devices. Microsoft Defender for Endpoint Tutorials & simulations provides organizations with valuable resources to enhance their understanding and proficiency in using the platform effectively. These tutorials and simulations offer hands-on guidance and practical scenarios to help security teams maximize the capabilities of Microsoft Defender for Endpoint and improve their incident response capabilities.

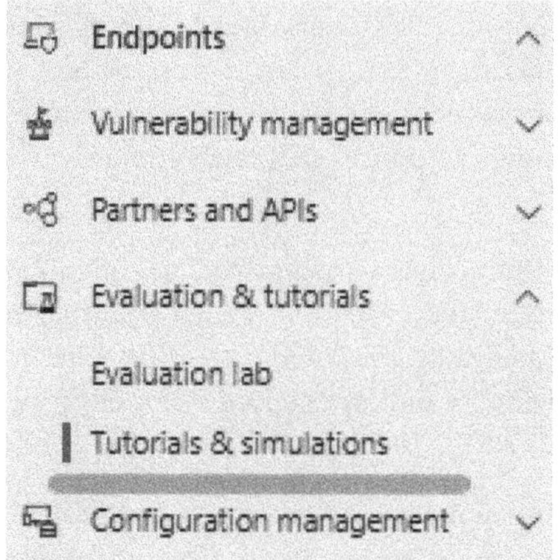

Figure 4.15 – Endpoint Tutorials and simulations

You can use different simulations, such as the following, for testing:

- Microsoft
- Atomic Red Team
- AttackIQ
- SafeBreach

Atomic Red Team, AttackIQ, and SafeBreach are all powerful platforms that can be integrated with Microsoft Defender for Endpoint to enhance an organization's threat detection and response capabilities.

Atomic Red Team is an open source testing framework that provides a library of adversary emulation techniques and detection tests. It enables organizations to validate the effectiveness of their security controls by simulating real-world attack scenarios. Integrating Atomic Red Team with Microsoft Defender for Endpoint allows security teams to create custom detection rules based on these attack simulations, enabling proactive detection and response to potential threats.

AttackIQ is a comprehensive breach and attack simulation platform that helps organizations continuously assess and validate their security posture. It allows security teams to emulate sophisticated attacks and measure the effectiveness of their security controls in real time. By integrating AttackIQ with Microsoft Defender for Endpoint, organizations can gain deeper insights into their security capabilities, identify potential vulnerabilities, and strengthen their overall defense against cyber threats.

SafeBreach is a breach and attack simulation platform that allows organizations to simulate real-world attacks and test the effectiveness of their security controls. It provides a wide range of attack scenarios and continuously evaluates an organization's security posture. By integrating SafeBreach with Microsoft Defender for Endpoint, security teams can validate the efficacy of their security controls, identify gaps or weaknesses, and optimize their incident response capabilities.

By leveraging the capabilities of Atomic Red Team, AttackIQ, and SafeBreach in conjunction with Microsoft Defender for Endpoint, organizations can proactively test, validate, and optimize their security defenses. These integrations enable security teams to simulate real-world attacks, detect vulnerabilities, and enhance incident response readiness, ultimately bolstering the overall security posture of the organization.

The tutorials provide step-by-step instructions and demonstrations on various features and functionalities of Microsoft Defender for Endpoint. They cover topics such as setting up the platform, configuring security policies, performing threat investigations, and responding to security incidents. These tutorials are designed to cater to both beginners and experienced users, ensuring that users of all skill levels can benefit from the resources.

Simulations, on the other hand, offer interactive scenarios that replicate real-world security incidents. These simulations enable security teams to practice their incident response skills in a controlled environment. They present different attack scenarios, such as malware infections, data breaches, or advanced persistent threats, and guide users through the process of detecting, investigating, and mitigating these incidents using Microsoft Defender for Endpoint. By engaging in these simulations, security teams can develop their incident response capabilities, refine their decision-making skills, and become more proficient in leveraging the platform's features to defend against emerging threats.

The tutorials and simulations are designed to be highly interactive and engaging. They often include quizzes, challenges, and feedback mechanisms to reinforce learning and encourage active participation. This gamified approach not only enhances the learning experience but also helps users retain knowledge and apply it effectively in real-world situations.

Microsoft provides these tutorials and simulations through various mediums, including online documentation, video tutorials, virtual labs, and interactive training modules. These resources are regularly updated to align with the latest features and enhancements of Microsoft Defender for Endpoint, ensuring that users have access to the most relevant and up-to-date information.

By leveraging these tutorials and simulations, organizations can derive significant benefits. They can accelerate the onboarding process for new security team members, enable existing team members to expand their knowledge and skills, and foster a culture of continuous learning and improvement within the organization. Moreover, these resources can help organizations optimize their use of Microsoft Defender for Endpoint, leading to more effective threat detection, faster incident response, and an improved overall security posture.

In conclusion, Microsoft Defender for Endpoint Tutorials & simulations provides organizations with valuable resources to enhance their proficiency in leveraging the platform's capabilities. These resources offer step-by-step instructions, practical scenarios, and interactive simulations to improve incident response skills and maximize the effectiveness of Microsoft Defender for Endpoint. By investing in these tutorials and simulations, organizations can empower their security teams to become more knowledgeable, skilled, and efficient in defending against evolving cybersecurity threats.

Creating simulations in Microsoft Defender for Endpoint

Creating simulations in Microsoft Defender for Endpoint involves leveraging the platform's capabilities to simulate real-world attack scenarios and assess the effectiveness of your security controls. Here is a high-level overview of the process:

1. Create and add a device for simulation.

Figure 4.16 – Evaluation lab

Prior to integrating a device into your evaluation lab, it's essential to specify the type of virtual machine you wish to test. As shown in the following screenshot, there's a variety of virtual machines available for your testing purposes.

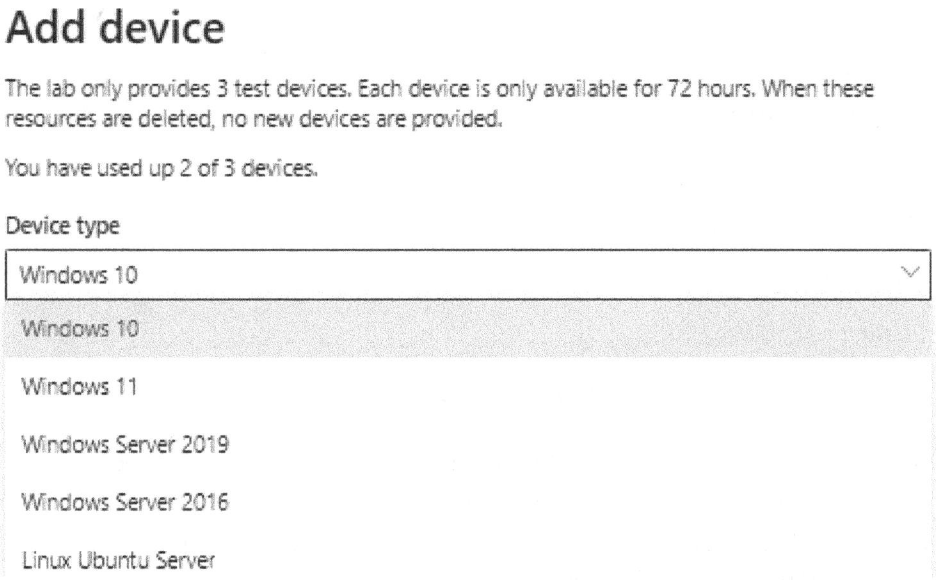

Add device

The lab only provides 3 test devices. Each device is only available for 72 hours. When these resources are deleted, no new devices are provided.

You have used up 2 of 3 devices.

Device type

Windows 10

Windows 10

Windows 11

Windows Server 2019

Windows Server 2016

Linux Ubuntu Server

Figure 4.17 – Add a device to an evaluation lab

2. Select available tools for the device type.

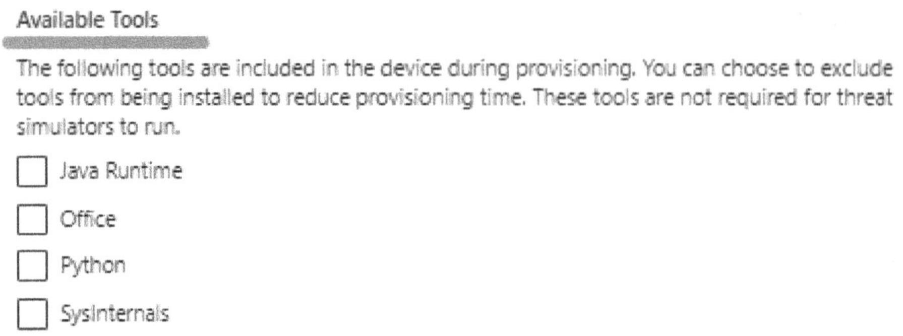

Available Tools

The following tools are included in the device during provisioning. You can choose to exclude tools from being installed to reduce provisioning time. These tools are not required for threat simulators to run.

- [ ] Java Runtime
- [ ] Office
- [ ] Python
- [ ] SysInternals

Figure 4.18 – Add tools to a device in an evaluation lab

3. On the **Add device** page, copy the username and password and device name. Bear in mind that simulations are available for 72 hours only.

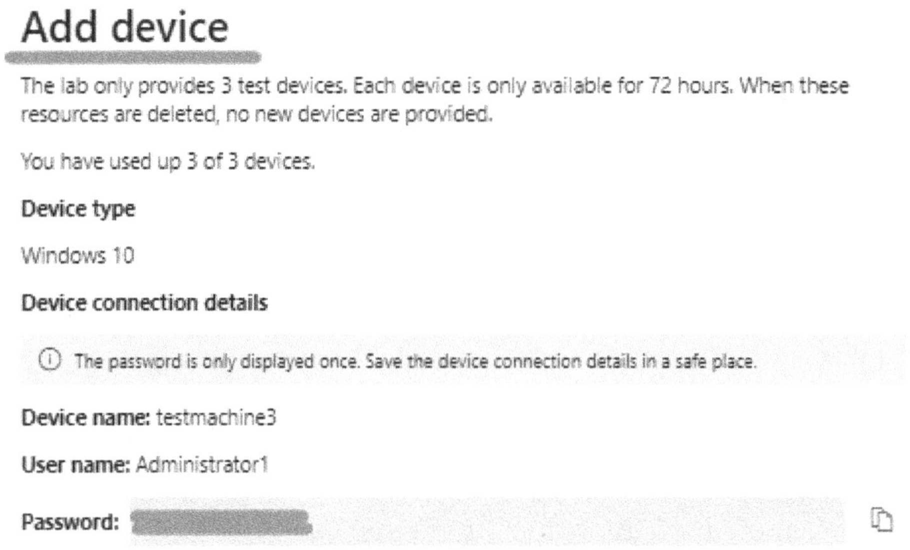

Add device

The lab only provides 3 test devices. Each device is only available for 72 hours. When these resources are deleted, no new devices are provided.

You have used up 3 of 3 devices.

Device type

Windows 10

Device connection details

ⓘ The password is only displayed once. Save the device connection details in a safe place.

Device name: testmachine3

User name: Administrator1

Password:

Figure 4.19 – Add evaluation device

4. Determine the specific objectives of the simulation. Consider the types of attacks or scenarios you want to simulate, the security controls you want to test, and the goals you want to achieve.
5. Choose attack techniques that align with your objectives. Microsoft Defender for Endpoint provides a wide range of built-in attack techniques that you can leverage. These techniques emulate real-world threats and help you assess the detection and response capabilities of your security infrastructure.

6. Within the Microsoft Defender security center, navigate to the **Attack surface reduction | Simulations** section. Here, you can configure and customize simulations based on your selected techniques and objectives. Specify the devices or groups of devices on which you want to run the simulations.

Figure 4.20 – Evaluation lab

7. Start the simulations to execute the chosen attack techniques against the designated devices. Microsoft Defender for Endpoint will emulate the attacks and monitor how your security controls respond. It will generate alerts and notifications for any detected activities.

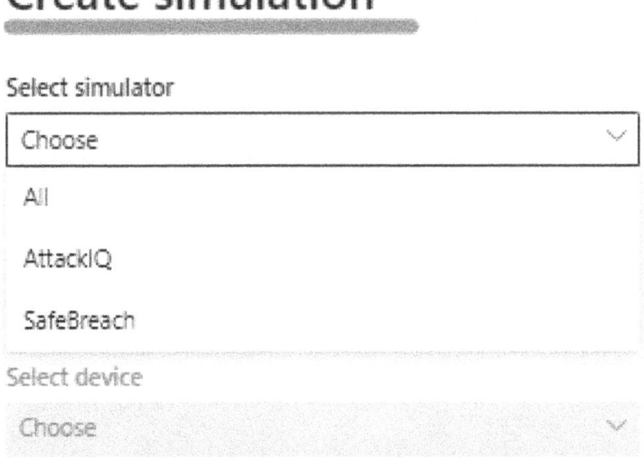

Figure 4.21 – Create simulation

8. After the simulations have run, review the results and analyze the data provided by Microsoft Defender for Endpoint. Look for any vulnerabilities or weaknesses in your security controls. Pay attention to the detection and response capabilities and identify areas that require improvement.

9. Based on the insights gained from the simulation results, take appropriate actions to remediate vulnerabilities and optimize your security controls. This may involve adjusting configurations, updating security policies, or enhancing your incident response processes.

It is important to note that the specific steps and options for creating simulations may vary based on the version and configuration of Microsoft Defender for Endpoint. Therefore, referring to Microsoft's official documentation and guidance is highly recommended to ensure accurate and up-to-date information tailored to your specific environment.

How to create web content filtering

To create web content filtering in Microsoft Defender for Endpoint, you can follow these steps:

1. Sign in to the Microsoft Defender security center with appropriate administrative credentials, then navigate to the security portal and select **Settings** then **Endpoints**.
2. Under **Rules**, select **Web content filtering** and click on + **Add Policy**.

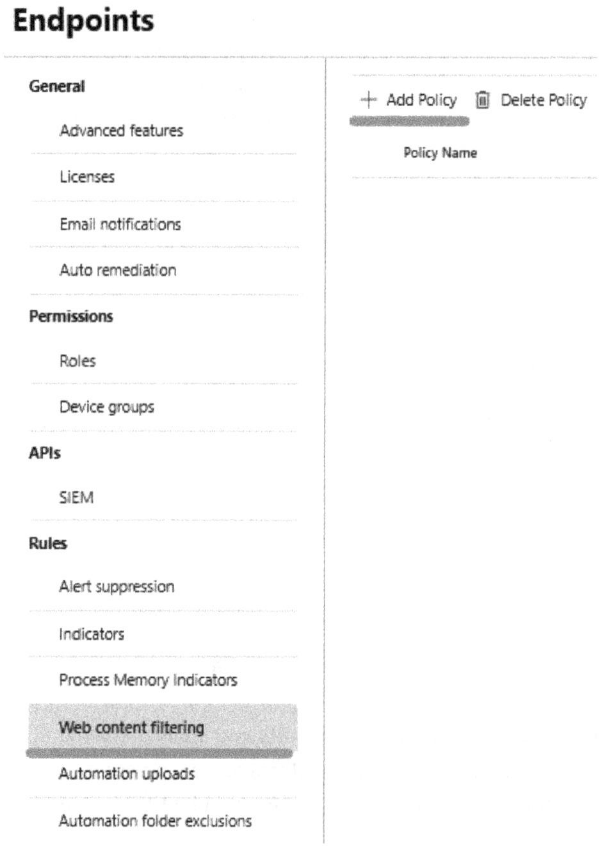

Figure 4.22 – Adding a web content filtering policy

3. Provide a name and description for the policy to help identify and describe its purpose.
4. Configure the policy settings based on your desired web content filtering requirements. You can choose from different categories and actions to allow, block, or warn users when accessing specific types of websites. For example, you can block categories such as adult content, gambling, or social media, or customize the policy to fit your organization's needs.

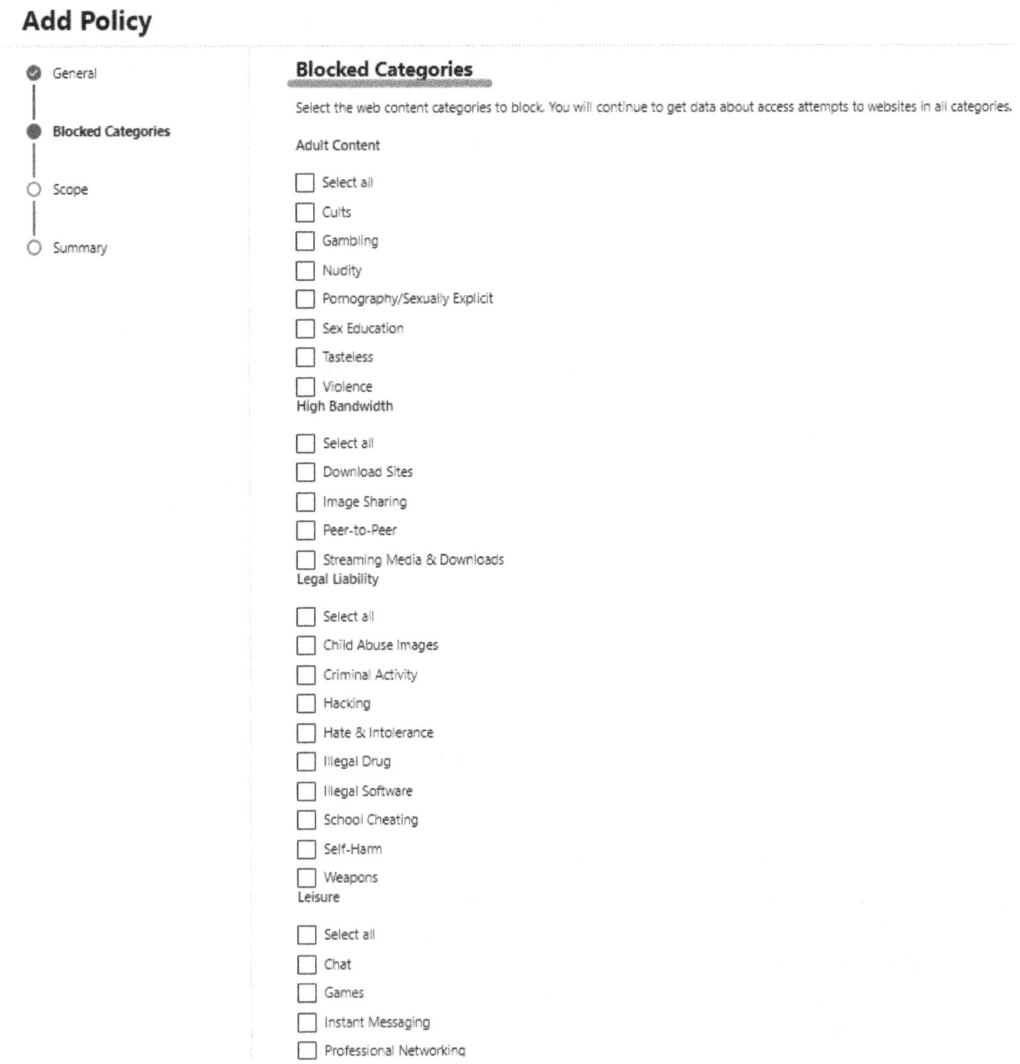

Add Policy

- General
- Blocked Categories
- Scope
- Summary

Blocked Categories

Select the web content categories to block. You will continue to get data about access attempts to websites in all categories.

Adult Content

- [ ] Select all
- [ ] Cults
- [ ] Gambling
- [ ] Nudity
- [ ] Pornography/Sexually Explicit
- [ ] Sex Education
- [ ] Tasteless
- [ ] Violence

High Bandwidth

- [ ] Select all
- [ ] Download Sites
- [ ] Image Sharing
- [ ] Peer-to-Peer
- [ ] Streaming Media & Downloads

Legal Liability

- [ ] Select all
- [ ] Child Abuse Images
- [ ] Criminal Activity
- [ ] Hacking
- [ ] Hate & Intolerance
- [ ] Illegal Drug
- [ ] Illegal Software
- [ ] School Cheating
- [ ] Self-Harm
- [ ] Weapons

Leisure

- [ ] Select all
- [ ] Chat
- [ ] Games
- [ ] Instant Messaging
- [ ] Professional Networking

Figure 4.23 – Web content filtering policy

You can also create custom allow or block lists to specify individual URLs or domains that should be permitted or denied access.

5. Adjust the settings for user notifications and reporting as needed. You can choose to display a customizable warning page to users when a blocked website is accessed and define the level of detail in reporting.
6. Review and confirm the policy settings. Ensure they align with your organization's security and compliance requirements.

Once you are satisfied with the policy configuration, save and activate the policy. It will be applied to the managed devices in your organization. Monitor and manage the web content filtering policy from the **Web content filtering** page. You can modify, disable, or delete policies, as necessary.

It is important to note that the specific steps and options for creating web content filtering policies may vary based on the version and configuration of Microsoft Defender for Endpoint.

Microsoft Defender **File Content Analysis** is a feature within the Microsoft Defender for Endpoint suite that focuses on analyzing and detecting potentially malicious files. It utilizes advanced machine learning models and threat intelligence to assess the content of files and identify any indicators of compromise or suspicious behavior. By leveraging a combination of static and dynamic analysis techniques, Microsoft Defender **File Content Analysis** helps organizations proactively detect and respond to file-based threats, protecting their systems and data from potential malware, ransomware, and other malicious file-based attacks.

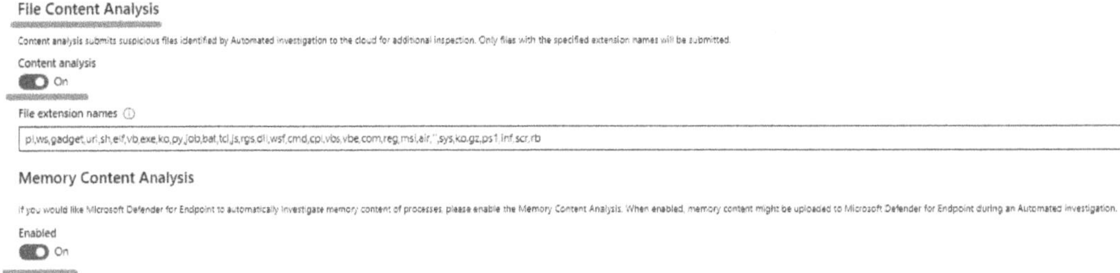

Figure 4.24 – File Content Analysis

The Microsoft Defender for Endpoint enforcement scope refers to the extent to which security policies and actions are applied to protect endpoints within an organization. It allows administrators to define and configure the specific devices or groups of devices to which enforcement actions should be applied. By setting the enforcement scope, organizations can tailor their security measures to target specific subsets of endpoints based on factors such as department, location, or user role. This granular control ensures that security policies and actions are effectively implemented where they are most needed, optimizing security measures and minimizing disruptions to the broader environment. You can easily use Microsoft Defender for Endpoint to enforce a security configuration defined in Intune.

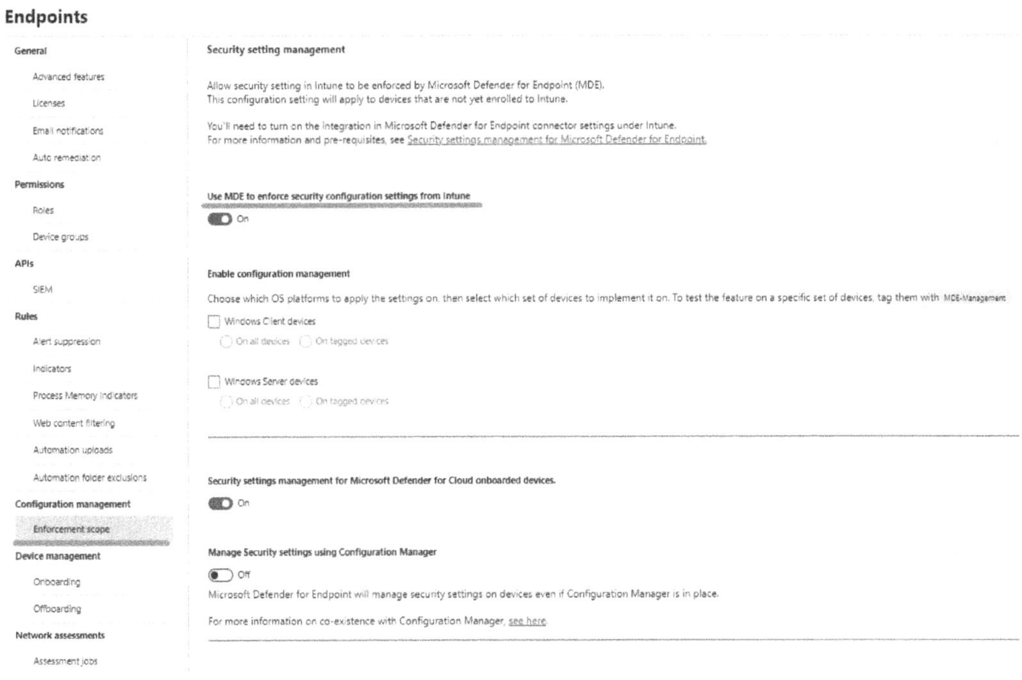

Figure 4.25 – Configure Enforcement scope

Microsoft Defender for Endpoint Co-management Authority

Microsoft Defender for Endpoint **Co-management Authority** is a feature in Microsoft Endpoint Configuration Manager that provides a mechanism for managing both traditional client management and modern management for Windows 10 devices. Co-management allows organizations to take advantage of the benefits of both traditional management and modern management (based on Microsoft Intune) for their Windows 10 devices. For example, an organization can use Configuration Manager to manage the traditional aspects of their devices, such as software distribution, while using Microsoft Intune to manage modern aspects, such as **mobile device management** (**MDM**) and **conditional access** (**CA**).

The Co-management Authority feature determines which management solution has authoritative control over specific management tasks for a given device. For example, an organization may choose to have Configuration Manager be the authoritative solution for software distribution and Intune be the authoritative solution for MDM. Having a clear understanding of the authoritative solution for each management task helps ensure that the management solutions work together seamlessly and provide a consistent experience for both IT administrators and users. By using Microsoft Defender for Endpoint Co-management Authority, organizations can take advantage of the best of both traditional and modern management to effectively manage and secure their devices.

Here are the general steps to configure Microsoft Defender for Endpoint Co-management Authority:

1. **Set up Microsoft Intune and Configuration Manager**: Before you can configure co-management, you need to have both Microsoft Intune and Configuration Manager set up and working in your environment.
2. **Enable co-management in Configuration Manager**: In the Configuration Manager console, navigate to administration workspace and select **Co-management**. Then, select **Configure co-management** and follow the wizard to enable co-management.
3. **Assign Configuration Manager to be the primary management authority**: In the Configuration Manager console, navigate to administration workspace and select **Co-management**. Then, select the **Devices** tab and choose the Windows 10 devices that you want to co-manage. In the **Properties** pane, under **Primary management authority**, select **Configuration Manager**.
4. **Assign Intune as the primary management authority**: In the Configuration Manager console, navigate to administration workspace and select **Co-management**. Then, select the **Devices** tab, and choose the Windows 10 devices that you want to co-manage. In the **Properties** pane, under **Primary management authority**, select **Microsoft Intune**.
5. **Configure and deploy policies**: Once you have assigned a primary management authority, you can use Configuration Manager and Microsoft Intune to configure and deploy policies for your Windows 10 devices.
6. **Monitor the co-management process**: In the Configuration Manager console, navigate to the monitoring workspace and select **Co-management** to monitor the status of your co-managed devices.

> **Note**
>
> These steps are a general guide, and the specific steps you need to follow to configure co-management may vary based on your organization's specific requirements and environment. It is recommended to thoroughly test the co-management process in a lab environment before deploying to production.

Let's embark on a journey to understand the steps of configuring System Center Configuration Manager and Microsoft Defender for Endpoint. This guide will walk you through the essential setup steps, ensuring optimal performance and security for your organization's IT infrastructure.

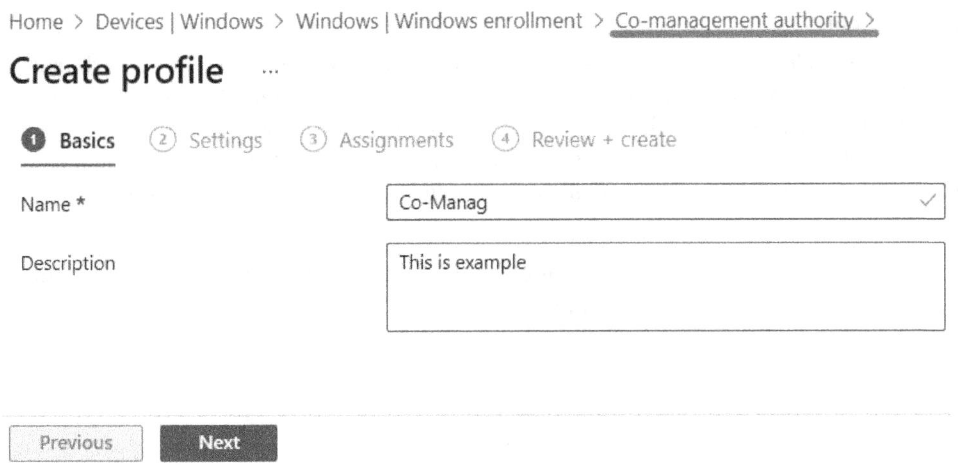

Home > Devices | Windows > Windows | Windows enrollment > Co-management authority >

Create profile ...

1 Basics 2 Settings 3 Assignments 4 Review + create

Name * Co-Manag

Description This is example

Previous Next

Figure 4.26 – Create a profile for Co-Management Authority

On the next tab, **Settings**, select **Yes** for the **Automatically install Configuration Manager agent** option, and under **Advanced**, leave **No** for the **Override co-management policy and use Intune for all workloads** option:

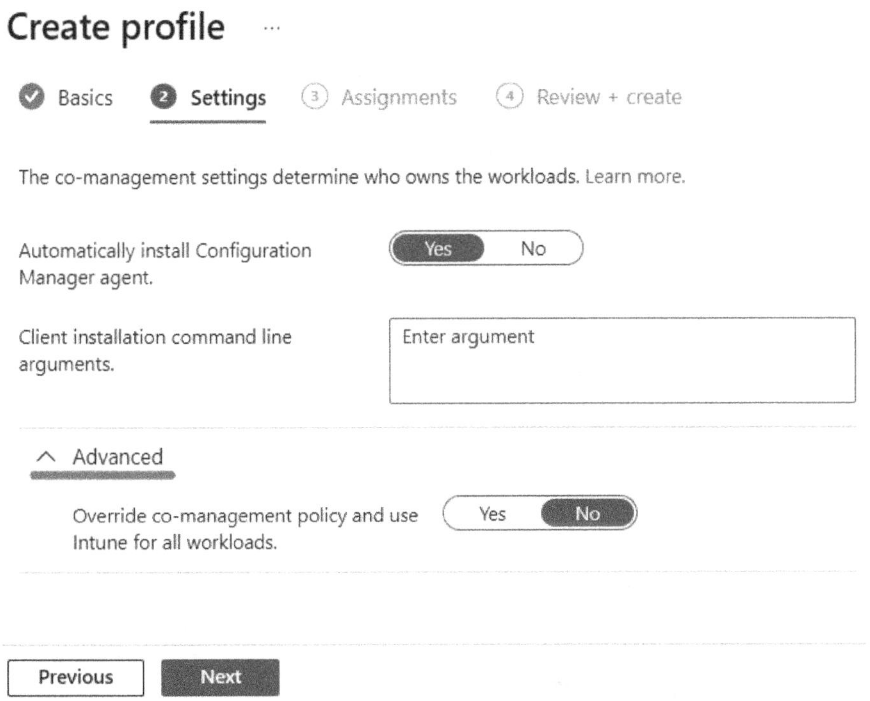

Create profile ...

Basics 2 Settings 3 Assignments 4 Review + create

The co-management settings determine who owns the workloads. Learn more.

Automatically install Configuration Manager agent. Yes No

Client installation command line arguments. Enter argument

Advanced

Override co-management policy and use Intune for all workloads. Yes No

Previous Next

Figure 4.27 – Define settings for Co-management Authority

Important note

Selecting **Yes** or **No** under **Override co-management policy and use Intune for all workloads** depends on the company's decision on what they want to use. For example, if a company has decided to use Microsoft Defender for Endpoint only for laptops and wants to control them via Endpoint, but the rest of the devices will still be under the control of System Center Configuration Manager, they would choose **Yes**, and all devices would be under Intune for all workloads.

In the next step, define for which groups this co-management enrollment will be used. Again, all groups should be created on Microsoft Entra ID:

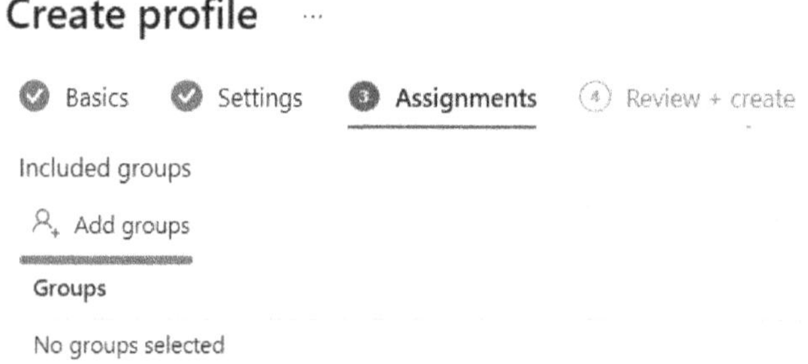

Figure 4.28 – Define groups

Review and press **Create**:

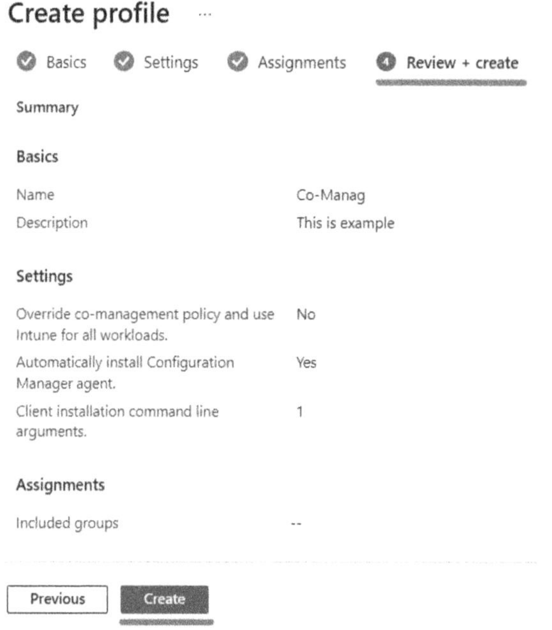

Figure 4.29 – Review co-management profile settings

Configuring a compliance policy for Windows devices

Configuring compliance policies for Windows devices in Microsoft Intune admin center involves the following steps:

1. **Create a compliance policy**: In the Microsoft Intune admin center, go to the **Devices** tab and select **Compliance policies**. Click + **Create Policy** and select **Windows 10 and later** as the platform. Choose the settings you want to enforce, such as password requirements, encryption, and software updates.
2. **Define compliance rules**: After creating the policy, define the compliance rules that will be used to evaluate device compliance. For example, you can define a rule that requires devices to have a password of a certain length and complexity.
3. **Assign the compliance policy**: Assign the compliance policy to a group of devices. You can assign the policy to all Windows devices or specific groups based on device ownership or other criteria.
4. **Monitor compliance**: After devices are assigned the compliance policy, Microsoft Intune admin center will evaluate compliance based on the defined rules. You can monitor compliance in the Microsoft Intune admin center, and act for non-compliant devices, such as sending notifications or blocking access to resources.

Overall, configuring compliance policies for Windows devices in Microsoft Intune admin center is a step in ensuring the security and compliance of your organization's devices and data.

Configuring a configuration profile for Windows devices

Configuring configuration profiles for Windows devices in Microsoft Intune admin center involves the following steps:

1. **Create a configuration profile**: In the Microsoft Intune admin center, go to the **Devices** tab and select **Configuration profiles**. Click **Create Profile** and select **Windows 10 and later** as the platform. Choose the settings you want to configure, such as device restrictions, network settings, and application management.
2. **Define profile settings**: After creating the profile, define the settings that will be applied to devices. For example, you can configure a policy that prevents users from accessing the control panel or restricts access to specific websites.
3. **Assign the configuration profile**: Assign the configuration profile to a group of devices. You can assign the profile to all Windows devices or to specific groups based on device ownership or other criteria.
4. **Monitor profile settings**: After devices are assigned the configuration profile, Microsoft Intune admin center will apply the settings to the devices. You can monitor the status of the profiles in the Microsoft Intune admin center and take action for devices that are not properly configured.

Configuring configuration profiles for Windows devices in Microsoft Intune admin center is an important step in ensuring that devices are properly configured and managed. By defining and enforcing policies, you can help protect your organization's devices and data, as well as streamline device management and configuration across your organization.

Windows 365

Windows 365 is a cloud-based operating system that provides a secure and efficient way to access Windows desktops from anywhere. Here are the steps to configure Windows 365 for Microsoft Defender for Endpoint:

1. **Set up Microsoft Defender for Endpoint**: First, you need to set up Microsoft Defender for Endpoint. You can do this by signing up for a Microsoft Defender for Endpoint account, deploying the Microsoft Defender for Endpoint agent to your devices, and configuring policies to protect your organization against cyber threats.
2. **Configure Windows 365 to use Microsoft Defender for Endpoint**: To configure Windows 365 to use Microsoft Defender for Endpoint, you need to create a policy in the Microsoft Endpoint Manager console.

   Go to **Devices** and select **Policies**. Click **Create Policy** and select **Windows 10 and later** as the platform. Under **Endpoint Protection**, select **Microsoft Defender for Endpoint** as the security solution. You can also configure additional settings, such as allowing or blocking specific applications, and set up remediation actions for detected threats.
3. **Assign the policy to Windows 365 devices**: Once you have created the policy, assign it to the group of Windows 365 devices you want to protect. Go to **Devices** and select **All Devices**. Select the devices you want to assign the policy to, and then click **Assignments**. Select the policy you created in the previous step, and then click **Save**.
4. **Monitor device compliance**: After you have assigned the policy to your Windows 365 devices, you can monitor device compliance in the Microsoft Endpoint Manager console. You can view alerts and reports on threats and compliance issues and take action to remediate any issues that arise.

By following these steps, you can configure Windows 365 for Microsoft Defender for Endpoint.

Enrollment device platform restrictions

Enrollment device platform restrictions in the Microsoft Intune admin center allow you to set restrictions on which platforms are allowed to enroll in your organization's Defender for Endpoint instance. Here are the steps to set up enrollment device platform restrictions:

1. Sign in to the Microsoft Intune admin center with an account that has the necessary permissions to manage device enrollment.

2. In the navigation pane, select **Settings** and then **Devices**.
3. Under **Enrollment restrictions**, click **+ Create restriction** (choose a platform – Android, Windows, macOS, or iOS):

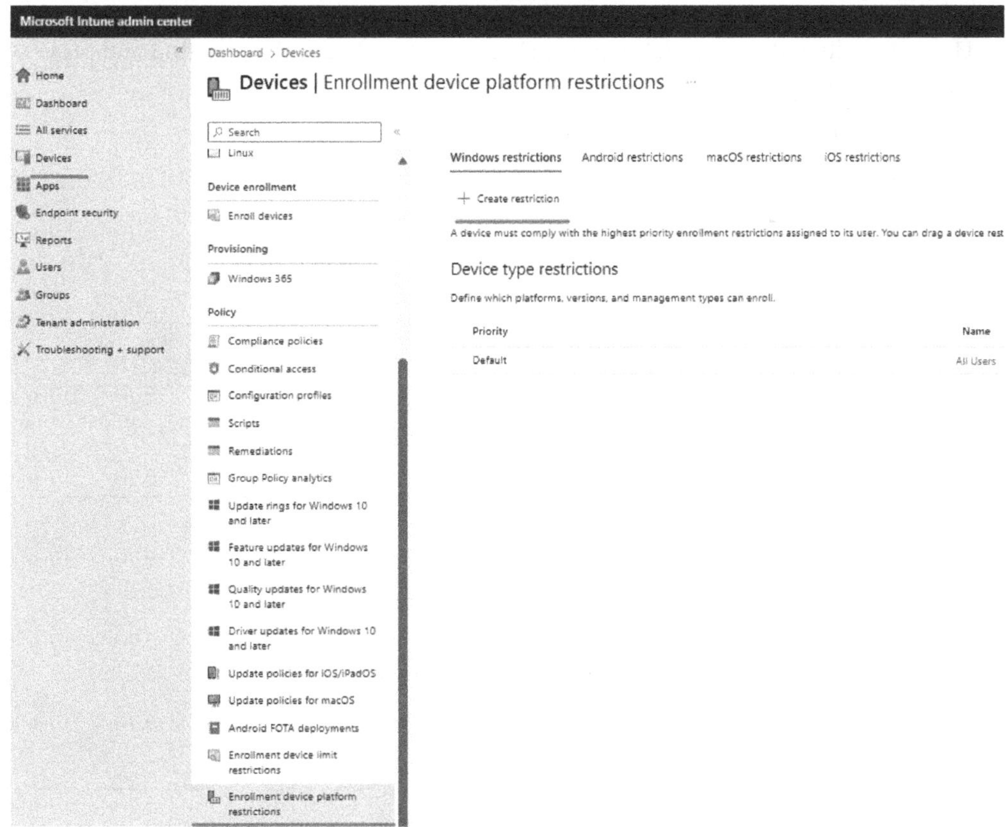

Figure 4.30 – Enrollment device platform restriction

4. Select the platform(s) you want to restrict enrollment for.
5. Select the type of restriction you want to set:
   - **Allow**: Only devices with the selected platform will be allowed to enroll
   - **Block**: Devices with the selected platform will not be allowed to enroll

> **Warning**
>
> Devices with the selected platform will be allowed to enroll, but you will receive a warning message.

6. Save your changes.

Creating an Android restriction

Managing device restrictions is a crucial aspect of mobile device management, and with Microsoft Intune, creating specific restrictions for Android devices becomes seamless and efficient. Let's follow these steps:

1. Under **Enrollment device platform restrictions**, select **Android restriction** and press + **Create Restriction**.
2. Add a name and description.

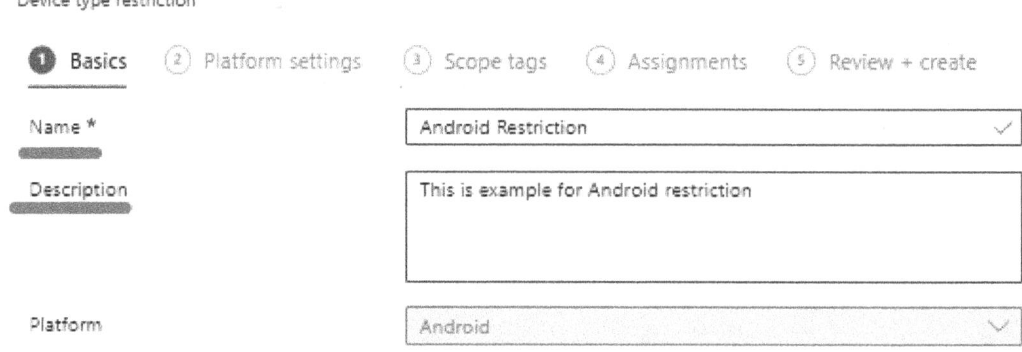

Figure 4.31 – Android restriction

3. Under **Platform settings**, define the Android type and press **Next**.

Figure 4.32 – Create restriction

4. Define scope tags.
5. Assign preferred groups (a security group must be created on Microsoft Entra ID).
6. Review your Android restriction and press **Create**.

For all other platforms (Windows, macOS, and iOS), the steps are the same as those just shown.

With enrollment device platform restrictions set up for Microsoft Defender for Endpoint, you can better control the types of devices that are allowed to enroll in your organization's Defender for Endpoint instance. Supported devices are Android, Windows 10, Windows 11, iOS, and macOS. This can help improve your organization's overall security posture by limiting the risk of potential security threats from devices that do not meet your organization's device platform standards.

Enrollment device limit restrictions

Enrollment device limit restrictions in the Microsoft Intune admin center allow you to set limits on the number of devices that users can enroll in your organization's Defender for Endpoint instance. Here are the steps to set up enrollment device limit restrictions for Microsoft Defender for Endpoint:

1. Sign in to the Microsoft Defender for Endpoint portal with an account that has the necessary permissions to manage device enrollment.
2. In the navigation panel, select **Devices**, and under **Policy**, select **Enrollment Device Limit Restriction**.
3. Under **Enrollment restrictions**, click **Add device limit restriction.**
4. Enter the maximum number of devices you want to allow to enroll in your organization's Defender for Endpoint instance. The default number of allowed devices per user is 15, but you can change this as per your company policy requirements:

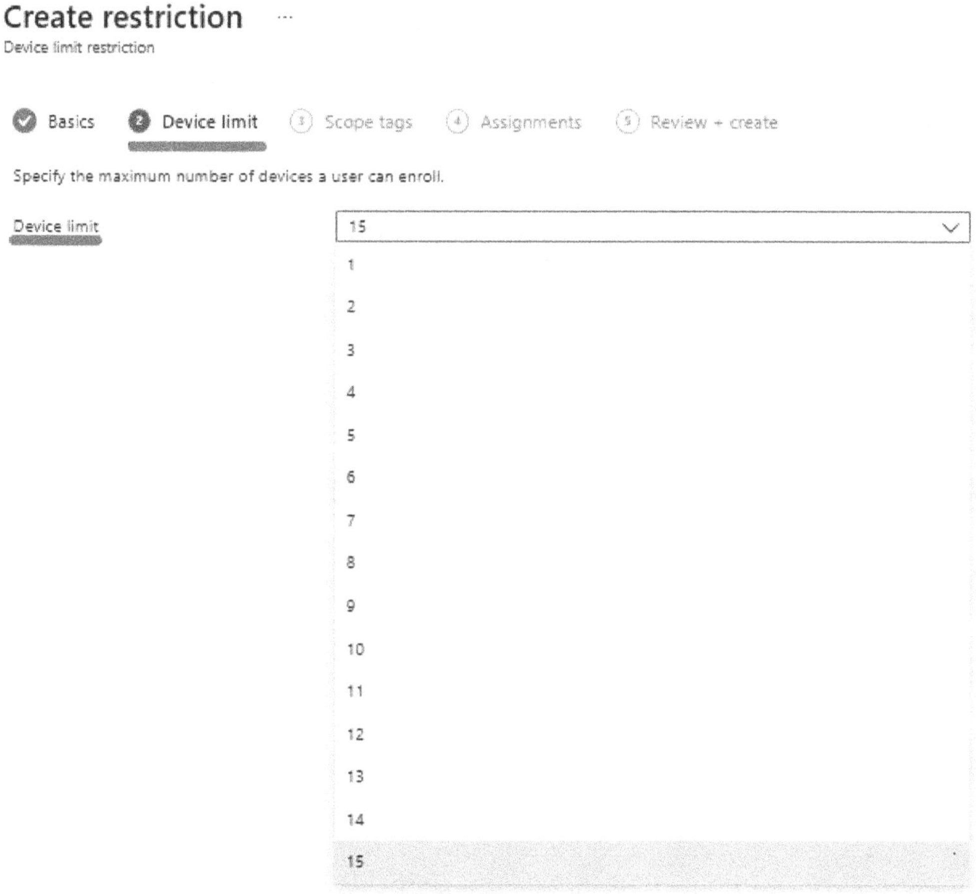

Figure 4.33 – Define device limits

5. Add scope tags.
6. Define assignments.
7. Save your changes.

With enrollment device limit restrictions set up for Microsoft Intune, you can better control the number of devices that can enroll in your organization's Defender for Endpoint instance. Sometimes it is not recommended to have 15 devices per user allowed to be enrolled into Endpoint. But bear in mind that some C-level positions require more devices. For those users, create a security group and create a new restriction policy. This can help improve your organization's overall security posture by limiting the risk of potential security threats from devices that are not properly managed and maintained.

Configuring quality updates for Windows 10 and later in Intune

Creating a profile for quality updates for Windows 10 and later in the Microsoft Intune admin center allows you to configure settings for how these updates are installed and managed on devices in your organization. Here are the steps to create a profile for quality updates:

1. Sign in to the Microsoft Intune admin center and navigate to **Devices** | **Policy**.
2. Select **Quality updates for Windows 10 and later** as the platform.
3. Select + **Create profile**.
4. Configure the settings you want for quality updates, such as whether to install updates automatically or manually, whether to defer an update, and how long to defer them for.

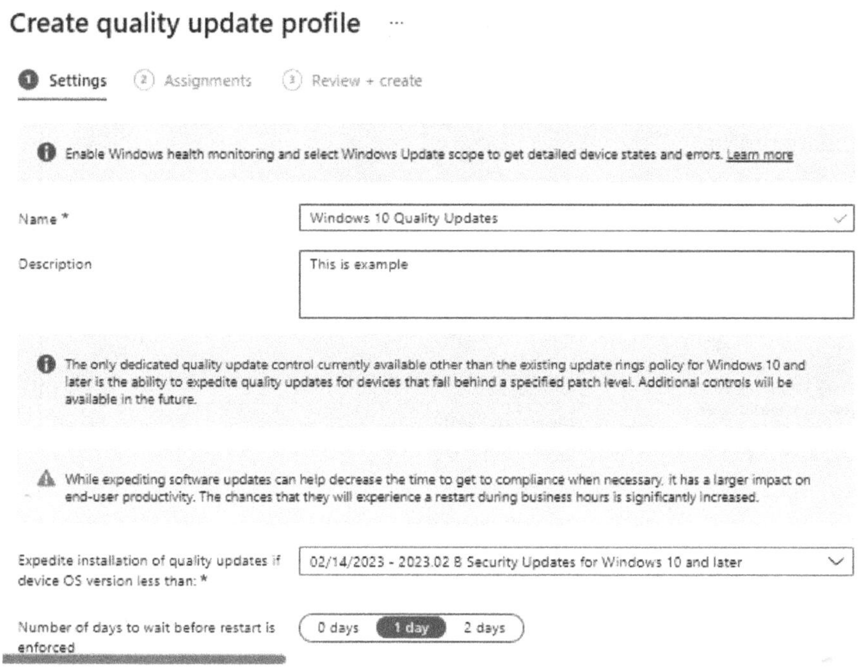

Figure 4.34 – Create quality update

5. Define group assignment.
6. Save your changes.

Once you have created the profile for quality updates, you can assign it to the devices in your organization for which you want to manage quality updates. To assign the profile, go to the **Assignments** section of the profile and select the group of devices you want to apply the profile to.

By creating a profile for quality updates in the Microsoft Intune admin center, you can better manage and maintain the security of the devices in your organization by ensuring that critical security updates are installed and managed in a way that meets your organization's requirements.

How to create a profile for update policies for iOS/iPadOS in Intune

Creating a profile for update policies for iOS/iPadOS in the Microsoft Intune admin center allows you to configure settings for how updates are installed and managed on iOS/iPadOS devices in your organization. Here are the steps to create a profile for update policies:

1. Sign in to the Microsoft Intune admin center and navigate to **Devices | Update policies for iOS/iPadOS**.
2. Select **+Create profile**.

3. Define a name and add a description. Then press **Next**.
4. Configure the settings you want for **Select version to install** and **Schedule type**:

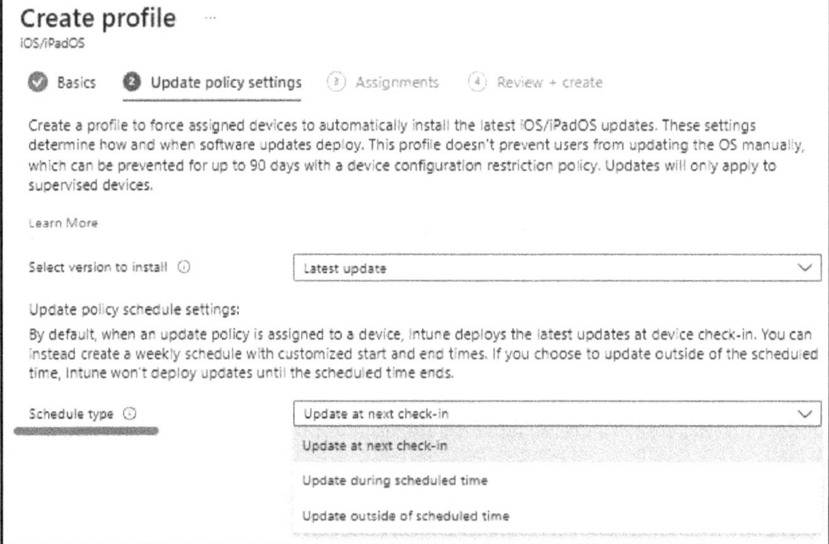

Figure 4.35 – Create an update policy for iOS/iPadOS

5. Save your changes.

Once you have created the profile for update policies, you can assign it to the iOS/iPadOS devices in your organization that you want to manage updates for. To assign the profile, go to the **Assignments** section of the profile and select the group of devices you want to apply the profile to.

By creating a profile for update policies in the Microsoft Intune admin center, you can better manage and maintain the security of the iOS/iPadOS devices in your organization by ensuring that critical security updates are installed and managed in a way that meets your organization's requirements.

How to create a profile for update policies for macOS in the Intune portal

Creating a profile for update policies for macOS in the Microsoft Intune admin center allows you to configure settings for how updates are installed and managed on macOS devices in your organization. Here are the steps to create a profile for update policies:

1. Sign in to the Microsoft Endpoint Manager admin center and navigate to **Devices** | **Update policy for macOS**.
2. Select + **Create profile**.
3. Define the name and add a description, then press **Next**.
4. Under **Update policy settings**, define critical, firmware, configuration, and other updates. Note that the options shown in the following screenshot are the same for all configurations:

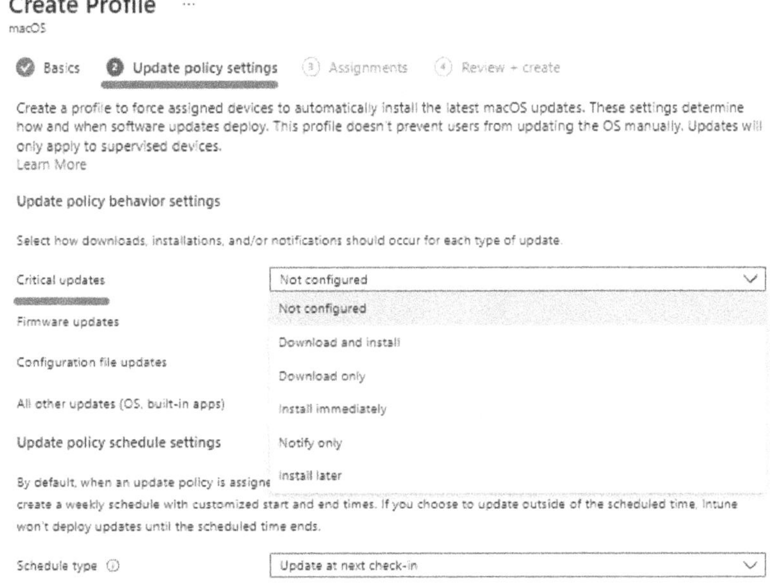

Figure 4.36 – Update policy settings

5. Configure the settings you want for update policies, such as whether to automatically install updates, whether to allow the installation of beta updates, and how long to defer updates for.
6. Save your changes.

Once you have created the profile for update policies, you can assign it to the macOS devices in your organization that you want to manage updates for. To assign the profile, go to the **Assignments** section of the profile and select the group of devices you want to apply the profile to.

By creating a profile for update policies in the Microsoft Intune admin center, you can better manage and maintain the security of the macOS devices in your organization by ensuring that critical security updates are installed and managed in a way that meets your organization's requirements.

How to create app protection policies in the Microsoft Intune admin portal

Creating an app protection policy in the Microsoft Intune admin center allows you to protect the data and applications on mobile devices in your organization by defining policies that restrict access to sensitive data and applications based on various conditions. Here are the steps to create an app protection policy:

1. Sign in to the Microsoft Intune admin center and navigate to **Apps** | **App protection policy**.
2. Click + **Create policy** and choose the platform you want to create the policy for, such as Android, iOS, or Windows:

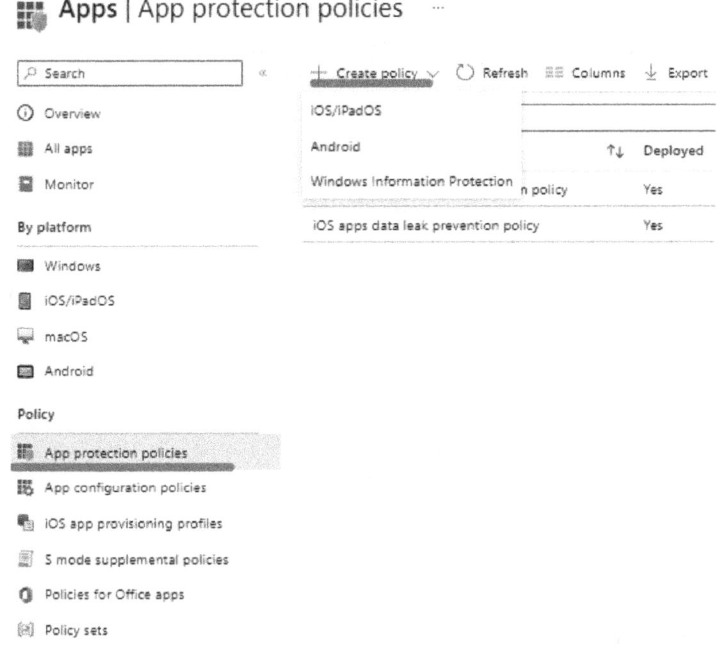

Figure 4.37 – App protection policy

3. Enter a name and description for the policy (the following screenshot is an example for Windows-targeted apps):

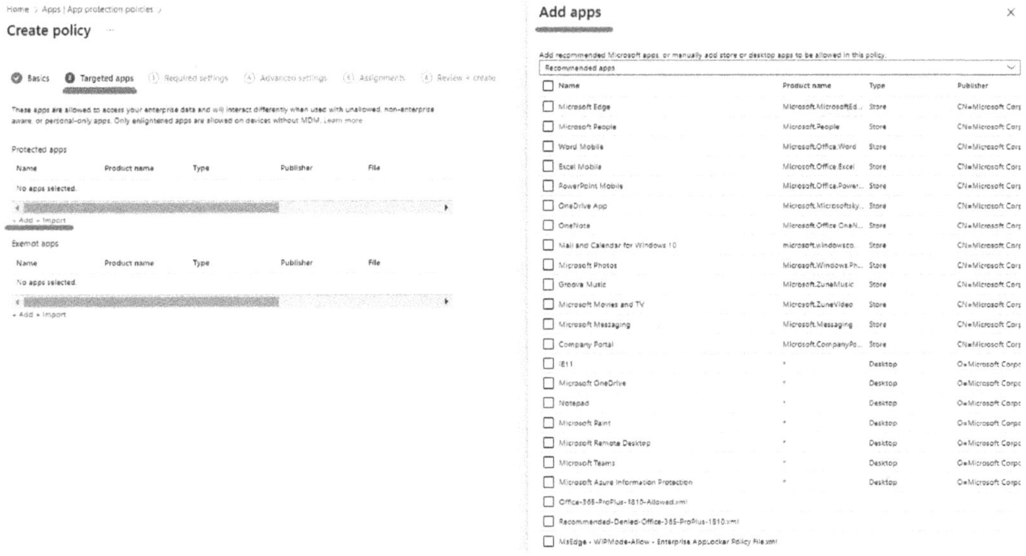

Figure 4.38 – App protection policy

4. After selecting apps in the previous step, on the **Required settings** page, define the policy settings you want to apply, such as which apps should be protected, whether to require a PIN or biometric authentication to access protected apps, and whether to restrict copy and paste or other data sharing between protected apps and non-protected apps:

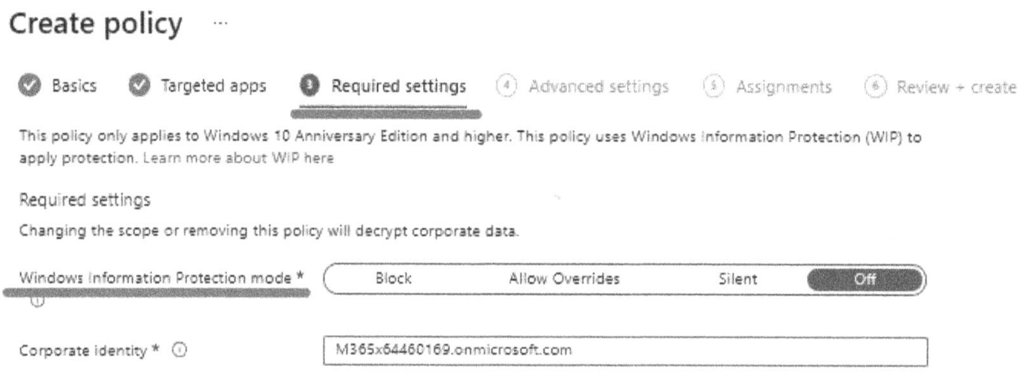

Figure 4.39 – Required settings for an app protection policy

> **Explanation of Windows Information Protection modes**
>
> **Off**: No action is logged, and the user is free to relocate data of protected apps.
>
> **Silent**: These actions are logged, but the user is free to relocate data of protected apps.
>
> **Allow Overrides**: The actions are logged, but the user has information about relocating data from protected apps.
>
> **Block**: Block relocating data.

5. Under **Advanced settings**, add a network boundary, define **Data protection**, and press **Next**:

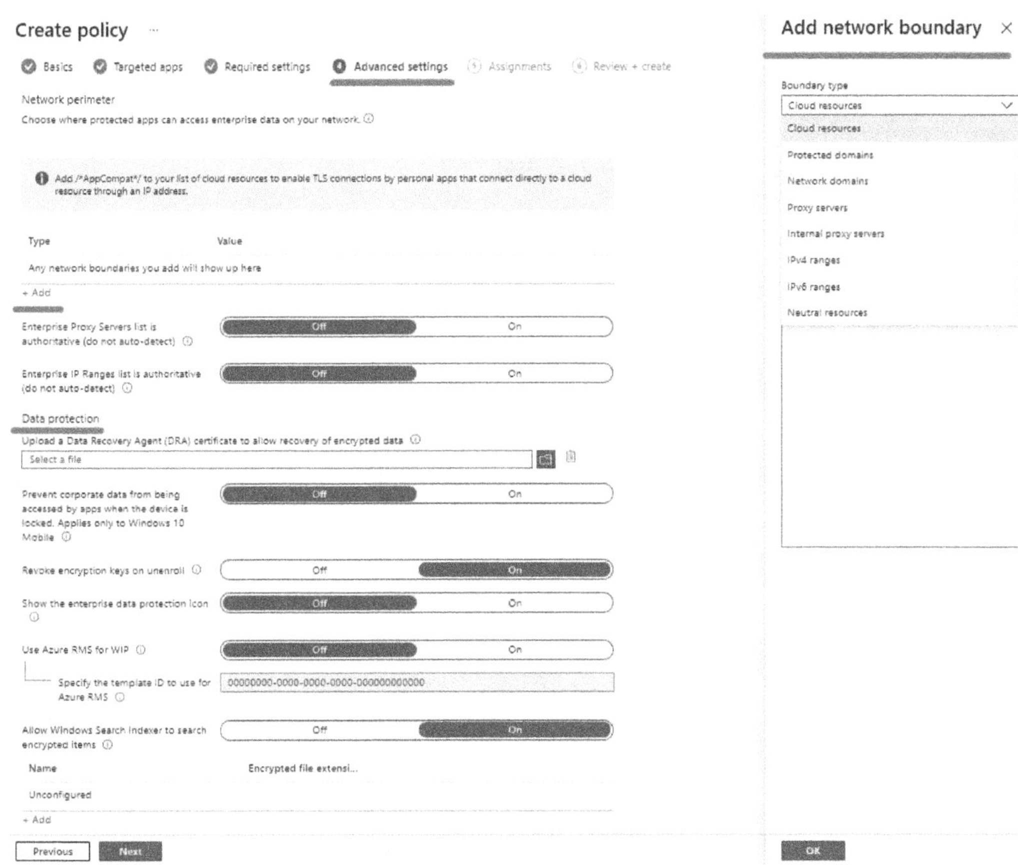

Figure 4.40 – App protection policy

6. Define **Assignments**.
7. Save your changes.

For Android, iOS, and macOS platforms, select the same steps, but under **Apps**, define **Target to apps on all device types** and **Target policy to**.

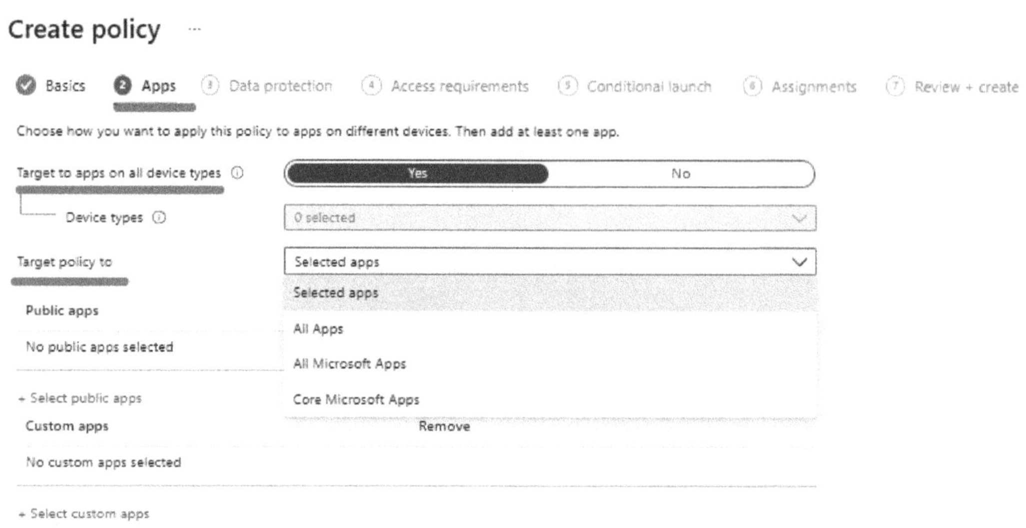

Figure 4.41 – Define target apps

For Android, you can select one of the device types:

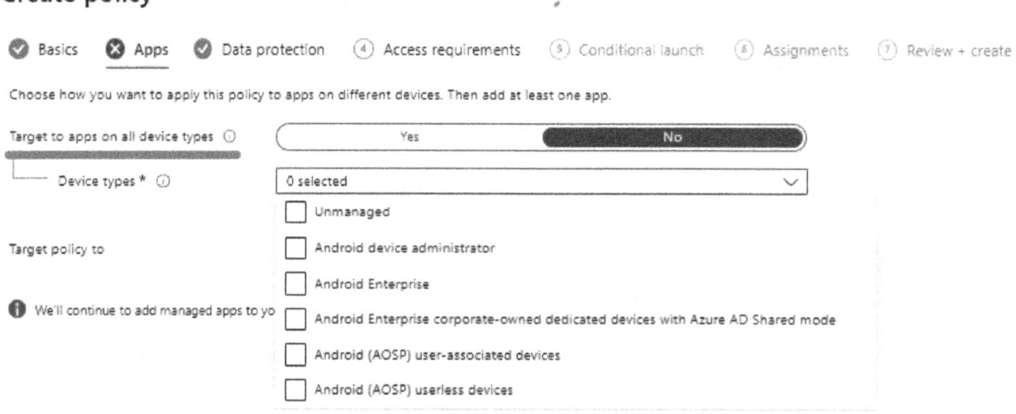

Figure 4.42 – Define device type in App protection policies

Data protection defines options for controls and restrictions. This section presents the policy on how users work with selected data in the apps. When you provide the following configuration, under the **Access requirements** tab, define how users access apps:

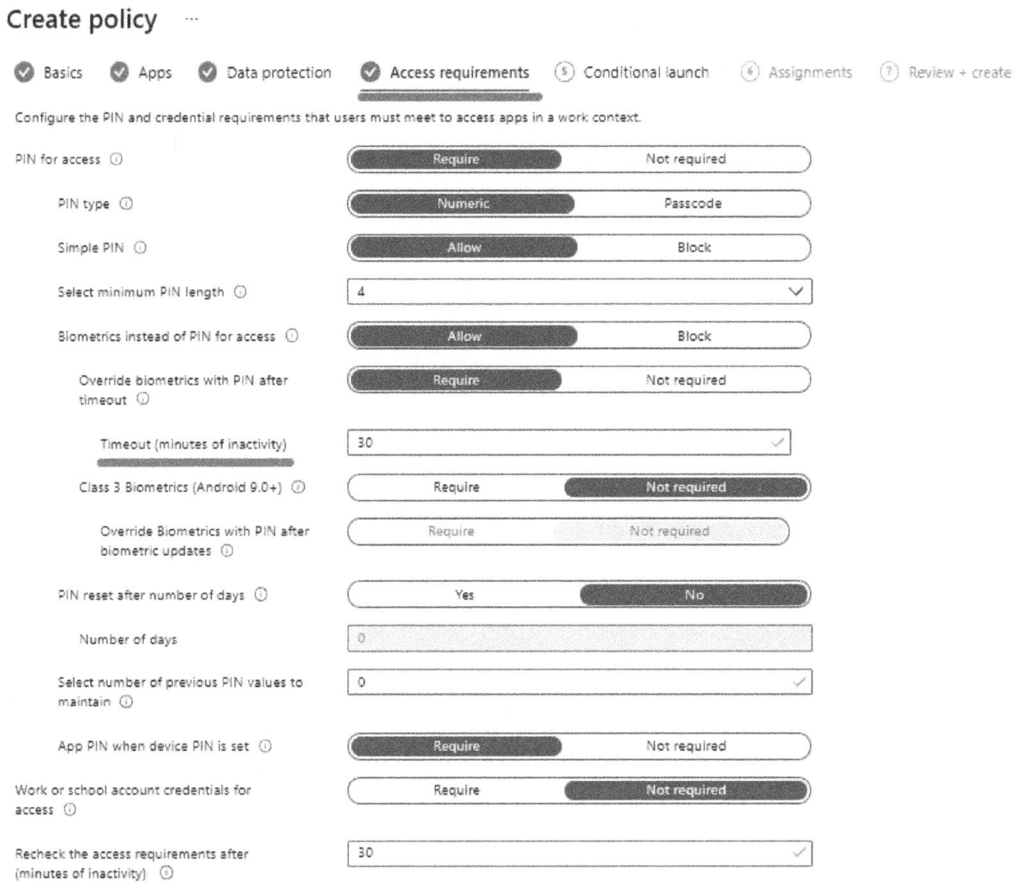

Create policy ...

Basics Apps Data protection Access requirements (5) Conditional launch (6) Assignments (7) Review + create

Configure the PIN and credential requirements that users must meet to access apps in a work context.

PIN for access — Require | Not required

PIN type — Numeric | Passcode

Simple PIN — Allow | Block

Select minimum PIN length — 4

Biometrics instead of PIN for access — Allow | Block

Override biometrics with PIN after timeout — Require | Not required

Timeout (minutes of inactivity) — 30

Class 3 Biometrics (Android 9.0+) — Require | Not required

Override Biometrics with PIN after biometric updates — Require | Not required

PIN reset after number of days — Yes | No

Number of days — 0

Select number of previous PIN values to maintain — 0

App PIN when device PIN is set — Require | Not required

Work or school account credentials for access — Require | Not required

Recheck the access requirements after (minutes of inactivity) — 30

Figure 4.43 – Access requirements

It's recommended to decrease **Timeout (minutes of inactivity)** from the default of 30 minutes to 10 minutes.

Under **Conditional launch**, define app condition settings for the PIN, offline grace period, minimal app version, and disabled accounts, as well as settings for device conditions:

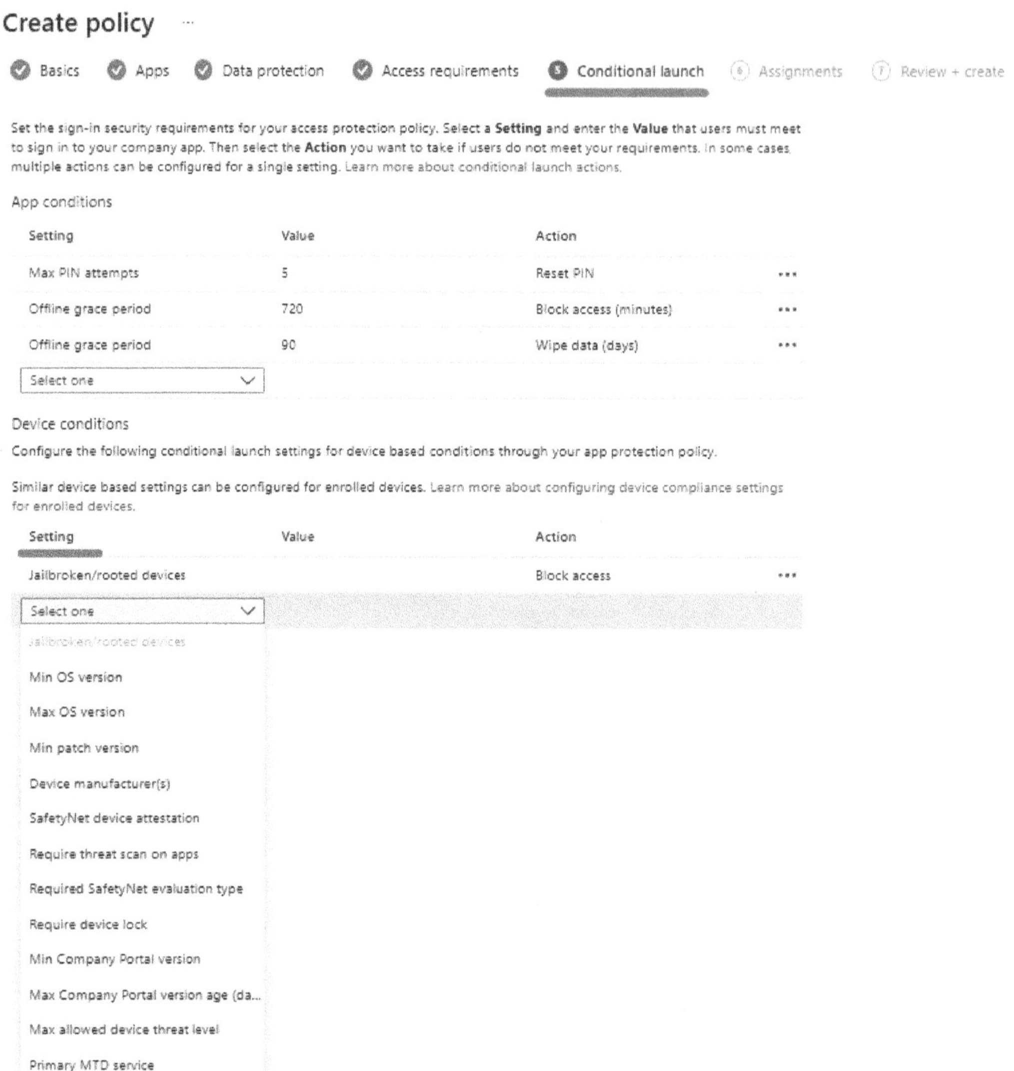

Figure 4.44 – Define conditional launch

Once you have created the app protection policy, you can assign it to the devices in your organization that you want to apply the policy to. To assign the policy, go to the **Assignments** section of the policy and select the group of devices you want to apply the policy to.

An app protection policy in the Microsoft Intune admin center is an important part of the Microsoft Endpoint solution and can help your organization ensure that sensitive data and applications on mobile devices in your organization are protected from unauthorized access and use.

How to create app configuration policies

Creating an app configuration policy in the Microsoft Intune admin center allows you to configure settings for specific apps on mobile devices in your organization, such as specifying default app settings or configuring specific app features. Here are the steps to create an app configuration policy:

1. Sign in to the Microsoft Intune admin center and navigate to **Apps** | **App configuration policies**.
2. Click **Create policy** and choose the platform you want to create the policy for, such as Android or iOS.
3. Enter a name and description for the policy.
4. Choose the app you want to configure from the list of supported apps or select **Other App** if the app you want to configure is not listed.
5. Configure the settings you want for the selected app, such as specifying default app settings or configuring specific app features:

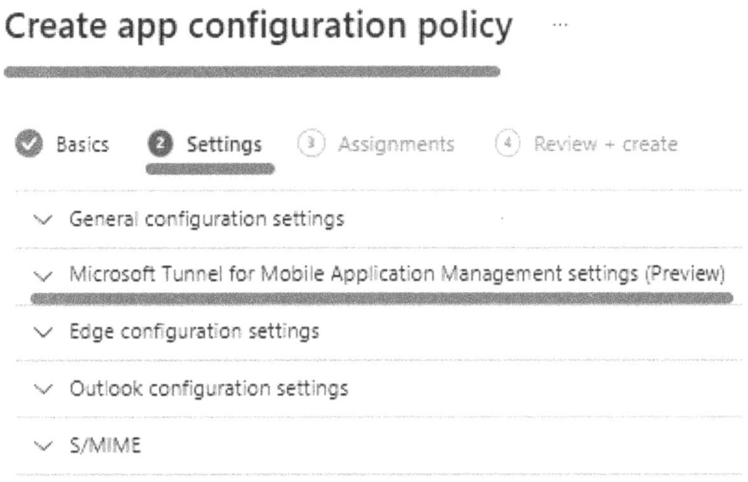

Figure 4.45 – Create app configuration policy

6. Define the conditions that should trigger the policy, such as whether the device is enrolled in Intune or managed by Microsoft Defender for Endpoint.
7. Define the actions that should be taken when the policy is triggered, such as sending an email notification or blocking access to the app.
8. Save your changes.

Once you have created the app configuration policy, you can assign it to the devices in your organization that you want to apply the policy to. To assign the policy, go to the **Assignments** section of the policy and select the group of devices you want to apply the policy to.

By creating an app configuration policy in the Microsoft Intune admin center, you can ensure that specific apps on mobile devices in your organization are configured in a way that meets your organization's requirements, such as ensuring that default app settings are consistent across all devices or configuring specific features of an app to meet your organization's needs.

How to create policies for Office apps in the Intune admin portal

Creating policies for Office apps in the Microsoft Intune admin center allows you to configure and manage the behavior of the Office apps on devices in your organization, such as controlling access to Office files, enabling or disabling specific features, or managing document-sharing settings. Here are the steps to create policies for Office apps:

1. Sign in to the Microsoft Intune admin center and navigate to **Apps**. Under **Policy**, select **Policies for Office Apps**.
2. Click **Create profile** and choose the platform you want to create the profile for, such as Windows or macOS.
3. Enter a name and description for the profile.
4. Configure the settings you want for the selected Office version, such as controlling access to Office files, enabling, or disabling specific features, or managing document-sharing settings:

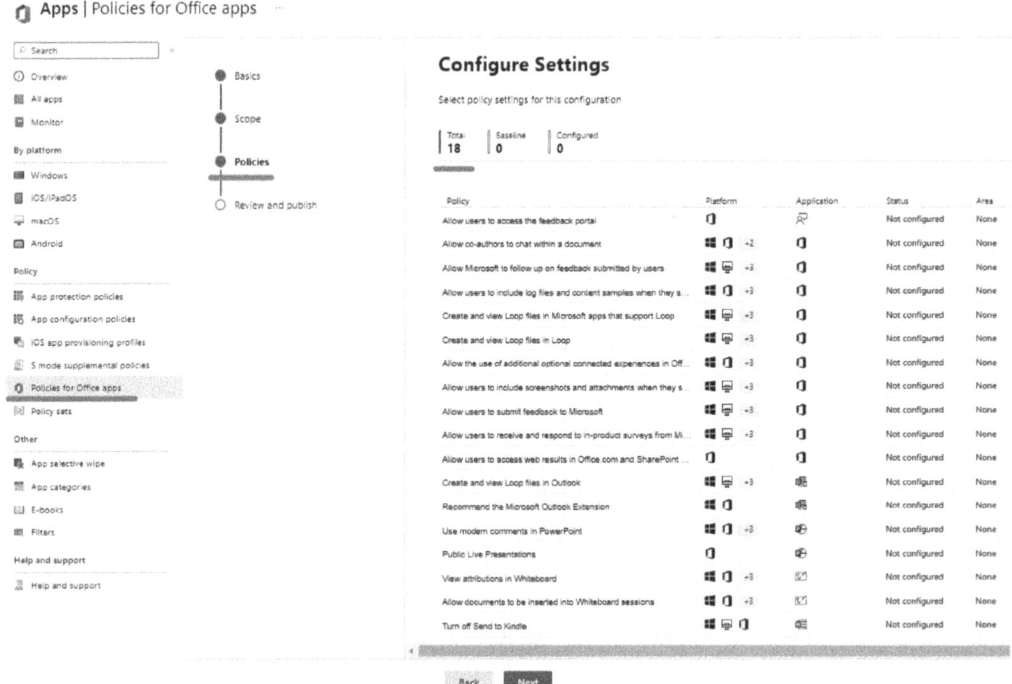

Figure 4.46 – Define policies for Office apps

5. Save your changes.

You can manage and maintain the security of the Office apps on devices in your organization better by ensuring that critical security settings are configured in a way that meets your organization's requirements. That is the main reason it is recommended to create policies for Office apps in Microsoft Defender for Endpoint.

Endpoint Security

Confused? Microsoft Defender for Endpoint or Endpoint Security? Microsoft Defender for Endpoint and Endpoint Security are both security solutions offered by Microsoft, but they have some important differences. Microsoft Defender for Endpoint is an advanced endpoint protection platform that helps to prevent, detect, investigate, and respond to advanced threats on devices and networks. It provides real-time protection against viruses, malware, and other cyberattacks. It also includes features such as behavioral analysis, cloud-powered protection, and automated security intelligence, as we already mentioned in the introduction. Defender for Endpoint is designed for organizations of all sizes, and it offers centralized management and reporting capabilities.

On the other hand, Endpoint Security is a more basic security solution that provides antivirus and anti-malware protection for Windows 10 devices. It is included in the Microsoft 365 Business Premium and Microsoft 365 E3/E5 subscriptions, and it is designed for small to medium-sized businesses that don't require the advanced features of Defender for Endpoint.

As you can see in the following screenshot, on Endpoint Security, you will find different security options that you can configure:

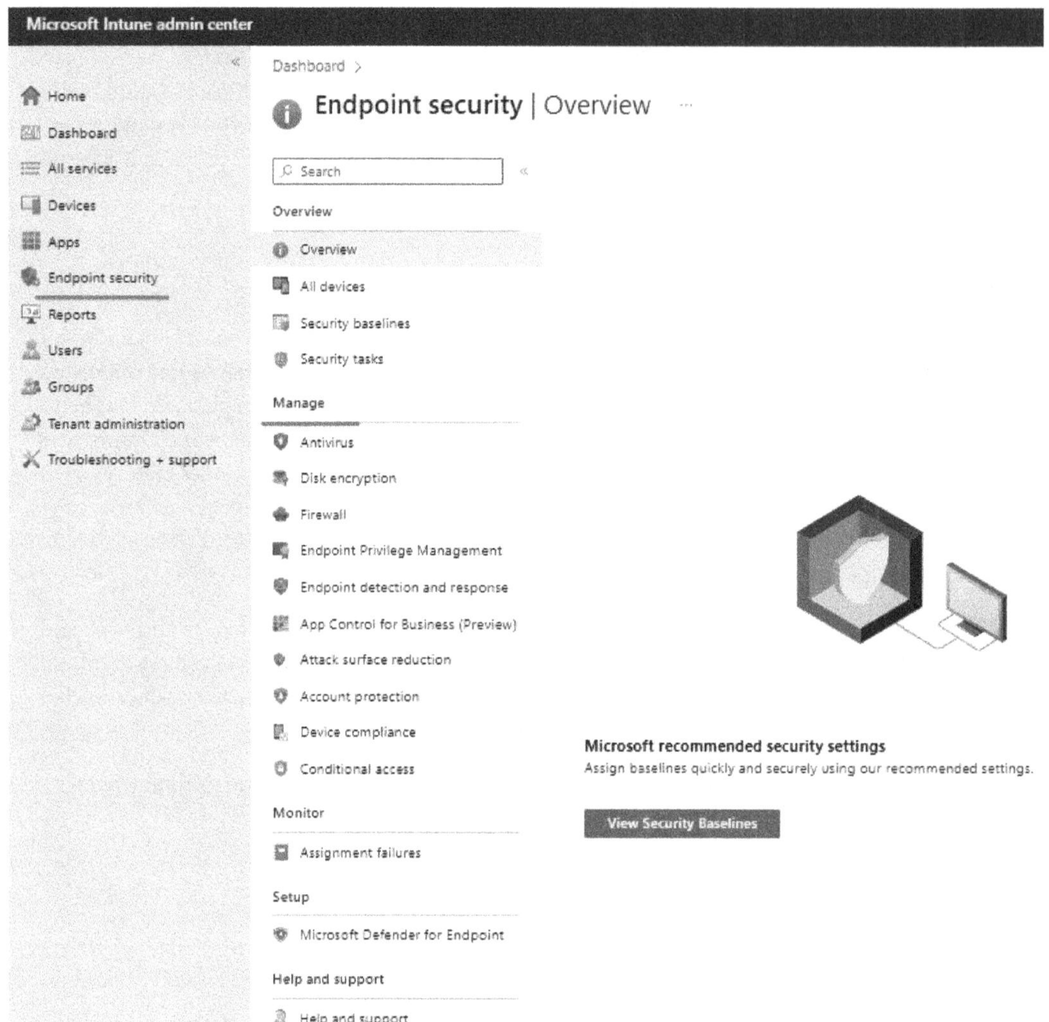

Figure 4.47 – Endpoint security in the Microsoft Intune admin center

So, let's see how you can easily configure each of the security settings and provide more effective protection on your devices enrolled in the Microsoft Intune admin center and Microsoft Defender for Endpoint.

On the Endpoint Security dashboard overview, you will find three steps for quick configuration of some of the security settings:

- **Microsoft recommended security settings**
- **Simplified security policies**
- **Remediate endpoint weaknesses**

Figure 4.48 – Configure security baselines

Click on **View Security Baselines** and you will find settings for creating different profiles for the following:

- Security baseline for Windows 10 and later
- Microsoft Defender for Endpoint baseline
- Microsoft Edge baseline
- Windows 365 security baseline (at the time of writing this book, this option is still in preview)

Creating a profile for a security baseline for Windows 10 and later

After clicking on **+Create profile** and adding a name and description, under **Configuration Settings**, you will find options for different security configurations, such as **Device Lock**, **Firewall**, **System**, and **Windows PowerShell**. One of the most important options that you need to configure is **Device Lock**:

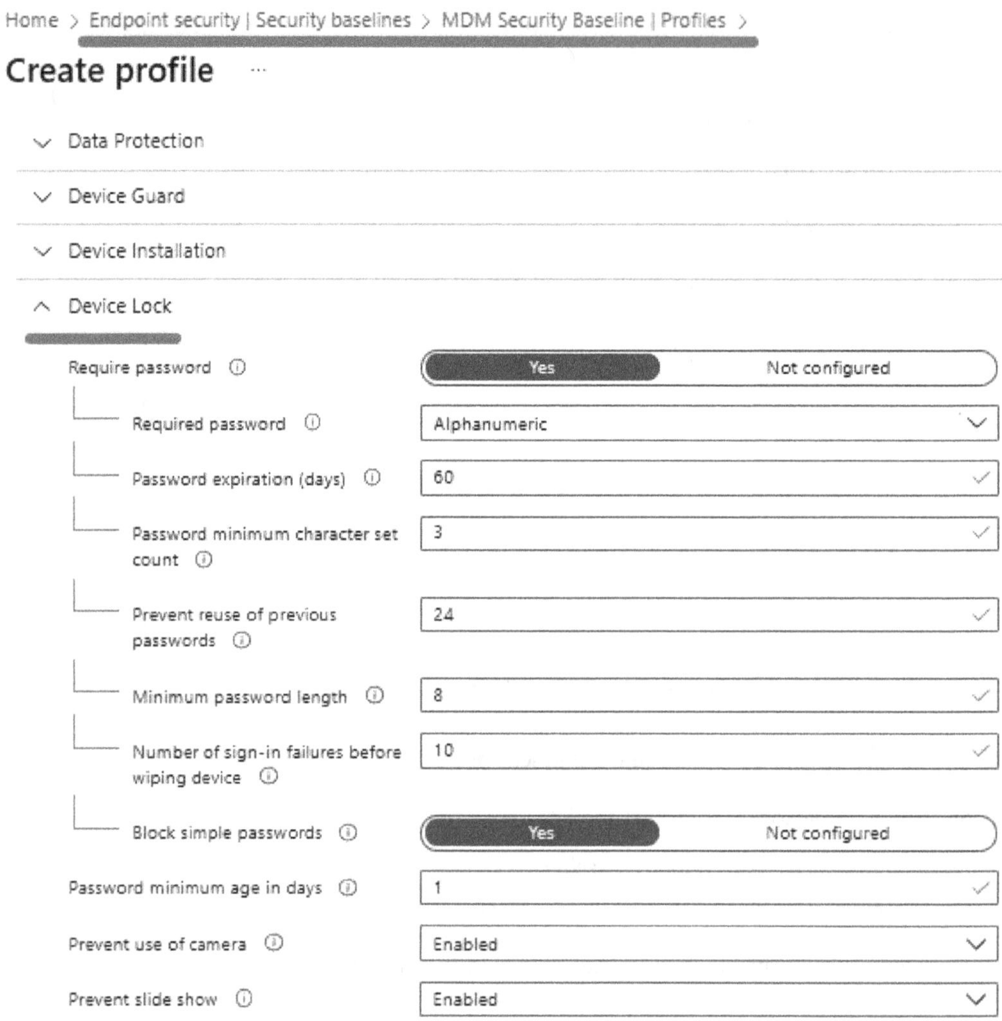

Home > Endpoint security | Security baselines > MDM Security Baseline | Profiles >

Create profile ...

Data Protection

Device Guard

Device Installation

Device Lock

Require password	Yes / Not configured
Required password	Alphanumeric
Password expiration (days)	60
Password minimum character set count	3
Prevent reuse of previous passwords	24
Minimum password length	8
Number of sign-in failures before wiping device	10
Block simple passwords	Yes / Not configured
Password minimum age in days	1
Prevent use of camera	Enabled
Prevent slide show	Enabled

Figure 4.49 – Create profile

As you can see, this section is no different than when you configure a password policy through a group policy on Active Directory on-premises.

Important note

If you have Active Directory in hybrid deployment (Active Directory on-premises and Microsoft Entra ID), you can use your group policy for password and applied to all enrolled devices in Microsoft Defender for Endpoint. But if you only have Microsoft Entra ID and you want to deploy your own password policy to all enrolled devices in Microsoft Defender for Endpoint, you will need to configure this through security baselines.

Creating a Microsoft Defender for Endpoint baseline

On the other side, the Microsoft Defender for Endpoint baseline is a set of recommended security settings that help organizations strengthen their security posture and protect their devices and data from various cyber threats. It is a security configuration baseline that provides a starting point for implementing security best practices in Microsoft Defender for Endpoint. The Microsoft Defender for Endpoint baseline consists of a set of security recommendations that cover different aspects of security, including device and user management, ASR rules, firewall protection, application control, and device protection. These recommendations are designed to help organizations secure their endpoints and reduce the risk of cyberattacks:

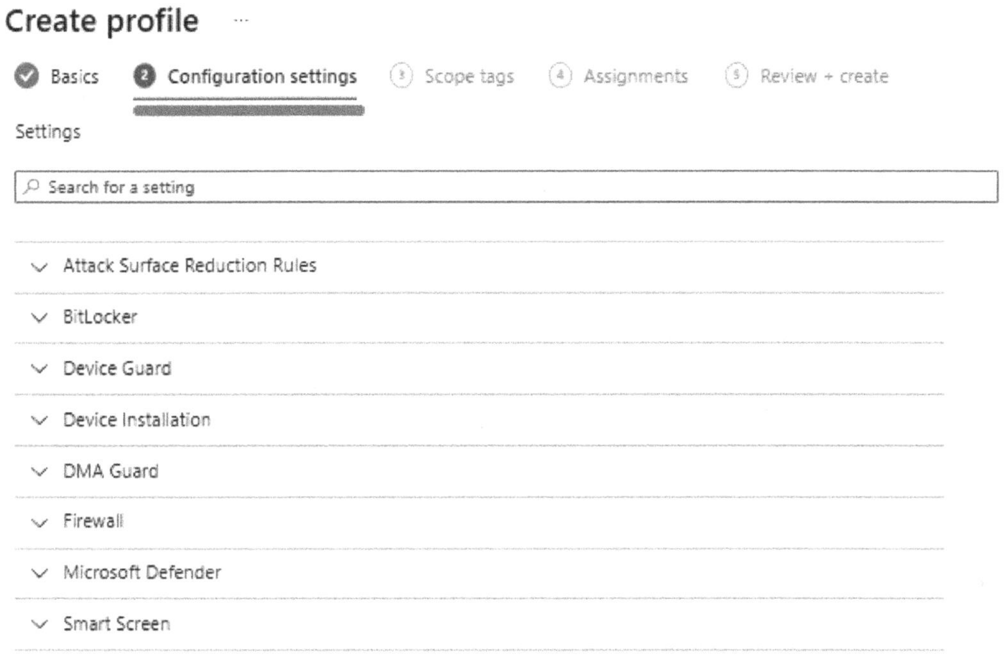

Create profile ...

Basics | Configuration settings | Scope tags | Assignments | Review + create

Settings

Search for a setting

Attack Surface Reduction Rules
BitLocker
Device Guard
Device Installation
DMA Guard
Firewall
Microsoft Defender
Smart Screen

Figure 4.50 – Microsoft Defender for Endpoint baseline

Implementing the Microsoft Defender for Endpoint baseline will provide organizations with a stronger security posture and reduce the likelihood of a successful cyberattack. The baseline is designed to be flexible and customizable to meet the specific needs of each organization, and it can be adjusted as needed to address new threats and vulnerabilities. Also, organizations can change profiles anytime and adjust them to their own needs at a specific time.

Creating a Microsoft Edge baseline

The Microsoft Edge baseline is a part of Endpoint Security and contains a set of recommended security settings for Microsoft Edge. The Microsoft Edge baseline helps organizations implement security best practices and protect their users and data from various online threats. The Microsoft Edge baseline includes a set of security recommendations covering different aspects of security, including user data protection, browsing security, network protection, and device protection. These recommendations are designed to help organizations configure their Microsoft Edge browsers in a way that reduces the risk of any internet attacks. Like the previous setting, the organization can create different profiles for different Azure AD groups:

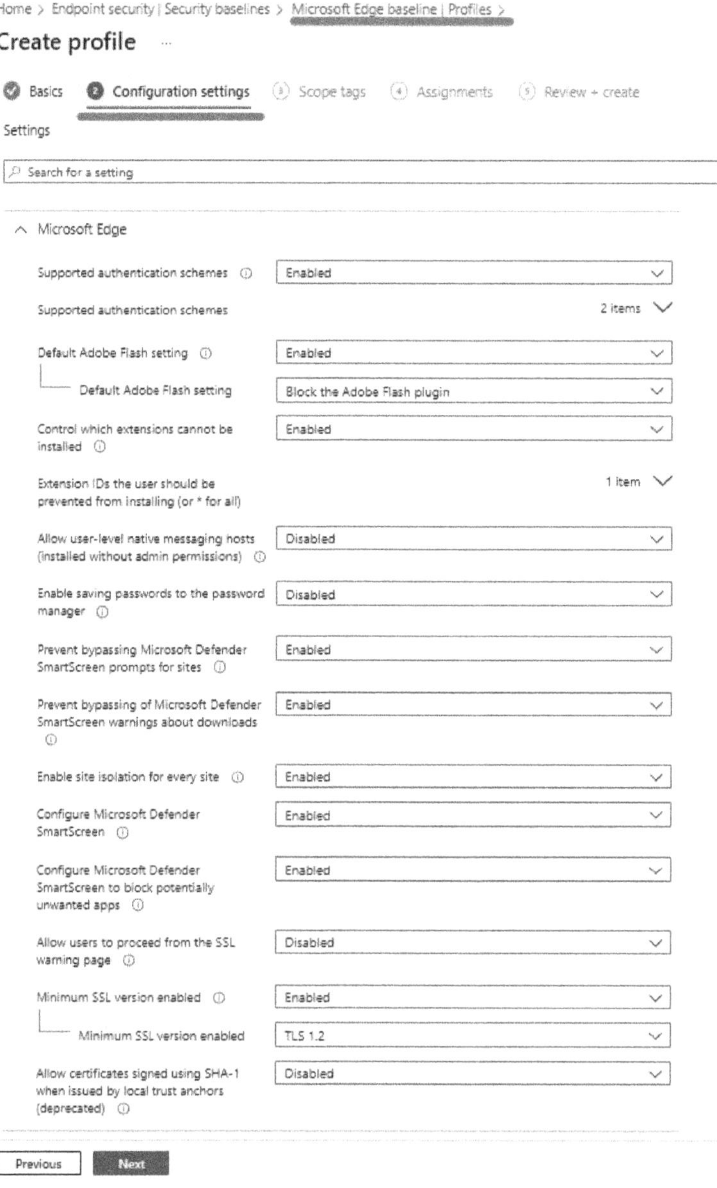

Figure 4.51 – Microsoft Edge baseline

Organizations can enhance and improve the security of their web browsing experience and reduce possible successful attacks such as viruses, phishing, malware, and other online threats. The Microsoft Edge baseline is designed to be flexible and customizable to meet the specific needs of each organization, and it can be adjusted as needed to address new threats and vulnerabilities. Any configuration, of course, depends on the organization's needs and requirements.

Creating a Windows 365 security baseline

Windows 365 is a cloud-based service that allows users to access a virtualized Windows desktop experience on any device, including PCs, tablets, and mobile devices. To ensure the security of Windows 365, Microsoft has developed a set of security baselines that provide a minimum level of security that organizations should implement to protect their Windows 365 environment. The Windows 365 security baseline is a set of recommended security settings and configurations for Windows 365 that help organizations secure their virtual desktops and maintain a consistent security posture across their environment. The security baseline is based on industry best practices and is updated regularly to address new and emerging security threats. The Windows 365 security baseline includes a set of group policy settings that can be applied to virtual desktops to enforce security policies such as password complexity, user account control, and encryption. The baseline also includes a set of security features that can be enabled, such as Windows Defender Antivirus and Windows Firewall, to protect virtual desktops from malware and unauthorized access.

In addition to the security baseline, Microsoft also provides security guidance and tools to help organizations secure their Windows 365 environment, including the Microsoft Security Compliance Toolkit, which provides recommended security configurations and policies for Windows 365.

If you have any Microsoft Windows 365 (Business or Enterprise) deployment in your environment and are looking for efficient protection, the Windows 365 security baseline is the perfect solution to implement.

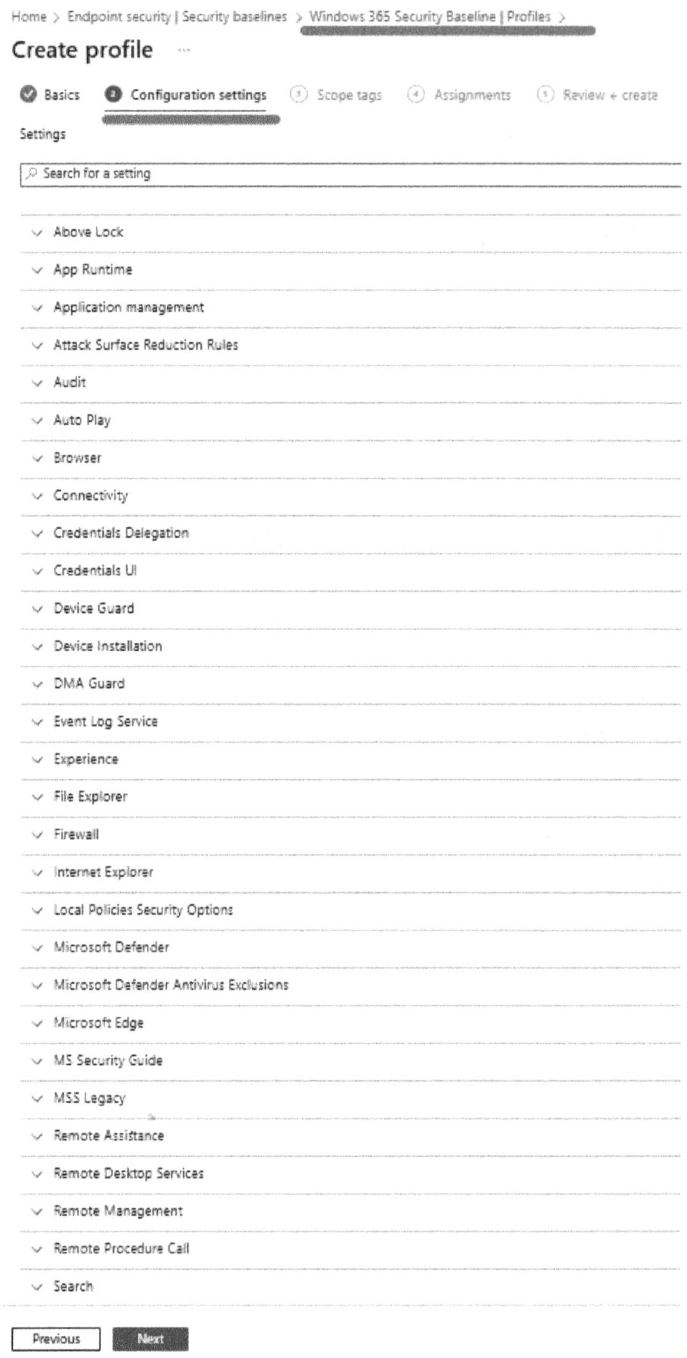

Home > Endpoint security | Security baselines > Windows 365 Security Baseline | Profiles >

Create profile ...

Basics
Configuration settings
3 Scope tags
4 Assignments
5 Review + create

Settings

Search for a setting

Above Lock
App Runtime
Application management
Attack Surface Reduction Rules
Audit
Auto Play
Browser
Connectivity
Credentials Delegation
Credentials UI
Device Guard
Device Installation
DMA Guard
Event Log Service
Experience
File Explorer
Firewall
Internet Explorer
Local Policies Security Options
Microsoft Defender
Microsoft Defender Antivirus Exclusions
Microsoft Edge
MS Security Guide
MSS Legacy
Remote Assistance
Remote Desktop Services
Remote Management
Remote Procedure Call
Search

Previous
Next

Figure 4.52 – Windows 365 security baseline

Managing and creating different policies under Endpoint Security

Besides security baselines, Microsoft Intune, under Endpoint Security, provides the option to create different policies for the following:

- Antivirus
- Disk encryption
- Firewall
- Endpoint detection and response
- Attack surface reduction
- Account protection
- Device compliance
- Conditional access

Let's see how you can create and implement different policies in your environment and protect your devices more in everyday work. But before starting with configuration policies, it would be good to check which version of Endpoint Security you have implemented on your tenant. Go to **Tenant Administration** | **Tenant Status** and check under **Tenant Details** which **Service release** version is implemented:

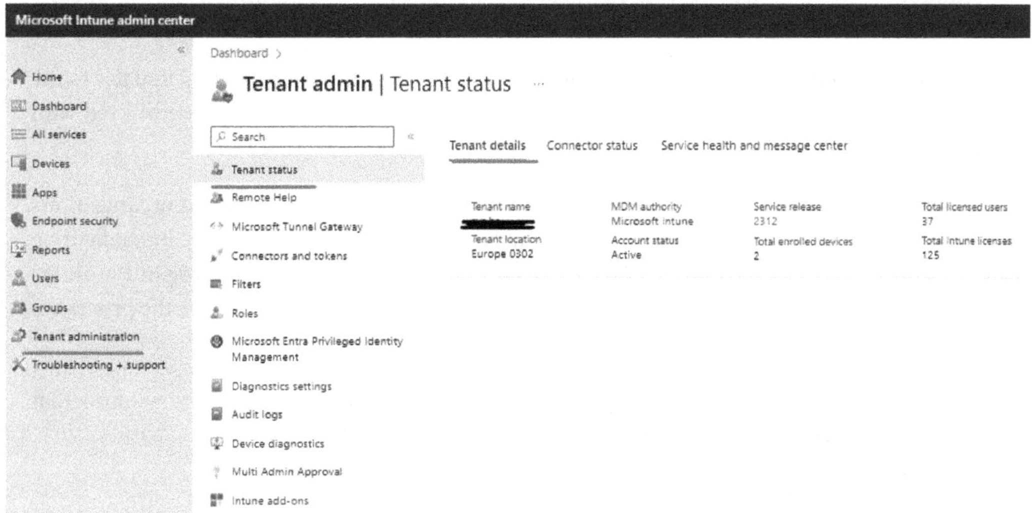

Figure 4.53 – Tenant administration

You can find more information about the version and updates by clicking on the number under **Service release**.

Configuring an antivirus policy in the Intune portal

As we mentioned earlier, Microsoft Endpoint Security is a suite of security tools and features designed to protect devices and data within an organization. One of the key components of Endpoint Security is the antivirus policy, which helps protect against malware, viruses, and other malicious software.

An antivirus policy is a set of rules and settings that dictate how the antivirus software behaves on devices within an organization. In Microsoft Endpoint Security, the antivirus policy is used to configure and manage the antivirus protection on devices running Windows 10, Windows Server, and macOS.

Some of the key elements that make up an antivirus policy in Microsoft Endpoint Security are as follows:

- **Malware detection**: The antivirus policy defines how the antivirus software detects and responds to malware threats. This includes setting up real-time scanning, scheduling regular scans, and specifying what types of files or devices should be scanned.
- **Threat remediation**: The antivirus policy also outlines what actions should be taken when a threat is detected. For example, it might quarantine or delete infected files, or block access to malicious websites.
- **Reporting**: The policy can be used to set up reporting and alerting so that security teams can be notified of any threats or suspicious activity.
- **Exclusions**: Sometimes it may be necessary to exclude certain files or directories from being scanned by the antivirus software. The antivirus policy allows administrators to specify these exclusions.
- **Update management**: The antivirus policy also includes settings for managing updates to the antivirus software and virus definitions. This ensures that devices are always protected with the latest security updates.

The antivirus policy in Microsoft Intune admin center is a critical component of an organization's security strategy, helping to protect against malware and other malicious software threats. By configuring and managing these policies, administrators can ensure that devices within their organization are kept secure and up to date by using next-generation antivirus solutions. Let's explore the process of configuring an Antivirus Policy within the Microsoft Intune admin center:

1. Click on **Antivirus** and under **AV policies**, click on + **Create Policy**. On the window that opens, select a platform and profile. Supported platforms are the following:
   - Windows 10, Windows 11, and Windows Server
   - macOS

- Windows 10, Windows 11, and Windows Server (Configuration Manager)

Figure 4.54 – Endpoint security antivirus

Windows Defender Antivirus is the next-generation protection component of Microsoft Defender for Endpoint. Next-generation protection brings together machine learning, big data analysis, in-depth threat resistance research, and cloud infrastructure to protect devices in your enterprise organization.

2. Click **Create**.
3. After providing a name (required) and description, click **Next**. On the opened **Configuration settings** tab, check the options that you can configure. Keep in mind that you have the option to create different antivirus policies and apply them to different security groups. The following screenshot provides a short example of options that you can configure.

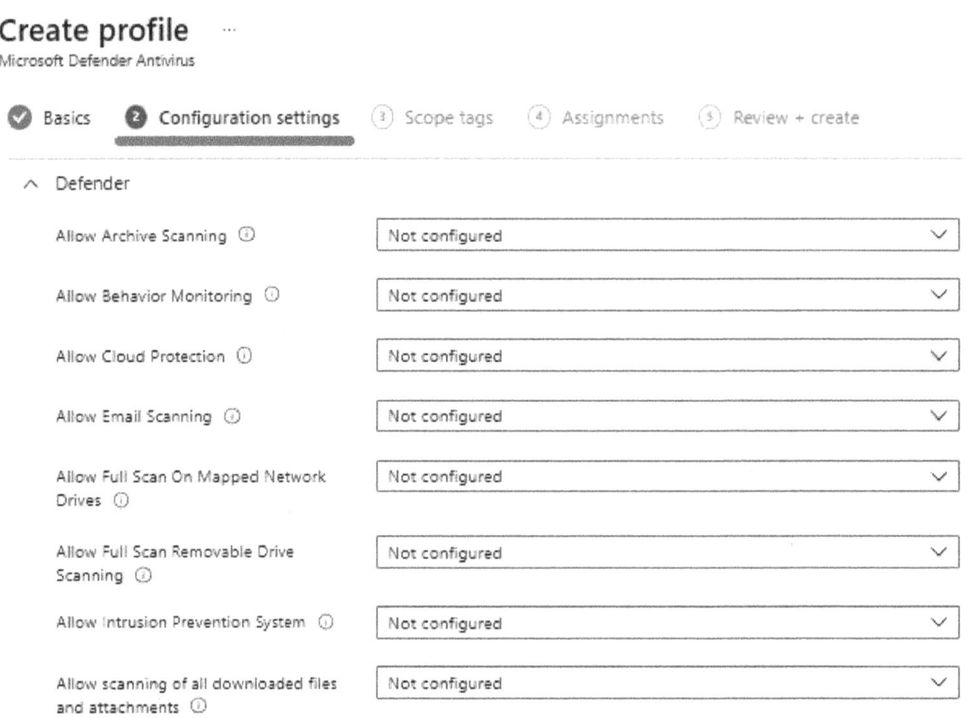

Figure 4.55 – Configuration settings for antivirus

4. Define the settings under **Scope tags** and **Assignment** and click **Create**. Depending on your organization's needs, you can create many antivirus profiles for different groups of users.

   If you select macOS as a platform, only one option for a profile is available for configuration:

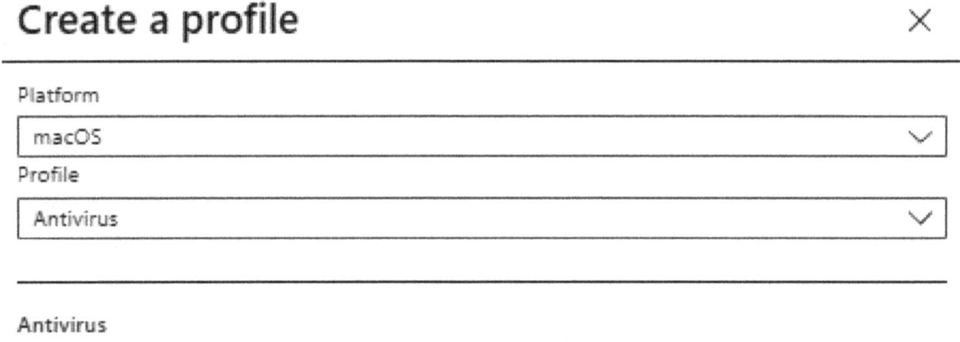

Figure 4.56 – Create a profile

5. Same as for the Windows profile, define the name and description for the macOS antivirus policy and configure the settings per your needs:

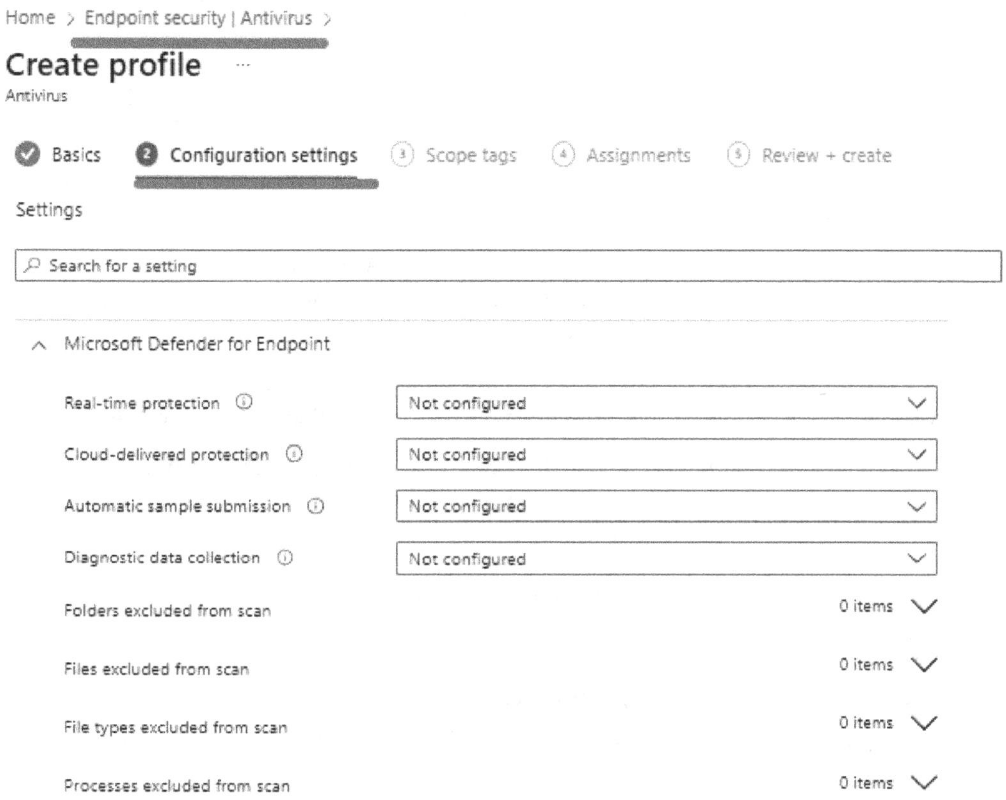

Home > Endpoint security | Antivirus >

Create profile ...

Antivirus

Basics 2 Configuration settings 3 Scope tags 4 Assignments 5 Review + create

Settings

Search for a setting

Microsoft Defender for Endpoint

Real-time protection: Not configured

Cloud-delivered protection: Not configured

Automatic sample submission: Not configured

Diagnostic data collection: Not configured

Folders excluded from scan: 0 items

Files excluded from scan: 0 items

File types excluded from scan: 0 items

Processes excluded from scan: 0 items

Figure 4.57 – Define a name and description for the macOS antivirus policy

Once you find the settings window, look for options that allow you to configure the following:

- **Scheduled scans**: Configure the software to perform scheduled scans of your system. You can specify the frequency and time of the scans.
- **Real-time protection**: Enable real-time scanning to monitor your system for any threats in real time.
- **Diagnostic data collection**: Configure the software to send any detected threats automatically to Microsoft.
- **Exclusions**: Exclude any files or folders that you know are safe from being scanned by the software.

Configuring disk encryption

Microsoft Endpoint disk encryption is a feature in Microsoft Intune that allows organizations to encrypt the hard drives of their managed devices to protect sensitive data from unauthorized access. Disk encryption is important for several reasons:

- **Data protection**: Disk encryption ensures that sensitive data stored on a device's hard drive is protected against unauthorized access. This is important because if an unauthorized person gains access to the device, they will not be able to read or access the data without the encryption key or password.
- **Compliance**: Many regulations and standards, such as HIPAA and GDPR, require the protection of sensitive data. Disk encryption can help organizations comply with these regulations by ensuring that sensitive data is protected in case of device theft or loss.
- **Theft prevention**: If a device is lost or stolen, the encrypted data on the hard drive will be inaccessible to unauthorized users, preventing the data from falling into the wrong hands.
- **Peace of mind**: Disk encryption can provide peace of mind to organizations and individuals that their sensitive data is protected. This can help reduce anxiety and stress related to data breaches and unauthorized access to sensitive information.

Here are the steps to configure Microsoft Endpoint disk encryption:

1. Sign in to the Microsoft Intune admin center using your admin credentials.
2. Go to **Endpoint security** | **Disk encryption** and click on + **Create Policy**.
3. Select **Windows 10 and later** or **macOS** as the platform and **Endpoint protection** as the profile type:

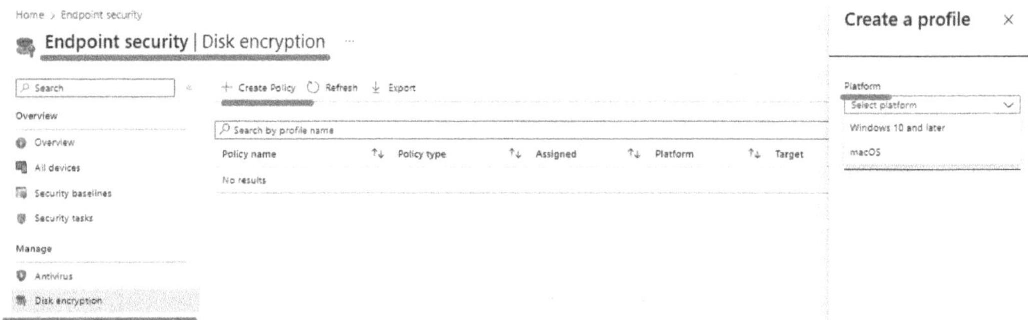

Figure 4.58 – Endpoint security disk encryption

4. Choose **BitLocker (Windows 10)** as the encryption type and configure the settings as per your requirements.

5. In the **Configuration settings** section, you can choose whether to use base, fixed, OS drive, or removable drive settings.

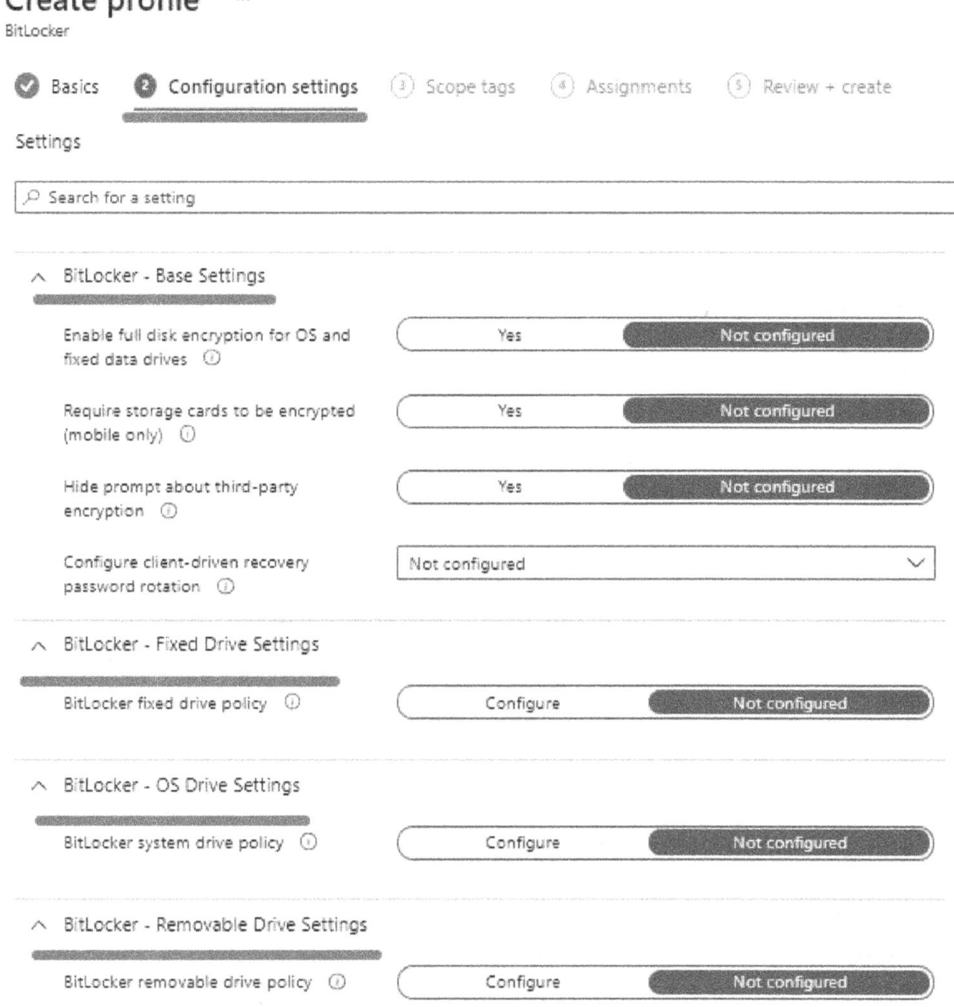

Figure 4.59 – Create profile for disk encryption

6. Assign the policy to the target devices or groups to apply the encryption settings.
7. Review and save the policy.

Once the policy is applied, the devices will automatically encrypt their hard drives using the specified settings. You can monitor the encryption status of devices in the Microsoft Endpoint Manager admin center.

Configuring a firewall policy

Microsoft Endpoint Security Firewall is a feature in Microsoft Intune that allows organizations to create firewall policies to control inbound and outbound traffic on their managed devices. Besides configuring a firewall policy, you have the option to check MDM device running Windows 10 or later with the **Firewall** option off. From that report, you can create and assign different firewall policies, based on your needs.

Here are the steps to configure a Microsoft Endpoint Firewall policy:

1. Sign in to the Microsoft Endpoint Manager admin center using your admin credentials.
2. Go to **Endpoint Security | Firewall** and click on + **Create Profile**.
3. Select **Windows 10, Windows 11 and Windows Server** as the platform and choose **Microsoft Defender Firewall** as a platform. Then, press **Create**:

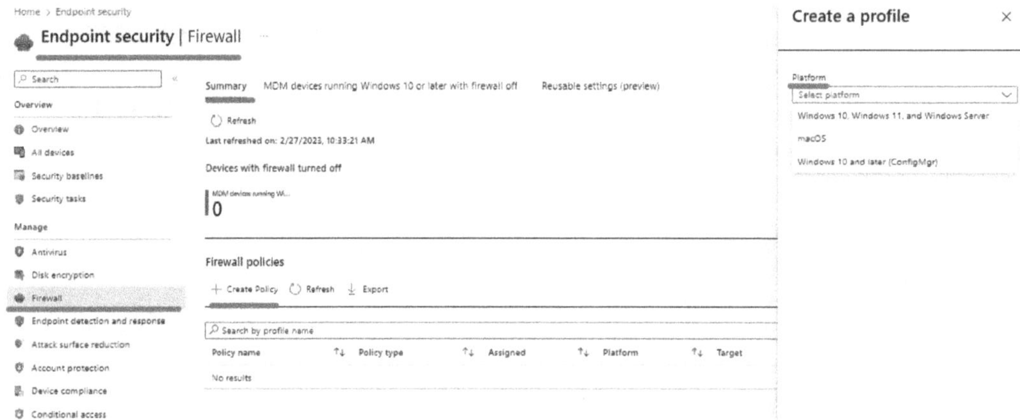

Figure 4.60 – Endpoint security Firewall configuration

4. After giving a name and description, click **Next** and define the configuration settings (the following screenshot contains fewer options than reality):

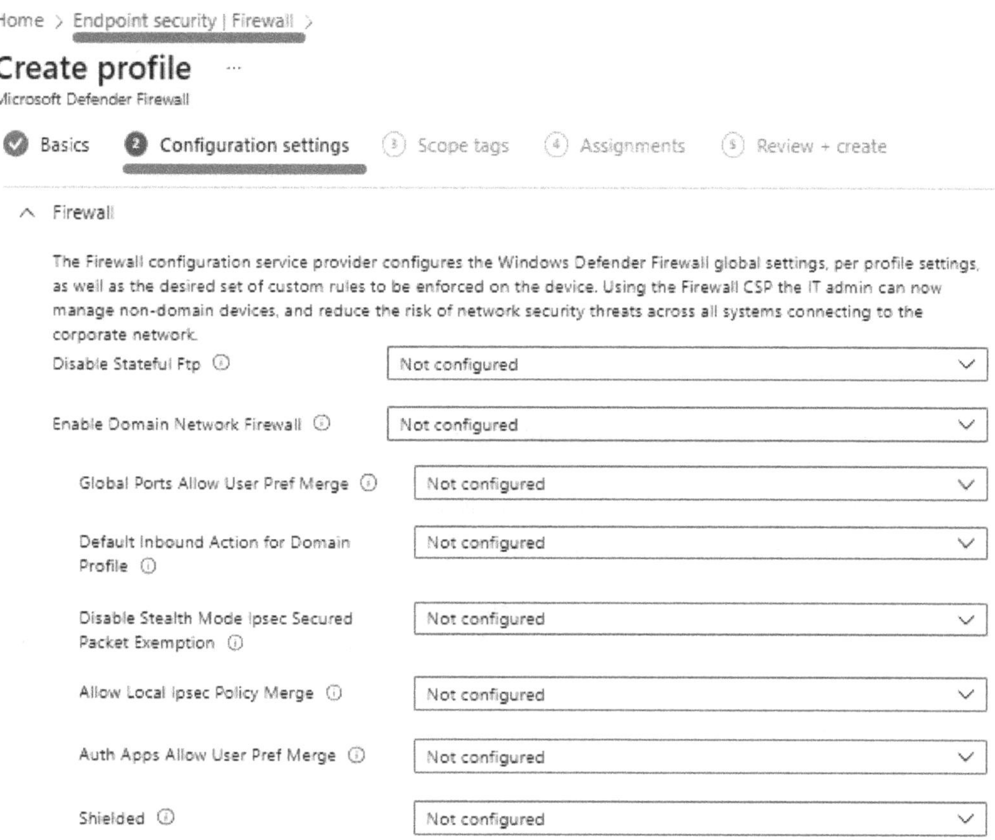

Figure 4.61 – Configuration settings

5. Assign the policy to the target devices or groups to apply the firewall settings.
6. Review and save the policy.

Once the policy is applied, the devices will automatically enforce the firewall settings specified in the policy. You can monitor the firewall status of devices in the Microsoft Intune admin center.

Setting up endpoint detection and response

Microsoft EDR is a feature in Microsoft Defender for Endpoint that helps organizations detect and respond to security threats on their managed devices. In Microsoft Defender for Endpoint, this solution is available for the Windows platform only. Here are the steps to create an EDR policy:

1. Sign in to the Microsoft Defender for Endpoint portal using your admin credentials.
2. Go to **Endpoint security** | **Endpoint detection and response** and click on + **Create Policy**. Configure the settings as per your requirements:

Figure 4.62 – Endpoint detection and response

3. After defining the name and description, click **Next**.
4. Under **Configuration settings**, enable all three options:

   A. **Microsoft Defender for Endpoint client configuration package type** (this Microsoft detection and response capabilities provide advanced attack detections that are **near real time** (NRT) and actionable)

   B. **Sample Sharing**

   C. **Telemetry Reporting Frequency**

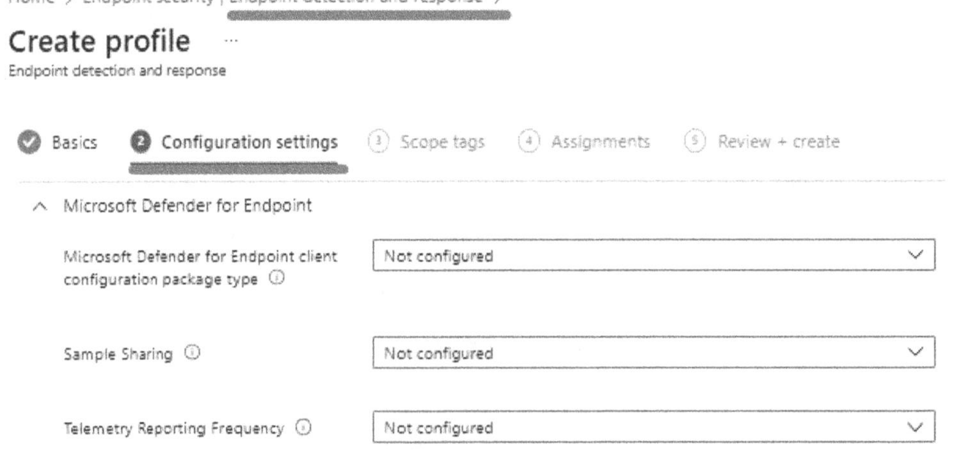

Figure 4.63 – Create profile

5. Add scope tags, if you need to, and assignments on users or groups.
6. Review and press **Create**.

Once the policy is applied, the devices will automatically enforce the EDR settings specified in the policy. You can monitor the security status of devices in the Microsoft Intune admin portal and receive alerts and notifications about security threats.

Configuring attack surface reduction

Microsoft Endpoint ASR policies are a set of security measures designed to reduce the attack surface of Windows-based endpoints. These policies are included in Microsoft Intune, a comprehensive security solution that provides endpoint protection, detection, and response capabilities. ASR policies use a combination of rules and policies to limit the exposure of endpoints to various threats, such as malware and exploits. At the time of writing, ASR can be implemented only for Windows 10 and later platforms. These policies work by restricting the execution of certain processes and behaviors that are commonly exploited by attackers, and by blocking the use of potentially dangerous applications. ASR policies are highly customizable, and administrators can configure them to meet the specific needs of their organization. ASR policies include the following:

- ASR rules
- Exploit protection
- Device control
- App and browser isolation
- Web protection (Microsoft Edge Legacy)
- Application control

By implementing ASR policies, organizations can significantly reduce the risk of endpoint compromise and protect their sensitive data and assets from cyberattacks.

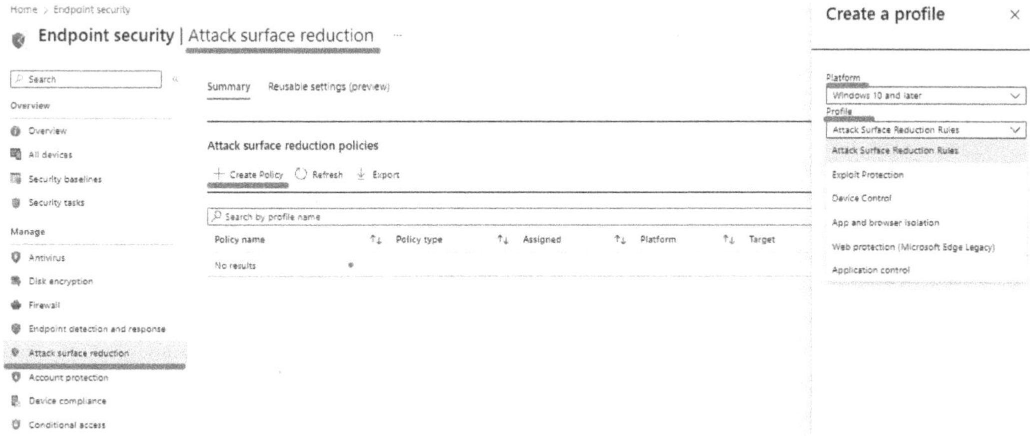

Figure 4.64 – Configure Attack surface reduction

To create an ASR policy, simply choose a platform and profile. After adding a name and description, press **Next**, and for the chosen profile, define configuration settings. You can select different ASR policies for different users and groups.

Configuring account protection

Microsoft Endpoint account protection is a set of security measures designed to protect user accounts and identities from cyber threats. It is a part of the Microsoft Defender for Endpoint suite (Microsoft Defender for Endpoint and Intune) of security solutions, which provides comprehensive protection for endpoints, including PCs, servers, and mobile devices. Endpoint account protection uses a variety of techniques, including the following:

- **Multi-factor authentication** (**MFA**): This requires users to provide an additional form of authentication, such as a code or biometric factor, in addition to their password, to access their accounts
- **Conditional access**: This allows administrators to control access to corporate resources based on various criteria, such as user location, device type, and risk level
- **Passwordless authentication**: This allows users to sign in without passwords by using biometric authentication, such as facial recognition or fingerprint scans
- **Identity protection**: This uses machine learning algorithms to detect and respond to suspicious sign-in attempts and other anomalous activities associated with user accounts
- **Privileged access management**: This limits access to sensitive resources by granting permissions only when needed and for a limited time

Endpoint account protection is configured in the following way:

1. Click on **Endpoint Security**, and under **Manage**, select **Account Protection.**
2. Click on + **Create Policy** and select **Platform** and **Profile** values:

   A. **Platform**:

      - **Windows 10 or later versions**

   B. **Profile**:

      - **Local User Group Membership**
      - **Account Protection**

3. Define **Name** and **Description** and press **Next**.
4. Define a configuration for the chosen profile (account protection configuration settings are shown in the following screenshot).

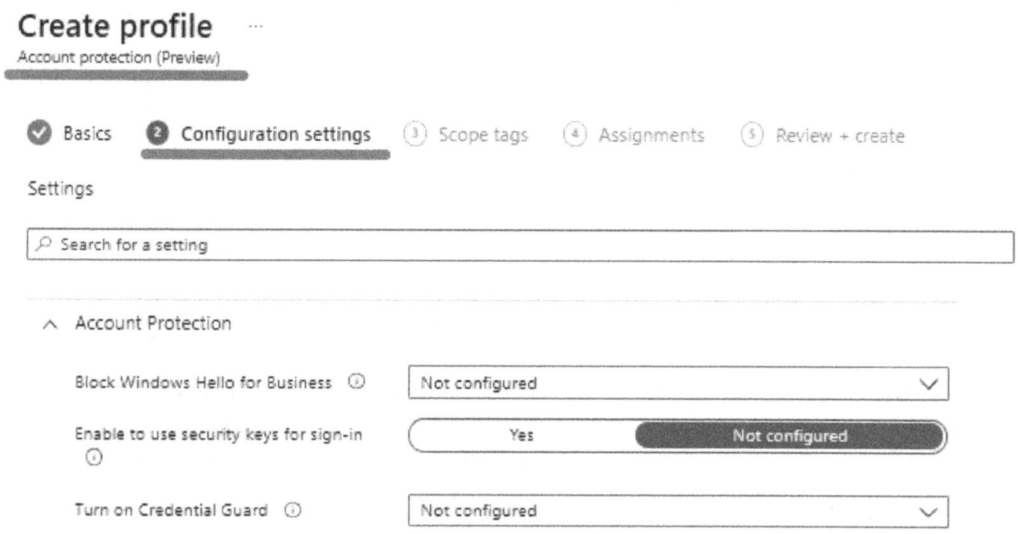

Create profile
Account protection (Preview)

Basics · Configuration settings · Scope tags · Assignments · Review + create

Settings

Search for a setting

Account Protection

Block Windows Hello for Business: Not configured

Enable to use security keys for sign-in: Yes / Not configured

Turn on Credential Guard: Not configured

Figure 4.65 – Account protection

5. Add scope tags, if you need to, and assignments on users or groups.
6. Review and press **Create**.

Configuring device compliance

Configuring Microsoft Endpoint device compliance involves setting up policies and rules that determine the security requirements that devices must meet to be considered compliant. This is an important aspect of endpoint security as it ensures that devices accessing corporate resources meet certain security standards and are less vulnerable to attacks.

Microsoft Endpoint device compliance is a feature within Microsoft Intune that enables organizations to enforce policies and rules to ensure that devices accessing corporate resources meet certain security standards. It allows administrators to define and manage compliance policies, monitor the compliance status, and remediate any devices that are out of compliance. Endpoint device compliance ensures that devices are secure and protected against threats by ensuring that they meet present security standards. As an administrator, you can configure different policies, notifications, and compliance policy settings. You can create different policies for the following platforms, as you can see in the following screenshot:

Figure 4.66 – Compliance policies

When you configure device compliance, you can define for each platform the minimum and maximum operating system that can be used in your organization. Of course, you can apply different device compliance rules for different users and groups. For Linux devices, you can upload scripts:

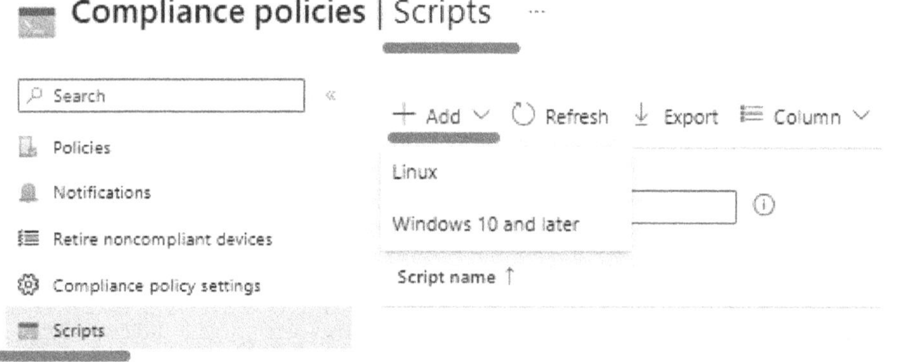

Figure 4.67 – Scripts for compliance policies

Endpoint Security device compliance provides a comprehensive approach to device security that helps organizations to have detailed insights into the compliance of the devices used in the organization. By implementing Endpoint device compliance, organizations can ensure that all devices accessing their resources meet certain security standards, which helps to reduce the attack surface.

Configuring Conditional Access policies

Microsoft Endpoint **Conditional Access** (**CA**) policies are a set of security controls that can be applied to devices and apps accessing corporate resources. These policies allow administrators to define the conditions under which a user can access a particular resource, such as a file or an application, based on factors such as the user's identity, the device being used, and the location from which the user is accessing the resource.

Endpoint CA policies can be used to enforce security requirements such as MFA, device compliance checks, and network location restrictions. For example, an organization can create a policy that requires users to use a company-managed device, have up-to-date antivirus software, and be located within a specific geographic area before they can access certain applications or data.

An easier way to configure Endpoint Security CA is to click on + **New Policy From Template** and check all templates available for implementation. In many cases, you will find predefined policies that you can use in your organization.

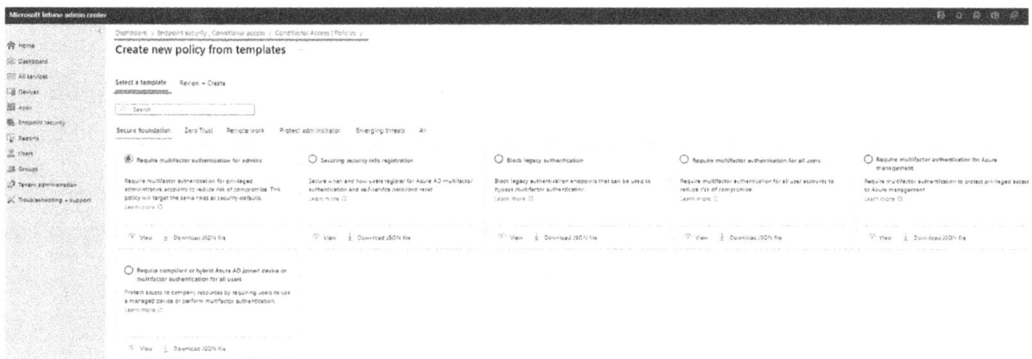

Figure 4.68 – CA policy

Most of this can be configured from the Microsoft Entra ID portal, but if you are planning to have CA for different devices, you can configure from the Endpoint Security portal.

Depending on your needs, you can configure terms of use and upload text with different CA policies.

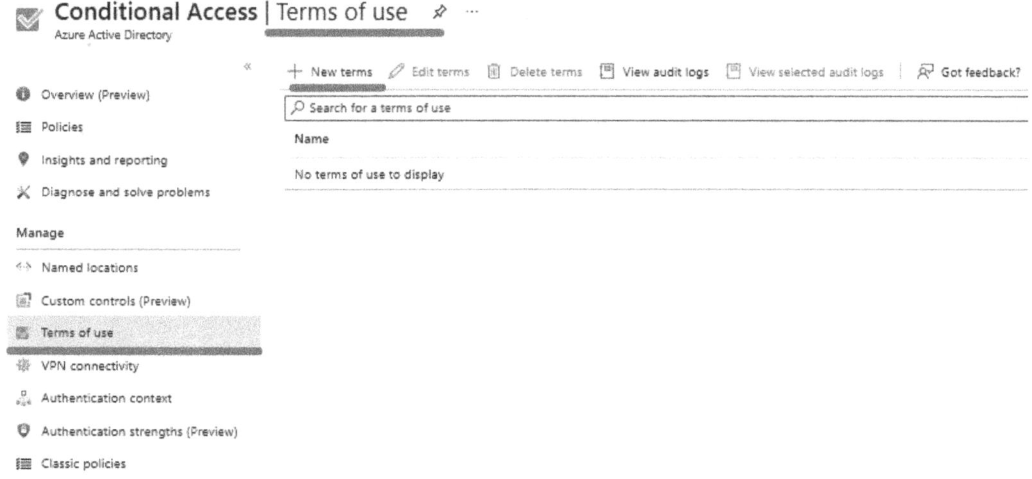

Figure 4.69 – CA terms of use

Click on **+ New terms** and define what you want to have inside your own terms of use. Keep in mind that you need to select the CA policy on which you want to enforce new terms of use.

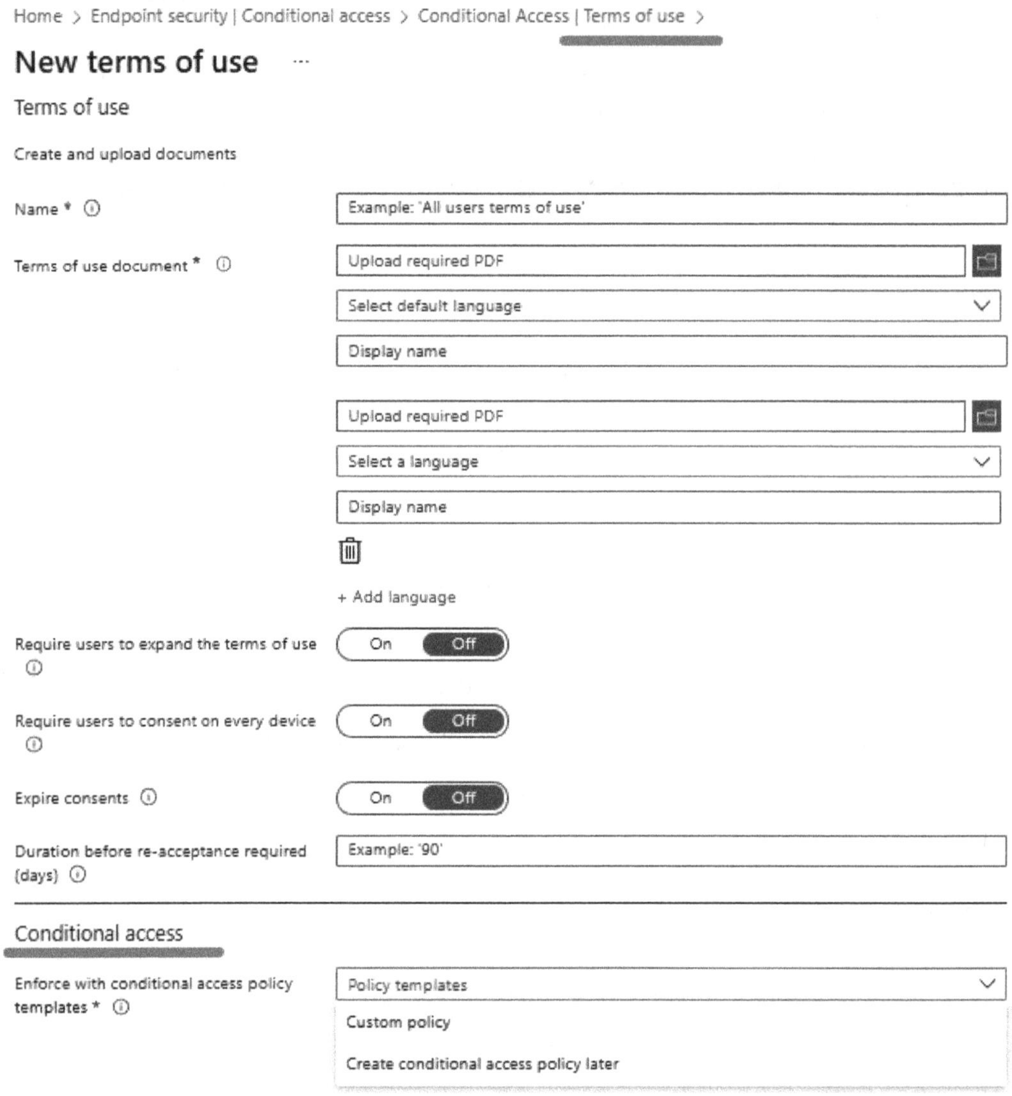

Home > Endpoint security | Conditional access > Conditional Access | Terms of use >

New terms of use ...

Terms of use

Create and upload documents

Name * Example: 'All users terms of use'

Terms of use document * Upload required PDF

Select default language

Display name

Upload required PDF

Select a language

Display name

+ Add language

Require users to expand the terms of use On Off

Require users to consent on every device On Off

Expire consents On Off

Duration before re-acceptance required (days) Example: '90'

Conditional access

Enforce with conditional access policy templates * Policy templates

Custom policy

Create conditional access policy later

Figure 4.70 – Define terms of use

By using Endpoint CA policies, organizations can provide a higher level of security for their data and resources while still allowing employees to access the tools they need to do their jobs. Microsoft Endpoint CA policies are part of the Microsoft Endpoint Manager suite of tools, which allows administrators to manage and secure devices, apps, and data across multiple platforms and devices.

In conclusion, Microsoft Endpoint Security is a comprehensive and integrated solution that helps organizations protect their devices and data from a wide range of cyber threats and can be configured in the Intune portal. With its advanced capabilities and features, it provides a multi-layered defense mechanism that can quickly detect and respond to security incidents.

One of the key features of Microsoft Endpoint Security is its antivirus capabilities. The solution uses advanced machine learning algorithms and real-time threat or NRT intelligence to detect and remove viruses, malware, and other types of malicious software. This not only helps to protect devices from infection but also prevents malware from spreading to other devices on the network. In addition to antivirus, Microsoft Endpoint Security also includes a powerful firewall that can be configured to block incoming and outgoing traffic based on a set of rules. This helps to prevent unauthorized access to the network and can also be used to block access to specific websites or applications. Another important key feature of Microsoft Defender for Endpoint is its EDR capabilities. The solution uses advanced behavioral analytics to detect suspicious activity on devices and can quickly respond to security incidents. This helps organizations identify and contain threats before they can cause significant damage.

Moreover, Microsoft Endpoint Security integrates with other Microsoft security solutions, such as Microsoft Defender for Endpoint and Microsoft Defender for Cloud Apps. This provides a unified security platform that helps organizations to manage and respond to security incidents effectively. The solution also integrates with Microsoft Intune, which allows organizations to manage devices and apply security policies from a single console.

Overall, Microsoft Endpoint Security is a powerful solution that can be integrated with your System Center Configuration Manager and can help organizations to secure their devices and data in a fast-changing threat landscape. With its advanced capabilities and integration with other Microsoft security solutions, it is a valuable investment for any organization that takes security seriously. By using Microsoft Endpoint Security, organizations can have peace of mind knowing that their devices and data are protected by a comprehensive and integrated security solution.

Summary

Microsoft Defender for Endpoint with Microsoft Intune represents a crucial cybersecurity solution in today's dynamic threat landscape. It is designed to address the diverse and evolving security challenges faced by organizations. Formerly known as Windows Defender ATP, this platform specifically focuses on defending endpoint devices, which are on the front line in the battle against cyber threats.

In a world where cyberattacks are constantly evolving in sophistication, Microsoft Defender for Endpoint offers an extensive toolkit to combat these challenges effectively. With its advanced threat protection capabilities, it guards against a wide spectrum of threats, including malware, ransomware, and zero-day attacks.

One of its standout features is the EDR functionality, which empowers organizations to not only identify but also respond swiftly to security incidents. This capability enhances an organization's ability to investigate and remediate threats promptly, reducing the potential impact of breaches.

Furthermore, the platform helps organizations reduce their attack surface through techniques such as ASR and secure configuration management. These features minimize vulnerabilities and create a more resilient security posture. Microsoft's expansive threat intelligence network further strengthens the platform by providing up-to-date threat information, ensuring that organizations are equipped to counter the latest threats effectively. The inclusion of security analytics and threat and vulnerability management tools helps organizations gain insights into their security postures, enabling them to identify and remediate vulnerabilities proactively.

The platform seamlessly integrates with Microsoft 365 services, creating a unified security ecosystem. This integration enhances visibility and coordination across various security components.

Lastly, the platform offers centralized management capabilities, simplifying security operations by allowing organizations to manage policies, configurations, and threat responses from a single console.

In summary, Microsoft Defender for Endpoint is a robust cybersecurity solution that plays an important role in an organization's defense against ever-evolving and increasingly sophisticated digital threats. It serves as a cornerstone of proactive threat detection, incident response, and risk mitigation in today's fast-paced digital landscape.

In the upcoming chapter, we will take a journey into the world of data governance and management with a focus on Microsoft Purview. This innovative platform is designed to revolutionize the way organizations handle their data assets, providing a comprehensive solution for discovering, classifying, and governing data. As we explore the features and capabilities of Microsoft Purview, you'll discover how it equips businesses with the tools they need to harness the full power of their data, promoting informed decision-making, enhancing data security, and optimizing their data ecosystem for success in the digital age.

5

Getting Started with Microsoft Purview

In today's data-driven landscape, where information flows very fast and businesses rely on data insights to make informed decisions, managing and harnessing the power of data has become paramount. Microsoft Purview, a dynamic and innovative solution in the realm of data governance and management, is poised to revolutionize how organizations handle their data assets.

This chapter serves as your gateway into the world of Microsoft Purview, offering a comprehensive introduction to its fundamental concepts, features, and functionalities. Whether you're an IT professional, a data analyst, a business leader, or someone with a keen interest in the possibilities of data, this chapter will equip you with the foundational knowledge needed to embark on a journey of discovery within the realm of Microsoft Purview.

So, let's begin our exploration of Microsoft Purview, unlocking the doors to a world where data becomes not just a valuable asset but also a strategic advantage. We will cover the following topics in this chapter:

- A Microsoft Purview introduction
- Configuring Microsoft Purview
- Classifiers in Microsoft 365 Purview
- Content search
- Data loss prevention

About Microsoft Purview

Microsoft Purview is a data management platform that enables organizations to discover, manage, and govern their data assets across on-premises, multi-cloud, and SaaS environments. It is a cloud-based solution that integrates with various data sources and provides a unified view of data across an organization. In this article, we will explore the key features of Microsoft Purview, how it works, and its benefits.

Here are the key features of Microsoft Purview:

- **Data discovery**: Microsoft Purview enables organizations to discover and inventory their data assets across multiple data sources, including structured, unstructured, and semi-structured data. The platform provides a centralized metadata repository that provides a unified view of data assets across an organization. With this, organizations can quickly find and understand the data they have and assess its quality, lineage, and sensitivity.
- **Data cataloging**: Once the data is discovered, Microsoft Purview provides an automated cataloging process that organizes the data assets into a hierarchical order. This helps organizations to better understand their data assets and quickly locate relevant data.
- **Data lineage**: Microsoft Purview tracks data lineage, showing how data moves through an organization, including where it originated, how it has been transformed, and where it is currently stored. This feature is essential for organizations that need to understand how data is being used and to ensure compliance with regulations such as GDPR, CCPA, and HIPAA.
- **Data governance**: Microsoft Purview provides tools for data governance, including data classification, data protection, and data access control. This feature enables organizations to ensure that their data is secure and meets regulatory requirements.
- **Integration with Microsoft Power Platform**: Microsoft Purview integrates with Microsoft Power Platform, enabling users to leverage the platform's low-code capabilities to create custom solutions and automate workflows.

Now, let's dive into the workings of Microsoft Purview and explore how this innovative platform work with data discovery and management.

How it works...

Microsoft Purview uses connectors to ingest metadata from various data sources, including on-premises, multi-cloud, and SaaS environments. The metadata is then organized into a hierarchical taxonomy using an automated cataloguing process. The platform uses machine learning to enrich metadata with additional information, such as data lineage and sensitivity. This feature enables users to quickly find and understand data assets, assess data quality, and ensure compliance with regulations.

Microsoft Purview provides a unified view of an organization's data assets, enabling users to search and discover relevant data quickly. Users can also collaborate and share data assets with other users, improving data discovery and use across the organization.

Benefits

Now, let's shift our focus to the real-world perks that Microsoft Purview offers businesses, bringing a host of compelling benefits to the forefront of how we handle and oversee our valuable data.

- **Improved data discovery and understanding**: Microsoft Purview provides a unified view of an organization's data assets, enabling users to quickly find and understand relevant data.
- **Improved data governance and compliance**: Microsoft Purview provides tools for data classification, data protection, and data access control, enabling organizations to ensure that their data is secure and meets regulatory requirements.
- **Improved collaboration and sharing**: Microsoft Purview enables users to collaborate and share data assets with other users, improving data discovery and use across an organization.
- **Improved data quality**: Microsoft Purview uses machine learning to enrich metadata with additional information, improving data quality and enabling users to assess data quality more effectively.
- **Lower cost and complexity**: Microsoft Purview is a cloud-based solution that provides a centralized metadata repository, reducing the cost and complexity of managing data across multiple data sources.

In conclusion, Microsoft Purview is a powerful data management platform that enables organizations to discover, manage, and govern their data assets across on-premises, multi-cloud, and SaaS environments. The platform provides a unified view of an organization's data assets, improving data discovery and understanding, data governance and compliance, collaboration and sharing, and data quality.

Technical and license requirements

Microsoft Purview compliance is a suite of solutions that helps organizations manage and meet their regulatory and compliance requirements. It includes various solutions, such as Microsoft 365 Compliance Center, Microsoft Information Protection, eDiscovery, LegalHold and Microsoft Compliance Manager. Before implementing Microsoft Compliance, it is essential to ensure that your organization meets the technical and license requirements.

The technical requirements for this chapter are as follows:

- **Supported browsers**: Microsoft Compliance requires the use of a modern web browser, such as Microsoft Edge, Google Chrome, or Mozilla Firefox
- **Azure Active Directory**: **Azure Active Directory** (**AAD**) is required to provide authentication and authorization for users to access the Compliance solutions
- **Network connectivity**: Microsoft Compliance requires network connectivity to access the Compliance solutions and for data transfer between the solutions and the user's devices
- **Data sources**: Microsoft Compliance solutions support various data sources, including Microsoft 365, Microsoft Azure, and third-party applications and services

Microsoft Compliance requires a license to use. The license is available in various options, depending on the specific solution and the features and capabilities required by the organization. The following are some of the licensing options for Microsoft Compliance:

- **Microsoft 365 E5 Compliance**: This license includes all the compliance solutions and features, such as Microsoft 365 Compliance Center, Microsoft Information Protection, and Microsoft Compliance Manager
- **Microsoft Information Protection and Governance**: This license includes Microsoft Information Protection and some features of Microsoft 365 Compliance Center
- **Microsoft Compliance Manager**: This license includes Microsoft Compliance Manager and some features of Microsoft 365 Compliance Center
- **Microsoft Cloud App Security**: This license includes Microsoft Defender Cloud App Security, which provides advanced threat protection and compliance capabilities for cloud applications and services

Microsoft Purview licenses are available as a subscription-based model, with different pricing options based on the number of users and the selected features.

To manage Microsoft Purview effectively, you will need to assign specific AAD roles to users or groups. These roles provide the necessary permissions to perform various tasks and operations within Microsoft Purview. The required AAD roles for Microsoft Purview include the following:

- Compliance administrator
- Compliance data administrators
- Global reader
- Information protection
- Information protection admins
- Information protection analyst
- Information protection investigators
- Information protection readers
- Organization management
- Records management
- Security administrator
- Security operator
- Security reader

It is worth noting that these roles are specific to Microsoft Purview and are separate from the AAD roles that are generally used to manage Azure resources. To assign these roles to users or groups, you can navigate to the Azure AD portal or use Azure PowerShell or Azure CLI commands.

Bear in mind that the specific role names and permissions may be subject to change, and it's always advisable to refer to the official Microsoft documentation or consult Microsoft support for the most up-to-date information on Azure AD roles for Microsoft Purview.

In conclusion, before implementing Microsoft Compliance, it is essential to ensure that your organization meets the technical requirements, including the supported browsers, AAD, network connectivity, and data sources. Additionally, it is essential to ensure that you have the required license for Microsoft Compliance, depending on the specific solution and the features and capabilities required by your organization.

> **Important note**
>
> Microsoft Compliance and Azure Purview are two different solutions provided by Microsoft. While both solutions are designed to help organizations manage their data and meet their compliance requirements, they have different purposes and functionalities. In summary, while Microsoft Compliance and Azure Purview share some common objectives in helping organizations manage their data and meet their compliance requirements, they have different functionalities and purposes. Microsoft Compliance focuses on providing solutions for regulatory and compliance requirements, while Azure Purview focuses on providing a data governance solution that helps organizations discover, understand, and manage their data assets.

Configuring Microsoft Purview

Compliance Manager is a tool provided by Microsoft that helps organizations assess and manage their regulatory compliance requirements within the Microsoft cloud ecosystem. It provides a centralized dashboard to track and manage compliance activities, assess risks, and monitor progress toward meeting regulatory standards.

Compliance Manager is directly integrated into the Microsoft Purview portal; both tools serve different purposes in managing data and compliance. Microsoft Purview focuses on data discovery, classification, and governance, while Compliance Manager is more geared toward compliance management across various Microsoft services.

Compliance Score

Microsoft Purview's Compliance Score is a powerful tool that enables organizations to assess their compliance with various regulatory requirements and industry standards. It provides a comprehensive view of an organization's compliance posture, highlighting areas where improvements can be made and helping to prioritize remediation efforts. This tool is part of the Microsoft Purview platform, which is designed to help organizations manage and govern their data across on-premises, multi-cloud, and SaaS environments. One of the key benefits of Microsoft Purview's Compliance Score is that it provides a centralized view of an organization's compliance posture across different regulatory frameworks and standards. This includes standards such as GDPR, HIPAA, ISO 27001, NIST, and others. The tool aggregates compliance data from various sources, such as Microsoft Cloud App Security and Microsoft 365 compliance portal, to provide a unified view of an organization's compliance posture.

Another key benefit of Microsoft Purview's Compliance Score is that it enables organizations to track their compliance progress over time. The tool provides a Compliance Score that ranges from 0 to 1,000, with higher scores indicating better compliance posture. This score is calculated based on various factors, such as an organization's compliance controls, policies, and procedures, as well as its implementation of security controls and risk management practices.

In addition to providing a Compliance Score, Microsoft Purview's Compliance Score also provides detailed insights into an organization's compliance posture. It highlights areas where the organization is doing well and areas where improvements can be made. This helps organizations prioritize their remediation efforts and focus on the areas that are most critical to their compliance posture.

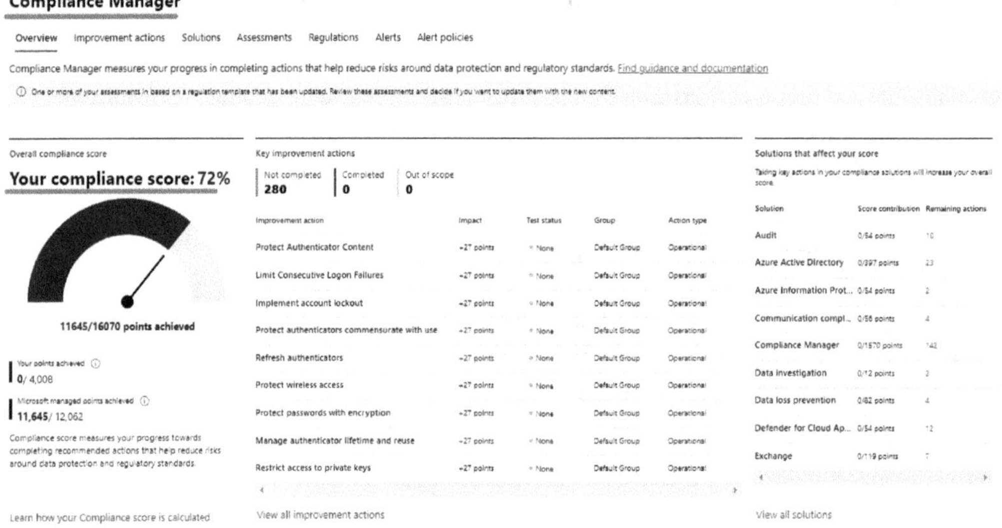

Figure 5.1 – Compliance Manager

Improving your Compliance Score in Microsoft Purview involves implementing a range of best practices and security controls across different areas of an organization's IT environment. Here are some general steps that can help improve the Compliance Score:

1. **Identify the compliance requirements**: The first step is to identify the regulatory requirements and industry standards that are applicable to an organization. This involves conducting a comprehensive risk assessment and reviewing the organization's policies, procedures, and controls.

2. **Develop a compliance program**: Once the compliance requirements have been identified, the organization should develop a compliance program that includes policies, procedures, and controls to meet those requirements. This may involve implementing technical controls such as access controls, encryption, and data loss prevention, as well as administrative controls such as training and awareness programs.
3. **Implement technical controls**: Implementing technical controls is an essential aspect of improving compliance posture. This may involve implementing security controls such as firewalls, intrusion detection/prevention systems, and endpoint protection. It may also involve implementing data governance solutions such as data classification and data lineage tools.
4. **Train employees**: Employees play a crucial role in maintaining compliance posture. Organizations should provide regular training and awareness programs to ensure employees understand their responsibilities and how to comply with regulatory requirements.
5. **Monitor compliance**: Monitoring compliance is critical to maintaining a good compliance posture. This involves implementing a robust monitoring and reporting framework that provides real-time visibility into compliance events. It may also involve conducting regular compliance audits and assessments.
6. **Continuous improvement**: Compliance posture is not a one-time activity but requires continuous improvement. Organizations should regularly review and update their compliance program to reflect changes in regulatory requirements, new threats, and emerging best practices.

By following these steps, organizations can improve their compliance posture and increase their Compliance Score in Microsoft Purview. Microsoft Purview's Compliance Score provides valuable insights and recommendations, helping organizations prioritize their efforts and identify areas where they need to improve.

Microsoft Purview's Compliance Score is designed to be easy to use and deploy. It integrates with Microsoft Azure and other Microsoft services, making it easy to incorporate into existing workflows and processes. The tool also provides actionable recommendations and guidance to help organizations improve their compliance posture.

Overall, Microsoft Purview's Compliance Score is a powerful tool that can help organizations assess their compliance posture and prioritize their remediation efforts. It provides a centralized view of an organization's compliance posture across different regulatory frameworks and standards, enabling organizations to track their compliance progress over time. With its detailed insights and actionable recommendations, Microsoft Purview's Compliance Score can help organizations improve their compliance posture and reduce the risk of non-compliance. There are more than 280 items that can help organizations to improve their compliance.

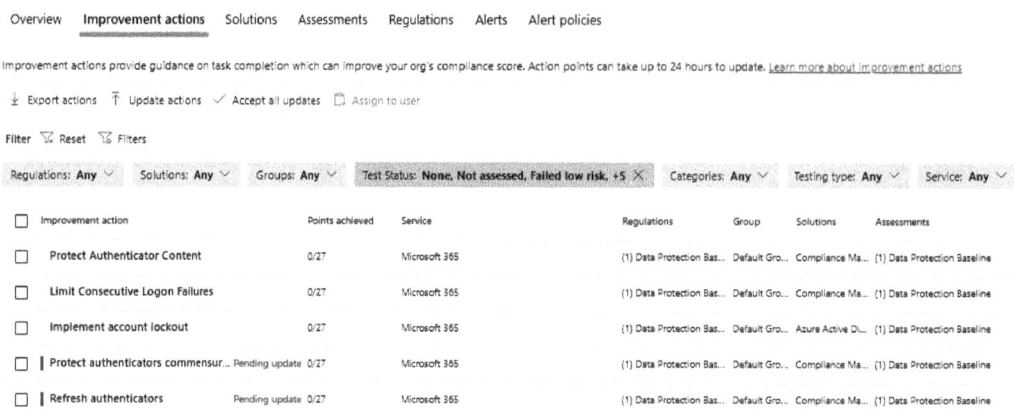

Figure 5.2 – Improvement actions

Each improvement in the Compliance Score requires several actions to be taken before implementation:

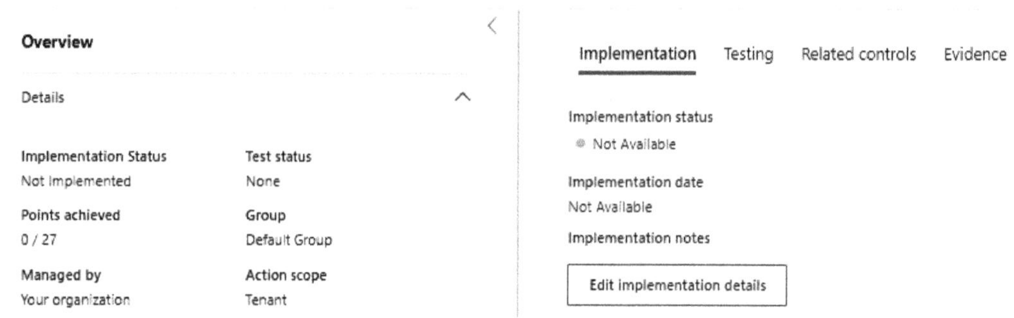

Figure 5.3 – An improvement action example

Let's use an example of implementing an account lockout and outline the necessary steps to take before implementation:

1. **Define the account lockout policy**: Clearly define the account lockout policy, including parameters such as the number of allowed failed login attempts, lockout duration, and reset procedures. This policy should align with industry best practices and regulatory requirements.
2. **Review user account management**: Assess the current user account management practices and ensure that they align with the account lockout policy. Review the user account creation, modification, and deactivation processes to ensure that they include the necessary checks and controls.

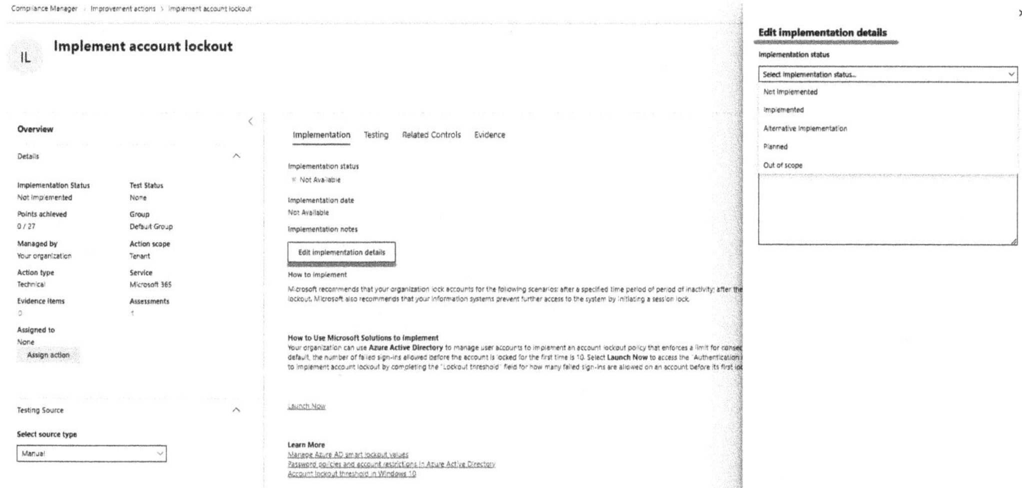

Figure 5.4 – Implement account lockout

3. **Update security awareness training**: Educate employees about the account lockout policy and the importance of safeguarding their credentials. Incorporate account lockout procedures into security awareness training to promote adherence to the policy, and mitigate risks associated with unauthorized access attempts.
4. **Test system compatibility**: Verify the compatibility of the account lockout mechanism with the existing IT infrastructure. Ensure that the account lockout functionality is supported by the relevant systems, such as operating systems, identity providers, and authentication mechanisms.

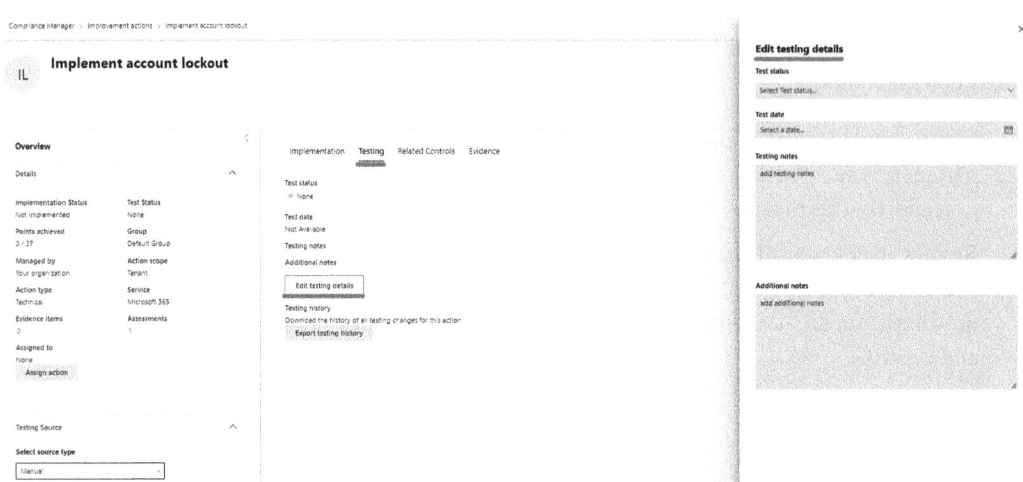

Figure 5.5 – Implement account lockout

5. **Implement monitoring and alerting**: Establish a system for monitoring and alerting on account lockout events. Configure logs and alerts to notify administrators of lockout incidents, enabling them to promptly investigate and respond to potential security breaches or suspicious activities.
6. **Develop incident response procedures**: Define incident response procedures specific to account lockouts. Determine the steps to be taken in the event of a lockout, including identification, investigation, remediation, and communication. This will help minimize downtime and mitigate potential security incidents.
7. **Communicate the change**: This is particularly important, as it is crucial to notify employees and relevant stakeholders about the upcoming implementation of the account lockout policy. Clearly communicate the rationale, benefits, and any changes in user behavior or processes that may result from the implementation.
8. **Test and pilot**: Before full-scale implementation, conduct thorough testing and a pilot phase. Test the account lockout functionality in a controlled environment to identify and address any potential issues or conflicts with existing systems or workflows.
9. **Deploy and monitor**: Once the necessary preparations have been completed, deploy the account lockout policy across the organization. Continuously monitor the effectiveness of the implementation and adjust as needed to ensure compliance, addressing any emerging challenges.

By following these steps and addressing the associated details, organizations can successfully implement the **Account Lockout** feature and make progress toward improving their Compliance Score.

The Compliance Manager dashboard

Within the Compliance Manager dashboard, you can perform the following activities:

- **Compliance Score**: This provides an overall assessment of your organization's compliance posture based on the implementation of controls and adherence to regulatory standards. Compliance Score evaluates controls across Microsoft 365, Azure, and Dynamics 365. As illustrated in the following screenshot, the dashboard provides a comprehensive overview of your Compliance Score:

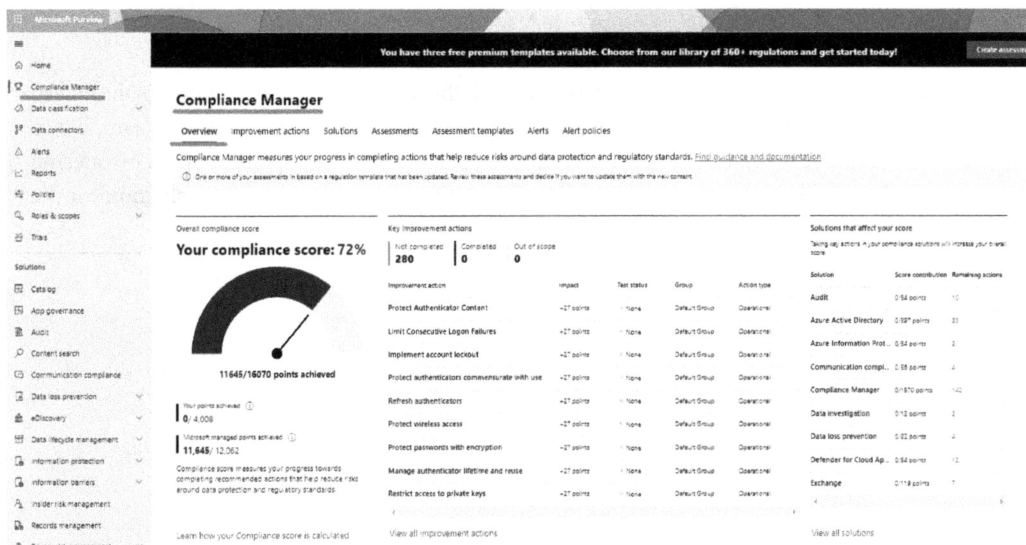

Figure 5.6 – Compliance Manager overview

- **Assessments**: Compliance Manager enables you to create and manage assessments to evaluate your organization's compliance with specific regulations or standards. These assessments include a set of questions and controls that need to be addressed to ensure compliance. In the context of Compliance Manager assessments, as illustrated in the following screenshot, the dashboard provides a comprehensive overview of your assessments:

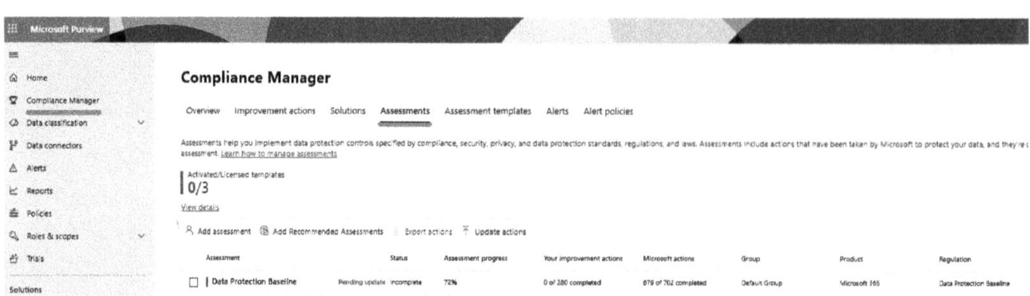

Figure 5.7 – Compliance Manager | Assessments

- **Solutions**: Compliance Manager allows you to track the implementation of controls solutions to improve your Compliance Score. Also, as you can see in the following screenshot, Compliance Manager empowers you to proactively track and enhance your Compliance Score by offering features that enable you to assign control owners, establish due dates, and closely monitor the progress of control implementation, through prepared solutions:

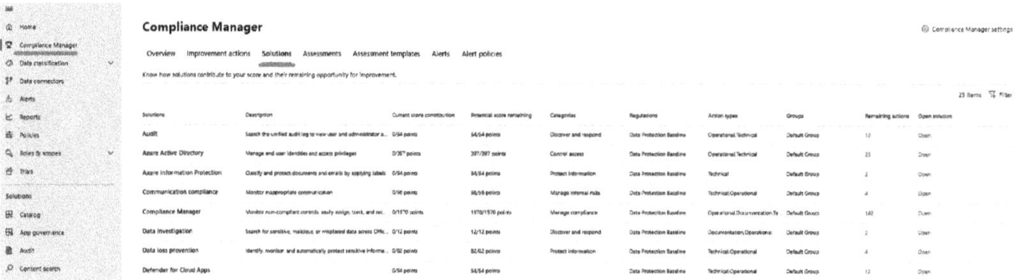

Figure 5.8 – Compliance Manager | Solutions

- **Regulatory requirements**: It provides a library of regulatory standards and frameworks that you can select to evaluate your organization's compliance posture. This includes standards such as GDPR, ISO 27001, and HIPAA.
- **Compliance reports and alerts**: You can generate compliance reports to showcase your organization's adherence to specific regulations or standards. These reports can be shared with auditors or stakeholders to demonstrate compliance efforts. As you can see in the following screenshot, you can configure different alerts about Compliance Manager events:

Figure 5.9 – Compliance Manager | Alert policies

It's important to note that while Compliance Manager provides valuable tools for managing compliance, it doesn't directly integrate with Microsoft Purview. However, you can use both tools in conjunction to enhance your organization's data management and compliance capabilities.

As always, it's recommended to refer to the official Microsoft documentation and the latest updates to understand the most up-to-date features and functionalities of both Compliance Manager and Microsoft Purview.

Adding assessments

To add assessments in Microsoft Compliance, you can use the Microsoft 365 Compliance Center. Assessments help you evaluate and track your organization's compliance with specific regulations, industry standards, or internal policies. Follow these steps to add assessments:

1. **Access the Microsoft 365 Compliance Center**: Go to the Microsoft 365 Compliance Center by visiting the following URL- `https://compliance.microsoft.com/`. Sign in with your Microsoft 365 administrator account.
2. **Navigate to the Assessments section**: In **Compliance Manager**, locate the **Assessments** option. This can usually be found in the left-hand navigation menu.
3. **Create a new assessment**: Click on **Assessments** to enter the assessments management area. Here, you will see a list of existing assessments. To create a new one, click on the **Add assessment** button:

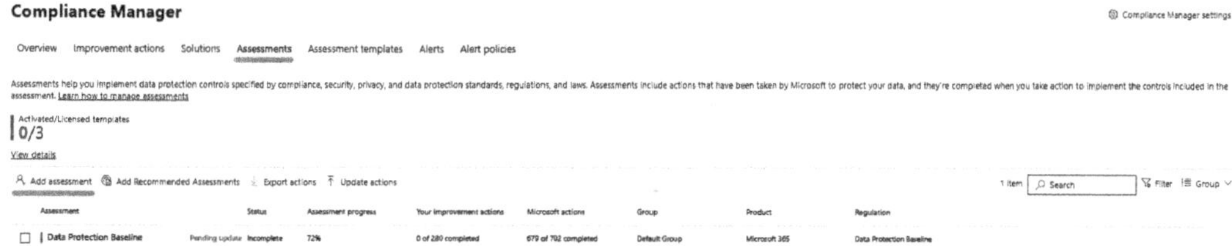

Figure 5.10 – Add assessment in Compliance Manager

4. **Configure the assessment**: In the assessment creation form, you will need to provide the following details:

   A. **Base your assessment on a template**: Choose a template from the list:

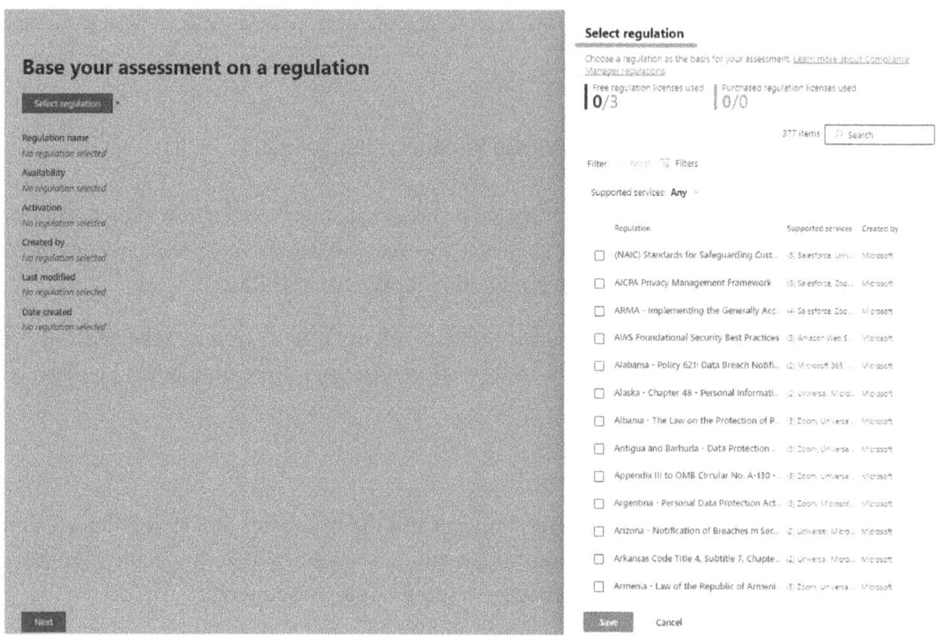

Figure 5.11 – Configure an assessment with a template

   B. **Product, name and group**: Define the product, assessment name, and assessment group:

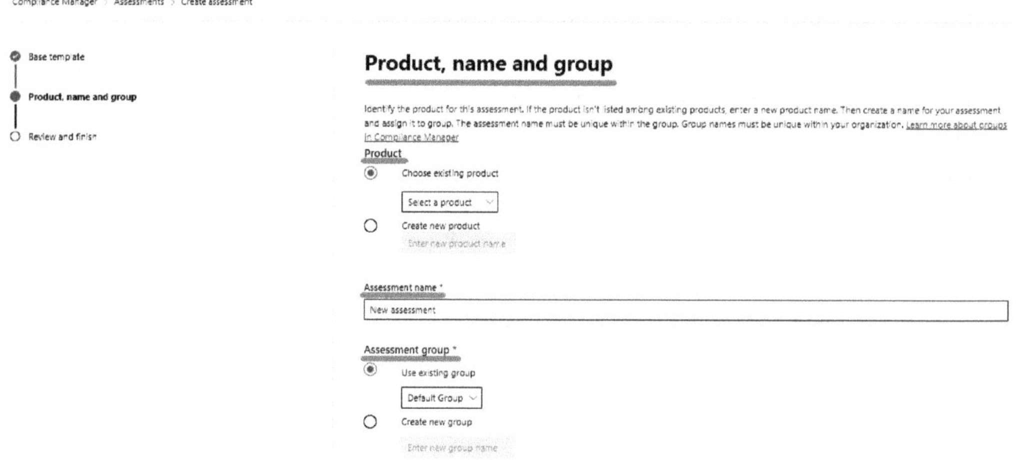

Figure 5.12 – Define the product, name, and group in the assessment

C. **Review and finish**: Carefully review the configured settings to ensure they align with your compliance requirements. Once verified, click on the **Create Assessment** button to create the assessment.

5. **Manage and track assessments**: After creating the assessment, you can manage and track its progress from the **Assessments management** area. You can assign participants, monitor completion status, review assessment responses, and generate reports.

It's important to note that the specific steps and options may vary slightly, depending on the version of Microsoft Compliance and the available features. It is recommended to refer to the Microsoft 365 Compliance Center documentation or reach out to Microsoft support for the most up-to-date instructions and guidance.

Creating alert policies

To create alert policies in Microsoft Compliance, you can utilize the Microsoft 365 Compliance Center. The Compliance Center offers a centralized location to manage compliance-related activities across various Microsoft 365 services. Follow these steps to create alert policies:

1. **Access the Microsoft 365 Purview (formerly Compliance) Admin portal**: Navigate to the Microsoft 365 Compliance Center by visiting the following URL: `https://compliance.microsoft.com/`. Sign in with your Microsoft 365 administrator account.
2. **Navigate to the Alert policies section**: In the Compliance Center, locate the **Alert policies** option. This can usually be found in the left-hand navigation menu.
3. **Create a new alert policy**: Click on **Alert policies** to enter the alert policies management area. Here, you will find a list of existing alert policies. To create a new one, click on the **+ Add** button:

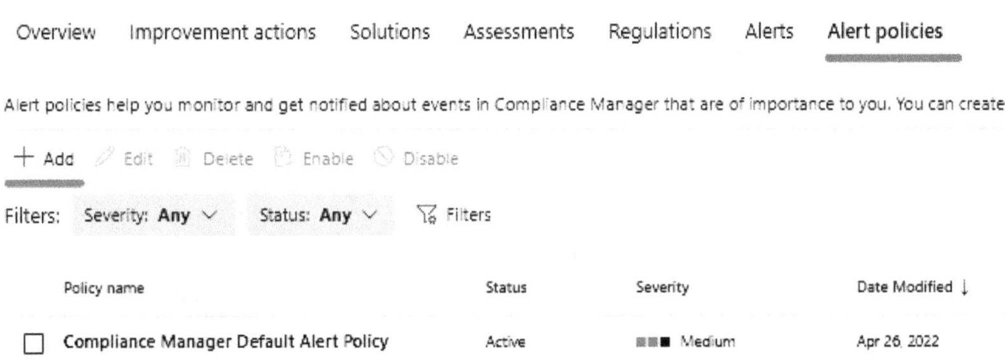

Figure 5.13 – Adding an alert policy in Compliance Manager

4. **Configure the alert policy**: In the policy creation form, you will need to provide the following details:

   A. **Policy Name**: Enter a descriptive name for the alert policy to identify its purpose.

   B. **Description**: Optionally, provide additional information or context for the alert policy.

   C. **Choose conditions for the policy**: Specify the conditions or triggers that will activate the alert. This could include events such as data breaches, suspicious user activities, or policy violations.

Figure 5.14 – Define conditions for the alert policy

   D. **Define outcomes when a match is detected**: Set the severity and frequency for the alerts when triggered.

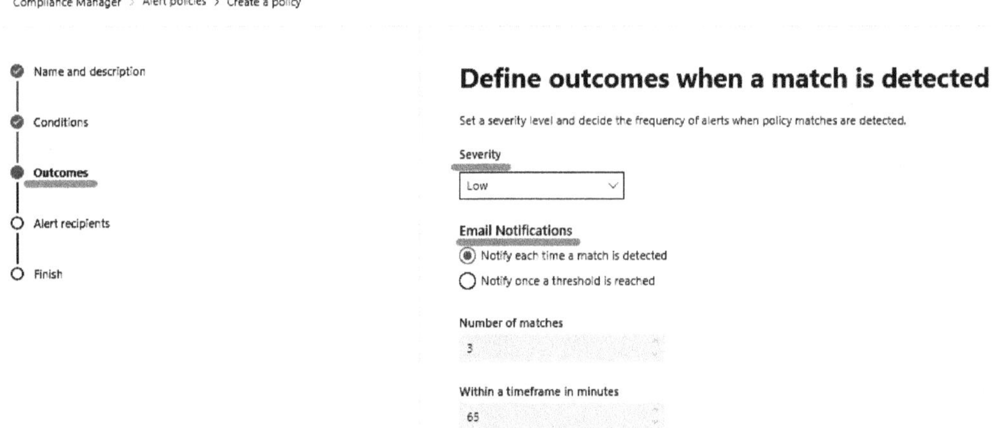

Figure 5.15 – Configure the severity and email notifications for the alert policy

   E. **Review and save**: Carefully review the configured settings to ensure they align with your compliance requirements. Once verified, click on the **Create policy** button to create the alert policy.

5. **Manage and monitor alert policies**: After creating the alert policy, you can further manage and monitor it from the alert policies management area. You can modify existing policies, create additional ones, or review the alerts triggered by the policies.

It's important to note that the specific steps and options may vary slightly, depending on the version of Microsoft Compliance and the available features. It is recommended to refer to the Microsoft 365 Compliance Center documentation or reach out to Microsoft support for the most up-to-date instructions and guidance.

Data classification

Data classification is a critical process in any organization's data governance and compliance strategy. It involves identifying and categorizing data based on its sensitivity, value, and regulatory requirements to ensure proper protection and handling. Microsoft 365 Compliance provides several tools and features to support data classification and labeling, including automatic classification and labeling, manual labeling, and advanced data protection capabilities.

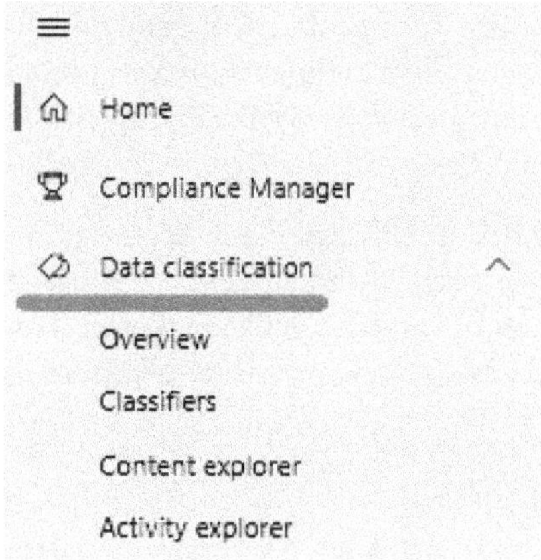

Figure 5.16 – The Data classification portal

The data classification **Overview** portal in Microsoft Purview serves as a centralized hub for efficiently managing and understanding your organization's data. It offers a comprehensive snapshot of data classification, enabling you to identify sensitive information, track data lineage, and assess compliance with data governance policies. This powerful tool empowers administrators to make informed decisions about data handling and protection strategies within their enterprise.

Figure 5.17 – An overview of labels and sensitive information

In conclusion, effective data classification is pivotal for maintaining data integrity and compliance. Now, let's seamlessly transition into exploring how automatic data classification and labeling further streamline this process, enhancing efficiency and accuracy in data governance.

Automatic data classification and labeling

Microsoft 365 Compliance offers automatic data classification and labeling, based on predefined sensitivity labels that can be applied to documents, emails, and other content. Sensitivity labels are used to indicate the level of protection and handling requirements for a given piece of data and can be customized to fit an organization's specific needs. For example, a sensitivity label can be created for "confidential" data, which requires encryption and restricted access.

Once sensitivity labels are defined, they can be automatically applied to data using Microsoft's intelligent labeling capabilities. This process uses machine learning algorithms to analyze the content of documents and emails, identifying sensitive information and applying the appropriate label automatically. This approach helps streamline data classification and labeling efforts, reduce human error, and ensure consistent protection across all content.

Manual data labelling

In addition to automatic labeling, Microsoft 365 Compliance also supports manual labeling. This approach allows users to manually apply sensitivity labels to content, based on their knowledge and understanding of the data's sensitivity. Manual labeling is especially useful for data that is not easily classified automatically, such as images or audio files.

Manual labeling can be done directly within Microsoft Office applications such as Word, Excel, and PowerPoint. Users can select the sensitivity label from a drop-down menu and apply the label to the document. This approach provides users with greater control and flexibility over data classification, ensuring that data is classified appropriately regardless of its format.

Advanced data protection capabilities

Beyond classification and labeling, Microsoft 365 Compliance also offers advanced data protection capabilities to ensure sensitive data is appropriately protected. Key features include **Data Loss Prevention (DLP)** policies, information barriers, and encryption.

DLP policies enable organizations to identify and prevent the sharing of sensitive data. These policies can be configured to prevent the sharing of data via email, instant messaging, or other communication channels. For example, a DLP policy can be configured to block the sharing of credit card numbers or social security numbers.

Information barriers help prevent conflicts of interest and inappropriate communication by limiting communication between specific groups of users. This capability can be used to enforce ethical walls between departments or prevent the sharing of sensitive information between teams.

Encryption is another critical data protection capability offered by Microsoft 365 Compliance. Encryption ensures that data is only accessible by authorized users and prevents unauthorized access if there are data breaches or theft.

In conclusion, data classification is a critical process in any organization's data governance and compliance strategy. Microsoft 365 Compliance offers several tools and features to support data classification and labeling, including automatic classification and labeling, manual labeling, and advanced data protection capabilities. By leveraging these capabilities, organizations can ensure that sensitive data is appropriately classified, labeled, and protected, enabling them to meet their regulatory and compliance requirements.

Classifiers in Microsoft 365 Purview

Microsoft 365 Purview is a comprehensive data governance solution that allows organizations to discover, understand, and manage their data assets. As part of its data management capabilities, Microsoft 365 Purview offers data classification features. These classification features enable organizations to categorize and label their data assets, based on predefined or custom classification rules. Data classification plays a crucial role in data governance by providing insights into the sensitivity, importance, and compliance requirements of data. It helps organizations identify and protect sensitive information, implement appropriate access controls, and ensure regulatory compliance.

In Microsoft 365 Purview, classifiers are used to automatically classify data based on predefined patterns, keywords, or metadata attributes. These classifiers are predefined rules or policies that are applied to data assets during the discovery and cataloging process.

In current versions of Microsoft Purview, you can find three different types of classifiers, as shown in *Figure 5.18*:

- Trainable classifiers (93 predefined templates)
- Sensitive info types (313 predefined templates)

- **Exact data match** (**EDM**) classifiers

Figure 5.18 – Create different classifiers

The classification capabilities in Microsoft 365 Purview allow organizations to create and manage classifiers to suit their specific needs. They can define classification rules based on regular expressions, keywords, or patterns that match specific data patterns. For example, organizations can create classifiers to identify **personally identifiable information** (**PII**), such as social security numbers or credit card numbers, sensitive financial data, intellectual property, or any other custom data patterns relevant to their industry or business.

When data assets are ingested into Microsoft 365 Purview, the classifiers are applied to automatically assign appropriate labels or tags to the data, based on the defined classification rules. These labels help users quickly identify and understand the nature of the data, its sensitivity, and any associated compliance requirements.

Furthermore, the classification information provided by Microsoft 365 Purview can be leveraged by other services and tools within the Microsoft 365 ecosystem. For example, the data classification labels can be used to enforce DLP policies, where certain actions or sharing of sensitive data can be restricted based on the classification labels.

In conclusion, classifiers in Microsoft 365 Purview provide a powerful mechanism for automatically categorizing and labeling data, based on predefined rules. These classification capabilities enhance data governance, enabling organizations to better understand and manage their data assets, implement appropriate security measures, and ensure regulatory compliance.

Configuring sensitive info types

Sensitive info types in Microsoft Purview can be configured through the data classification feature. The data classification feature provides a comprehensive set of sensitive info types that can be used to classify and protect sensitive data. Sensitive info types are pre-configured patterns or rules that identify specific types of sensitive data, such as credit card numbers, social security numbers, or other types of PII.

Here are the steps to configure sensitive info types in Microsoft Purview:

1. Navigate to the Microsoft Purview portal and sign in with your account.

2. Click on the **Data classification** tab and select the **Classifiers** option.
3. Click on the **Sensitive info types** tab to view the pre-configured sensitive info types.

Classifiers

Figure 5.19 – Creating sensitive classifiers

4. Review the list of sensitive info types, selecting the ones that are relevant to your organization's needs.
5. Click on + **Create sensitive info type** if you need to define your own custom patterns for sensitive data. Add a name and description (both are required fields) and click **Next**.
6. Define the custom sensitive info type by specifying the pattern and any additional metadata or context that should be associated with it.
7. Click on + **Create pattern** and define the new pattern:

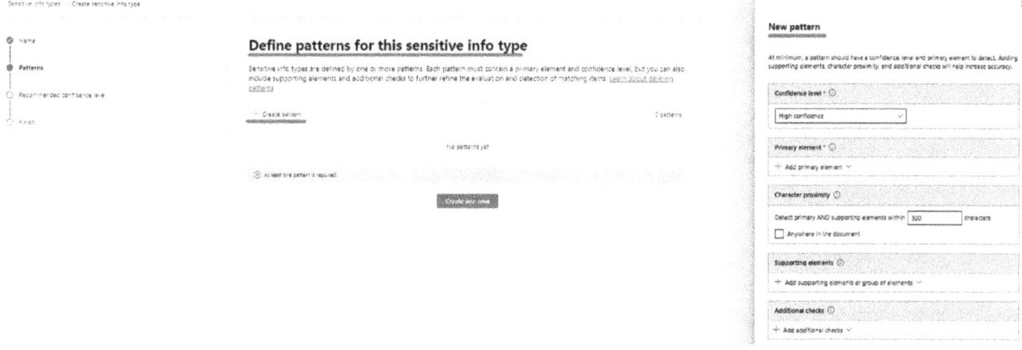

Figure 5.20 – Defining pattern

8. In this section, do the following:

   A. Define the confidence level

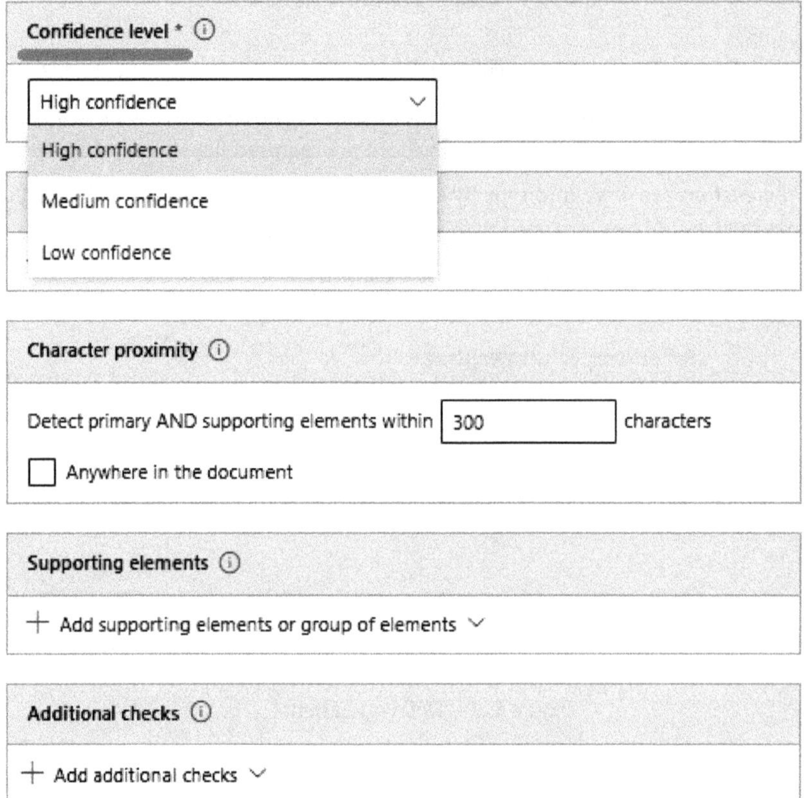

Figure 5.21 – Defining the confidence level

B. Define the pattern element

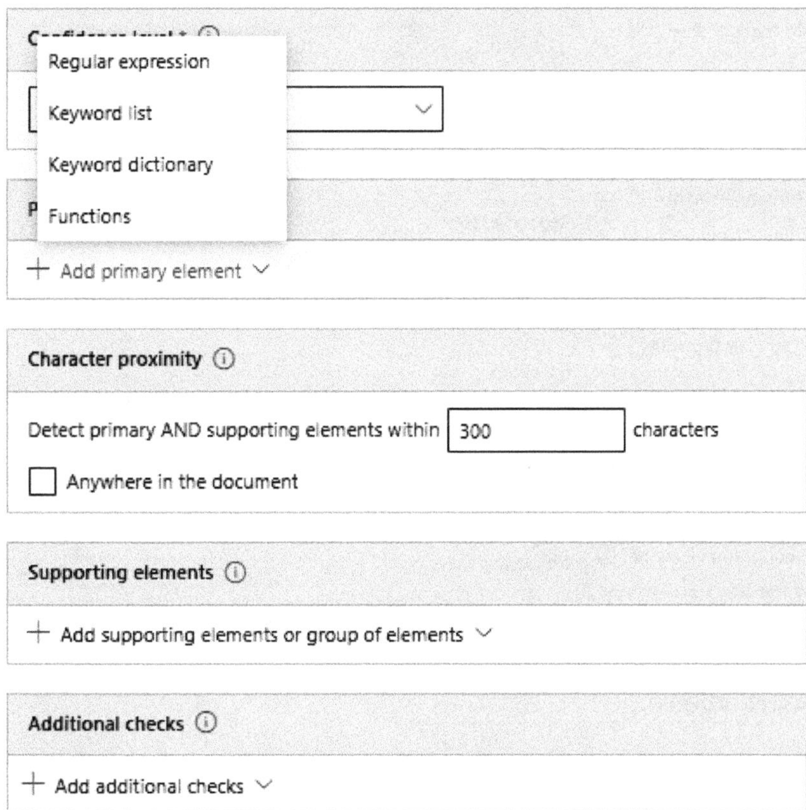

Figure 5.22 – Defining the pattern element

C. **Define the recommended action**: Check the **Anywhere in the document** box (this option will search more detailed documents)

D. Define the supporting elements

New pattern

At minimum, a pattern should have a confidence level and primary element to detect. Adding supporting elements, character proximity, and additional checks will help increase accuracy.

Confidence level * ⓘ

Medium confidence

Primary element * ⓘ

+ Add primary element

Elements

Regular expression

Keyword list

Keyword dictionary

Functions

Groups

Any of these

All of these

Not any of these

Character proximity ⓘ

Detect primary AND suppo characters

Anywhere in the docur

Supporting elements ⓘ

+ Add supporting elements or group of elements

Additional checks ⓘ

+ Add additional checks

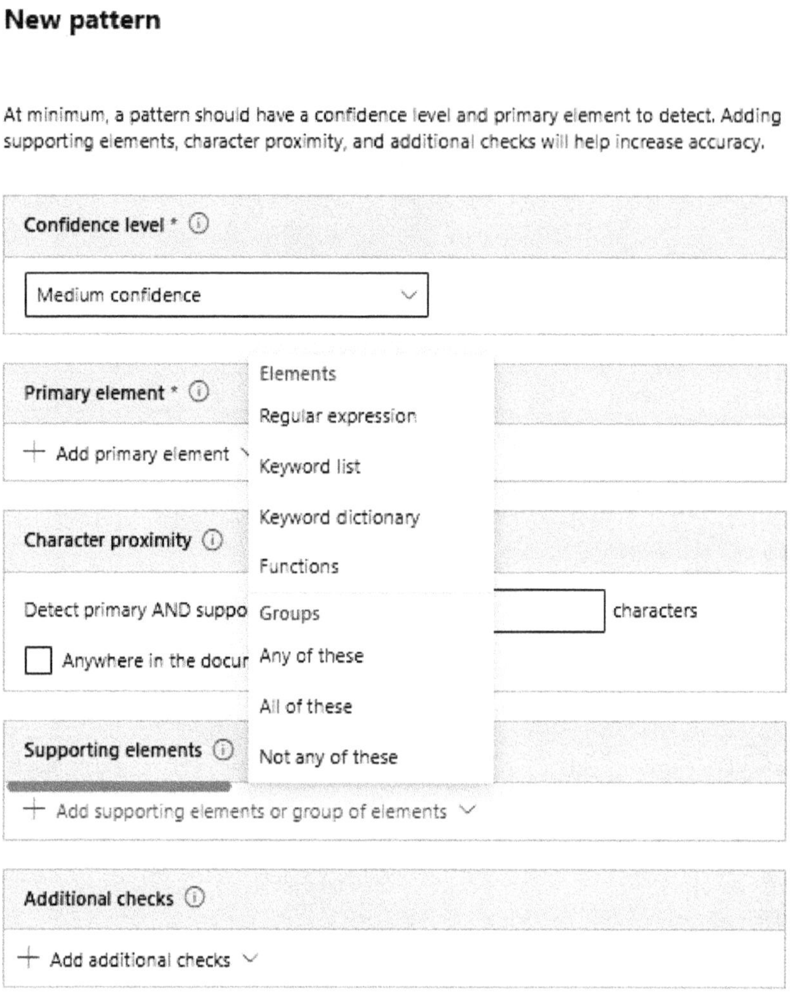

Figure 5.23 – Defining the supporting elements

E. Add additional checks

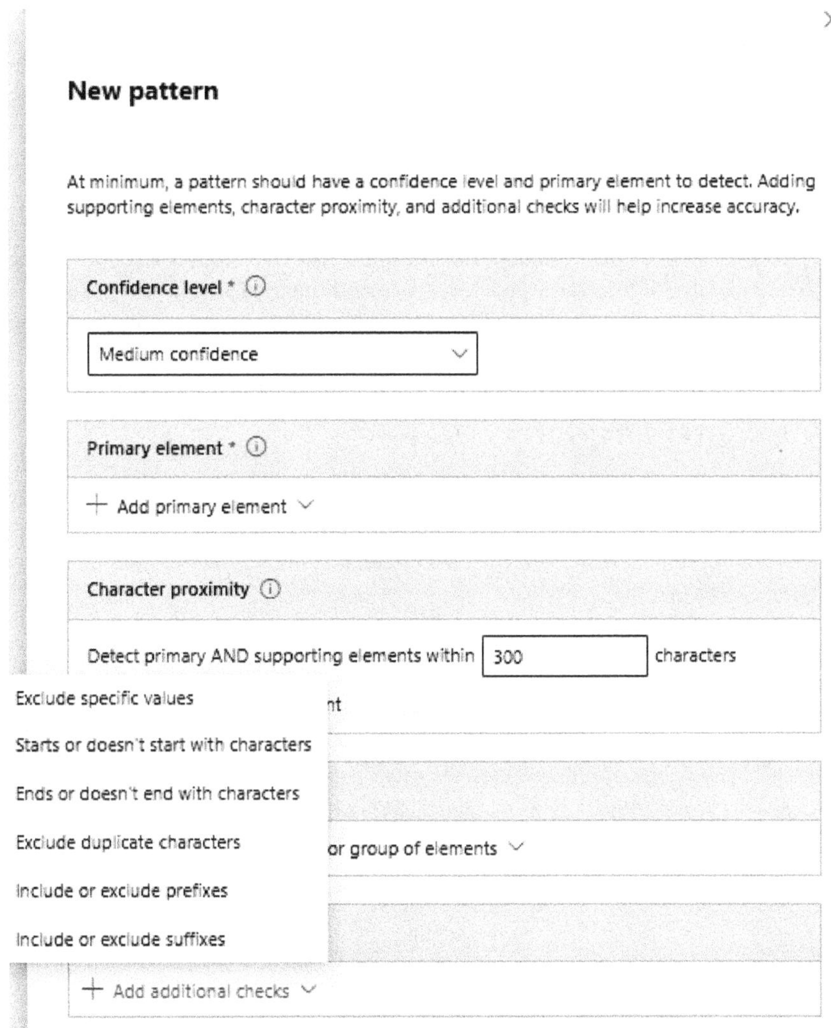

Figure 5.24 – Adding additional checks

F. Once you have selected or defined the sensitive info types, you can apply them to your data sources by creating or updating data classification rules

G. Define the criteria for the rule, including the sensitive info types that should be detected, the scope of the rule, and any other conditions or filters

9. Save the rule and apply it to the relevant data sources

Once you have configured the sensitive info types and created data classification rules, the Microsoft Purview system will scan the data sources for sensitive information and apply the appropriate labels or tags based on the defined rules. This information can then be used to support compliance, data protection, and other data management tasks.

It is important to note that while Microsoft Purview provides a wide range of pre-configured sensitive info types, organizations may need to define their own custom types, based on their specific data and regulatory requirements. Additionally, the configuration steps may vary, depending on the specific version and features of Microsoft Purview. It is recommended to refer to the latest Microsoft documentation or consult Microsoft support for the most up-to-date information on configuring sensitive info types in Microsoft Purview.

Configuring content explorer

Content explorer is a powerful feature within Microsoft Purview that empowers organizations to discover, explore, and manage their data assets effectively. Serving as a unified interface, content explorer provides a comprehensive view of the data estate, facilitating data governance, compliance, and data-driven decision-making.

At its core, content explorer in Microsoft Purview offers the following key capabilities:

- **Data catalog**: Content explorer serves as a centralized catalog for all data assets within an organization. It enables users to search, filter, and browse through a wide range of data sources, including files, databases, and data lakes. The catalog provides valuable details about each data asset, such as its source, location, metadata, and classification information:

Figure 5.25 – Content explorer in Microsoft Purview

- **Data lineage**: Understanding the lineage and relationships between data assets is critical for effective data management. Content explorer provides data lineage capabilities, allowing users to track the flow of data from its origin to various systems and processes. This knowledge facilitates impact analysis, change management, and maintaining data integrity.

- **Search and discovery**: The robust search functionality in Content Explorer empowers users to locate specific data assets quickly. Users can utilize keywords, metadata filters, and advanced search options to pinpoint the data they need. This streamlines data discovery and accelerates access to relevant information.

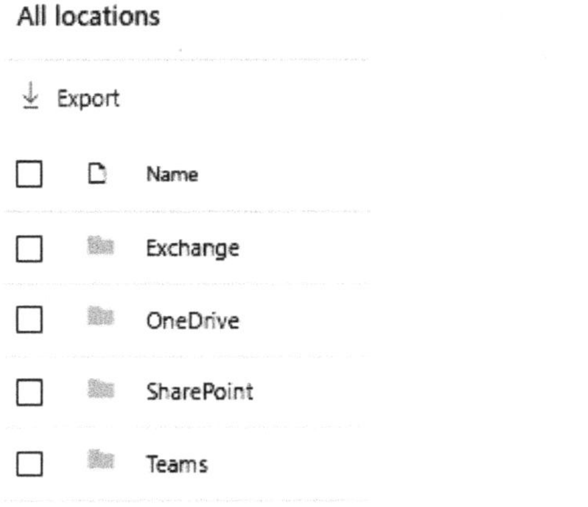

Figure 5.26 – Content explorer – search and discovery

- **Data profiling**: Content explorer offers data profiling capabilities to assess the structure, quality, and content of data assets. By performing statistical analysis, identifying patterns, and evaluating data quality metrics, users gain insights into the health and characteristics of their data. This understanding supports data cleansing, standardization, and enhancement initiatives.
- **Classification and labels**: Content explorer plays a pivotal role in data classification and labeling. It enables organizations to apply predefined or custom classification rules to data assets. By automatically categorizing and labeling data based on sensitivity, compliance requirements, or other criteria, content explorer enhances data governance, privacy, and security practices.

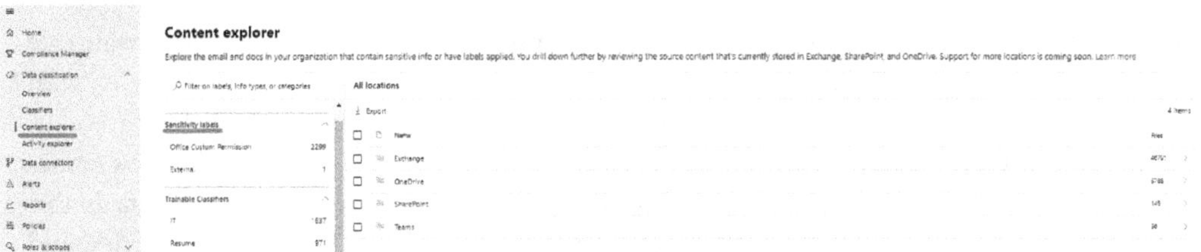

Figure 5.27 – Defining the sensitivity label

- **Data insights**: By leveraging artificial intelligence and machine learning technologies, content explorer offers data insights. It can automatically identify patterns, correlations, and anomalies within the data, enabling users to derive valuable insights. These insights support decision-making, uncover business opportunities, and drive innovation.

- **Data actions**: Content explorer allows users to take actions directly from the interface. It provides capabilities to initiate data protection policies, access requests, data sharing controls, or other data management actions, based on the information and insights provided. This streamlines workflows and enhances operational efficiency.

By leveraging content explorer in Microsoft Purview, organizations can gain better visibility, control, and understanding of their data assets. It facilitates compliance with regulations, supports data governance frameworks, and enables data-driven decision-making. Additionally, the ability to explore and manage data assets in a unified interface simplifies data management tasks and improves overall data management maturity.

For more information about user activity, click on **Activity explorer** in the left-hand navigation menu, and check out all the details about accessing sensitive info types in your organization:

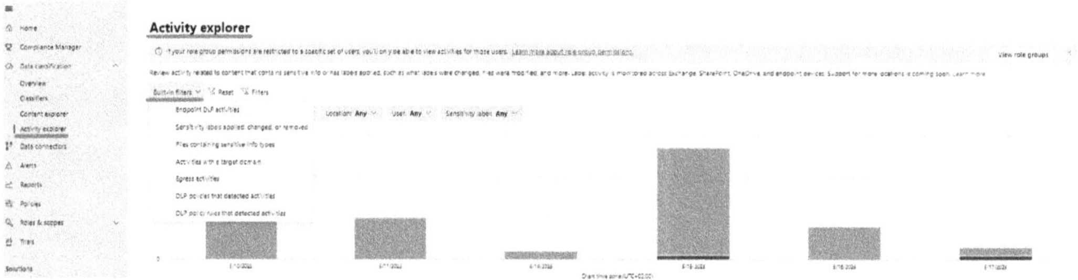

Figure 5.28 – The Activity explorer dashboard

Having covered data classifiers, the spotlight now turns to Content search, a feature within Microsoft Purview that plays one of the most important roles in data governance and accessibility.

Content search

In today's digital age, organizations generate vast amounts of data daily. This data holds valuable insights that can drive informed decision-making and enhance business operations. However, with the exponential growth of data, it has become increasingly challenging for businesses to locate, access, and protect relevant information efficiently. This is where Content search in Microsoft Purview comes into play, offering a powerful solution to effectively manage and extract value from data assets. In this part of the chapter, we will explore the importance of using Content search in Microsoft Purview and how it can revolutionize data discovery and utilization.

Streamlining data discovery

One of the primary benefits of Content search in Microsoft Purview is its ability to streamline data discovery processes. Purview acts as a central hub, enabling Compliance Administrators to search across various data sources, a Microsoft 365 location (e.g., Exchange Online, SharePoint Online, OneDrive for

Business, Teams, etc.), cloud storage, data lakes, and even unstructured data such as documents and images. By leveraging advanced search capabilities, including keyword search, filtering, and faceted navigation, Compliance Administrators can quickly locate the specific data they need, regardless of its location or format. This streamlined data discovery process brings immense value to organizations. It saves time and effort spent on manually searching through disparate systems, databases, or file shares. With Content search, Compliance Administrators can access a comprehensive view of a user's data landscape, ensuring they make informed decisions based on accurate and up-to-date information. This empowers organizations to harness the full potential of their data assets and extract valuable insights that drive business growth.

> **Important note**
>
> To ensure access to user information through the Content search option in Microsoft Purview, it is necessary to assign the Compliance Administrator with additional roles. These roles can be assigned by the Global Administrator, with the understanding that any roles added for compliance purposes will trigger email notifications to all Global Administrators. This process helps to maintain transparency and accountability within an organization when granting access to sensitive user information.

Enhancing data governance and compliance

Data governance and compliance are critical considerations for organizations in today's regulatory landscape. Failure to comply with data regulations can lead to severe consequences, including legal penalties, reputational damage, and loss of customer trust. Microsoft Purview's Content search plays a crucial role in enhancing data governance and compliance practices.

By enabling comprehensive search capabilities across all data sources, Purview allows organizations to identify sensitive or regulated data. Content search helps locate PII, sensitive financial data, or other critical business information, ensuring that proper safeguards and controls are in place to protect it. Additionally, Purview assists in meeting regulatory requirements by providing an audit trail of data access and usage, enabling organizations to demonstrate compliance during audits or investigations.

In today's data-driven world, the ability to discover, manage, and utilize data is paramount quickly and efficiently. Content search in Microsoft Purview provides organizations with a powerful tool to overcome data management challenges and unlock the full potential of their data assets. By streamlining data discovery, enhancing data governance, and promoting collaboration, Content search revolutionizes the way organizations harness their data, enabling them to make informed decisions, comply with regulations, and achieve sustainable growth in a rapidly evolving business landscape. Embracing Content search in Microsoft Purview is a crucial step toward maximizing the value of data and staying ahead in the digital era.

However, there are several reasons why a Compliance Administrator *should not* be a part of the IT department. Let's look at what those reasons are.

Independence and objectivity

Compliance Administrators play a critical role in ensuring adherence to regulatory requirements and internal policies. By keeping them separate from the IT department, their independence and objectivity can be better maintained. Placing compliance responsibilities within IT may lead to conflicts of interest, as IT departments primarily focus on system functionality, efficiency, and operational needs. By separating compliance functions, the Compliance Administrator can objectively assess and monitor compliance without being influenced by IT-specific considerations.

Regulatory oversight and accountability

Compliance Administrators have the responsibility to oversee and ensure compliance with various regulatory frameworks, industry standards, and internal policies. By being independent of the IT department, they can provide a higher level of oversight and hold all departments, including IT, accountable for compliance. Placing compliance responsibilities within IT may create conflicts of interest, as IT departments might prioritize technical requirements and operational efficiency over compliance concerns.

Risk mitigation and control

Compliance Administrators are tasked with identifying, assessing, and mitigating risks related to non-compliance. By being separated from the IT department, they can objectively evaluate the adequacy and effectiveness of IT controls and processes. This separation helps avoid situations where IT departments might inadvertently overlook compliance risks due to their focus on technical operations. Compliance Administrators can provide an independent perspective on the effectiveness of IT controls and make recommendations for improvements, mitigating compliance risks.

A comprehensive compliance oversight

Compliance is a multi-faceted function that encompasses various aspects beyond IT, such as legal, finance, human resources, and data privacy. Placing compliance within the IT department may limit its scope and effectiveness. By having a separate Compliance Administrator, organizations can ensure that compliance considerations extend beyond technology-related areas and cover all aspects of a business. This holistic approach helps to develop comprehensive compliance programs and ensures that compliance requirements are met across an organization.

Collaboration and cross-functional alignment

Separating the Compliance Administrator from the IT department promotes collaboration and cross-functional alignment. Compliance Administrators can work closely with IT departments to understand technical capabilities and limitations, incorporating compliance requirements into IT processes. This collaboration is more effective when both parties bring their unique expertise and perspectives to the table. Having an independent Compliance Administrator encourages open communication, fosters a culture of compliance, and ensures that compliance considerations are adequately addressed in IT-related decisions.

In summary, keeping the Compliance Administrator separate from the IT department allows for greater independence, objectivity, regulatory oversight, risk mitigation, comprehensive compliance oversight, and collaboration. This separation ensures that compliance is effectively addressed throughout an organization, with due consideration to all relevant regulations, standards, and policies.

For more information about required roles and assigned members, just click on **Roles & scopes** in the left-hand navigation menu:

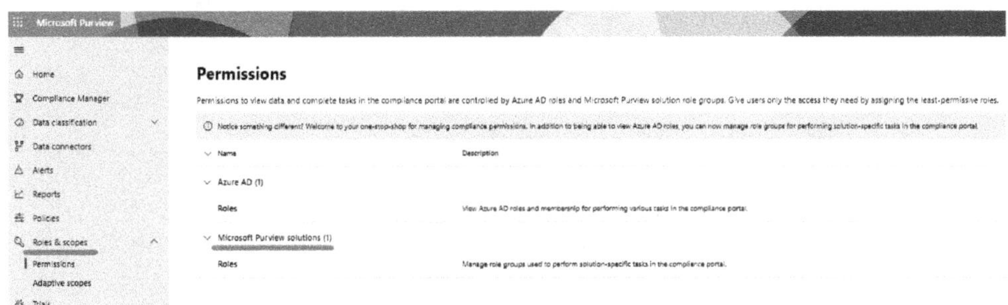

Figure 5.29 – Configuring roles for Content search

Here is an example of a Compliance Administrator:

Figure 5.30 – Compliance Administrator role features

To configure Content search in Microsoft Purview, follow these steps:

1. Log on to the Microsoft Purview portal with Admin rights.
2. Click on **Content search**.

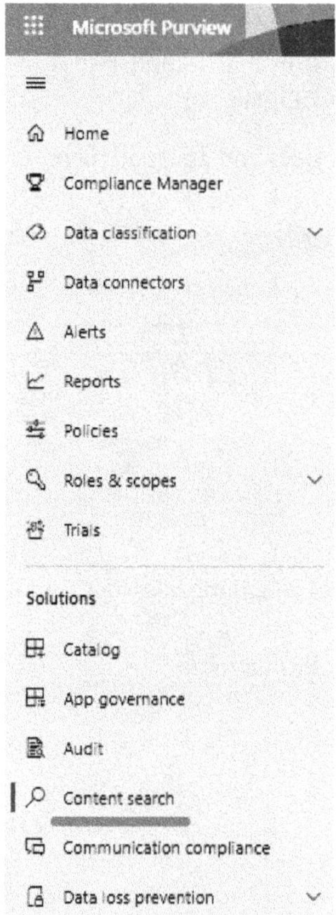

Figure 5.31 – Content search portal

3. Click on + **New search** to create a new Content search case.

Content search

Search your organization for content in emails, documents, Skype for Business conversations, and more. You can then preview and export the search results.

Search Export

+ New search ⤓ Download list ⟳ Refresh

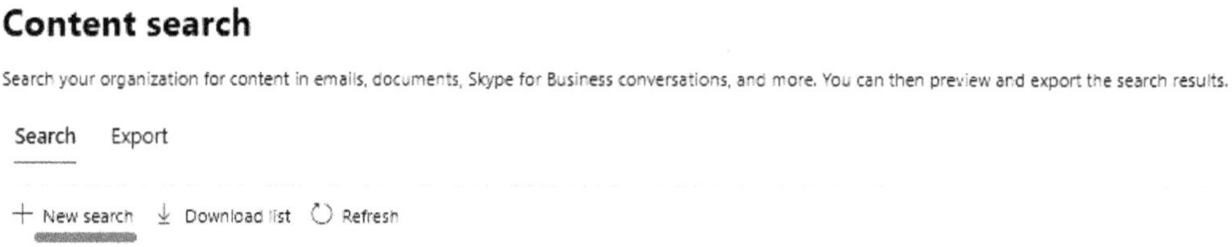

Figure 5.32 – Configuring a new Content search case

4. Define a name and description for the case.
5. Configure the location for Content search (Exchange Mailbox, which includes Microsoft 365 groups, and Teams and Yammer user messages or SharePoint sites, which include OneDrive sites, Microsoft 365 group sites, Teams sites and Yammer networks).

> **Note**
>
> You can add an on-premises user for a search, but you will need to configure and add app content additionally (keep in mind that an on-premises user *must* be synchronized with AAD).

Figure 5.33 – Define locations for the Content search task

6. Configure the search conditions (the typed-in words in the following screenshot are examples only):

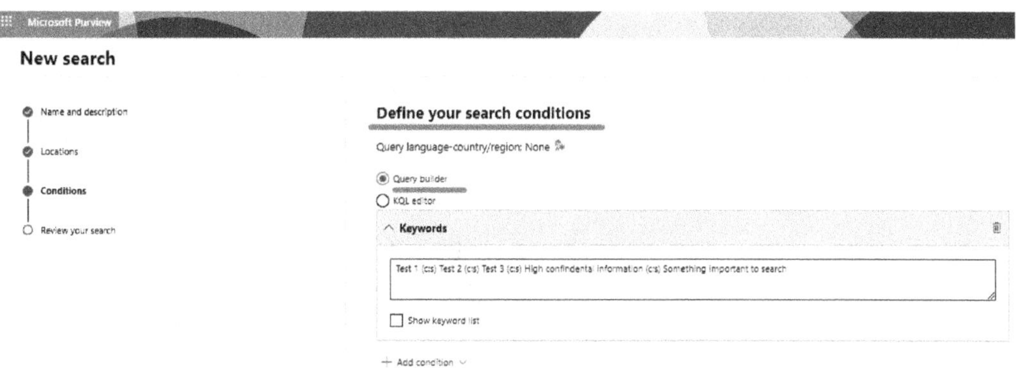

Figure 5.34 – Define the search conditions

7. Add conditions, for a more granular content search:

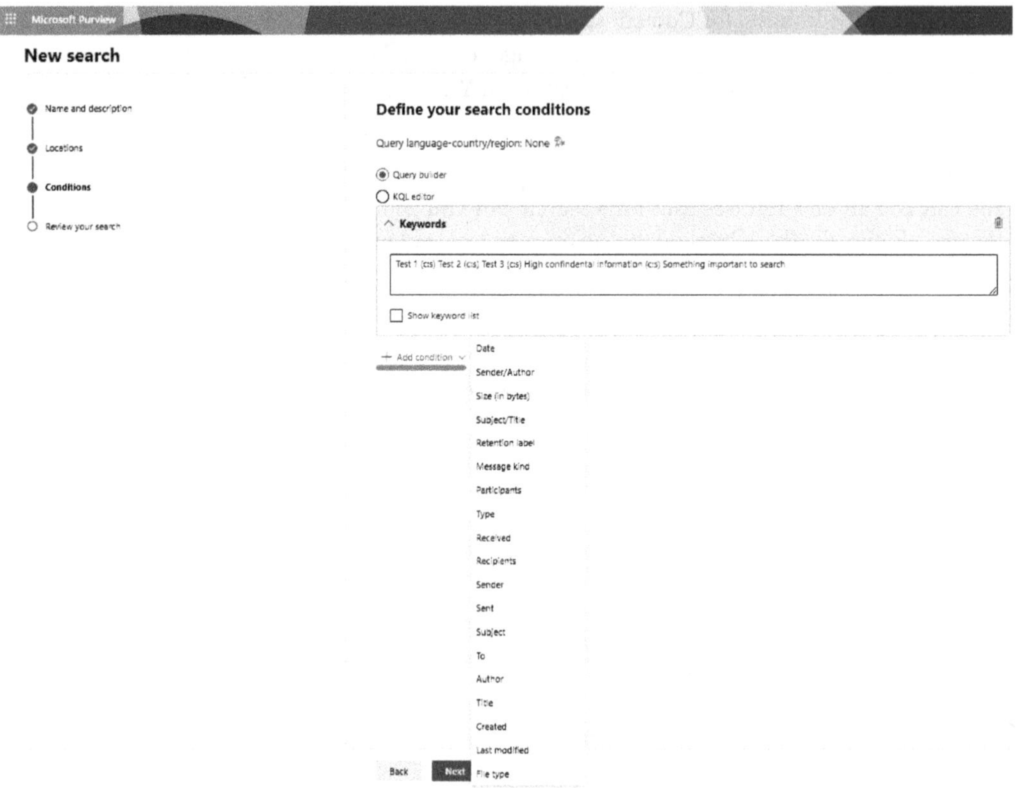

Figure 5.35 – Add different conditions for the Content search task

8. Review your search and submit.

In Microsoft Purview, the Compliance Administrator role is typically assigned to individuals within the following organization departments:

- **Compliance and legal department**: The compliance and legal department is responsible for ensuring that an organization complies with relevant regulations, industry standards, and internal policies. Assigning a Compliance Administrator role to individuals within this department enables them to oversee and manage the compliance aspects of Content search. They can define search policies, access controls, and data classification rules to align with regulatory requirements and mitigate compliance risks.
- **IT security and governance department**: The IT security and governance department plays a crucial role in safeguarding an organization's data assets and managing access controls. Assigning a Compliance Administrator role to individuals within this department allows them to enforce

security policies related to Content search. They can define user access permissions, manage encryption settings, and monitor data usage to ensure compliance with data protection and privacy regulations.

- **Data governance and data management department**: The data governance and data management department focuses on managing an organization's data assets, ensuring data quality, and establishing data governance frameworks. Assigning a Compliance Administrator role to individuals within this department empowers them to define data classification schemes, metadata standards, and data retention policies for Content search. They can collaborate with other departments to establish data governance practices and ensure compliance in data discovery and analysis.
- **Internal audit department**: The internal audit department is responsible for assessing and evaluating an organization's internal controls, processes, and compliance with policies and regulations. Assigning a Compliance Administrator role to individuals within this department enables them to conduct audits and reviews related to Content search. They can monitor access logs, perform compliance checks, and ensure that the organization is meeting its regulatory obligations in data discovery and search activities.
- **Risk management department**: The risk management department focuses on identifying, assessing, and mitigating risks across an organization. Assigning a Compliance Administrator role to individuals within this department allows them to assess the compliance risks associated with Content search. They can collaborate with other departments to identify potential vulnerabilities, implement risk mitigation measures, and ensure that the organization's data discovery and search activities align with risk management strategies.

It is important to note that the specific departments and roles may vary depending on an organization's structure, industry, and compliance requirements. The key is to assign the Compliance Administrator role to individuals who have the necessary expertise in compliance, data governance, security, and risk management to effectively manage and oversee Content search in Microsoft Purview.

Recommended action

For better control of who can access user's information through the Content Search service, it is recommended to use AAD's **Privileged Identity Management** (**PIM**). Using PIM to assign sensitive admin roles in Microsoft 365 is highly recommended for several reasons:

- **Just-in-time access**: PIM enables the concept of *just-in-time*" access, which means that users are granted administrative privileges only when they need them and for a limited time. This reduces the risk of unauthorized or prolonged access to sensitive administrative roles, minimizing the window of opportunity for potential security breaches.

- **The least privilege principle**: Following the principle of least privilege is a crucial security practice. PIM allows organizations to assign administrative privileges on a temporary basis, granting users the minimum required access rights to perform their tasks. This helps prevent unnecessary exposure of sensitive administrative capabilities, reducing the attack surface and mitigating the potential impact of compromised accounts.
- **Access reviews and auditing**: PIM provides features for access reviews and auditing, allowing organizations to regularly review and verify the need for ongoing administrative access. Access reviews ensure that privileged roles are assigned to the right individuals or groups and are continuously monitored for appropriateness. Audit logs capture and track all privileged role activations and deactivations, providing a clear record of administrative activities for compliance and security purposes.
- **A justification and approval workflow**: PIM introduces a workflow for requesting and approving privileged role activations. Users who require administrative access can submit access requests through PIM, which are then reviewed and approved by appropriate stakeholders. This adds an additional layer of accountability and oversight, ensuring that access to sensitive admin roles is granted based on business justifications and proper authorization.
- **Time-bound access**: With PIM, privileged role assignments are time-bound, meaning that administrative access is automatically revoked after the specified duration. This reduces the risk of stale or forgotten privileged access rights, enhancing security by limiting the window of opportunity for potential attacks.
- **Privileged access monitoring**: PIM enables the monitoring and detection of privileged access usage. It provides visibility into who has activated privileged roles and when, allowing organizations to detect any unusual or unauthorized activities. This monitoring capability enhances incident response and helps identify and mitigate potential security incidents promptly.
- **Compliance and regulatory requirements**: Many compliance frameworks and regulations require organizations to implement controls and monitoring around privileged access. Using PIM to assign sensitive admin roles in Microsoft 365 aligns with these requirements, providing a systematic and auditable approach to manage and control privileged access.

In summary, using AAD's PIM to assign sensitive admin roles in Microsoft 365 provides numerous benefits, including just-in-time access, adhering to the principle of least privilege, access reviews and auditing, justification and approval workflows, time-bound access, privileged access monitoring, and compliance with regulatory requirements. Implementing PIM enhances security, reduces the risk of unauthorized access, and improves overall governance and control over privileged roles in Microsoft 365 environments.

Data loss prevention

DLP plays a crucial role in safeguarding sensitive information and preventing data breaches within organizations. With the increasing reliance on cloud-based solutions, Microsoft has introduced a service called Microsoft 365 Purview Data Loss Prevention, designed to enhance data visibility, classification, and protection. In this part of the book, we will explore the concept of DLP in Microsoft 365 Purview and its significance in ensuring data security.

Microsoft 365 Purview is an advanced data governance platform that enables organizations to gain insights into their data landscape. It leverages **artificial intelligence** (**AI**) and **machine learning** (**ML**) capabilities to scan, classify, and protect data across various sources, such as cloud applications, on-premises systems, and even third-party repositories. By providing a comprehensive view of data usage and identifying sensitive information, Purview helps organizations establish effective data protection strategies.

One of the key features of Microsoft 365 Purview is its ability to discover and classify data based on predefined policies and regulatory requirements. Organizations can define custom policies or use built-in templates to identify sensitive data such as PII, financial records, health information, and intellectual property. Purview employs sophisticated algorithms to scan and analyze data, regardless of its location, and automatically apply classification labels, based on the identified content. This allows organizations to understand the nature of their data and take appropriate measures to secure it.

Once data is classified, Microsoft 365 Purview provides robust DLP capabilities to prevent unauthorized disclosure or leakage of sensitive information. It offers a range of built-in or customizable policy rules that organizations can enforce to control data sharing and usage. For example, administrators can configure policies to block or quarantine emails containing sensitive information, prevent unauthorized file sharing, or detect and remediate data exfiltration attempts. Purview integrates seamlessly with other Microsoft 365 applications, such as Microsoft Teams, SharePoint, and OneDrive for Business, ensuring consistent protection across the entire collaboration and data sharing ecosystem.

In addition to preventing data loss, Microsoft 365 Purview assists organizations in meeting compliance requirements by offering comprehensive auditing and reporting capabilities. It maintains a centralized audit log that tracks user activities, data accesses, and policy violations, providing visibility into data usage patterns and potential security risks. Purview generates detailed reports and analytics, empowering organizations to assess their compliance posture, identify areas of improvement, and demonstrate adherence to regulatory frameworks.

Furthermore, Microsoft 365 Purview incorporates advanced threat intelligence and anomaly detection mechanisms to proactively identify and mitigate data security risks. By continuously monitoring data activity and applying AI-driven algorithms, Purview can detect suspicious behavior, unusual data access patterns, or abnormal data movement. It raises alerts and triggers automated responses to mitigate potential data breaches or unauthorized access attempts, helping organizations prevent security incidents before they occur.

To ensure scalability and flexibility, Microsoft 365 Purview offers integration capabilities with third-party data protection solutions. This allows organizations to leverage existing investments in security tools and extend the reach of their DLP strategies. Purview's open architecture enables seamless integration with various **security information and event management** (**SIEM**) systems, DLP solutions, and other security controls, facilitating a unified and holistic approach to data protection.

In conclusion, DLP in Microsoft 365 Purview is a comprehensive and robust solution that empowers organizations to gain visibility into their data landscape, classify sensitive information, and protect it from unauthorized access or leakage. By leveraging AI and ML capabilities, Purview enables organizations to proactively monitor data activity, enforce policies, and detect potential security risks.

Let's explore the configuration of DLP in Microsoft 365 Purview. However, before we dive into the setup process, it's essential to establish the requisite additional admin roles. These roles grant the necessary permissions and access for configuring and monitoring DLP policies and actions effectively. Here are the administrator roles that are typically involved in DLP in Microsoft Purview:

- **Global Administrator**: The Global Administrator role is the highest level of administrative access in Microsoft 365. Global Administrators have full control over all administrative features and settings, including the ability to configure DLP policies in Microsoft Purview. This role is responsible for managing user roles, assigning permissions, and overseeing the overall security and compliance of an organization's data.
- **Compliance Administrator**: The Compliance Administrator role is focused on managing compliance features and settings in Microsoft 365. This role includes responsibilities related to data protection, retention, and compliance across various Microsoft services, including Purview. Compliance Administrators have the authority to create and manage DLP policies and configure DLP settings specific to an organization's compliance requirements.
- **Data Loss Prevention Administrator**: The Data Loss Prevention Administrator role is specifically dedicated to managing DLP policies and controls. This role is responsible for configuring and fine-tuning DLP policies in Microsoft Purview to protect sensitive data and prevent unauthorized disclosure or leakage. Data Loss Prevention Administrators can define policy rules, customize policy templates, and monitor DLP incidents and reports.
- **Security Administrator**: The Security Administrator role focuses on managing security-related features and settings in Microsoft 365. In the context of DLP in Microsoft Purview, Security Administrators play a crucial role in defining security policies, implementing access controls, and ensuring data protection across an organization. They work closely with other administrators to align DLP policies with broader security strategies.

It's important to note that these roles can be customized and assigned based on the specific needs and organizational structure. Additionally, the availability and naming of these roles may vary, depending on the version of Microsoft 365 and the specific licensing plan in use.

Creating a DLP policy in Microsoft Purview is a straightforward process. By following these steps, you can set up a basic DLP policy to protect your sensitive data:

1. **Sign in to Microsoft Purview**: Access the Microsoft Purview portal using your administrator credentials.
2. **Navigate to the Data loss prevention Policies section**: Once logged in, locate and select the **Policies** option in the **Microsoft Purview** portal. This is where you can manage and create DLP policies.

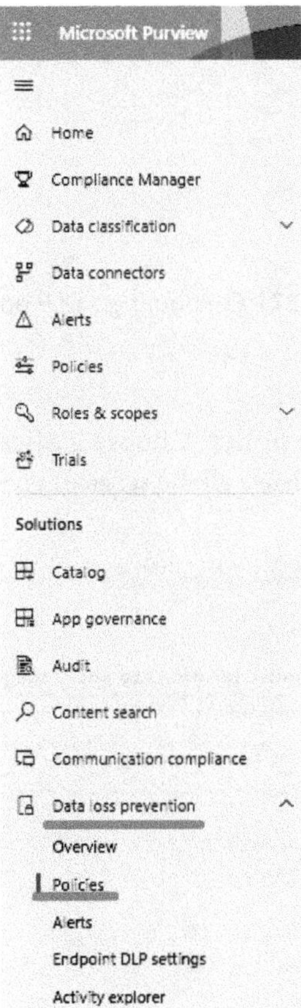

Figure 5.36 – The DLP portal

3. **Create a new DLP policy**: Click on + **Create Policy** in the admin portal, under **Policies**.
4. **Start with a template or create a custom policy**: This helps you identify and understand the purpose of the policy. Define a category and country region if you need to.

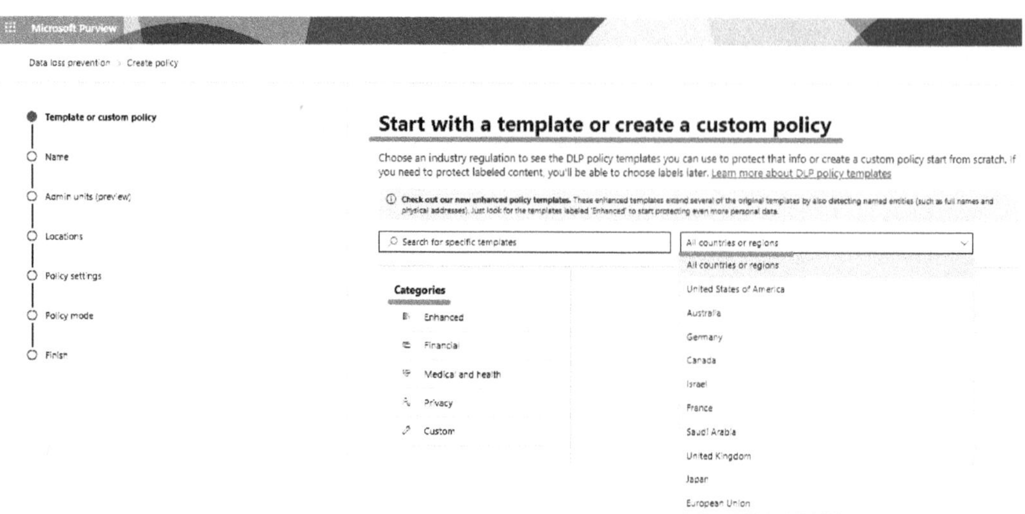

Figure 5.37 – Configuring a DLP policy

5. Assign admin units.
6. **Choose a location to apply the policy**: Choose a Microsoft 365 location where you will apply the created policy. You can leave all the services on by default or choose where to apply, according to your needs:

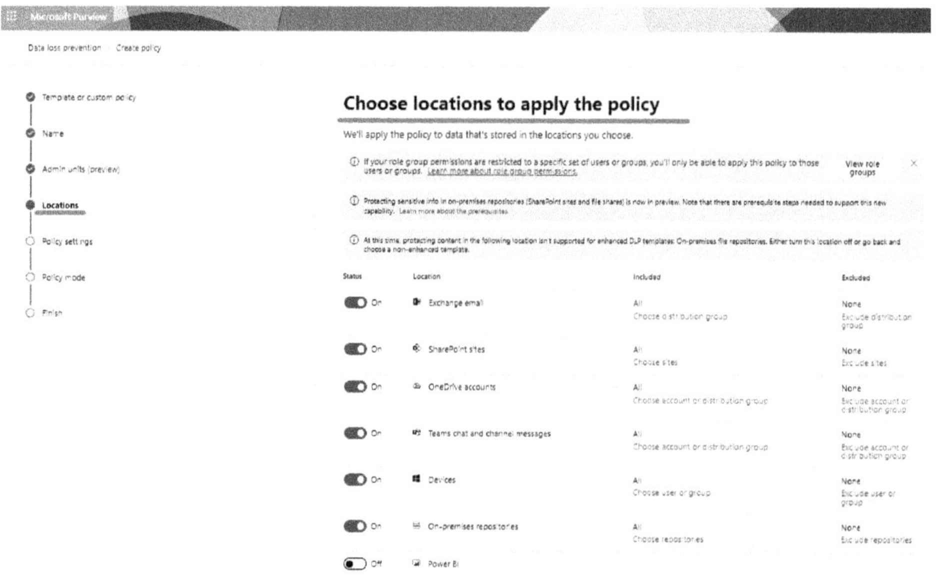

Figure 5.38 – Choose a location for the DLP policy

If you wish to add on-premises repositories, click on **Choose repositories** and type the correct path to the repository (for example: `\\server\share`):

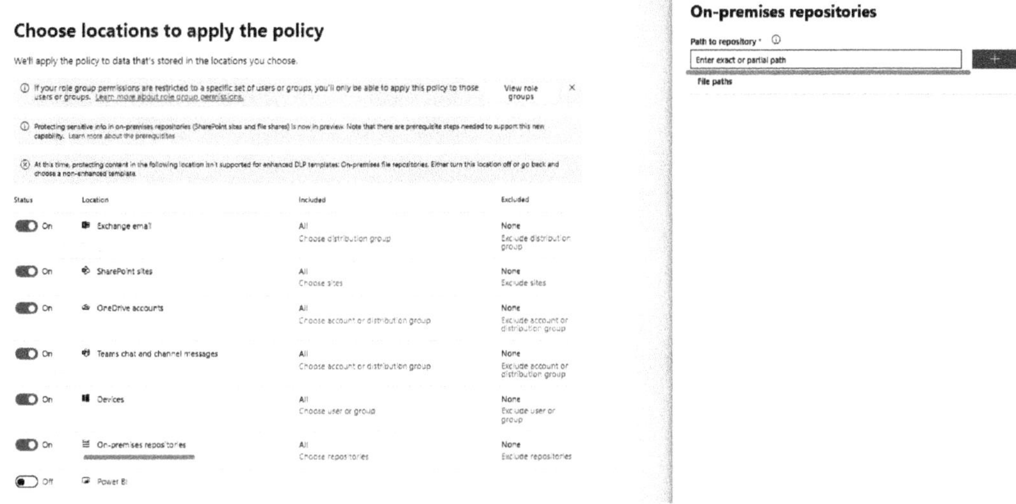

Figure 5.39 – Adding a DLP policy for on-premises repositories

7. **Policy settings**: Customize advanced DLP rules to identify the types of sensitive data you want to protect. Microsoft Purview offers a wide range of built-in sensitive data types, such as credit card numbers, social security numbers, or PII. You can also create custom data types if needed:

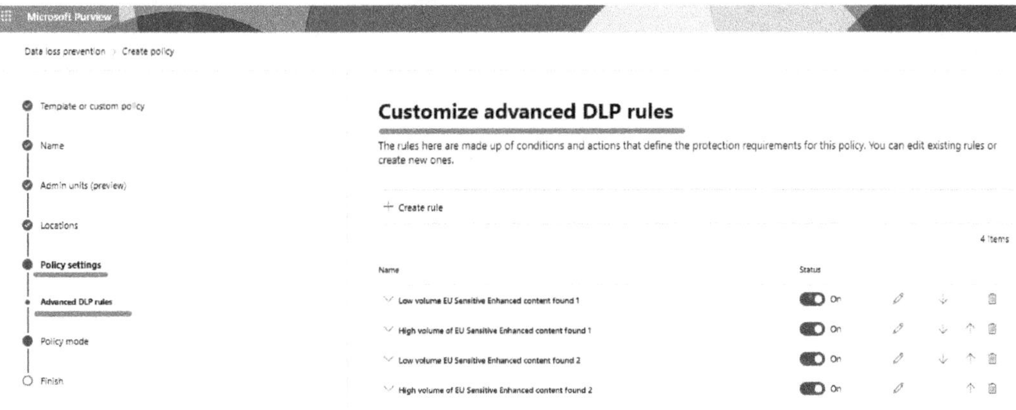

Figure 5.40 – Define advanced DLP rules

8. **Policy mode**: After creating a DLP policy in Microsoft Purview, it is important to define how the policy should be handled before releasing it into production. To ensure the policy's effectiveness, testing it is highly recommended. By following the following steps, you can test your created policy and gather valuable information to fine-tune its settings:

   A. **Enable test mode**: Before activating the DLP policy, enable the **Show policy tips while in test mode** checkbox. This option provides valuable information and notifications about policy violations without taking immediate action. It allows you to assess the impact of the policy on your organization's data and user interactions without blocking or alerting users.

   B. **Test with sample data**: Utilize sample data that closely resembles the type of content your organization handles. This can include sample documents, emails, or other relevant data sources:

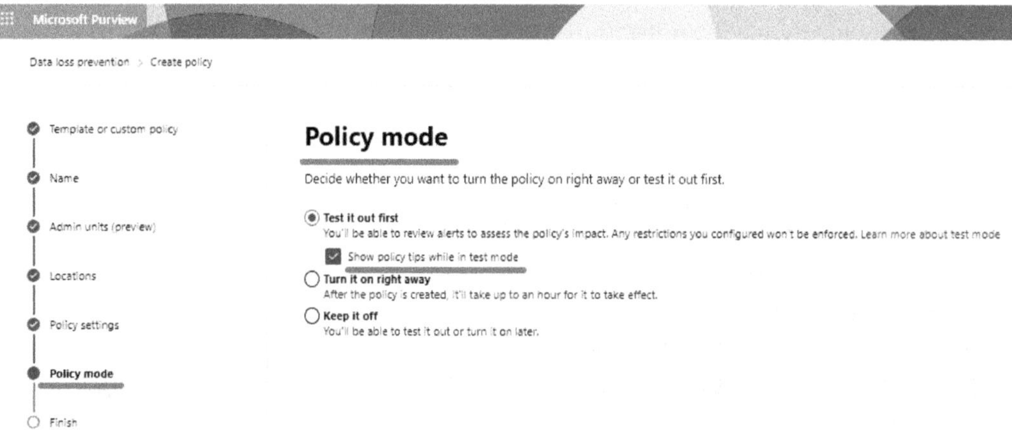

Figure 5.41 – Define the policy mode

9. Review your policy and create it.

As we navigate the landscape of data governance, let's put our attention to another crucial aspect by exploring how automatic data classification and labeling set the stage for robust EndPoint **Data Loss Prevention** (**DLP**) settings.

Endpoint DLP settings

Endpoint DLP settings in Microsoft Purview refer to the configuration options that allow you to extend DLP measures to endpoints, such as desktops, laptops, or mobile devices, within your organization. These settings enable you to protect sensitive data from being leaked or mishandled at the endpoint level:

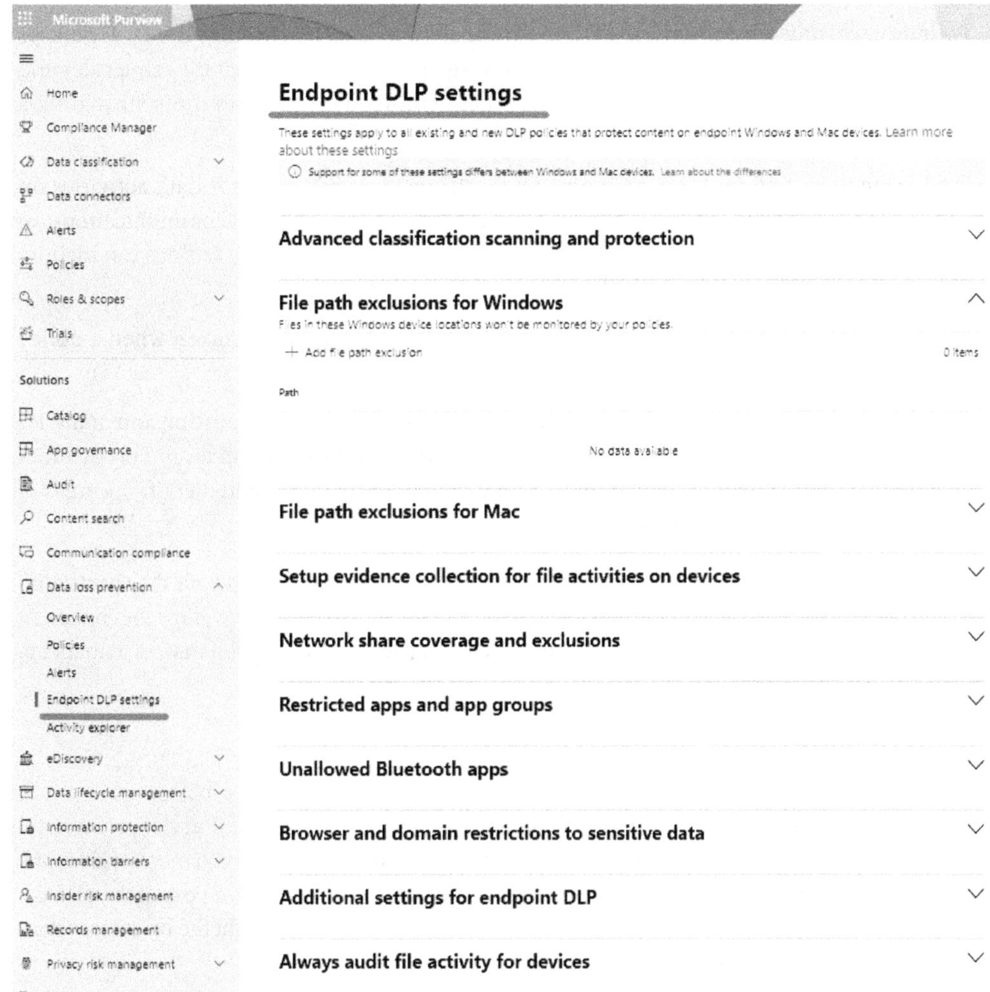

Figure 5.42 – Endpoint DLP settings

Here is a simple explanation of endpoint DLP settings in Microsoft Purview:

- **Endpoint protection**: Microsoft Purview provides options to install and configure endpoint agents on devices, enforcing data protection policies at the endpoint level. These agents monitor and analyze data activities on the endpoints to detect potential data breaches or policy violations.
- **Device management integration**: Microsoft Purview integrates with device management solutions, such as Microsoft Intune (formerly Microsoft Endpoint Manager), to manage and control endpoint devices centrally. This integration ensures consistent enforcement of DLP policies across all managed endpoints.

- **Policy synchronization**: Endpoint DLP settings allow you to synchronize the DLP policies defined in Microsoft Purview with the endpoint agents. This ensures that the same rules and conditions applied at the organizational level are enforced on the endpoints, providing a consistent approach to data protection.
- **Real-time monitoring**: With endpoint DLP settings, you can monitor data activities on endpoints in real time. This includes actions such as file transfers, email communications, or data uploads/downloads. By analyzing these activities, the endpoint DLP settings can identify and respond to potential data breaches or policy violations promptly.
- **Policy enforcement actions**: You can configure specific actions to be taken when a policy violation is detected on an endpoint.
- **Endpoint reporting and analytics**: Endpoint DLP settings provide reporting and analytics capabilities to gain insights into data protection activities at the endpoint level. This includes generating reports on policy violations, tracking data usage patterns, and identifying areas of improvement for DLP measures.

By utilizing endpoint DLP settings in Microsoft Purview, organizations can extend their data protection strategies to endpoints and mitigate the risk of data breaches or leaks. These settings allow for consistent policy enforcement, real-time monitoring, and centralized management of endpoint devices, enhancing overall data security and compliance.

Summary

In this chapter, we took a small journey to explore the rich landscape of Microsoft Purview, a powerful service designed to empower organizations in their data governance and management endeavors. Recognizing the complexity of Purview, we carefully curated a selection of key components to discuss, aiming to provide you with valuable insights into its essential elements and highlight the most important services that you can configure.

With its wide range of functionalities, integrations, and capabilities, Purview is a dynamic platform that constantly evolves to meet the ever-changing needs of data-driven organizations. Thus, our focus was on shedding light on the fundamental building blocks that underpin its operation.

One of the important objectives of Microsoft Purview is to facilitate robust data governance. By establishing comprehensive policies, organizations can enforce data quality standards, access controls, and regulatory compliance. We explored the mechanisms through which Purview enables the creation and enforcement of these policies, providing you with practical insights into configuring and managing them effectively.

Additionally, we covered and showed the importance of data classification and labeling within Purview. With an ever-increasing volume of data, automating the process of assigning labels and tags becomes imperative. We examined how Purview employs ML algorithms and predefined rules to streamline data categorization, leading to improved efficiency and accuracy in data organization and management.

Throughout our exploration, it is important to emphasize that Microsoft Purview is an evolving ecosystem. As new features and services are introduced, it is essential to stay abreast of the latest developments and innovations within the platform. Our intention was to equip you with a solid foundation, empowering you to adapt and explore the vast possibilities that Purview holds.

In conclusion, this chapter strived to provide you with an in-depth understanding of the essential components and services offered by Microsoft Purview. While acknowledging the impossibility of covering every part of service (such as Information Protection, eDiscovery, LegalHold, and information barriers), we hope we ignited your curiosity and showed you a path to explore and discover Microsoft Purview.

In the forthcoming chapter, we will take a journey through Microsoft Defender for CloudApps, giving you the opportunity to witness its robust capabilities in safeguarding both applications and users.

6
Microsoft Defender for Cloud Apps

In our increasingly digital world, where businesses and organizations rely on cloud-based applications and services for their daily operations, ensuring the security of data and applications in the cloud has become an utmost priority. This is where Microsoft Defender for Cloud Apps steps in as a guardian of your cloud-based assets, helping you navigate the complex landscape of cloud security threats and challenges. This chapter serves as your entry point into the realm of Microsoft Defender for Cloud Apps, offering a comprehensive introduction to its essential concepts, core features, and its vital role in safeguarding your cloud-based environment SaaS applications.

As we delve into this chapter, we will explore the fundamental principles that underlie Microsoft Defender for Cloud Apps, its integration with various cloud platforms, and how it empowers organizations to proactively detect, analyze, and respond to cloud-based threats. We will be covering the following topics in this chapter:

- Microsoft Defender for Cloud Apps introduction
- Configuring Microsoft Defender for Cloud Apps
- Managing OAuth applications with Microsoft Defender
- Managing files in Microsoft Defender for Cloud Apps
- Governance log
- Microsoft Defender for Cloud Apps policies

By the end of this chapter, you will have a solid knowledge of what Microsoft Defender for Cloud Apps brings to the table and how it can enhance your cloud security posture in an era where the cloud is the cornerstone of modern business operations.

Introducing Microsoft Defender for Cloud Apps

Microsoft Defender for Cloud Apps is a cloud-native security solution that provides advanced threat protection for your SaaS applications. It is designed to help organizations secure their cloud-based assets and protect them against a wide range of cyber threats, such as malware, phishing, ransomware, and other attacks.

Microsoft Defender for Cloud Apps is part of Microsoft Defender XDR, which includes Microsoft Defender for Endpoint, Microsoft Defender for Office 365, and Microsoft Defender for Identity. These solutions work together to provide a comprehensive, integrated approach to security that spans across endpoints, applications, identities, and data. With Microsoft Defender for Cloud Apps, organizations can gain visibility of the security of their cloud applications and services, detect and respond to threats in real time, and enforce security policies and controls to protect against unauthorized access and data breaches.

One of the key features of Microsoft Defender for Cloud Apps is its advanced threat detection capabilities. The solution uses a combination of machine learning, behavioral analysis, and threat intelligence to detect and block malicious activities in the cloud environment. It can identify suspicious behavior, such as attempts to exfiltrate data, lateral movement within a network, and suspicious login attempts, and automatically take action to prevent further damage.

Shadow IT poses a significant challenge for organizations, as employees often adopt unauthorized applications and services, potentially compromising security and compliance. Microsoft Defender for Cloud Apps emerges as a robust solution to identify, monitor, and manage shadow IT within cloud environments. This article explores the key features and strategies employed by Microsoft Defender for Cloud Apps in discovering and effectively handling shadow IT.

Shadow IT refers to the use of unauthorized IT systems, applications, or services without official approval, presenting a potential threat to an organization's data security and compliance. Commonly driven by the need for convenience or specific functionalities, shadow IT can introduce vulnerabilities that may go unnoticed by traditional security measures.

Discovering shadow IT with Microsoft Defender for Cloud Apps

With comprehensive visibility and advanced threat detection, Defender for Cloud Apps offers unparalleled insights into unauthorized cloud usage and potential security risks. Safeguard your digital assets and ensure compliance by proactively addressing Shadow IT with this powerful solution:

- **App discovery**: Microsoft Defender for Cloud Apps provides comprehensive visibility of the cloud applications used across an organization. It employs advanced techniques to discover both sanctioned and unsanctioned applications, offering a clear understanding of the extent of shadow IT.
- **Risk assessment**: The solution assesses the risk associated with each discovered application. Factors such as data exposure, compliance violations, and security vulnerabilities are considered, allowing organizations to prioritize mitigation efforts based on the level of risk posed by specific applications.

- **Policy enforcement**: Microsoft Defender for Cloud Apps empowers organizations to establish and enforce policies governing the usage of cloud applications. This includes the ability to block or limit access to high-risk applications, ensuring a more secure cloud environment.
- **Anomaly detection**: The solution incorporates advanced anomaly detection mechanisms to identify unusual user behavior or access patterns associated with shadow IT. This proactive approach enables organizations to detect and respond to potential security incidents promptly.

Discovering and managing shadow IT in Microsoft Defender for Cloud Apps

In the ever-evolving landscape of cloud computing, organizations face the challenge of managing and securing their digital environments. One of the persistent issues is the presence of shadow IT, where employees use unauthorized applications and services without IT approval. Microsoft Defender for Cloud Apps emerges as a powerful tool to discover and manage shadow IT, providing organizations with the visibility and control needed to enhance security and compliance.

Microsoft Defender for Cloud Apps employs advanced techniques to identify and discover all cloud applications used within an organization. The comprehensive discovery process encompasses both sanctioned and unsanctioned applications, offering a holistic view of the organization's cloud landscape. This visibility is crucial in understanding the extent of shadow IT and the potential security risks associated with unauthorized applications.

Once cloud applications are discovered, Microsoft Defender for Cloud Apps assesses the risk associated with each application. This assessment takes into consideration numerous factors, including data exposure, compliance violations, and security vulnerabilities. By assigning risk scores to different applications, organizations can prioritize their efforts to mitigate the most significant risks posed by shadow IT.

Beyond discovery and risk assessment, Microsoft Defender for Cloud Apps integrates advanced threat detection mechanisms. This includes the identification of anomalous user behavior, suspicious access patterns, and potential data exfiltration attempts related to shadow IT. With real-time threat detection, organizations can respond swiftly to security incidents and prevent potential data breaches.

Microsoft Defender for Cloud Apps also facilitates user education and awareness initiatives. By providing insights into the usage of various applications and associated risks, organizations can educate users about the importance of adhering to IT policies. This proactive approach contributes to a culture of security awareness, reducing the likelihood of Shadow IT occurrences.

In conclusion, Microsoft Defender for Cloud Apps offers a comprehensive solution for discovering and managing shadow IT in the cloud. By providing visibility, assessing risks, enforcing policies, and integrating advanced threat detection, the tool empowers organizations to take control of their cloud environment, enhance security, and ensure compliance with IT policies. Continuous monitoring and user education further contribute to a robust defense against the challenges posed by shadow IT in the modern digital landscape.

Another important feature of Microsoft Defender for Cloud Apps is its ability to integrate with other security solutions and tools. The solution supports a range of APIs and connectors, which allow it to work seamlessly with other Microsoft security products, as well as third-party security solutions. This integration enables organizations to achieve a more holistic and unified approach to security across their entire IT environment. Microsoft Defender for Cloud Apps also provides organizations with detailed insights and analytics about their cloud security posture. The solution offers a range of reporting and monitoring capabilities, which enable organizations to track their security status, identify trends and patterns, and make data-driven decisions to improve their security posture.

Technical and license requirements

Microsoft Defender for Cloud Apps is a cloud-native security solution that provides visibility of your cloud applications and detects and blocks threats targeting your cloud environment. The technical and license requirements for Microsoft Defender for Cloud Apps are as follows:

Technical requirements:

- **Supported cloud services**: Microsoft Defender for Cloud Apps currently supports these major cloud services: Microsoft 365, Google Workspace, Salesforce, Box, Dropbox, Citrix ShareFile, ServiceNow, and many more
- **Supported operating systems**: Microsoft Defender for Cloud Apps can be used on any operating system that supports a modern web browser
- **Required permissions**: To use Microsoft Defender for Cloud Apps, you must have the necessary permissions to connect to your cloud applications and to configure security policies

License requirements:

- **Microsoft 365 E5 or Microsoft 365 E5 Security**: Microsoft Defender for Cloud Apps is included in Microsoft 365 E5 or Microsoft 365 E5 Security licenses.
- **Standalone license**: If you don't have a Microsoft 365 E5 or Microsoft 365 E5 Security license, you can purchase a standalone license for Microsoft Defender for Cloud Apps.

> **Important note**
>
> To use Microsoft Defender for Cloud Apps, you need to have a supported cloud service and the necessary permissions to connect to your cloud applications. If you want to use Microsoft Defender for Cloud Apps on Microsoft 365 or Google Workspace, you need to have a Microsoft 365 E5 or Microsoft 365 E5 Security license. Otherwise, you can purchase a standalone license for Microsoft Defender for Cloud Apps.

Configuring Microsoft Defender for Cloud Apps

Microsoft Defender for Cloud Apps is a cloud-native security solution that helps organizations protect their cloud applications and services from cyber threats. Cloud Discovery is one of the key features of Microsoft Defender for Cloud Apps, which allows organizations to discover and gain visibility of their cloud apps and services. It offers advanced threat protection capabilities, including behavioral analytics, machine learning, and security intelligence, to detect and prevent cloud-based attacks.

Cloud apps have become an integral part of modern-day organizations, making it essential to monitor and manage their usage. Microsoft offers two solutions for discovering and monitoring cloud apps in an organization's environment: Microsoft Defender for Cloud Apps and Cloud App Discovery.

Cloud App Discovery works by analyzing network traffic between client devices and cloud applications to identify which cloud apps and services are being used within the organization. This information is then used to create a comprehensive inventory of all cloud apps and services used by the organization.

Microsoft Defender for Cloud Apps and Cloud App Discovery are two different solutions provided by Microsoft that help organizations discover and monitor cloud applications used in their environment. Here are some of the key differences between their discovery capabilities:

- **Scope**: Microsoft Defender for Cloud Apps is a comprehensive cloud app security solution that provides visibility and control over cloud apps across various cloud services and platforms, such as Office 365, Azure, and third-party cloud apps. On the other hand, Cloud App Discovery is focused on discovering and monitoring cloud apps used by users within an organization's network.
- **Data sources**: Microsoft Defender for Cloud Apps leverages a variety of data sources, such as API logs, network logs, and proxy logs, to discover and monitor cloud apps. Cloud App Discovery uses network traffic logs to identify cloud apps used by users within an organization's network.
- **Real-time monitoring**: Microsoft Defender for Cloud Apps provides real-time monitoring of cloud apps and their activities, including user activity monitoring, file activity monitoring, and access monitoring. Cloud App Discovery provides periodic reports on the cloud apps used by users within an organization's network.
- **Integration with other security solutions**: Microsoft Defender for Cloud Apps integrates with other Microsoft security solutions such as Microsoft Defender for Endpoint, Microsoft Sentinel, and Microsoft Defender for Cloud Apps, providing a comprehensive security solution for cloud environments. Cloud App Discovery does not integrate with other Microsoft security solutions.

Keep in mind that Microsoft Defender for Cloud Apps provides a more comprehensive and real-time discovery and monitoring solution for cloud apps used in an organization's environment, while Cloud App Discovery is focused on discovering and reporting on cloud apps used by users within an organization's network.

The Cloud App Discovery feature in Microsoft Defender for Cloud Apps provides several benefits to organizations, including the following:

- **Visibility**: Cloud App Discovery provides organizations with a complete inventory of all cloud apps and services being used within the organization, which can help them identify potential security risks and vulnerabilities.
- **Control**: Once an organization has identified all the cloud apps and services being used, it can take steps to control access to these applications, enforce policies, and manage data security.
- **Compliance**: Cloud Discovery helps organizations comply with various regulatory requirements, such as GDPR and CCPA, by providing a comprehensive view of all cloud apps and services used within the organization.

Cloud App Discovery is included in the following licenses:

- Microsoft Entra ID P1
- Microsoft 365 E3
- Microsoft 365 E5
- EM+S E3

App Category in Microsoft Defender for Cloud Apps is a feature that helps organizations classify and manage their cloud applications based on their business functions and security risks. With App Category, organizations can create custom categories for their cloud apps and services and apply policies and controls based on these categories.

App Category works by analyzing the metadata and behavior of cloud applications to determine their business function and security risks. This information is used to classify cloud apps and services into various categories, such as finance, human resources, marketing, social media, and collaboration. Once the cloud apps and services are categorized, organizations can apply policies and controls based on the category. For example, an organization may want to apply stricter data protection policies to cloud apps in the finance category compared to cloud apps in the marketing category.

App Category provides several benefits to organizations, including the following:

- **Improved visibility and control**: App Category provides organizations with a better understanding of their cloud application landscape, allowing them to prioritize their security efforts and apply appropriate controls.
- **Customization**: Organizations can create custom categories based on their specific business needs, allowing them to tailor their security policies and controls to their unique requirements.
- **Compliance**: App Category helps organizations comply with various regulatory requirements, such as GDPR and CCPA, by providing better visibility and control over their cloud applications and services.

App Category is a powerful feature of Microsoft Defender for Cloud Apps that helps organizations classify and manage their cloud applications based on their business function and security risks, enabling them to better manage their security posture and reduce the risk of cyber threats.

The new Cloud Apps portal has been removed from the previous site (`https://portal.cloudappsecurity.com`) and can be accessed through the security admin portal (Microsoft Defender portal) or using this link: `https://security.microsoft.com/cloudapps`. In the Microsoft Security admin portal, you can access Microsoft Defender for Cloud Apps, as shown in the following screenshot:

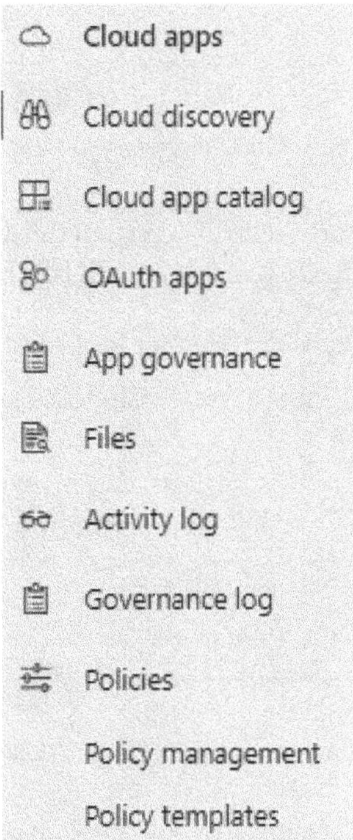

Figure 6.1 – Microsoft Defender for Cloud Apps portal

The default report can be found on the Microsoft Defender for Cloud Apps dashboard, where you can define different app categories through the **Apps**, **Users**, **IP Addresses**, **Traffic**, **Upload**, and **Transactions** sections:

Figure 6.2 – Cloud discovery in MDCA

In this part, you can create different reports, upload logs from third-party appliances, and create your own dashboard with specific reports. Create a snapshot with the following steps:

1. Click on **Cloud discovery** in Microsoft Defender for Cloud Apps.
2. Click on the **Actions** option and choose **Create Cloud Discovery snapshot report**:

Figure 6.3 – Cloud discovery snapshot report

3. In the following window, click **Next**:

Figure 6.4 – Create a new snapshot in MDCA

4. Give a report name and select your source for the report from the drop-down menu:

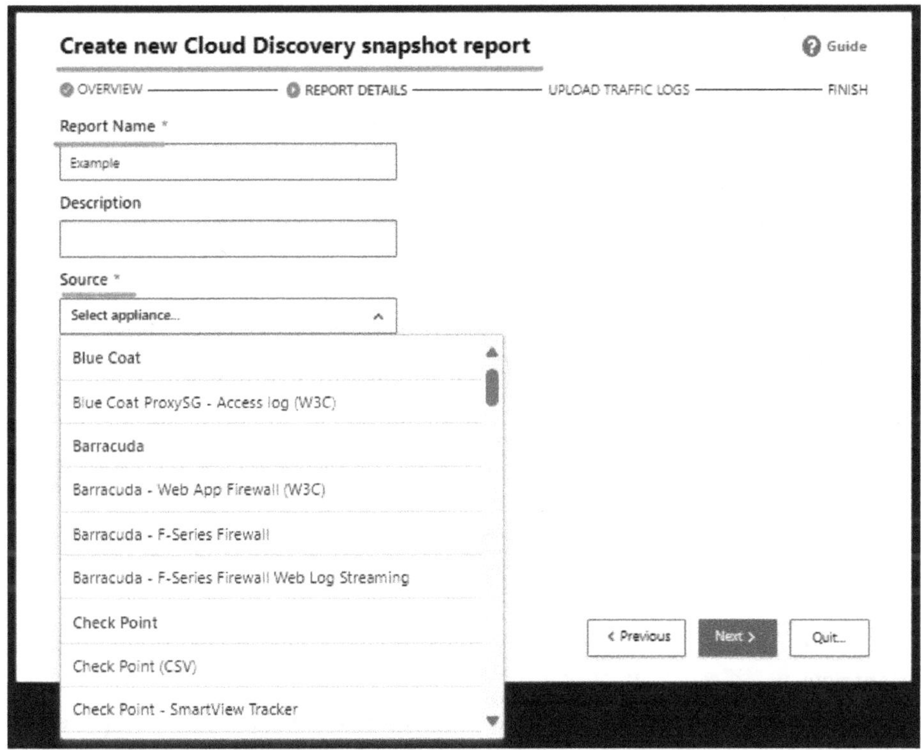

Figure 6.5 – Select source for snapshot report

Follow the instructions to verify your log format (FYI: Cisco Meraki – URLs log-in screenshot is an example):

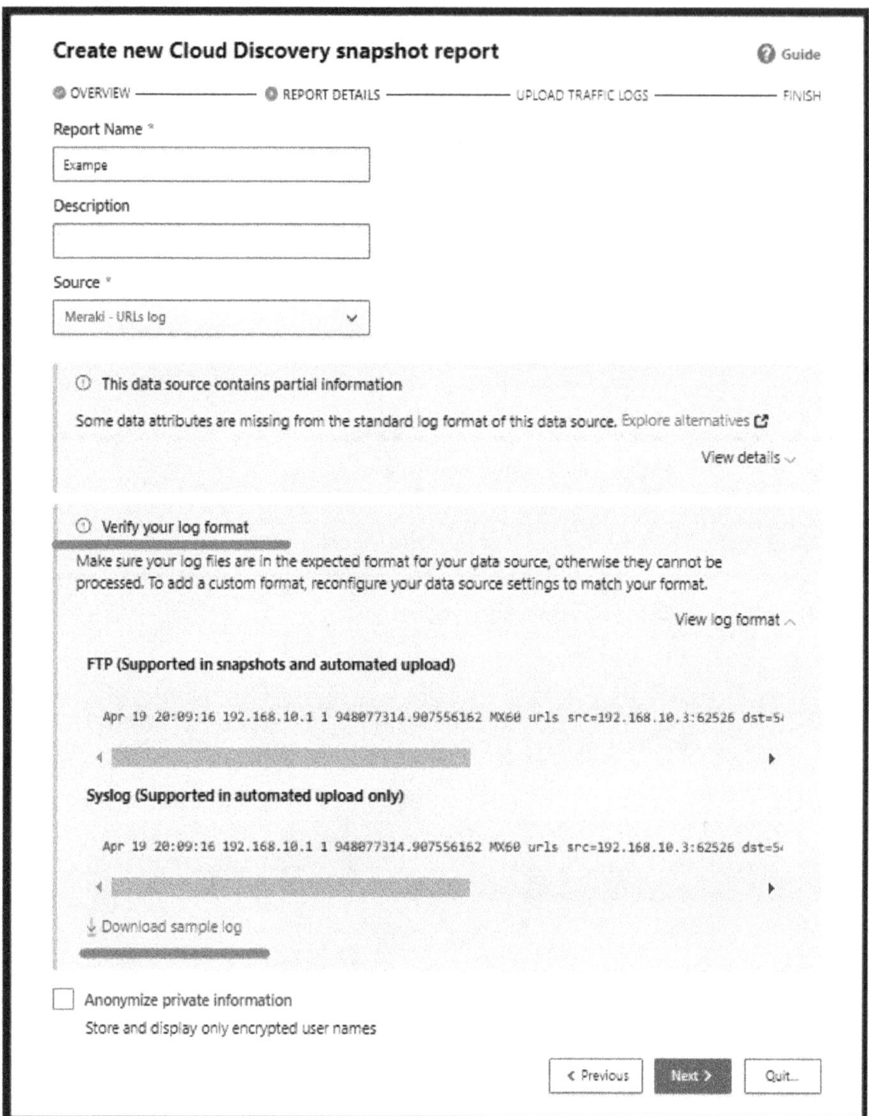

Figure 6.6 – Verify log format for snapshot report

Important note

If you don't know how to prepare logs for upload, use **Download sample log** (see the preceding screenshot) and correct your logs for upload to Microsoft Defender For Cloud Apps.

5. Click **Next** and upload traffic logs (up to 1 GB in size):

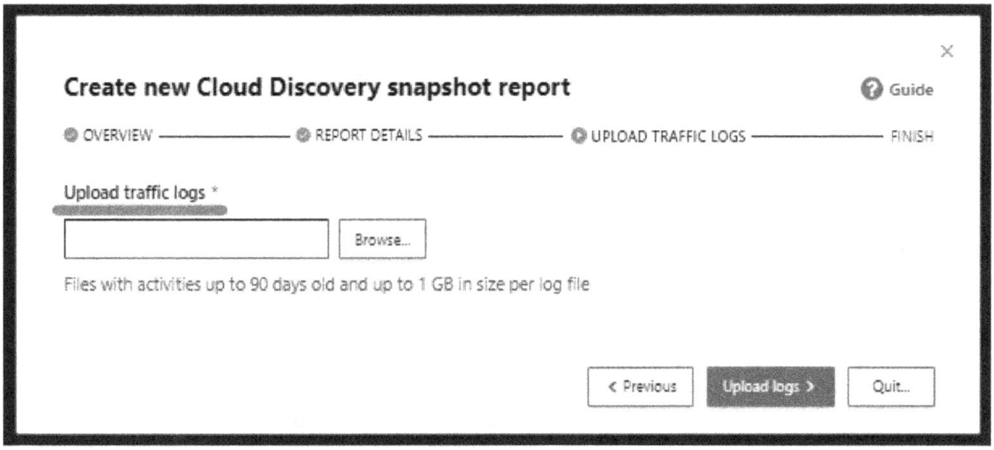

Figure 6.7 – Upload log file for snapshot report

6. Click **Finish** and check your reports.

Microsoft Defender for Cloud Apps supports a variety of third-party cloud-based applications and services, and it can collect logs from these services through the Cloud App Security data connector. Here are some examples of third-party logs that can be uploaded to Microsoft Defender for Cloud Apps:

- **Barracuda**: Microsoft Defender for Cloud Apps can collect logs from Barracuda, including login activity, report exports, and configuration changes
- **Check Point**: Microsoft Defender for Cloud Apps can collect logs from Check Point, including user activity, traffic, and sharing events
- **Dropbox**: Microsoft Defender for Cloud Apps can collect logs from Dropbox, including login activity, file uploads and downloads, and sharing events
- **Google Workspace**: Microsoft Defender for Cloud Apps can collect logs from various Google Workspace services, including Gmail, Google Drive, and Google Calendar
- **AWS**: Microsoft Defender for Cloud Apps can collect logs from various AWS services, including AWS CloudTrail, AWS Config, and Amazon S3
- **Cisco**: Microsoft Defender for Cloud Apps can collect logs from various Cisco appliances, including Cisco ASA Firewall, Cisco IronPort, Cisco Meraki, Cisco ASA FirePower, and so on
- **McAfee**: Microsoft Defender for Cloud Apps can collect logs from McAfee, including incident management events
- **Sophos**: Microsoft Defender for Cloud Apps can collect logs from different Sophos appliances such as Sophos SG, Sophos XG, and Sophos Cyberoam

Note that the specific logs that can be uploaded to Microsoft Defender for Cloud Apps may depend on the specific configuration of the third-party cloud-based applications and services that you are using. It is important to review the documentation for the Cloud App Security data connector and the specific third-party applications and services that you are using to ensure that you are sending the appropriate logs to Microsoft Defender for Cloud Apps.

Besides Cloud Discovery, through Microsoft Defender for Cloud Apps, you can find the Cloud app catalog. The Cloud app catalog in Microsoft Defender for Cloud Apps is a comprehensive database of cloud applications and services that have been analyzed and rated based on their security risks. The Cloud app catalog helps organizations gain visibility of the cloud apps and services being used within their environment and assess the risk associated with each app.

The Cloud app catalog includes information on thousands of cloud applications and services, including popular cloud services such as Microsoft Office 365, Salesforce, and Dropbox. For each cloud application and service, the Cloud app catalog provides a detailed security assessment that includes information on the following:

- **Data protection**: This includes an assessment of the data protection capabilities of the app or service, such as encryption, access controls, and data backup and recovery
- **Compliance**: The Cloud app catalog includes information on the compliance certifications and regulations that the app or service adheres to, such as GDPR, HIPAA, and PCI DSS
- **Security controls**: The Cloud app catalog assesses the security controls of the app or service, including authentication, authorization, and network security
- **Data usage and privacy**: This includes an assessment of the app or service's data usage policies and privacy practices

Using the Cloud app catalog, organizations can gain a better understanding of the security risks associated with the cloud apps and services being used within their environment. Organizations can also create policies and controls based on the risk level of each app or service, enabling them to better manage their security posture and reduce the risk of cyber threats.

In addition to the information on individual cloud applications and services, the Cloud app catalog also provides overall ratings for each app or service, based on their security risk level. These ratings can help organizations quickly assess the risk associated with each app or service and take appropriate action to manage that risk:

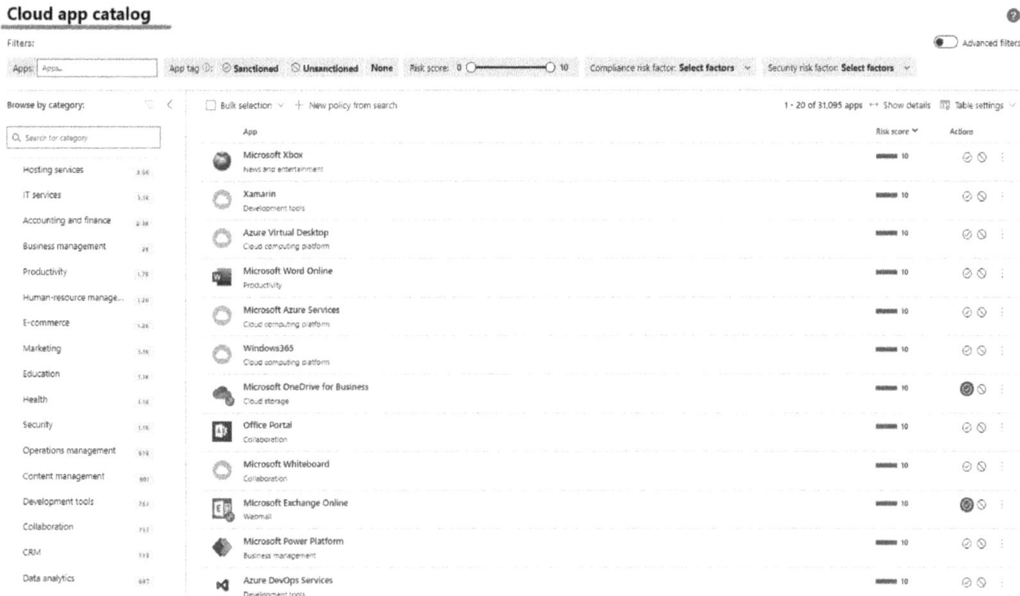

Figure 6.8 – Cloud App Catalog

Here are the steps to use the Microsoft Defender Cloud app catalog:

1. Log in to the Microsoft Defender for Cloud Apps portal using your Microsoft credentials.
2. Once logged in, click on the **Cloud app catalog** tab on the left-hand side of the screen.
3. You will be taken to the **Cloud app catalog** page where you can search for specific cloud apps and services by name or category.
4. To view the security assessment of a specific cloud app or service, click on the name of the app or service.
5. The Cloud app catalog will display a detailed security assessment that includes information on the data protection, compliance, security controls, and data usage and privacy of the app or service.
6. Based on the risk level associated with each app or service, organizations can create policies and controls to manage the risk.
7. Organizations can also use the overall rating provided by the Cloud app catalog to quickly assess the risk associated with each app or service and take appropriate action to manage that risk.

You can get more details and information about more than 31,000 apps if you click **Show details**. On the **Details** page, you will see all **GENERAL**, **SECURITY**, **COMPLIANCE**, and **LEGAL** information about the site. Following is an example for the Microsoft Xbox app (all green and a risk score of 10):

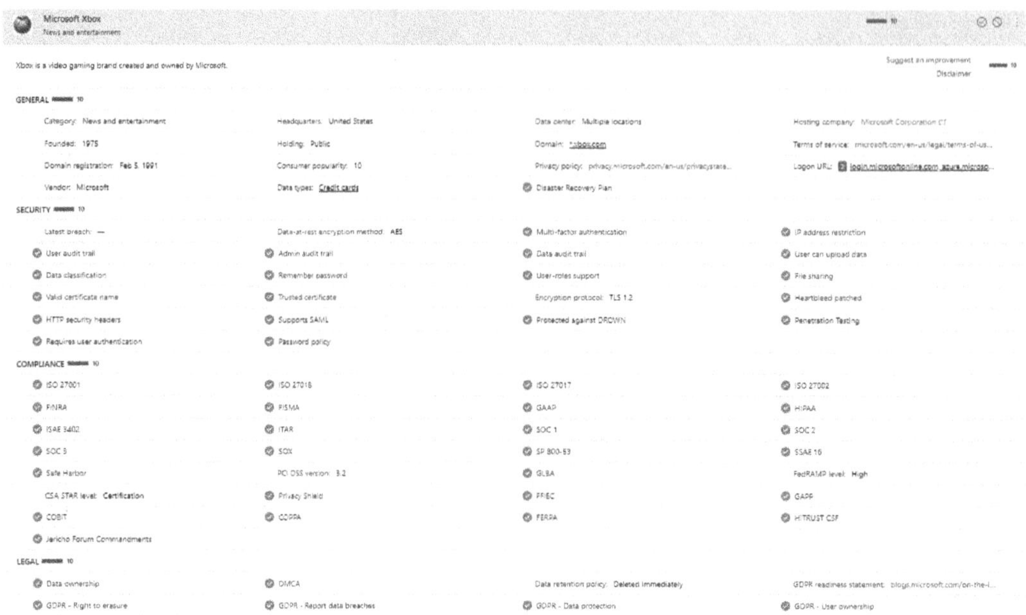

Figure 6.9 – Microsoft Xbox

Here is the one for the Dispatch app (with a risk score of 2):

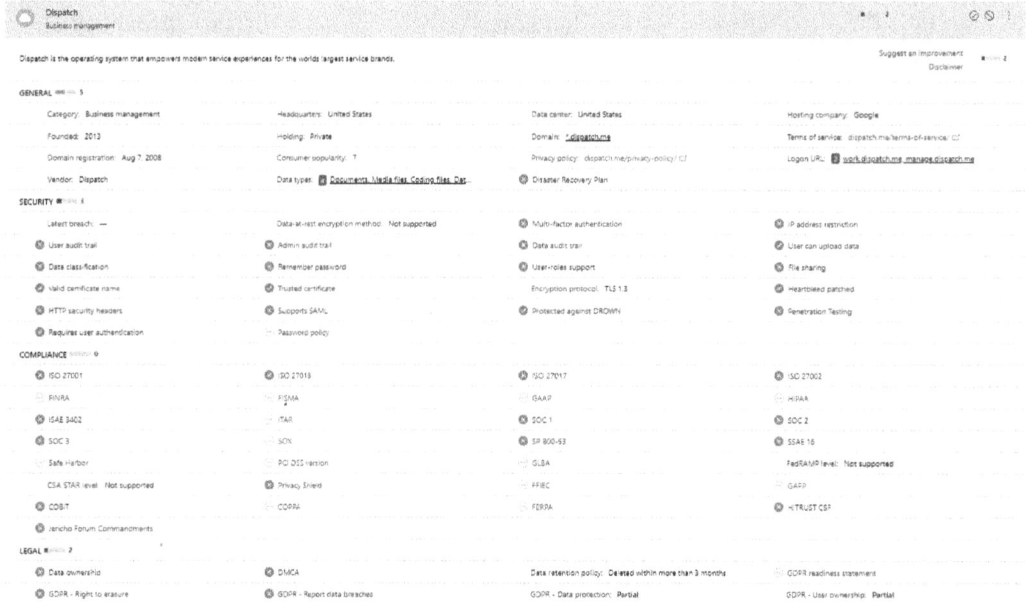

Figure 6.10 – Dispatch

For a better overview of newly discovered apps in your organization, use the **New policy from search** option.

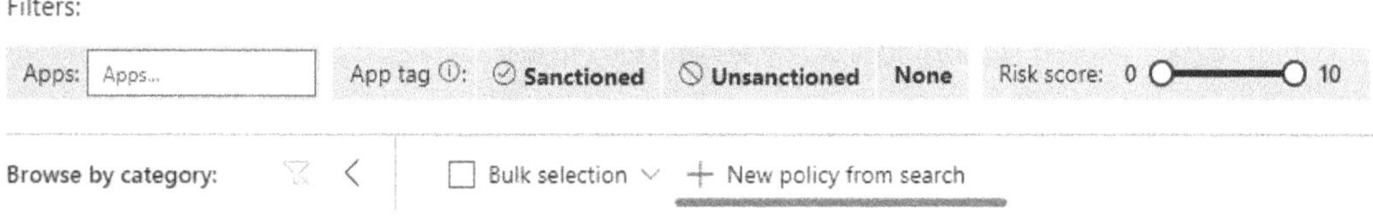

Figure 6.11 – Cloud app catalog

To create an app discovery policy in Cloud App Security, follow these steps:

1. Click on the **New policy from search** tab in the top menu bar.
2. Click on **Policy template** and select one of the options.

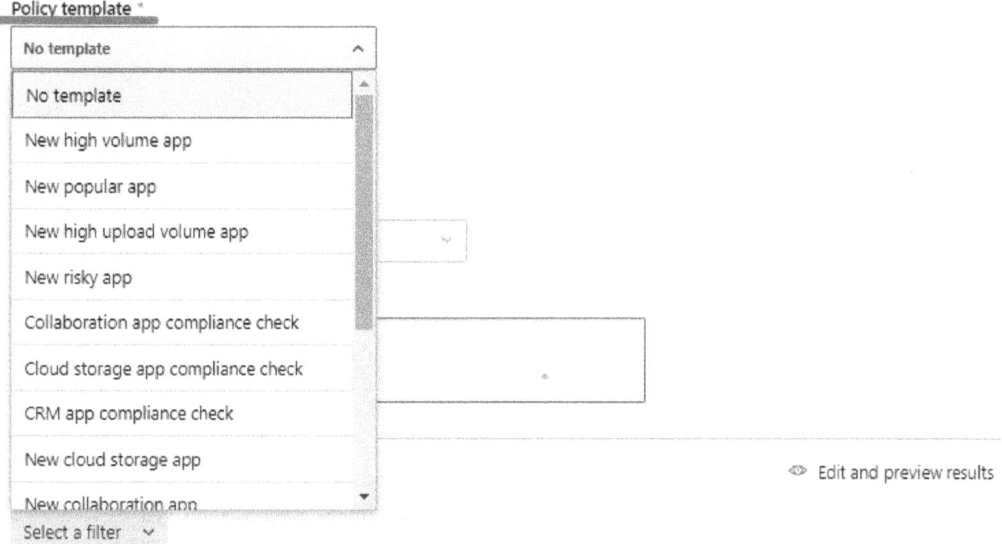

Figure 6.12 – Policy template for app discovery

3. Enter a name and description for the policy.

4. Set **Policy severity** and **Category**.

Figure 6.13 – Define severity for app discovery

5. Under **Apps matching all of the following**, select one of the filters from the drop-down menu or add more, if you need:

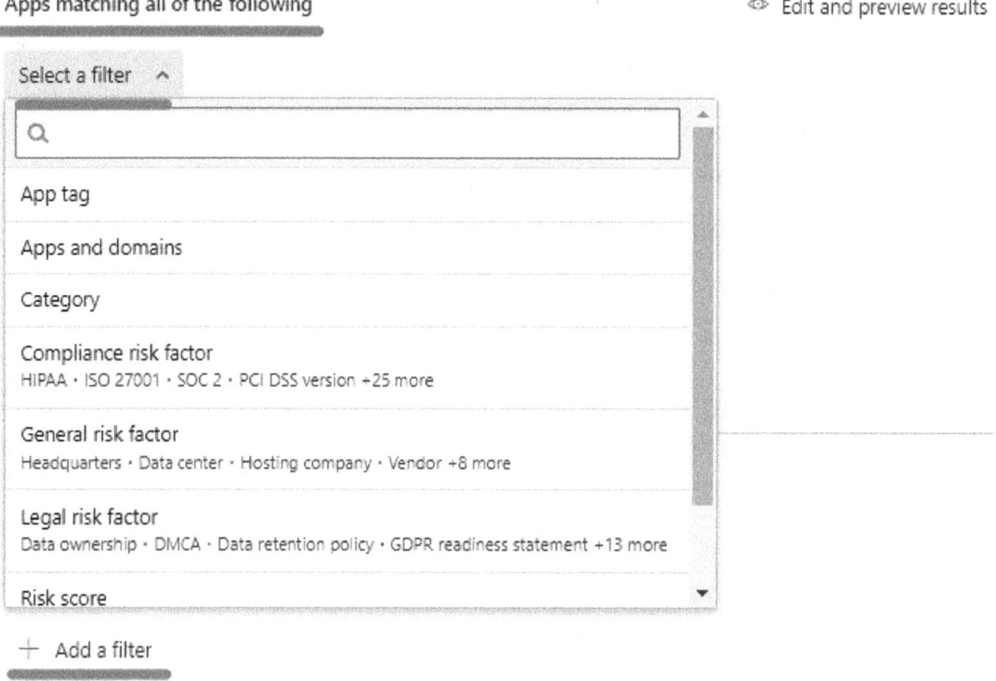

Figure 6.14 – App discovery filter

6. Under **App matching all of the following**, define the conditions under which the policy will trigger. For example, you could create a rule that triggers the policy if a user uploads sensitive data to a non-approved cloud app:

Figure 6.15 – Additional app discovery filter

7. Under **Alerts**, define the conditions under which the policy will create mail notifications, a daily alert limit per policy, and governance action. You can add a playbook in Power Automate (requires additional configuration in the Power Automate portal) if you want:

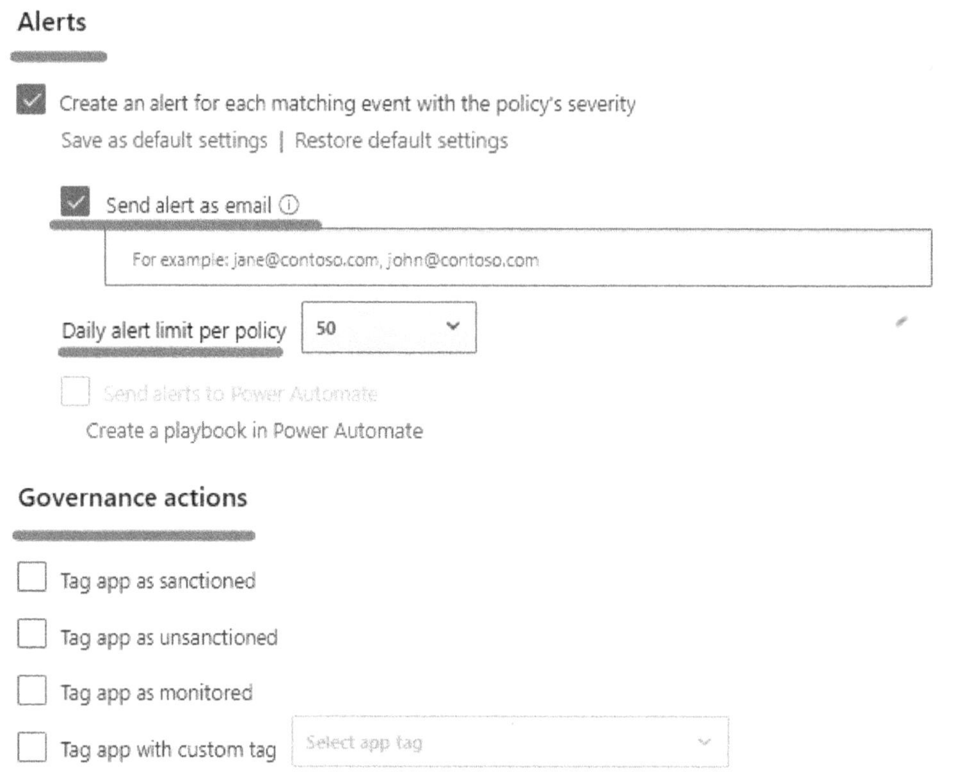

Figure 6.16 – Configure notifications for app discovery policy

8. Click **Create** to create the policy.

Once the policy is created, Cloud App Security will begin scanning your organization's cloud usage to identify any apps and services that match the criteria you specified. You can view the results of the app discovery policy in the Cloud App Security portal, under the **Discover** tab.

The Cloud app catalog is a powerful feature of Microsoft Defender for Cloud Apps that provides organizations with a comprehensive database of cloud applications and services, allowing them to better understand the security risks associated with their cloud environment and take appropriate action to manage those risks.

Managing OAuth applications with Microsoft Defender for Cloud Apps

Microsoft Defender for Cloud Apps allows you to manage OAuth apps for your organization. OAuth apps are third-party applications that access your organization's data using OAuth tokens. But what is an OAuth app?

OAuth (short for **Open Authorization**) is a standard protocol that allows users to grant third-party applications access to their resources without sharing their credentials. An OAuth app, also known as an OAuth client, is a third-party application that uses OAuth to access protected resources on behalf of the user. When a user grants an OAuth app access, the app receives an access token that allows it to access specific resources, such as data or services, without the user having to share their username and password. This access token is typically short-lived and can be revoked by the user at any time.

OAuth apps are commonly used by cloud services and web applications to access user data stored in other services, such as social media platforms or email providers. For example, a third-party email app may use OAuth to access a user's Gmail account, allowing the user to read and send emails from within the app without having to share their Gmail username and password with the app. OAuth provides a secure and standardized way for users to grant and revoke access to their resources, and for third-party apps to access those resources without compromising user credentials.

For a quick overview of OAuth apps by users, use options from the portal by selecting a username and a quick report will show you all the details about apps marked as approved or marked as banned:

Figure 6.17 – Manage OAuth apps

Here are the steps to manage OAuth apps in Microsoft Defender for Cloud Apps:

1. Click on **OAuth apps** in the Cloud Apps portal.

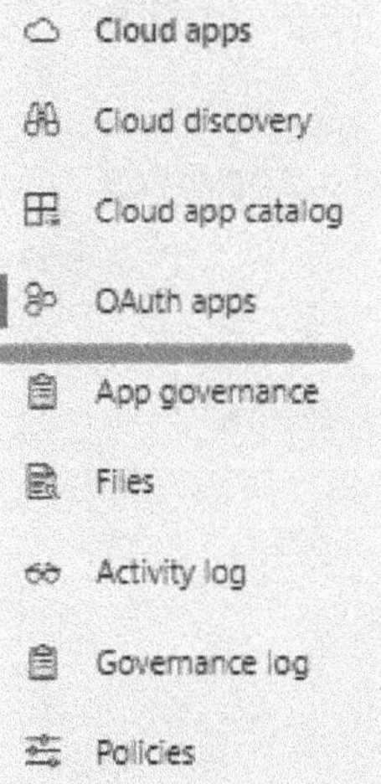

Figure 6.18 – OAuth apps in MDCA

2. Enable **Advanced filters** on the portal site.

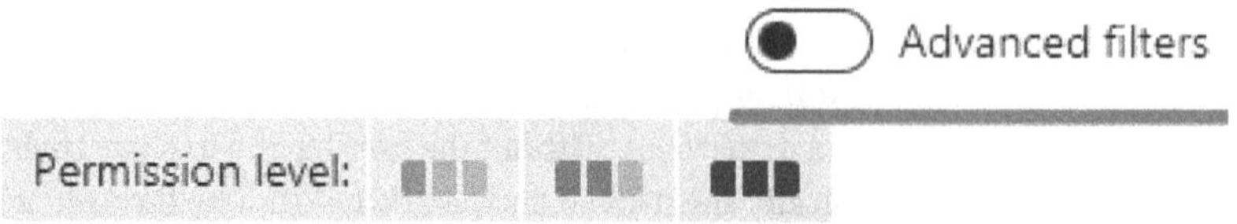

Figure 6.19 - Enabling Advanced filters

3. From **Queries**, create one of the predefined queries and add more filters if you need.

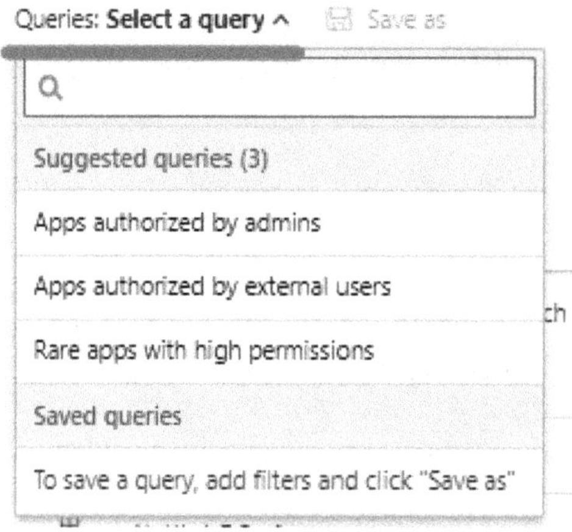

Figure 6.20 – Select a query

After selecting **Query** in **Manage OAuth apps**, click on **Select a filter** to specify your configuration preferences. Choose from filters such as **App**, **App state**, **Community use**, and others based on your query's requirements.

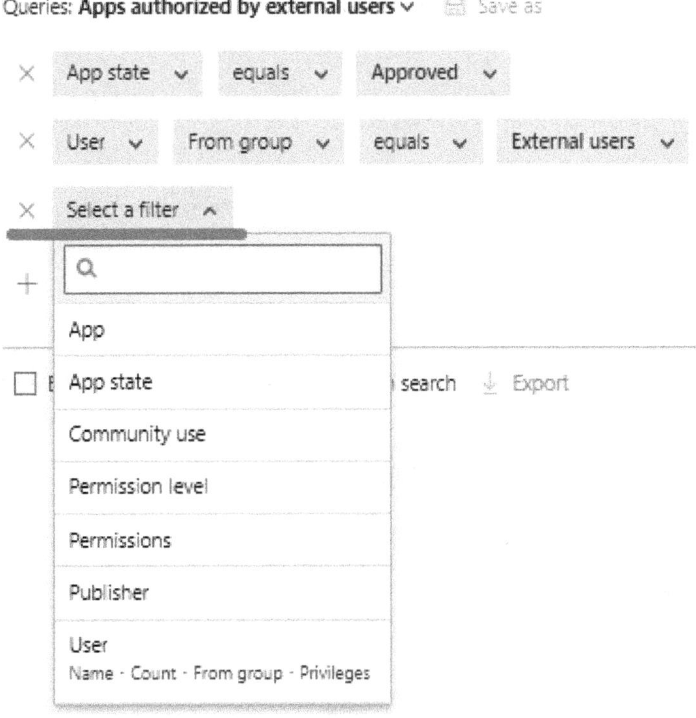

Figure 6.21 – Select filter for OAuth apps

1. Here, you can see a list of all the OAuth apps that have been granted access to your organization's data. You can filter the list by cloud app or by user.

   - To revoke access for an OAuth app, select the app from the list and click the **Revoke access** button. This will remove the OAuth token and prevent the app from accessing your organization's data.
   - To block an OAuth app, select the app from the list and click the **Block app** button. This will prevent the app from requesting new OAuth tokens and accessing your organization's data.
   - To allow an OAuth app, select the app from the list and click the **Allow app** button. This will enable the app to request new OAuth tokens and access your organization's data.

You can also create an OAuth app policy to automatically block or allow OAuth apps based on certain criteria. To do this, click on the **Policies** tab and select **OAuth app policy** from the **Add policy** dropdown. You can then define the criteria for the policy and choose whether to block or allow OAuth apps that match those criteria.

1. Click on **New policy from search:**

Figure 6.22 – Create new policy

2. Fill in the **Policy name** and **Description** fields and select the severity level from the **Policy severity** and **Category** menus:

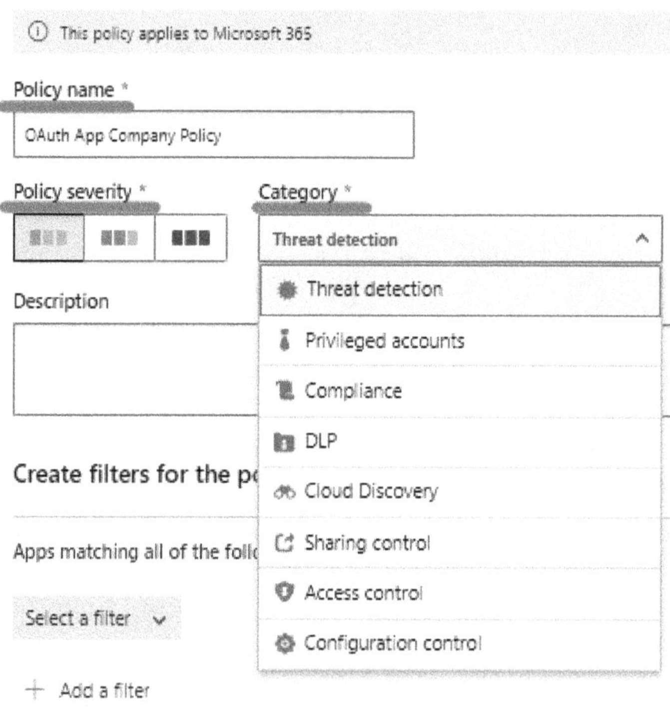

Figure 6.23 – Define category for new search

3. From **Create filters for the policy**, select **Filter** and add additional filters, if you need them:

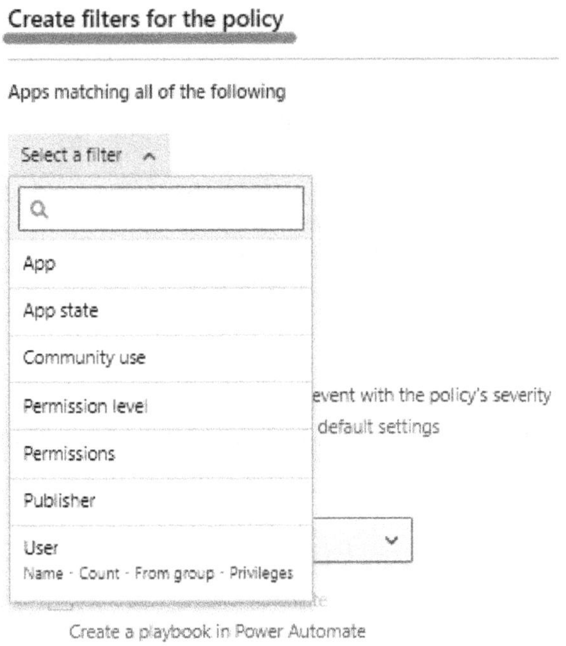

Create filters for the policy

Apps matching all of the following

Select a filter

App

App state

Community use

Permission level

Permissions

Publisher

User

Name · Count · From group · Privileges

event with the policy's severity

default settings

Create a playbook in Power Automate

Figure 6.24 – Define filter for new search policy

4. Define **Alerts** and **Governance actions**:

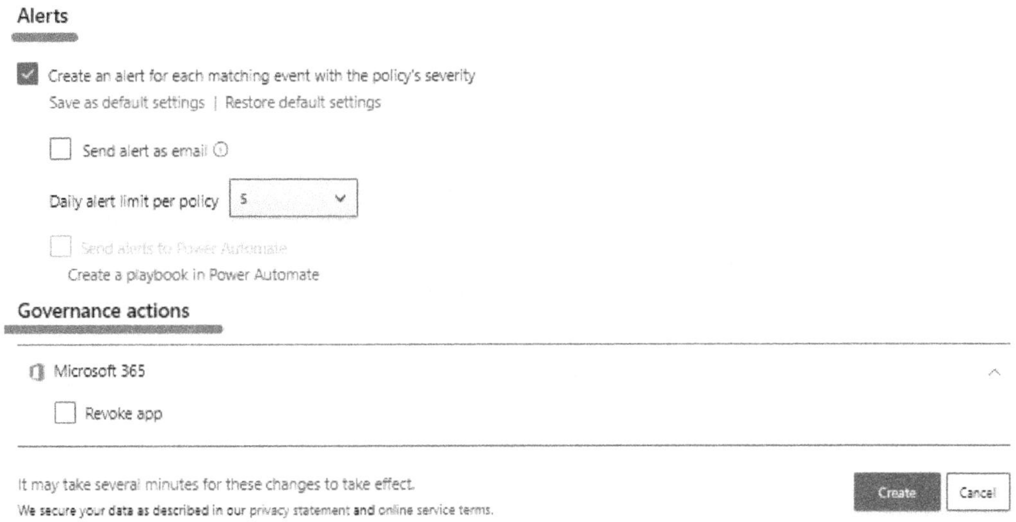

Alerts

Create an alert for each matching event with the policy's severity

Save as default settings | Restore default settings

Send alert as email

Daily alert limit per policy 5

Send alerts to Power Automate

Create a playbook in Power Automate

Governance actions

Microsoft 365

Revoke app

It may take several minutes for these changes to take effect.

We secure your data as described in our privacy statement and online service terms.

Create Cancel

Figure 6.25 – Configure alerts

5. Click **Create**.

> **Important note**
>
> The **Create a playbook in Power Automate** option requires additional configuration in the Power Automate portal. Microsoft Power Automate is a cloud-based service that allows users to create workflows and automate repetitive tasks across different applications and services. Formerly known as Microsoft Flow, Power Automate is part of the Microsoft Power Platform and is available as a standalone service or as part of Microsoft Office 365 and Dynamics 365. With Power Automate, users can create custom workflows that automate tasks such as data entry, file management, notifications, and approvals. Workflows can be triggered by various events, such as the creation of a new file or record, the receipt of an email, or a scheduled time.

By managing OAuth apps in Microsoft Defender for Cloud Apps, you can help ensure that only trusted and authorized applications have access to your organization's data. You can get all the details and permissions for any OAuth app by simply clicking on the app in the **Manage OAuth apps** portal:

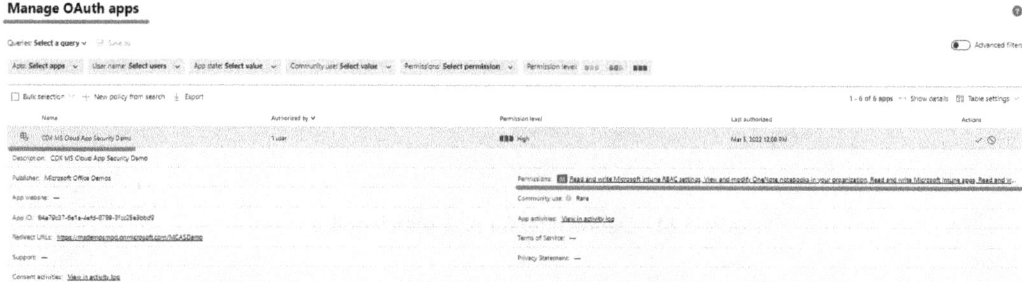

Figure 6.26 – Manage OAuth apps

Managing files in Microsoft Defender for Cloud Apps

Microsoft Defender for Cloud Apps allows organizations to provide protection and visibility for cloud-based applications and services. It allows you to manage and monitor file activities in your cloud applications, including OneDrive, SharePoint, Exchange Online, and Teams. You can simply create different policies for different purposes and manage activity for all your files stored online in a Microsoft 365 environment. You can create a policy to manage files in Microsoft Defender for Cloud Apps by following these steps:

1. Sign in to the Microsoft Defender Security Center (`https://securitycenter.windows.com/`).
2. In the left-hand pane, click on **Cloud apps** and then click on **Files**:

Figure 6.27 – Managing files in MDCA

3. On the **Files** management page, click on **Select a query** to view the list of predefined queries. Use **Advanced filters** on the right side if you need more options for search and selection:

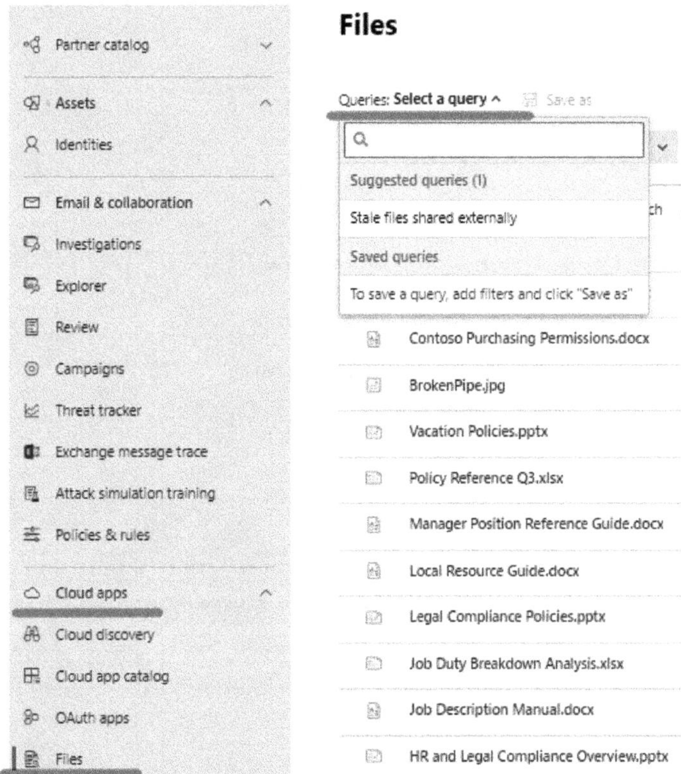

Figure 6.28 – Select query for files

4. To create a new file policy, click on **+ New policy from search**:

Figure 6.29 – Create new policy from search

5. In the **Create file policy** window, specify the policy name and select a policy template (selecting **No template** is also a possible option), policy name, and set **Policy severity** and **Category** for the policy:

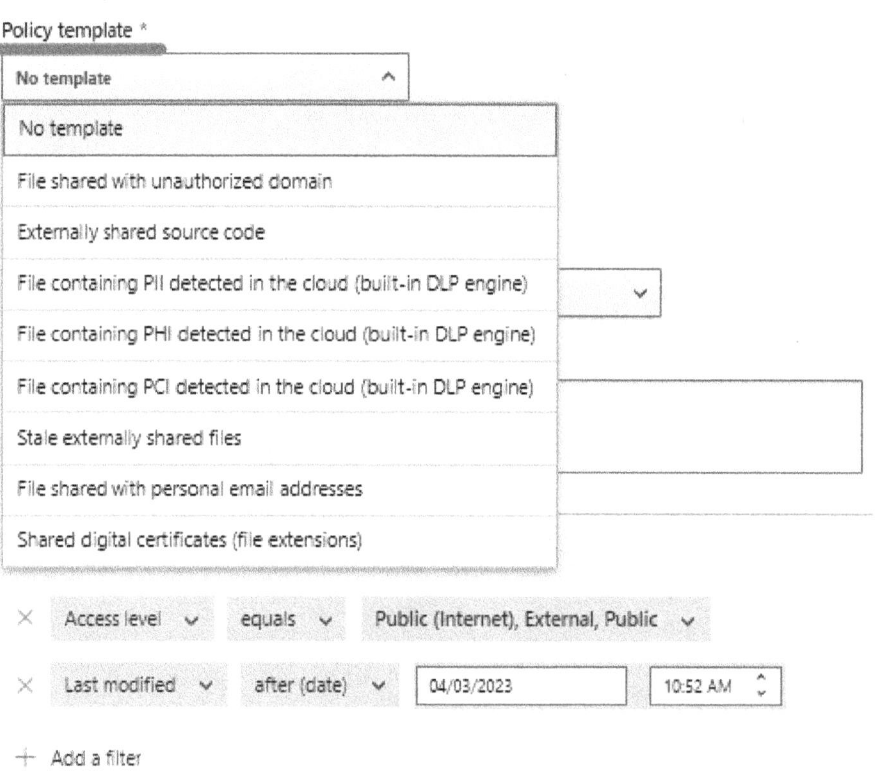

Figure 6.30 – File policy template

6. **Once you've chosen a template for a new file policy, proceed to specify the severity and category:**

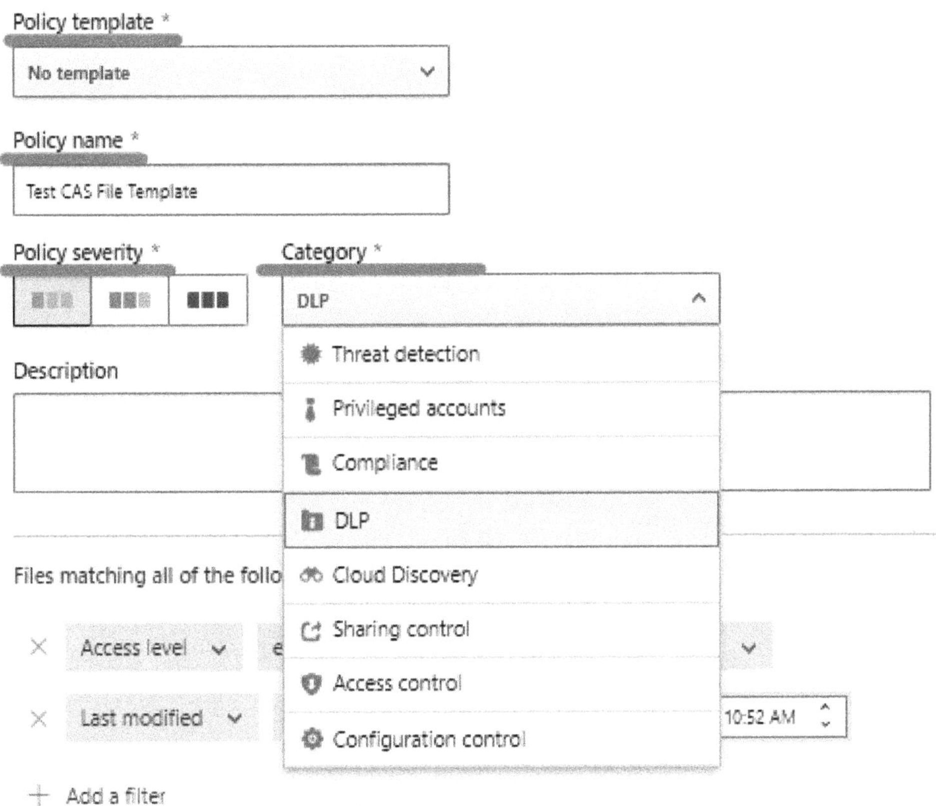

Figure 6.31 – Define severity and category

7. In the **Files matching all of the following** tab, define the conditions for the policy, such as file type, filename, and file location (the following example presents a file policy for all public, shared files):

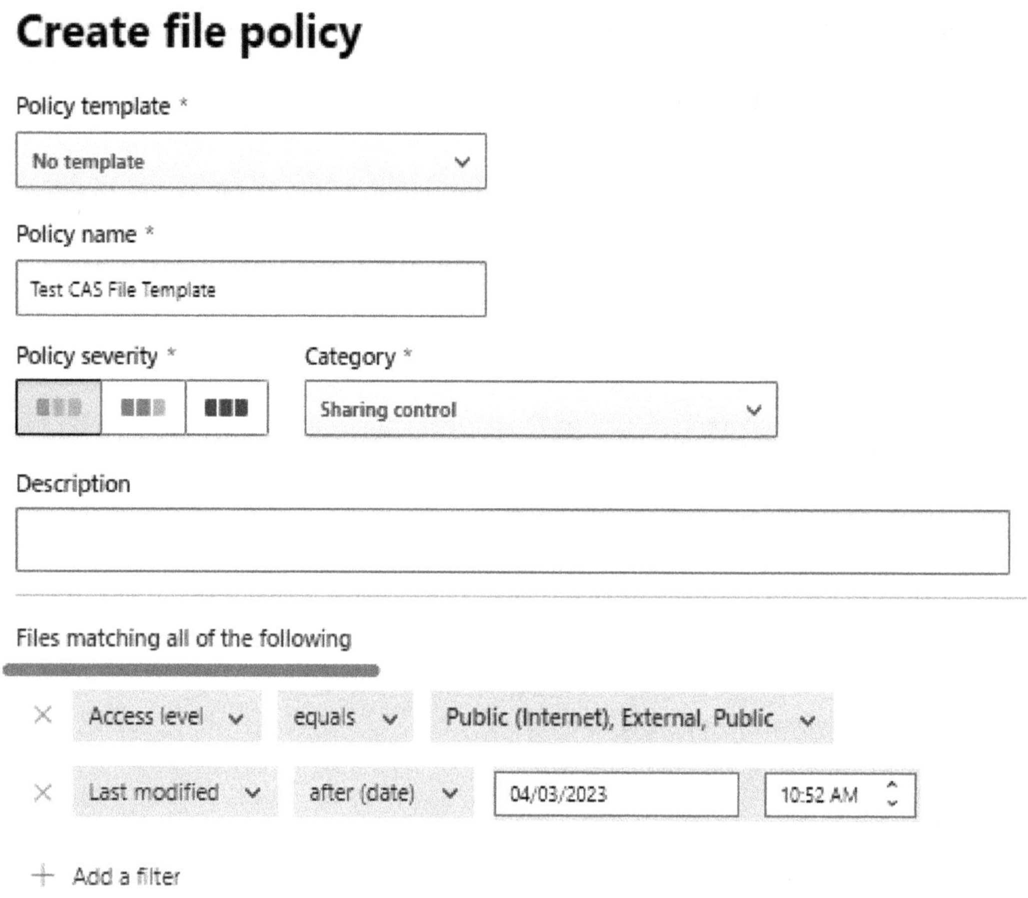

Figure 6.32 – Define additional filters

8. In the **Apply to** tab, specify the actions to be taken when the policy conditions are met, such as alerting or blocking access to the file. Select the files, user groups, and inspection method. Select **Create an alert for each matching file**:

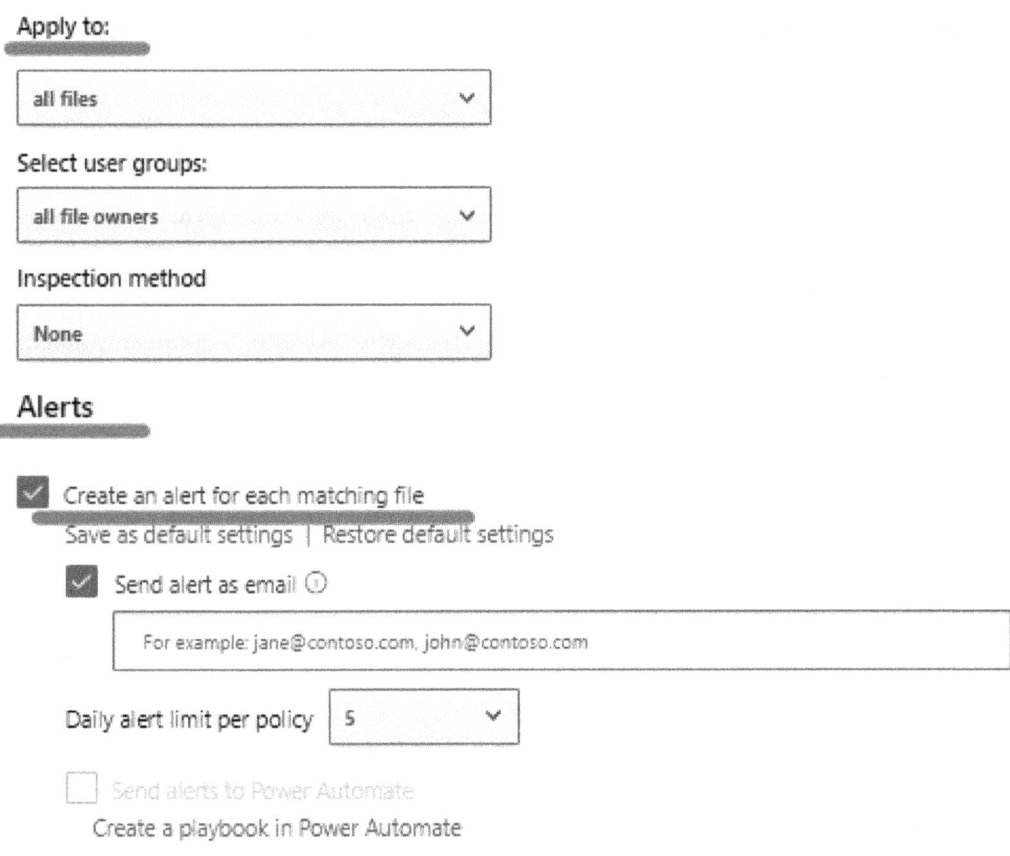

Figure 6.33 – Configure alerts and notifications

9. Save the policy by clicking on **Create**.

Important note

The created policy will be visible in the **Policy Management** section, not in the **Files** portal. The **Policy Management** portal is located under the **Policies** tab in the Cloud Apps portal.

To view the file activity logs, click on **Investigate** in the left-hand pane and then select **Logs**. On the **Logs** page, select the cloud app and the type of log you want to view, such as **File activity** or **File policy matches**.

Managing the activity log in Microsoft Defender for Cloud Apps

If you are already creating different policies for managing files in Microsoft Defender for Cloud Apps, now you can create a policy for monitoring different activities on selected files. Microsoft Defender for Cloud Apps provides an activity log that allows you to monitor and review events and activities performed in your cloud environment. Here are the steps to manage the activity log in Microsoft Defender for Cloud Apps:

1. Open the Microsoft Defender for Cloud Apps portal (the portal is located in the Security Admin Center) and sign in with your credentials.
2. In the left navigation menu, select **Activity log**.

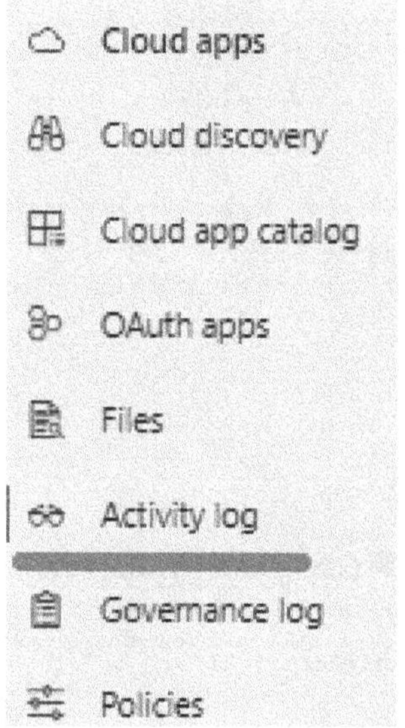

Figure 6.34 – Activity log in MDCA

3. On the **Activity log** page, you can filter the events based on date, severity, category, or service. Click on **Select a query** to choose one of the options for a quick overview.

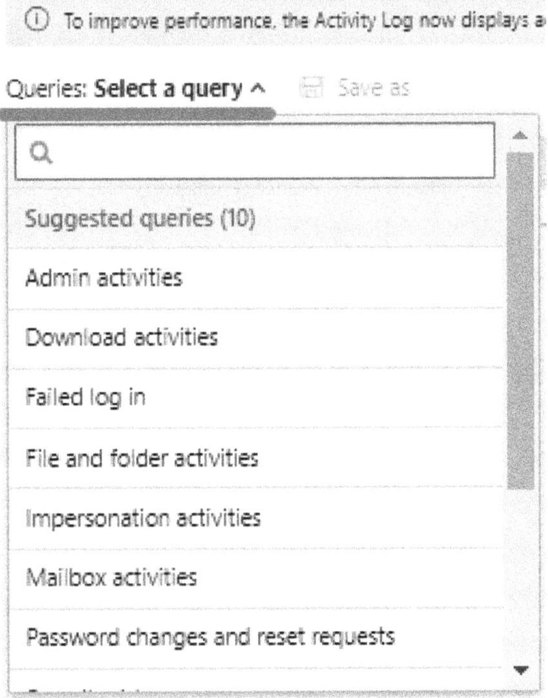

Figure 6.35 – Select a query

4. To customize the columns displayed in the activity log, select **Columns** and choose the fields you want to see:

Figure 6.36 – Define filters for activity report

> **Important note**
>
> If you want to investigate more than 15 days back, click on the top-right **Investigate 6 months back** option.

Figure 6.37 – Activity log report

5. You can also create an alert based on specific conditions by selecting + **New policy from search**.
6. Select one of the listed templates in the **Policy template** menu:

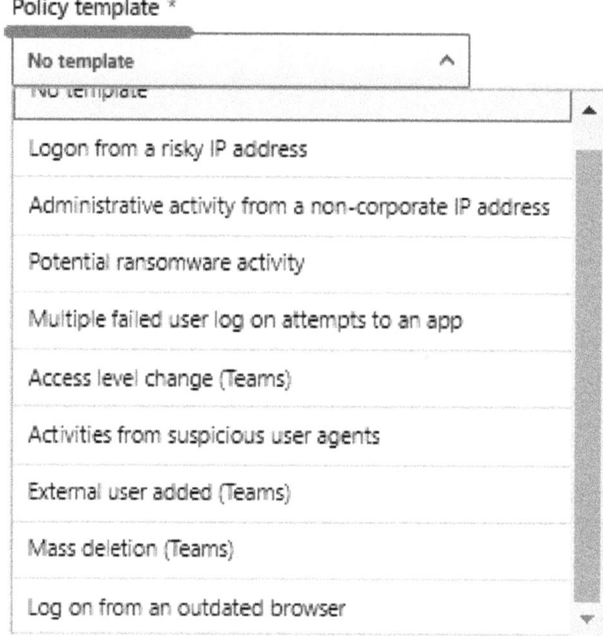

Figure 6.38 – Activity policy template

7. Give the policy a name, define **Policy severity**, and select **Category** (the following screenshot is an example with the selected **Potential ransomware activity** template):

Create activity policy
Policy template *
Potential ransomware activity
Policy name *
Potential ransomware activity
Policy severity *
Category *
Threat detection
Description
Alert when a user uploads files to
Threat detection
Privileged accounts
Compliance
DLP
Cloud Discovery
Sharing control
Access control
Configuration control
Create filters for the p
Act on:
Single activity
Every activity that matche
Repeated activity:
Repeated activity by a sin

Figure 6.39 – Define severity and category

> **Important note**
>
> If you select **Potential ransomware activity** for **Policy template**, leave all pre-defined **Activities matching all of the following** options as is. You can provide additional extensions, only if they are not already there. There are more than 80 predefined extensions added.

8. After defining the severity and category for a new activity report, you will need to configure the activities.

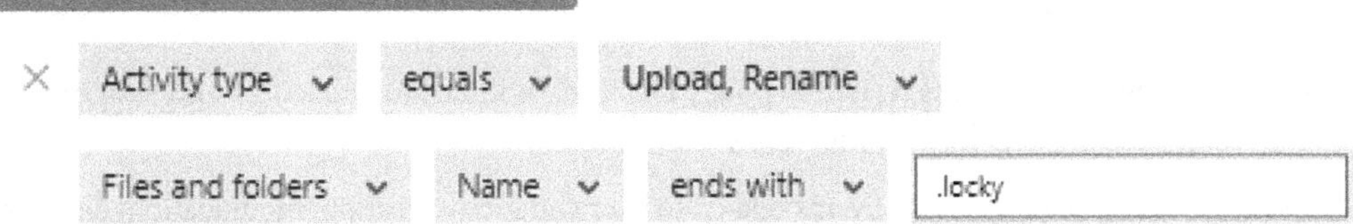

Figure 6.40 – Define activities

9. In **Alerts**, select the **Send alert as email** box and add an email address where notifications for the selected policy will be sent:

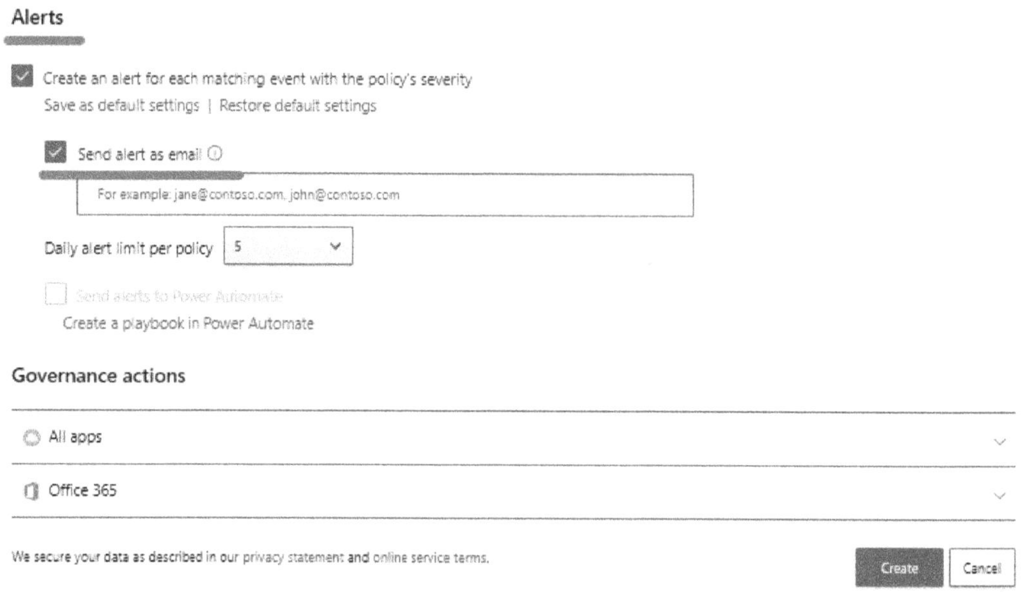

Alerts

Create an alert for each matching event with the policy's severity

Save as default settings | Restore default settings

Send alert as email

For example: jane@contoso.com, john@contoso.com

Daily alert limit per policy 5

Send alerts to Power Automate

Create a playbook in Power Automate

Governance actions

All apps

Office 365

We secure your data as described in our privacy statement and online service terms.

Create Cancel

Figure 6.41 – Define alerts and notifications

By managing the activity log in Microsoft Defender for Cloud Apps, you can monitor and review the events and activities in your cloud environment and take appropriate actions to prevent security incidents.

Governance log

The governance log in Microsoft Defender for Cloud Apps is a feature that enables administrators to track all administrative activities performed in the Defender for Cloud Apps portal. The governance log records events related to policy configurations, user and group management, and other administrative tasks, providing a detailed audit trail of all the changes made in the portal. This log is an essential component of a comprehensive cloud app security strategy, allowing organizations to monitor and investigate administrative activities in the portal and detect any suspicious or unauthorized activities.

The governance log captures various types of events related to the administration of Defender for Cloud Apps, including the following:

- **Policy management**: Events related to policy creation, modification, deletion, and assignment, including changes to policy settings and configurations
- **User and group management**: Events related to user and group creation, modification, deletion, and assignment, including changes to user and group permissions and access levels

- **Role management**: Events related to role creation, modification, deletion, and assignment, including changes to role permissions and access levels
- **Configuration changes**: Events related to changes made to the Defender for Cloud Apps portal configuration, including changes to notifications, alerts, and other settings

The governance log records details such as the user who performed the action, the time and date when the action was performed, and the outcome of the action. The log also captures the IP address and the location of the user who performed the action, allowing administrators to track the activities of users from different geographical locations.

The governance log can be accessed and viewed by administrators who have been granted the appropriate permissions in the Defender for Cloud Apps portal. The log can be searched and filtered based on various criteria, such as date range, username, and event type, making it easier for administrators to find the information they need. The log can also be exported to a CSV file, allowing administrators to perform further analysis and reporting:

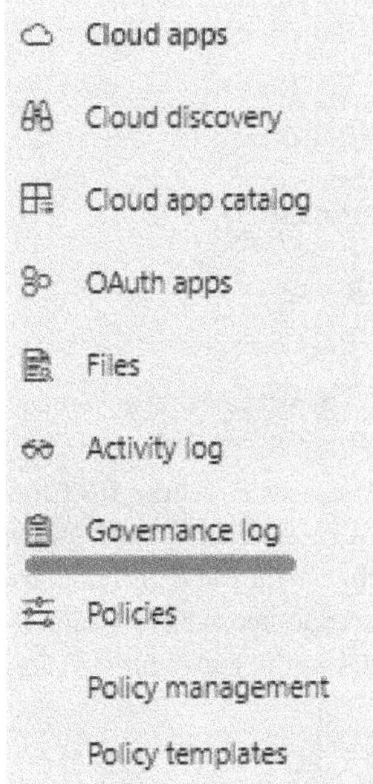

Figure 6.42 – Governance log portal

You can find more details by selecting **Action type** under **Filters**. There are over 60 predefined action types that you can use for an overview:

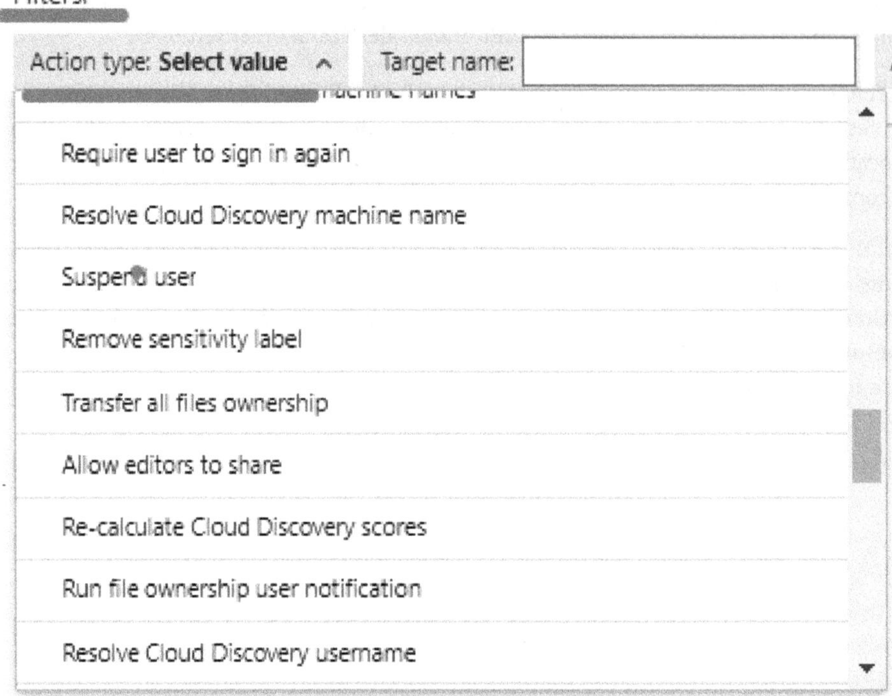

Figure 6.43 – Select value for governance log

In summary, the governance log in Microsoft Defender for Cloud Apps provides a detailed audit trail of all administrative activities performed in the portal, allowing organizations to monitor and investigate administrative activities in the portal and detect any suspicious or unauthorized activities. The log is an essential component of a comprehensive cloud app security strategy, providing visibility and control over administrative activities in the Defender for Cloud Apps portal.

Microsoft Defender for Cloud Apps policies

Microsoft Defender for Cloud Apps provides a comprehensive set of preconfigured policies to help organizations secure their Microsoft cloud environment. Policies are a set of rules and configurations that define how Microsoft Defender for Cloud Apps works and what actions it takes when it detects a security threat or vulnerability. Keep in mind that Microsoft Entra ID protection policies have been removed from the Defender for Cloud Apps policy list.

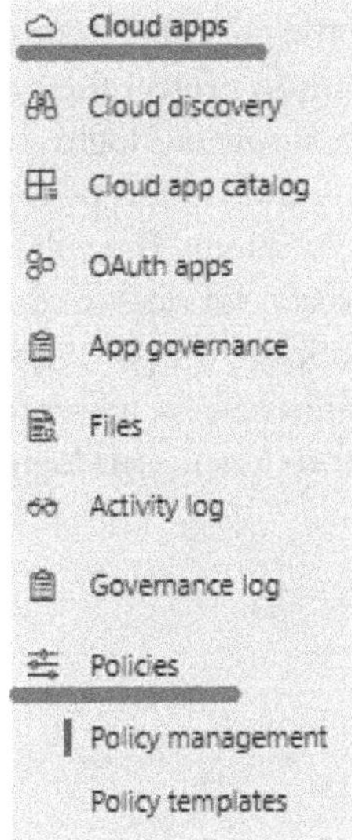

Figure 6.44 – MDCA policies

Microsoft Defender for Cloud Apps provides a wide range of preconfigured policies that organizations can use to secure their Microsoft cloud environment. The best policies to use with Microsoft Defender for Cloud Apps may vary depending on the specific needs and security requirements of an organization. Here is a small selection of predefined Microsoft Defender for Cloud Apps policies that you can use:

- **Suspicious inbox forwarding**: The **Suspicious inbox forwarding** policy is a security control feature in Microsoft Defender for Cloud Apps that helps organizations prevent unauthorized forwarding of emails from their Exchange Online environment to external email addresses. This policy can help protect sensitive information from being accidentally or intentionally forwarded to unauthorized recipients, including attackers. The policy works by monitoring emails that are forwarded from Exchange Online mailboxes and comparing them to predefined criteria. If an email meets the criteria for suspicious forwarding behavior, the policy will trigger an alert and take action to prevent further forwarding of the email.

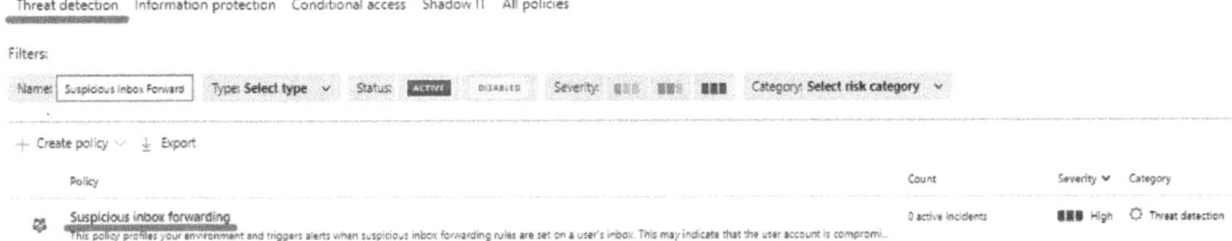

Figure 6.45 – Threat detection policy

- **Impossible travel**: The **Impossible travel** policy is a security control feature in Microsoft Defender for Cloud Apps that helps organizations protect their cloud-based data from unauthorized access. This policy detects and alerts suspicious login attempts that appear to have originated from multiple geographic locations within a short period, making it physically impossible for a user to have traveled between the locations. The policy works by analyzing login data from Microsoft Entra ID and other Microsoft services to identify patterns that suggest a possible breach or unauthorized access. Specifically, the policy compares the location and time of login attempts to determine whether it is possible for a user to have traveled between the locations in the time frame. If the policy detects suspicious login activity that meets this criterion, it generates an alert.

Figure 6.46 – Impossible travel policy

- **Unusual file deletion activity (by user)**: The **Unusual file deletion activity (by user)** policy is a security control feature in Microsoft Defender for Cloud Apps that helps organizations detect and respond to suspicious activity related to file deletion in their cloud environment. This policy is designed to detect when a user deletes a large number of files within a short period of time, which could indicate malicious activity such as data theft or destruction. The policy works by monitoring file activity in cloud storage services such as OneDrive for Business and SharePoint Online. When a user deletes a large number of files within a short period of time, the policy triggers an alert and takes action to prevent further deletion of files. Additionally, create a retention policy for all files in OneDrive for Business and SharePoint and provide even more security over files in your organization.

Figure 6.47 – Unusual file detection activity policy

- **Multiple failed login attempts**: The **Multiple failed login attempts** policy in Microsoft Defender for Cloud Apps is a security feature designed to protect against brute-force attacks on user accounts. This policy is used to detect when an attacker is trying to gain access to an account by repeatedly trying different passwords or login credentials. The policy works by monitoring login attempts to a user account in the cloud app and counting the number of failed attempts within a specified time period. If the number of failed attempts exceeds the threshold set in the policy, the account is locked out or flagged for further investigation. The policy is designed to be flexible, allowing administrators to set the threshold for failed login attempts and the duration of the time period during which login attempts are monitored. Administrators can also specify whether they want the account to be locked out or flagged for further investigation when the threshold is exceeded.

Figure 6.48 – Multiple failed login attempts policy

- **Unusual file share activity (by user)**: The **Unusual file share activity (by user)** policy in Microsoft Defender for Cloud Apps is a security feature that helps protect against data exfiltration and insider threats. This policy is designed to detect when a user is accessing and sharing files in a way that is unusual or outside of their normal behavior patterns. The policy works by monitoring user activity within a file share and comparing it to their historical behavior. If the user's activity is outside of their normal behavior patterns, the policy will flag the activity as unusual and notify administrators. For example, if a user typically accesses files during regular business hours, but suddenly begins accessing files in the middle of the night, the policy may flag this activity as unusual and alert the administrator. Similarly, if a user who typically only accesses a few files suddenly begins accessing a large number of files, this activity may also be flagged as unusual. Administrators can configure the policy to specify the threshold for what is considered unusual activity and determine the appropriate response, such as alerting or blocking the user's access to the file share.

Figure 6.49 – Unusual file share activity policy

- **Activity from infrequent country**: The **Activity from infrequent country** policy in Microsoft Defender for Cloud Apps is a security feature that helps organizations protect their data from potential threats originating from unfamiliar or risky locations. The policy is designed to detect when a user account logs in to a cloud application from a location that is infrequent or unusual, based on their past login history. The policy works by analyzing the location information associated with a user's login attempts to a cloud app and comparing it to their historical login patterns. If the location is deemed to be infrequent or unfamiliar, based on the user's past login history, the policy will flag the activity as potentially suspicious and notify administrators. For example, if a user has historically only logged in from the United States, but suddenly logs in from a location in a country where the organization has no business interests, the policy may flag this activity as potentially suspicious. Administrators can configure the policy to set the threshold for what is considered an infrequent location and determine the appropriate response, such as alerting or blocking the user's access to the cloud app.

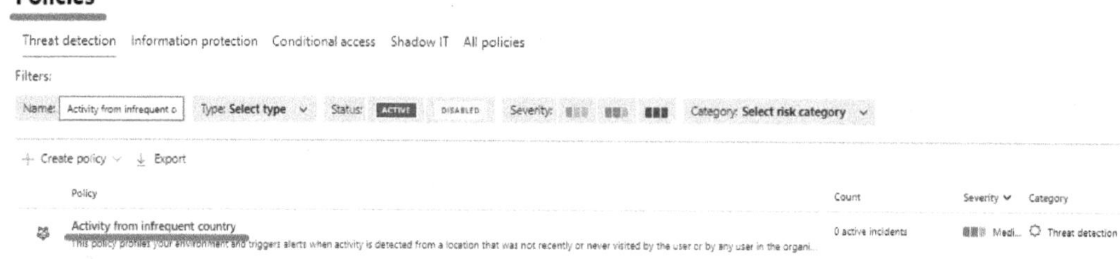

Figure 6.50 – Activity from infrequent country policy

These policies are just a few examples of the many preconfigured policies that Microsoft Defender for Cloud Apps offers. Organizations can choose which policies to enable or disable based on their specific security needs and requirements.

In the end, working with Microsoft Defender for Cloud Apps policies involves creating and configuring policies to secure your cloud environment, assigning policies to specific applications or services, and monitoring the policy status to ensure compliance. By following these steps, organizations can effectively use Microsoft Defender for Cloud Apps policies to secure their Microsoft cloud environment and protect against cyber threats.

Summary

In today's cloud-centric world, securing cloud applications and services has become a top priority for organizations. Microsoft Defender for Cloud Apps is a cloud-native security solution that can help organizations secure their Microsoft cloud environments against various cyber threats. It provides advanced security features, such as real-time protection, vulnerability assessments, and compliance management, which can significantly enhance an organization's security posture.

Even though Microsoft Defender for Cloud Apps is a cloud-native security solution that helps organizations secure their cloud applications and services against various cyber threats, it is very good to know the limitations of this service. Microsoft Defender for Cloud Apps provides protection for Microsoft cloud applications and services as well as different third-party applications that are widely used by organizations. Organizations should carefully evaluate their security needs and consider the limitations of Microsoft Defender for Cloud Apps before implementing it as their cloud security solution.

In summary, Microsoft Defender for Cloud Apps is a valuable tool for organizations looking to secure their Microsoft cloud environment SaaS applications. With its advanced threat protection, risk assessment, and compliance management capabilities, it can help organizations reduce their security risks and protect against cyber threats. Nevertheless, organizations should consider its limitations and weigh them against their specific security requirements before deploying Microsoft Defender for Cloud Apps.

7

Microsoft Defender Vulnerability Management

In an era where our daily lives are intricately intertwined with the digital realm, safeguarding sensitive data and critical systems has never been more crucial. Enter **Microsoft Defender Vulnerability Management**—a cybersecurity solution that's not just smart but also surprisingly user-friendly. Developed by the tech giant Microsoft Corporation, it's like your organization's digital guardian, protecting you from the ever-shifting landscape of cyber threats.

Picture this: a world where everything from your personal information to your business's sensitive data is just a click away from potential hackers and digital mischief-makers. In such a world, robust cybersecurity isn't just a choice; it's a necessity, and that's precisely where Microsoft Defender Vulnerability Management takes center stage. This powerful tool is more than just lines of code and algorithms. It's like the trusty knight guarding the kingdom's gates, ensuring that your digital assets remain safe and sound. Its mission is crystal clear: to identify, assess, and rectify vulnerabilities within your organization's IT infrastructure. Just like a diligent security team, it tirelessly scans, evaluates, and takes action to patch up potential weak spots, making sure your defenses are rock-solid.

But Microsoft Defender Vulnerability Management doesn't stop there; it's also your trusty counselor in the realm of modern cybersecurity. It doesn't just shield you from danger; it educates you about it. In this introduction, we're going to delve into the heart of this cybersecurity champion, uncovering the remarkable features and benefits that make it your steadfast ally in the ever-evolving battle against digital threats. So, let's embark on this journey together and illuminate the path to a safer, more secure digital world with Microsoft Defender Vulnerability Management.

In this chapter, we are going to cover the following main topics:

- Getting started with Microsoft Defender Vulnerability Management
- Recommendations and remediation
- Inventories and weaknesses

Getting started with Microsoft Defender Vulnerability Management

In the ever-evolving landscape of cybersecurity, organizations need reliable tools to help them identify and address vulnerabilities in their systems and networks. **Microsoft Defender Vulnerability Management** (**MDVM**) is a comprehensive solution designed to do just that. One of its key features is the **Microsoft Defender Vulnerability Management dashboard**, a central hub for tracking and mitigating vulnerabilities. In this article, we will explore the MDVM dashboard and discuss its capabilities, benefits, and how it can enhance an organization's security posture.

Microsoft Defender Vulnerability Management licensing and technical requirements

MDVM is a component of the broader Microsoft Defender for Endpoint security suite. Licensing for MDVM is typically associated with Microsoft Defender for Endpoint licensing, as MDVM is included as part of that suite. Microsoft offers various licensing options for Microsoft Defender for Endpoint, including the following:

- **Microsoft 365 E5**: Microsoft Defender for Endpoint, including MDVM, is included with Microsoft 365 E3 and E5 licensing.
- **Microsoft Defender for Endpoint, Plan 2**: Within Microsoft Defender for Endpoint, there are two different plans: Plan 1 and Plan 2. MDVM is included in Plan 2. If you have Plan 1, you will need to purchase an MDVM Add-On.
- **Microsoft Defender for cloud, Plan 2**: Among other features, MDVM is included in this MDC Plan 2 as well.
- **Enterprise agreements**: For larger enterprises or organizations with complex licensing needs, Microsoft offers Enterprise Agreements, which can include licensing for Microsoft Defender for Endpoint Plan 2, including MDVM.

It's important to note that licensing terms and options may change over time, and it's essential to consult Microsoft's official website or contact a Microsoft licensing expert for the most up-to-date information and to determine the most suitable licensing option for your organization's specific needs. Additionally, the licensing terms and pricing can vary based on factors such as the number of users, subscription duration, and any additional services or features required.

Key features and capabilities

MDVM provides advanced vulnerability and configuration assessment, as well as these additional capabilities:

- **Vulnerability assessment**: The dashboard offers a comprehensive view of the vulnerabilities present in an organization's environment. It categorizes vulnerabilities based on severity, CVE IDs, and affected assets, making it easier to prioritize the most critical issues.
- **Asset inventory**: MDVM provides an up-to-date inventory of assets, helping security teams understand the scope and potential impact of vulnerabilities.
- **Risk-based prioritization**: The dashboard uses a risk-based approach to prioritize vulnerabilities, considering factors such as exploitability and asset criticality. This helps organizations focus on fixing the vulnerabilities that pose the most significant threats.
- **Integration with Microsoft Security Center**: Integration with the broader Microsoft Security Center ecosystem ensures that security teams have a seamless experience in managing vulnerabilities alongside other security-related tasks.
- **Remediation workflows**: MDVM allows security professionals to create and track remediation tasks, helping them manage the patching and mitigation process efficiently.
- **Customizable reporting**: The dashboard provides customizable reporting options, enabling organizations to create reports tailored to their specific needs and compliance requirements.

Benefits of using the Vulnerability Management dashboard

Using a Vulnerability Management dashboard offers several significant benefits. It enhances an organization's security by providing a comprehensive view of vulnerabilities, helping to prioritize and address threats efficiently. This proactive approach reduces the risk of security breaches and minimizes the potential downtime associated with reactive fixes. The dashboard's reporting capabilities simplify compliance with regulatory requirements, making it easier to demonstrate adherence to security standards. Some of the benefits of using the Vulnerability Management dashboard are as follows:

- **Improved security posture**: By providing a clear view of vulnerabilities and their potential impact, MDVM empowers organizations to make informed decisions, leading to a stronger security posture.
- **Efficient resource allocation**: With prioritized vulnerabilities and streamlined remediation workflows, security teams can allocate their resources effectively and focus on what matters most.
- **Reduced downtime and risk**: The timely identification and remediation of vulnerabilities helps prevent security breaches and reduce the potential downtime associated with patching or mitigating vulnerabilities reactively.
- **Compliance and reporting**: The customizable reporting capabilities facilitate compliance with regulatory requirements, making it easier to demonstrate due diligence in securing the organization's assets.
- **Seamless integration**: Integration with other Microsoft security solutions creates a holistic security ecosystem, allowing organizations to benefit from a unified and coherent approach to cybersecurity.

The MDVM dashboard provides an excellent overview of essential and critical MDVM functionality, a clear overview of the most important data and scores, such as the exposure score, top security recommendations, top vulnerable software, device exposure distribution, top exposed devices, top exposed software, and many others.

The MDVM dashboard is a powerful tool for organizations looking to strengthen their security posture.

By providing a centralized platform to discover, prioritize, and remediate vulnerabilities, it helps security teams effectively manage the evolving threat landscape. Its risk-based prioritization, customizable reporting, and seamless integration with other Microsoft security tools make it an asset in the fight against cyber threats:

Figure 7.1 – MDVM dashboard

As the cyber threat landscape continues to evolve, having a robust vulnerability management solution, such as MDVM, is essential to maintaining a resilient and secure organization.

The minimum requirements for MDVM are the same as the minimum requirements for Microsoft Defender for Endpoint (MDE). The requirements for MDE are explained in more detail in *Chapter 4*.

In addition to the requirements, you have to ensure the devices you intend to monitor meet the following:

- Are onboarded for MDVM or MDE Plan 2
- Run supported operating systems and platforms (`https://learn.microsoft.com/en-gb/microsoft-365/security/defender-vulnerability-management/tvm-supported-os?view=o365-worldwide#capabilities-per-supported-operating-systems-os-and-platforms`)
- Are onboarded to **Intune** and Microsoft Endpoint Configuration Manager, if you want to take advantage of MDVM threat remediation capabilities

Permissions

MDVM supports assigning granular permissions, conforming to the best practices of Just Enough Administration. To access the permissions and roles blade in the Microsoft defender portal, you must have a Security Administrator or Global Administrator role in Azure Active Directory, that is, Microsoft Entra ID.

To view and manage permissions for vulnerability management, navigate to the **Microsoft 365 Defender** portal (`https://security.microsoft.com`) and log in using an account with a Global Administrator or a Security Administrator role assigned. In the navigation pane, select **Settings**, then **Endpoints**. The **Roles** page allows you to define and create administrative roles and permissions and contains the list of already defined roles to manage MDVM. To create an MDVM role, select **+Add role** and follow a very straightforward and simple procedure: choose the role name, describe the role and its purpose, and assign user groups:

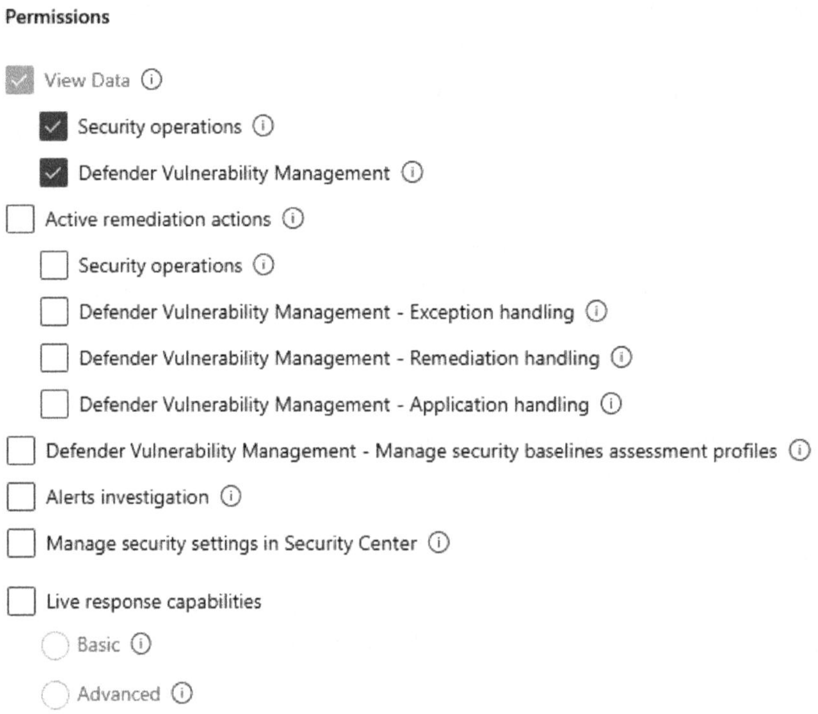

Permissions

- [x] View Data
  - [x] Security operations
  - [x] Defender Vulnerability Management
- [ ] Active remediation actions
  - [ ] Security operations
  - [ ] Defender Vulnerability Management - Exception handling
  - [ ] Defender Vulnerability Management - Remediation handling
  - [ ] Defender Vulnerability Management - Application handling
- [ ] Defender Vulnerability Management - Manage security baselines assessment profiles
- [ ] Alerts investigation
- [ ] Manage security settings in Security Center
- [ ] Live response capabilities
  - Basic
  - Advanced

Figure 7.2 – MDVM permissions

The permissions available in MDVM are well-defined and granular and allow you to allow user groups to perform the following actions, grouped by permissions and assigned operations:

1. **View data**:

   - **Security operations**: This allows you to view security operations data such as security operations dashboard, Incidents, Alerts, Automated investigations, Advanced Hunting security operations data schemas, Security operations reports, Evaluation lab, API explorer, Device page security operations tabs, and Device page MDVM tabs.
   - **Defender Vulnerability Management**: This allows you to view the MDVM dashboard, Security recommendations, MDVM remediations/exceptions, Software inventory, Software page, Weaknesses (vulnerabilities) page, Missing KBs, Software version distribution, Advanced Hunting MDVM data schemas, and Device page MDVM tabs.

2. **Active remediation actions**:

    - **Security operations**: This allows you to take response actions, approve or dismiss pending remediation actions, and manage allowed/blocked lists for automation.
    - **Defender Vulnerability Management - Exception handling**: This allows you to create new MDVM exceptions and manage active exceptions.
    - **Defender Vulnerability Management - Remediation handling**: This allows you to submit new MDVM remediation requests, create remediation tickets, and manage existing remediation activities.
    - **Defender Vulnerability Management - Application handling**: This allows you to apply immediate mitigation actions by blocking vulnerable applications, as part of the remediation activity; manage the blocked apps and perform unblock actions.

3. **Defender Vulnerability Management - Manage security baselines assessment profiles**: This option allows you to create and manage profiles so you can assess if your devices comply with security industry baselines.
4. **Alerts investigation**: Grants rights to manage alerts, initiate automated investigations, run scans, collect investigation packages, and manage device tags.
5. **Manage security settings in Security Center**: This option grants permission to configure alert suppression settings, manage folder exclusions for automation (applies globally), onboard and offboard devices, manage email notifications, and manage the evaluation lab.
6. **Live response capabilities**:

    - **Basic**: This permission allows you to start a live response session, perform read-only live response commands on a remote device, and download a file from the remote device.
    - **Advanced**: This option grants rights to upload a file to the remote device, view a script from the files library, and execute a script on the remote device from the files library.

Microsoft 365 Defender also supports defining custom roles using unified **role-based access control** (**RBAC**). Again, as mentioned earlier, with MDVM roles, you must be a Security Administrator or Global Administrator member to define unified RBAC roles. After activating the unified RBAC permission model, it will become the primary authorization model, and any custom roles that you created previously will no longer be valid; that is, they will no longer grant access to services and data in Microsoft 365.

To use the Microsoft Defender 365 unified RBAC roles model, you must activate it. In the Microsoft 365 Defender portal, select **Permissions**, then select **Settings**, followed by **Microsoft 365 Defender**. Select **Permissions and roles** to view the available options.

The following screenshot from Microsoft 365 Defender Permissions and roles contains the options to activate unified RBAC options on a variety of workloads and additional data sources.

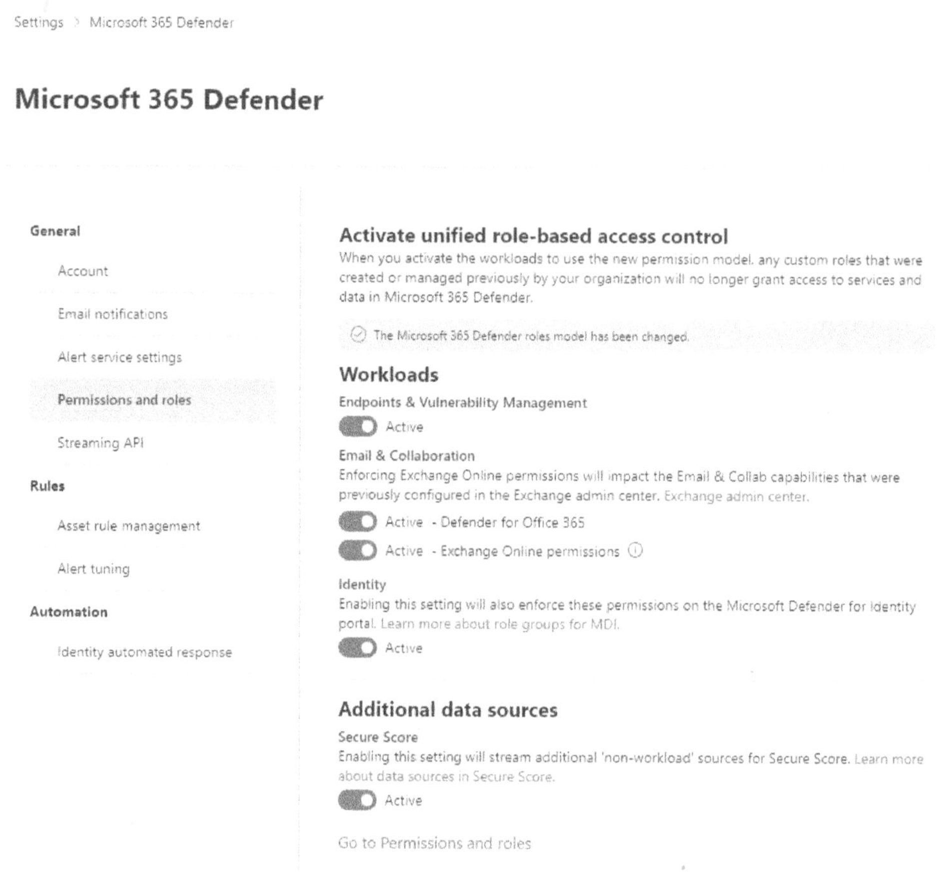

Figure 7.3 – Microsoft 365 Defender permissions and roles

To activate workloads to use unified role-based access control, you can choose **Endpoints & Vulnerability Management**, **Defender for Office 365**, **Exchange Online permissions**, and Microsoft Defender for **Identity**. Activating the **Secure Score** option will enable additional data sources to access Secure Score data, such as Docusign, GitHub, Okta, Salesforce, ServiceNow, Zoom, Microsoft Teams, and the Microsoft Defender "family" of products, to name a few.

After switching to the unified RBAC model, the next step would be to create custom roles that will define permissions for working with security operation, managing settings, authorization, and security operations.

To create a custom role, navigate to **Permissions**, select **Roles** under **Microsoft Defender XDR**. Select **+ Create a custom Role** to start creating a role by defining a role name and entering a role description. Click on **Next** to choose permissions from the permissions group. Select each permission group to bring up a blade allowing you to select permissions from a selected Permission group:

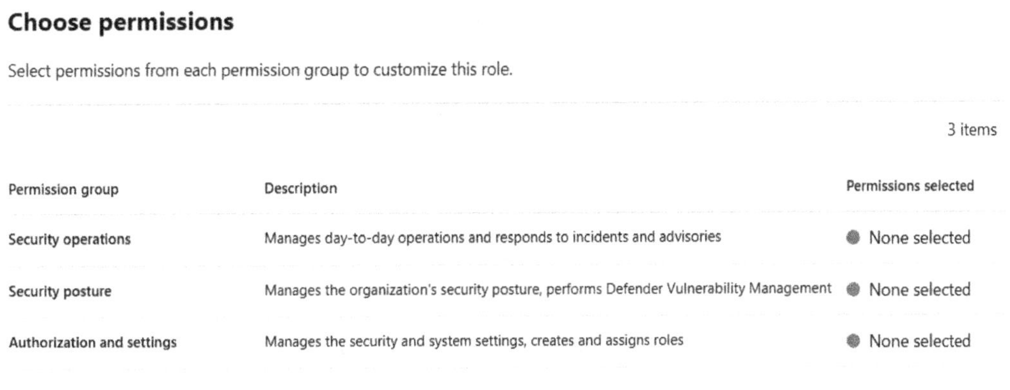

Choose permissions

Select permissions from each permission group to customize this role.

3 items

Permission group	Description	Permissions selected
Security operations	Manages day-to-day operations and responds to incidents and advisories	None selected
Security posture	Manages the organization's security posture, performs Defender Vulnerability Management	None selected
Authorization and settings	Manages the security and system settings, creates and assigns roles	None selected

Figure 7.4 – Microsoft Defender XDR permission groups

All three permission groups have these three permissions options in common:

- All read-only permissions
- All read and manage permissions
- Select custom permissions

The **Security operations** group of permissions contains permissions that control access to security and raw data, which is appropriate for users who act as security incident responders and security operations managers. Custom permissions include the following:

- **Security data basics (read)**: This enables you to view info about incidents, alerts, investigations, advanced hunting, **Microsoft Defender for Endpoint** (MDE), devices, submissions, evaluation lab, and reports.
- **Alerts (manage)**: This enables you to manage alerts, start automated investigations, run scans, collect investigation packages, and manage device tags.
- **Response (manage)**: This allows you to take response actions on a device, approve or dismiss pending remediation actions, and manage blocked and allowed lists for automation.
- **Basic live response (manage)**: This gives you permission to initiate a live response session, download files, and perform read-only actions on devices remotely.
- **Advanced live response (manage)**: This enables you to create live response sessions and perform advanced actions, including uploading files and running scripts on devices remotely.
- **File collection (manage)**: This enables you to collect or download relevant files for analysis, including executable files.

- **Email quarantine (manage)**: This allows you to view and release email from quarantine.
- **Email advanced actions (manage)**: This permits you to move or delete email actions to the junk email folder, deleted items, or inbox, including soft and hard deletes of emails.
- **Email message headers (read)**: This lets you view email and collaboration data in hunting scenarios, including advanced hunting, threat explorer, campaigns, and email entities.
- **Email content (read)**: This allows you to view and download email content.

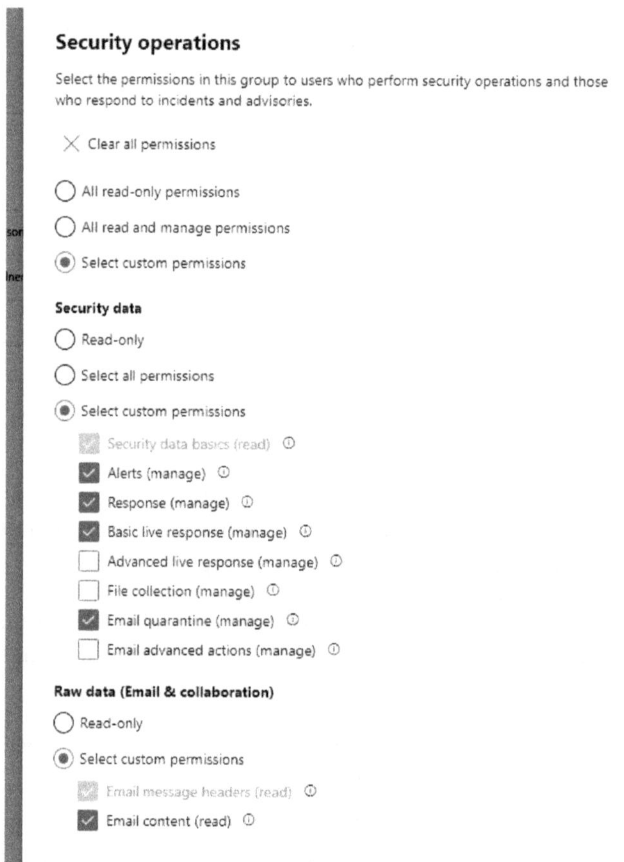

Figure 7.5 – Microsoft Defender XDR Security operations permissions

The **Security posture** group of permissions includes permissions to grant users rights to act on security recommendations and track appropriate actions. This group includes these custom permissions:

- **Vulnerability management (read)**: This enables you to view Defender Vulnerability Management data for software and software inventory, weaknesses, missing KBs, advanced hunting, security baselines assessment, and devices.

- **Exception handling (manage)**: This allows you to create security recommendation exceptions and manage active exceptions in Defender Vulnerability Management.
- **Remediation handling (manage)**: This permits you to create remediation tickets, submit new requests, and manage remediation activities in Defender Vulnerability Management.
- **Application handling (manage)**: This lets you manage vulnerable applications and software, including blocking and unblocking vulnerable applications and software in Defender Vulnerability Management.
- **Security baselines assessment (manage)**: This gives you permission to create and manage profiles that enable you to assess your devices' security industry standards compliance status.
- **Secure score (read)**: This enables you to view Secure Score data, including your current score, recommended actions, history, and metrics and trends.
- **Secure score (manage)**: This allows you to take actions to improve your Secure Score by editing the status and action plan, managing tags, and editing score zones.

The following screenshot shows Microsoft Defender XDR security posture permissions options:

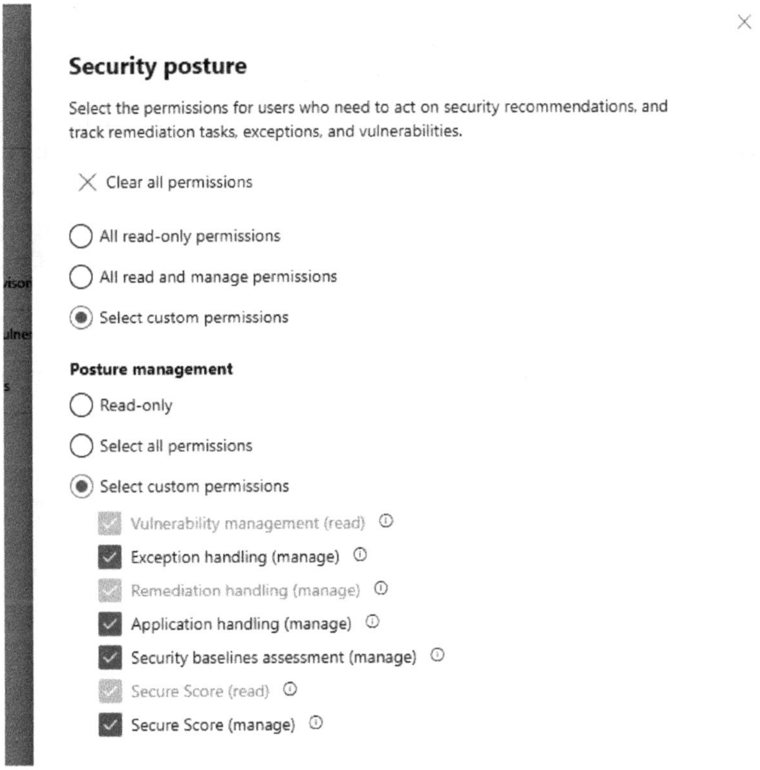

Figure 7.6 – Microsoft Defender XDR Security posture permissions

Authorization and settings: This comprises permissions that will allow users to configure the security and system settings and create and assign roles:

- **Authorization**: This contains the options to set permissions to view or manage device groups and custom and built-in roles.
- **Detection tuning (manage)**: This allows you to manage tasks related to detections in the Microsoft 365 Defender portal, including custom detections, alert suppression, and indicators of compromise.
- **Core security settings (read)**: This permits you to view general security settings for the Microsoft 365 Defender portal.
- **Core security settings (manage)**: This enables you to manage general security settings for the Microsoft 365 Defender portal.
- **System settings**: This defines permissions to view or manage general systems settings for the Microsoft 365 Defender portal, Defender for Office 365, and Defender for Identity.

> **Important note**
>
> You can find more information about Microsoft Defender for Endpoint RBAC roles management and Unified RBAC custom permissions at the following resources:
>
> Create and manage roles for role-based access control: `https://learn.microsoft.com/en-us/microsoft-365/security/defender-endpoint/user-roles?view=o365-worldwide`.
>
> Permissions in Microsoft Defender XDR Unified role-based access control (RBAC): `https://learn.microsoft.com/en-us/microsoft-365/security/defender/custom-permissions-details?view=o365-worldwide`.

The following screenshot shows Microsoft Defender XDR authorization and security settings options and permissions:

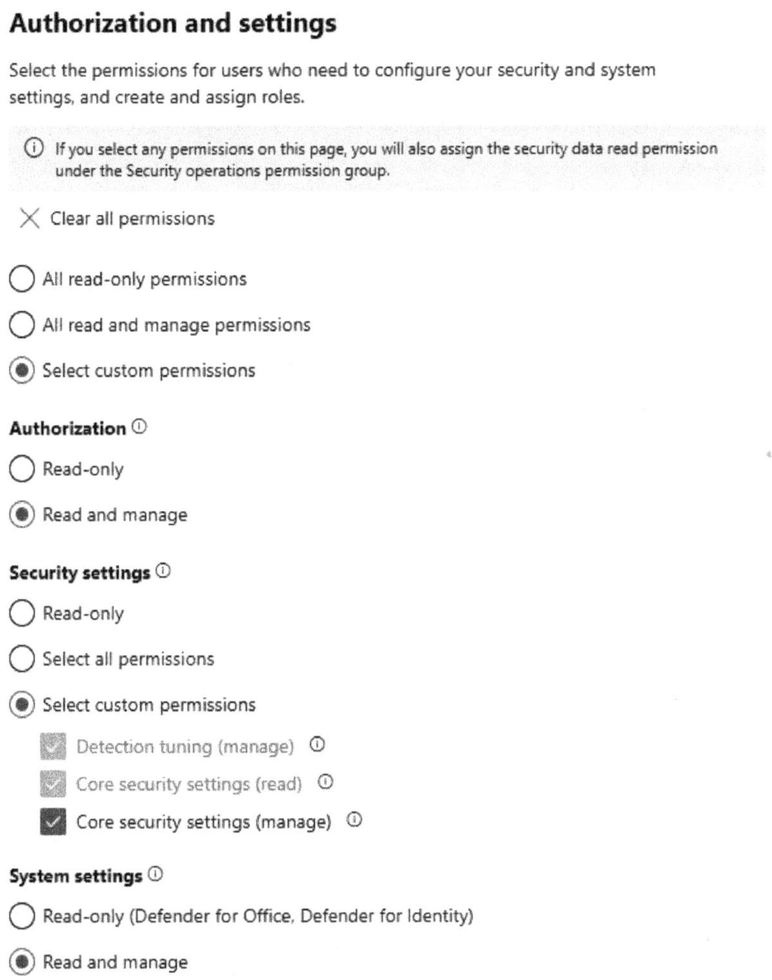

Authorization and settings

Select the permissions for users who need to configure your security and system settings, and create and assign roles.

ⓘ If you select any permissions on this page, you will also assign the security data read permission under the Security operations permission group.

× Clear all permissions

○ All read-only permissions

○ All read and manage permissions

◉ Select custom permissions

Authorization ⓘ

○ Read-only

◉ Read and manage

Security settings ⓘ

○ Read-only

○ Select all permissions

◉ Select custom permissions

☑ Detection tuning (manage) ⓘ

☑ Core security settings (read) ⓘ

☑ Core security settings (manage) ⓘ

System settings ⓘ

○ Read-only (Defender for Office, Defender for Identity)

◉ Read and manage

Figure 7.7 – Microsoft Defender XDR Authorization and settings options

After choosing the desired permissions, click **Next** to display **Assign users and data sources**, where you will assign roles to users and user groups, along with the resources to which these users and groups will have access. Select **Create assignments** to open the **Add assignment** blade and enter an **Assignment name**:

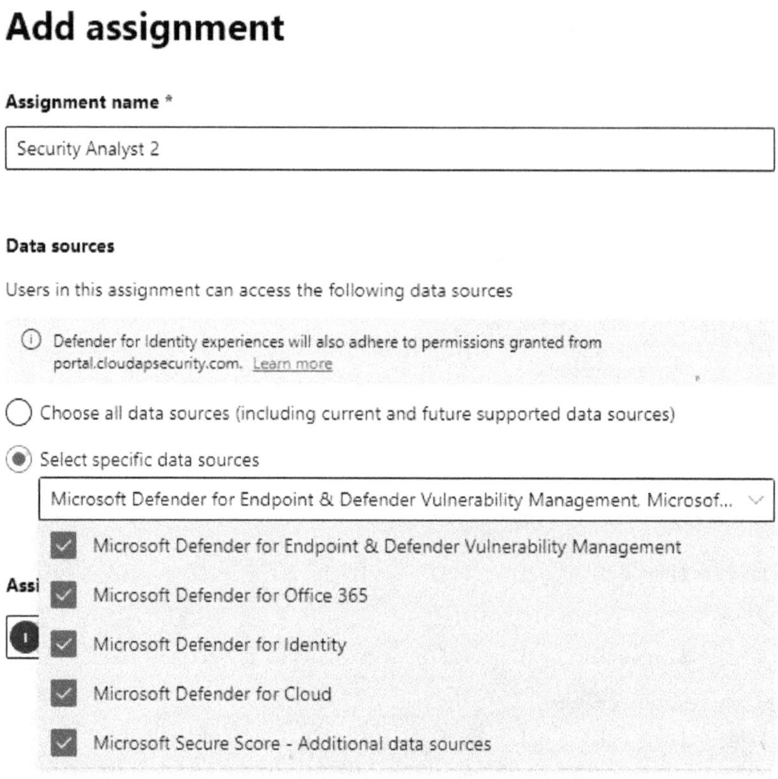

Add assignment

Assignment name *

Security Analyst 2

Data sources

Users in this assignment can access the following data sources

Defender for Identity experiences will also adhere to permissions granted from portal.cloudapsecurity.com. Learn more

Choose all data sources (including current and future supported data sources)

Select specific data sources

Microsoft Defender for Endpoint & Defender Vulnerability Management, Microsof...

Microsoft Defender for Endpoint & Defender Vulnerability Management

Microsoft Defender for Office 365

Microsoft Defender for Identity

Microsoft Defender for Cloud

Microsoft Secure Score - Additional data sources

Figure 7.8 – Assigning specific data sources

Choose whether users and groups will have access to all current and future supported data sources or select between specific data sources: Microsoft Defender for Endpoint and Defender Vulnerability Management, Microsoft Defender for Office 365, Microsoft Defender for Identity, Microsoft Defender for Cloud, and Microsoft Secure Score and additional data sources mentioned earlier in this chapter. Click on **Next** to review the selection and assignments, and if everything looks good, click on **Submit** to create a new role.

> **Important note**
>
> As many users have already set up Defender for Endpoint and Defender Vulnerability Management permissions, Microsoft has put up a comparison table or a mapping table of MDVM permissions to Microsoft Defender RBAC permissions to ease the transition between the two permission models. See page `https://learn.microsoft.com/en-gb/microsoft-365/security/defender/compare-rbac-roles` for more information.

MDVM is an integral part of the Microsoft Defender for Endpoint suite. It enables organizations to discover, prioritize, and remediate vulnerabilities in their network, ensuring that security risks are minimized. The Vulnerability Management dashboard serves as the primary interface for security teams to monitor and manage vulnerabilities.

Now that you have set up permissions and roles, the next step is to assess and inspect the device and software inventory, see the MDVM recommendations, and take action on the remediation of weaknesses.

Recommendations and remediation

An integral part of the MDVM is the **Devices** page, placed under the **Assets** category, where you can view all devices protected with Microsoft Defender for Endpoint—ones for which the software inventories will be assessed by MDVM—and all their details, such as risk and exposure level, tags, incidents and alerts, timeline, security recommendations, and security policies, as well as software inventory, discovered vulnerabilities, and much more.

> **Important note**
>
> More about Microsoft Defender for Endpoint, **Devices**, and related pages is described in more detail in *Chapter 4*. In this chapter, we will focus on MDVM features.

Security recommendations

The **Security recommendations** page contains information about protected devices' security recommendations, operating system versions and related OS components, the number of weaknesses found, remediation types and activities, impact on the secure score and overall security posture, the number of exposed devices, recommendations timeline, and tags associated with devices.

Security recommendations

Export

Filters: Status: Active +1

	Security recommendation	OS platform	Weaknesses	Related component
☑	Update Microsoft Windows Server 2019 (OS and built-in applications)	Windows	29	Microsoft Windows Server 2019
☐	Block persistence through WMI event subscription	Windows	1	Security controls (Attack Surface Reduction)
☐	Update Microsoft .net Framework	Windows	2	Microsoft .net Framework
☐	Update Microsoft Teams	Windows	1	Microsoft Teams
☐	Update Microsoft Windows Server 2016 (OS and built-in applications)	Windows	23	Microsoft Windows Server 2016
☐	Update Ubuntu Policykit-1 for Linux	Other	1	Ubuntu Policykit-1 for Linux
☐	Update Zoom Meetings	Windows	37	Zoom Meetings
☐	Update Openssl	Windows	22	Openssl

Figure 7.9 – MDVM Security recommendations page – Part 1 (left portion)

The **Threats** column contains two icons that can be either grayed out, which means there are no threats, or in red, which means a threat has been found. A bullseye icon represents a breach insight, where an active alert is found and associated with a security recommendation, while a red bug icon represents a threat insight, where a known public exploit is found and associated with this security recommendation:

OS platform	Weaknesses	Related component	Threats	Exposed devices	Remediation type	Remediation activities	Impact	Tags
Windows	29	Microsoft Windows Server 2019		2 / 2	Software update	0	▼ 14.76	+
Windows	1	Security controls (Attack Surface Reduction)		5 / 5	Configuration change	0	▼ 10.50	+ User impact assessment
Windows	2	Microsoft .net Framework		3 / 6	Software update	0	▼ 9.24	+ 0
Windows	1	Microsoft Teams		1 / 3	Software update	1	▼ 7.58	+ 0
Windows	23	Microsoft Windows Server 2016		1 / 1	Software update	0	▼ 7.38	+ 0
Other	1	Ubuntu Policykit-1 for Linux		1 / 4	Software update	0	▼ 6.88	+ 0
Windows	37	Zoom Meetings		2 / 3	Software update	0	▼ 6.64	+ 0
Windows	22	Openssl		2 / 6	Software update	0	▼ 6.34	+ 0
Windows	17	Microsoft Edge Chromium-based		2 / 5	Software update	0	▼ 6.16	+ 0

Figure 7.10 – MDVM Security recommendations page – Part 2 (right portion)

To view more detailed information about a security recommendation, click on a security recommendation to open a right-side pane, which contains multiple tabs: **General**, **Exposed devices**, **Installed devices**, and **Associated CVEs**:

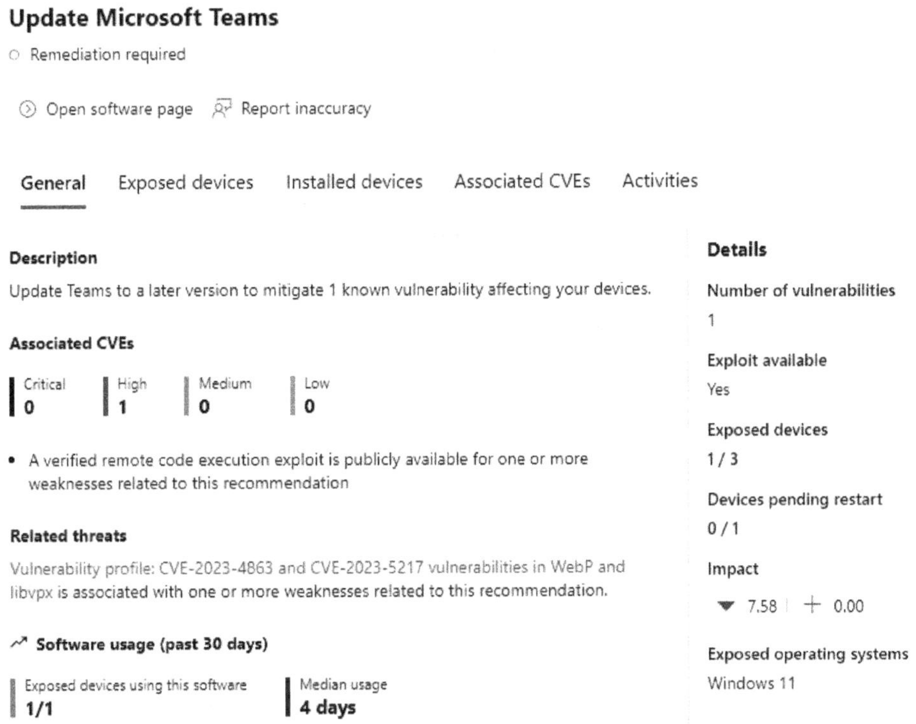

Figure 7.11 – A security recommendation details pane

The **General** tab contains a description of the recommendation, graphical, color-coded information, and distribution of associated CVEs, the threats related or associated with one or more weaknesses of the viewed recommendation, as well as details about vulnerabilities and exploits and impacts to the security score and security posture.

Software usage (past 30 days) displays the information about the median usage of the affected software on the affected devices in the past 30 days. This is a rather minuscule piece of information but very valuable for getting a bigger picture of how vulnerable software is used on exposed devices, and it helps in triaging and prioritizing remediation activities.

The information about **Exposed devices** and **Devices pending restart** is also available, where the first number indicates the number of exposed devices or the number of devices needed to be restarted, and the second number indicates the total number of devices:

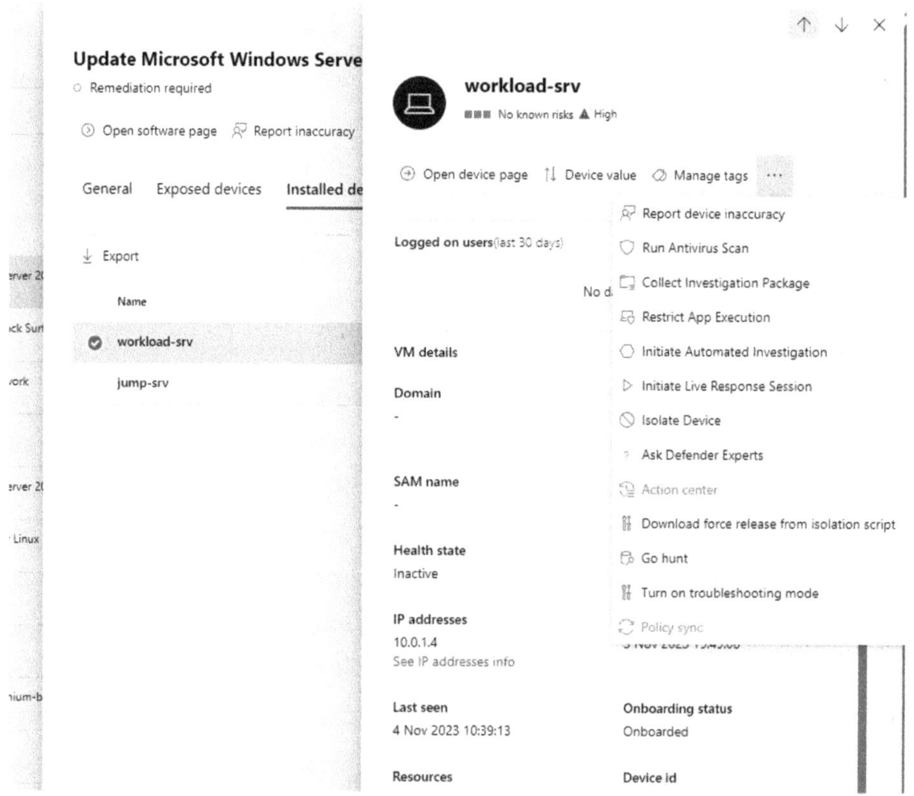

Figure 7.12 – A security recommendation details pane – Exposed devices tab

The list of devices is also available on the **Exposed devices** and **Installed devices** tabs and, very conveniently, these lists are clickable or selectable to open a blade with thorough, detailed information about a device and associated actions, such as those available under the **Devices** page, under the **Assets** category. We will look at the **Associated CVEs** tab very soon (later in this chapter).

The **Activities** tab will contain a list of remediation tasks (or activities) created for the security recommendation you are currently displaying.

Two buttons are available at the bottom of a security recommendation page: **Request remediation** and **Exception options**.

Click on the **Request remediation** button to fill in the remediation request so the users with appropriate permissions, whose task is to remediate the vulnerabilities, know what to prioritize and what recommendations to address. The **Remediation request** page includes the **Remediation options** categories Software update, Software uninstall, and Attention required, as well as **Remediation due date**, **Priority**, and a space to add any relevant notes to the request that might be valuable and informative to the remediation team.

For the devices that are joined to Azure Active Directory, there is an **Open a ticket in Intune (for AAD joined devices)** option available to select, too. This will add an entry to the Intune portal, where an administrator can approve remediation action. Click **Next** to review and **Submit** to complete the remediation request.

Select **Exception options** to create an exception for a security recommendation. This might be needed if a security recommendation is not relevant or you cannot (or do not) want to remediate a recommendation. After you click on **Submit**, you will create an exception, and that will change the recommendation status from **Active** to **Exception**. You must choose exception duration and one of the following justification reasons: Third-party control, Alternate mitigation, Risk accepted, or Planned remediation (grace).

Remediation tasks in Microsoft Intune

By connecting Intune with Microsoft Defender for Endpoint, you can use Defender for Endpoint's features for threat and vulnerability management to find and rank vulnerabilities. Then, you can apply Intune to fix the endpoint issues that Defender's vulnerability management feature detected. This connection enables a risk-based method for discovering and prioritizing vulnerabilities, which can enhance remediation speed across your environment.

Defender for Endpoint security admins check data on endpoint vulnerabilities in the Microsoft Defender Security Center console. After that, admins can create security tasks with a few clicks that mark the devices with vulnerabilities for fixing. The security tasks are sent right away to the Microsoft Intune Admin Center, where Intune admins can see them. The security task shows the kind of vulnerability, priority, status, and the actions to take to fix the vulnerability. Finally, the Intune administrator can decide to accept or reject the task:

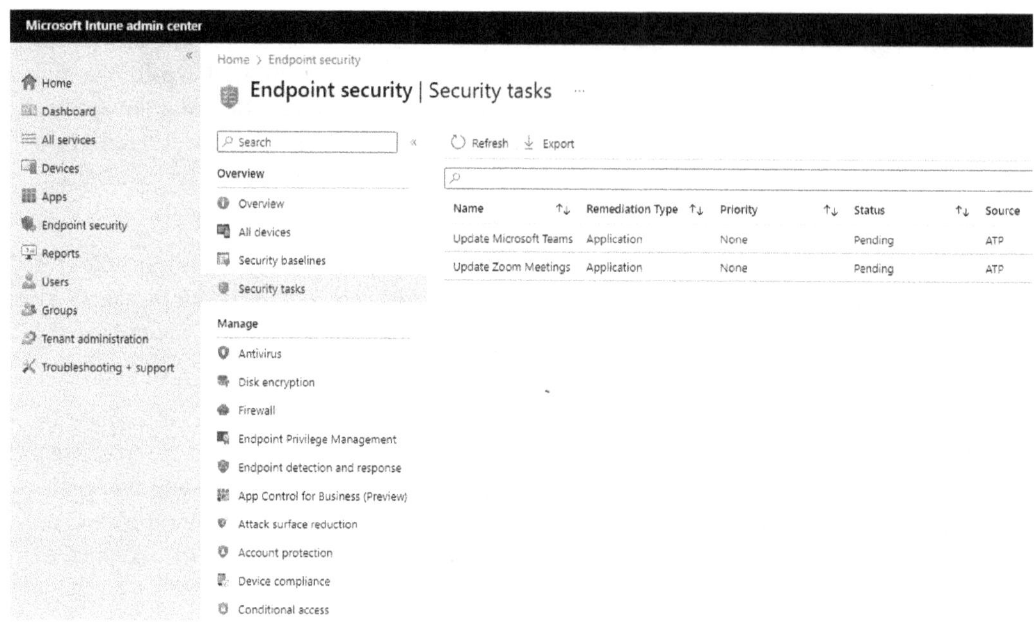

Figure 7.13 – Microsoft Endpoint security – Security tasks

Navigate to Microsoft Intune admin center at `https://intune.microsoft.com/`, select **Endpoint Security**, and click on **Security tasks** to display the list of tickets waiting for approval. Select a task to display its details and click on the **Accept** button to accept the task. In the **Are you sure you want to accept this task?** dialog box, fill in the task details (optional) and click **Yes**. The information about the accepted task is reflected in remediation activities, which helps teams and users who are working on remediation activities to track remediations better. To complete the task in Intune, open the task page and select **Complete**. Add an optional note and confirm the action with **Yes**. This will mark the ticket as complete in Intune.

Remediation

The **Remediation** page contains a list of **Activities** that are in progress or past due. Select a remediation activity to display more information on the right-side pane, where you can track a remediation activity, read the details, and view related recommendations, but also jump to the related component or the software page for more detailed information about the software you are inspecting.

After selecting a remediation activity from the list, a blade opens on the right side with the details of an activity, as shown in the following screenshot:

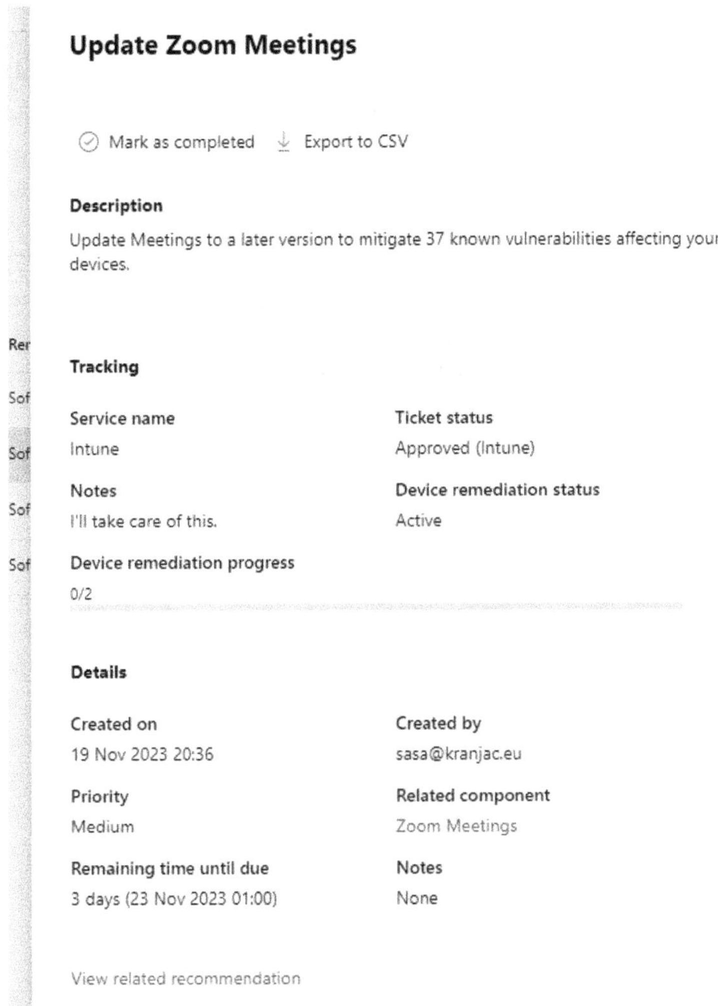

Figure 7.14 – Remediation activity details blade

After you have successfully remediated a vulnerability, click on **Mark as completed** to set the **Device remediation status** as **Completed**.

The **Exceptions** page lists all exceptions and, as always, when selecting an entry, displays the details about the exception where you can, in case you change your mind, cancel an exception or, alternatively, you can let the exception expire.

Inventories and weaknesses

To understand the software landscape throughout your organization's MDVM, use the **Inventories** page, where you can dive deeper into browser extensions usage and the state of certificates and firmware vulnerabilities, whereas the **Weaknesses** page contains a list of **common vulnerabilities exploits (CVEs)** currently applicable to your environment. Let's get into more detail about each of these two important MDVM pages.

Inventories

The vulnerability management **Inventory** page gives you an understanding of the software usage in your organization in the past 30 days. Similar to the **Recommendations** page, this software usage information page has the same columns, such as weaknesses, threats, vendors, and others, but here, this information is relevant to the median usage of the software rather than to the specific recommendation or a vulnerability:

Inventories

Software | Browser extensions (trial) | Certificates (trial) | Hardware & Firmware (trial)

Software
477

Export

477 items | Search | Filter | Customize columns

Filters: Product Code (CPE): Available

Name	OS platform	Vendor	Weaknesses	Threats	Exposed devices	Impact	Tags
Windows Server 2019	Windows	Microsoft	29		2 / 2	14.76	
.net Framework	Windows	Microsoft	2		3 / 6	9.24	
Teams	Windows	Microsoft	1		1 / 3	7.58	
Windows Server 2016	Windows	Microsoft	23		1 / 1	7.38	
Policykit-1 for Linux	Linux	Ubuntu	1		1 / 4	6.88	
Meetings	Windows	Zoom	37		2 / 3	6.64	
Openssl	Windows	Openssl	22		2 / 6	6.34	
Edge Chromium-based	Windows	Microsoft	17		2 / 5	6.16	
Odbc	Windows	Microsoft	12		2 / 2	6.16	
Vlc Media Player	Windows	Videolan	3		2 / 2	5.72	
Visual Studio 2022	Windows	Microsoft	6		1 / 2	5.68	
Git	Windows	Git-scm	19		1 / 1	3.56	
Python3-urllib3 for Linux	Linux	Ubuntu	3		1 / 4	3.24	
Notepad++	Windows	Notepad Plus P...	6		1 / 1	3.12	

Figure 7.15 – MDVM inventories page

On the Inventories page, besides the **Software** tab, three other tabs are available: **Browser extensions**, **Certificates**, and **Hardware & Firmware**. Naturally, selecting software or an application from a list opens a side information pane—commonly referred to as a flyout—that gives you more details about the software vulnerabilities, associated CVEs, and on which devices it is installed:

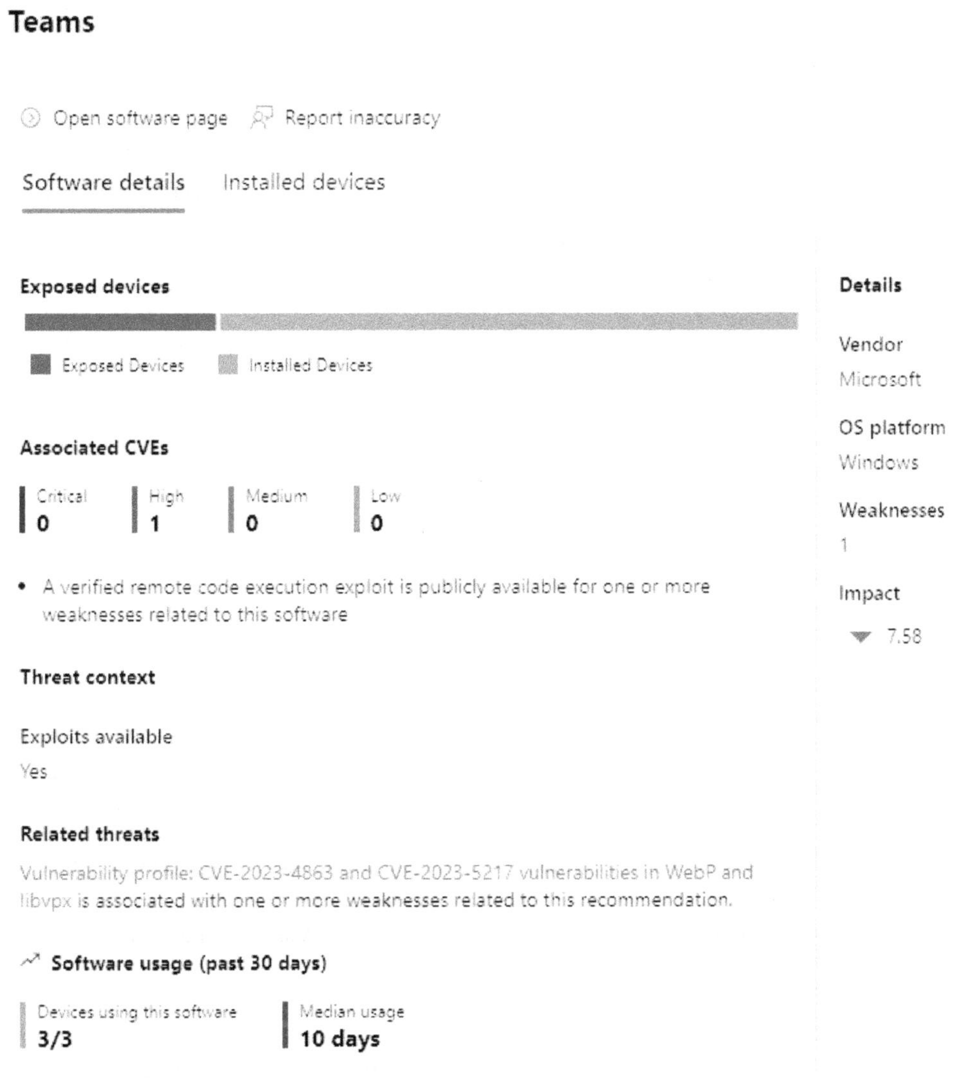

Figure 7.16 – MDVM software details pane

Located on top of the side pane is the **Open software page** button. It contains a wealth of information about the software, organized in tabs. The **Overview** tab hosts a summary and graphical display of discovered weaknesses, exposed devices, software usage in the past 30 days, and top events that happened in the last 7 days.

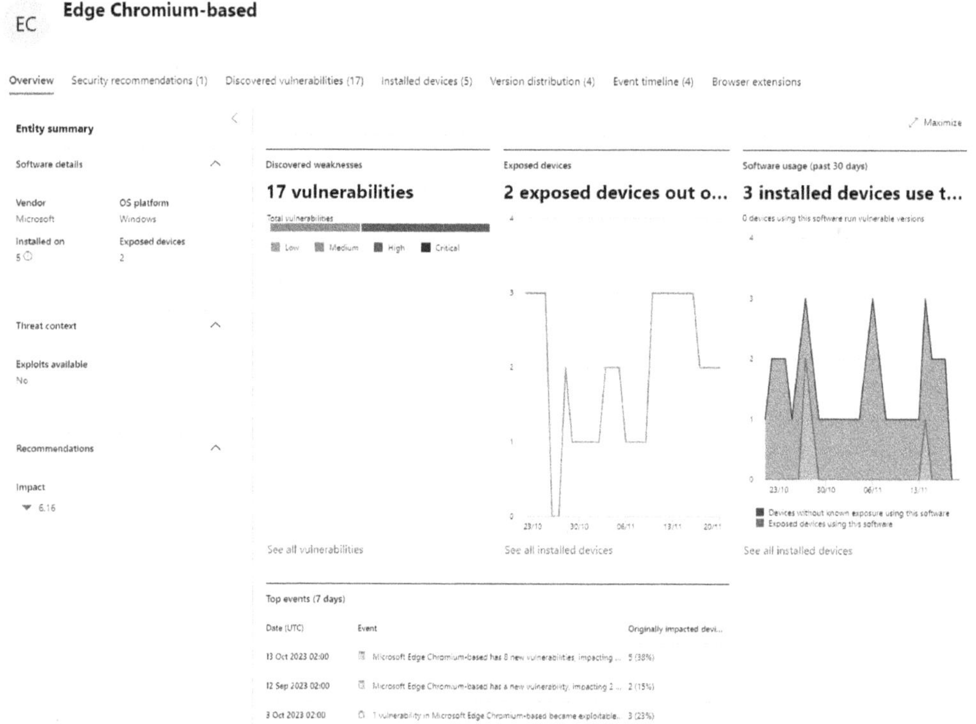

Figure 7.17– MDVM software page

Any information related to the software displayed is located under the tabs **Security recommendations** and **Discovered vulnerabilities**, which provide a list of devices where the software is installed, details about different software versions and their distribution across devices, any installed browser extensions, and the associated risks and vulnerabilities, and a timeline of events related to the software.

Weaknesses

Vulnerability Management in Microsoft Defender uses the same signals as endpoint protection in Defender for Endpoint to find and identify vulnerabilities.

On the Weaknesses page, you can see the software vulnerabilities that affect your devices. Each vulnerability has a **common vulnerabilities and exposures** (CVE) ID.

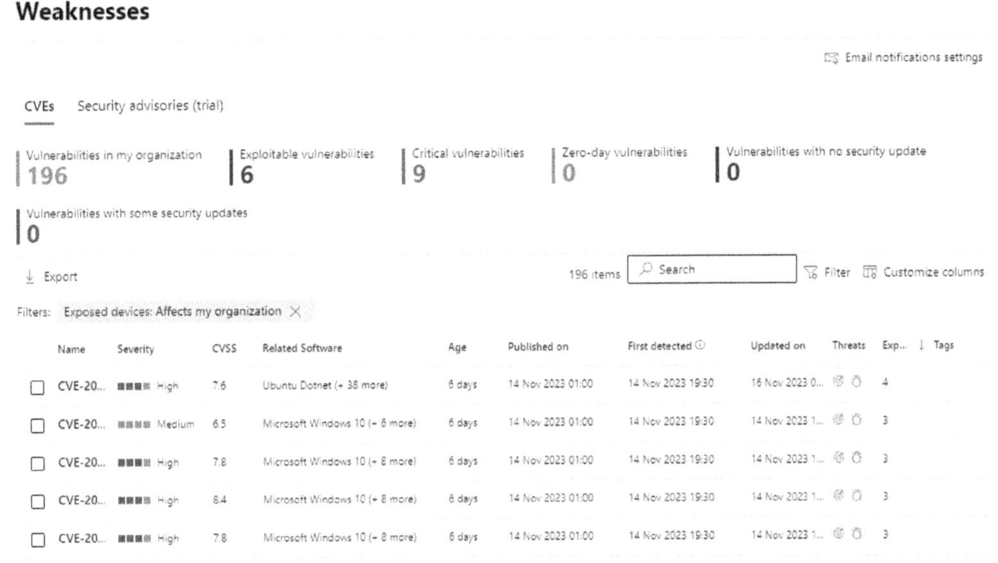

Figure 7.18 – MDVM Vulnerabilities page

You can also see other information, such as severity, **common vulnerability scoring system** (**CVSS**) rating, how common it is in your organization, related breaches, threat insights, and more.

To protect your assets and organization from risk, you need to fix the vulnerabilities in exposed devices. If you see `0` in the **Exposed Devices** column, that means your devices are not vulnerable.

Selecting a vulnerability shows additional details about a CVE. The side pane, or a flyout, opens with the **Vulnerability details** tab that shows detailed vulnerability information, a description of the vulnerability, a reference (if it exists, in the form of a URL), and a link to the threat analytics report. The **Exposed devices** tab has a list of affected devices, while the **Related software** tab contains a list of related software, possibly affected software versions and different distributions, for example. A different but insightful view of a vulnerability exposure is readily available after you click on **Open vulnerability page**.

For a security investigator or a user working with MDVM, finding out how threats and risks enter an organization is crucial. There is a dedicated page just for that.

Event timeline

Event timeline is a risk news feed that helps you understand how new vulnerabilities or exploits can increase the risk for your organization. You can see events that may affect your organization's risk level. For example, you can discover new vulnerabilities that have emerged, vulnerabilities that can be exploited, exploits that have been added to an exploit kit, and more:

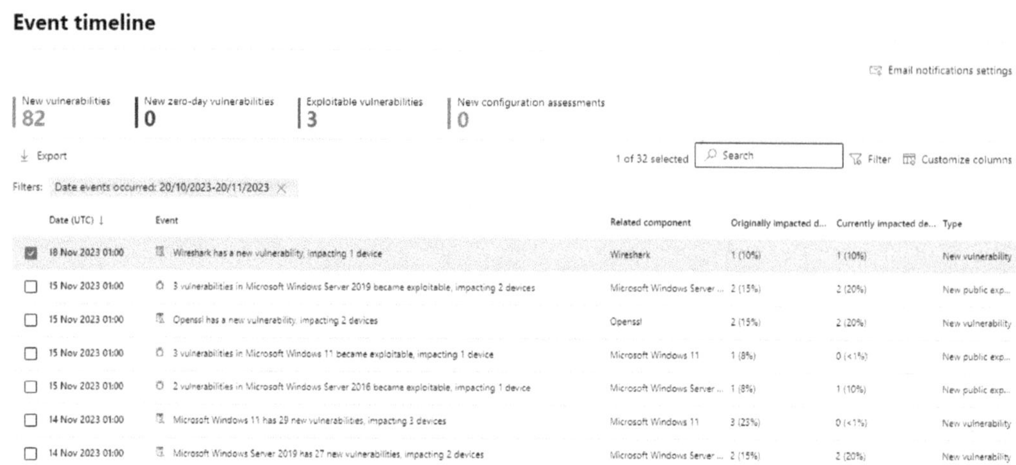

Figure 7.19 – MDVM event timeline page

The event timeline also shows you how your exposure score and Microsoft Secure Score for Devices change over time and what causes the changes. Events can have an impact on your devices or your score for devices. You can lower your exposure by taking action on the security recommendations that are most important.

To reduce cyber risk, you need a single solution that can manage risk-based vulnerability across your most important assets. You need to find, evaluate, fix, and monitor all your biggest vulnerabilities. MDVM gives you visibility into your assets, smart assessments of your vulnerabilities, and tools to fix them for Windows, macOS, Linux, Android, iOS, and network devices. Using Microsoft threat intelligence, breach likelihood predictions, business contexts, and device assessments, MDVM quickly and continuously ranks the most serious vulnerabilities of your most critical assets and gives you security recommendations to lower the risk.

Summary

MDVM is a cybersecurity solution that helps organizations identify, assess, and remediate vulnerabilities in their IT infrastructure. It integrates with Microsoft Defender for Endpoint and other Microsoft security tools to provide a comprehensive and user-friendly security platform. With Defender Vulnerability Management, you can enable your security and IT teams to work together and focus on the most urgent vulnerabilities and misconfigurations in your organization.

In the next chapter, we will cover Microsoft Defender for Identity, a cloud-based security solution that protects on-premises Active Directory environments from advanced and targeted attacks, monitors user activities, devices, and resources, and detects anomalies and threats using machine learning and behavioral analysis.

8

Microsoft Defender for Identity

In the ever-evolving landscape of cybersecurity, safeguarding your organization's digital infrastructure is paramount. This chapter introduces a critical tool in the arsenal of defense – Microsoft Defender for Identity. As we delve into the intricate world of cybersecurity, this chapter will illuminate the core concepts and functionalities of this robust security solution.

As we journey through this chapter, we'll unravel the secrets behind Microsoft Defender for Identity's essential elements, such as anomaly detection, risk assessment, and identity protection. You'll gain a complete grasp of how these tools team up to spot and tackle security issues early on. We'll also chat about the smartest ways to set up and tweak the system, making sure it fits seamlessly into your organization's security setup. When you reach the end of this chapter, you'll be all set with the knowledge and tools you need to beef up your security, safeguard your sensitive data, and stay one step ahead of cyber threats, ultimately fortifying the resilience of your digital world.

In this chapter, we will dive into essential aspects of Microsoft Defender for Identity, providing an in-depth understanding of key functionalities and configuration processes. We will cover the following topics:

- Configuring Microsoft Defender for Identity
- Configuring Sensors for Microsoft Defender for Identity
- Working with Detection Rules in Microsoft Defender for Identity
- Integration of Microsoft Defender for Identity and Microsoft Sentinel

Throughout this chapter, we aim to empower you with the knowledge and skills needed to navigate and use the full potential of Microsoft Defender for Identity. By the end, you'll be well-equipped to configure, optimize, and integrate these security features into your organization's identity infrastructure, improving your defenses against modern cyber threats.

Introducing Microsoft Defender for Identity

Microsoft Defender for Identity is a powerful cloud-based security solution that is designed to protect against advanced and targeted attacks on an organization's on-premises **Active Directory** (**AD**) environment. The solution provides a range of features and functionalities that help detect and respond to threats in real time, providing administrators with comprehensive visibility into their network and user activity.

One of the key benefits of Microsoft Defender for Identity is its ability to provide continuous monitoring of an organization's environment. By monitoring user activities, devices, and resources, the solution can quickly identify suspicious behavior and potential security threats. This is particularly important as the threat landscape is constantly evolving, and traditional security measures may not be sufficient to protect against sophisticated attacks.

Microsoft Defender for Identity uses advanced **machine learning** (**ML**) and behavioral analysis to detect anomalies and potential threats. The solution uses this data to build a profile of what constitutes normal behavior within an organization's environment, and it can quickly identify deviations from this baseline. This can include activities such as lateral movement, reconnaissance, and privilege escalation, which are common in advanced and targeted attacks.

In addition to threat detection, Microsoft Defender for Identity provides administrators with a detailed timeline of an attack. This helps to understand how the attack happened, what actions were taken, and the impact on the organization. This information is critical for determining an appropriate response and developing a strategy for preventing future attacks.

Microsoft Defender for Identity also offers automated response capabilities. This means that the solution can take action to block suspicious activities, isolate compromised devices, and reset user credentials. These actions are taken in real time, reducing the time required to respond to an attack and minimizing the impact on the organization.

Another important feature of Microsoft Defender for Identity is its integration with other security solutions. The solution can be integrated with Microsoft Sentinel and Microsoft Defender for Endpoint, providing a comprehensive security solution for organizations. This integration enables administrators to quickly detect and respond to threats across their entire network, from the endpoint to the cloud.

Overall, Microsoft Defender for Identity is an essential security solution for organizations that are looking to protect against advanced and targeted attacks. The solution provides continuous monitoring, threat detection, detailed timelines of attacks, automated response capabilities, and integration with other security solutions. These features help to provide comprehensive visibility into an organization's environment, and the ability to quickly respond to threats in real time. Microsoft Defender for Identity is also highly scalable, making it suitable for organizations of all sizes. Whether an organization has a small on-premises network or a large, complex environment, Microsoft Defender for Identity can provide the necessary protection to keep it secure.

In conclusion, Microsoft Defender for Identity is a highly effective cloud-based security solution that provides organizations with the ability to detect and respond to advanced and targeted attacks. The solution offers a range of features and functionalities that help to provide comprehensive visibility into an organization's environment and the ability to quickly respond to threats in real time. With its scalability and integration with other security solutions, Microsoft Defender for Identity is an essential tool for organizations looking to protect against sophisticated threats.

Technical and license requirements

Microsoft Defender for Identity is a cloud-based security solution that is designed to protect an organization's on-premises AD environment. To deploy Microsoft Defender for Identity, several technical and licensing requirements must be met.

The technical requirements are as follows:

- **Operating system**: Microsoft Defender for Identity can be installed on a server running Windows Server 2016 or later.
- **AD**: To use Microsoft Defender for Identity, an organization must have an on-premises AD environment. The solution integrates with AD to monitor user activities, devices, and resources.
- **Internet connectivity**: Microsoft Defender for Identity is a cloud-based solution, which means that it requires a stable internet connection to function properly. The solution communicates with the Microsoft cloud, where it analyzes data and provides real-time threat detection. Browser compatibility requires compliance with HTML5 standards.
- **Hardware requirements**: The hardware requirements for Microsoft Defender for Identity are relatively modest. The solution can run on a standard server with 8 GB of RAM and 4 CPU cores.
- **Network configuration**: To ensure that Microsoft Defender for Identity can communicate with the Microsoft cloud, organizations must allow outbound traffic to the following IP addresses and URLs:
    - `.crl.microsoft.com`
    - `.ctldl.windowsupdate.com`
    - `www.microsoft.com/pkiops/*`
    - `www.microsoft.com/pki/*`

To understand the compatibility and system requirements of Microsoft Defender for Identity, take a look at the following table, which outlines the supported Windows Server versions:

OS	Server with Desktop Experience	Server Core	Read-only domain controller (RODC)	Domain controller (DC)	AD Federation Services (ADFS)
Windows Server 2016	Yes	Yes	Yes	Yes	Yes
Windows Server 2019*	Yes	Yes	Yes	Yes	Yes
Windows Server 2022	Yes	Yes	Yes	Yes	Yes

Table 8.1 – Supported Windows versions

Note

The file version of `ntdsai.dll` must be version `10.0.17763.316` or newer.

Let's look into the license requirements now.

To use Microsoft Defender for Identity, organizations must have an appropriate license. The solution is available through Microsoft 365 E5, Microsoft 365 E5 Security, Microsoft **Enterprise Mobility + Security** (**EMS**) E5, and Microsoft 365 Defender plans. These plans provide a range of security solutions, including Microsoft Defender for Identity. For organizations that do not have an appropriate license, Microsoft provides a free trial of Microsoft Defender for Identity. The trial period lasts for 60 days, and it provides all the features and functionalities of the paid version.

In addition to the license requirements, organizations must also ensure that they have the necessary permissions to deploy Microsoft Defender for Identity. This includes permissions to install software on servers and to configure AD to integrate with the solution.

Microsoft Defender for Identity is a powerful security solution that requires relatively modest technical requirements. To deploy the solution, organizations must have an on-premises AD environment, a stable internet connection, and a server running Windows Server 2016 or later. In addition, organizations must have an appropriate license to use the solution. With its advanced threat detection capabilities and real-time response capabilities, Microsoft Defender for Identity is an essential security solution for organizations looking to protect against advanced and targeted attacks on their on-premises AD environment.

Important note

It is important to note that Microsoft Defender for Identity is only available as part of the **Microsoft 365 E5 suite and EMS E5** license. Organizations must have a valid Microsoft 365 E5 subscription to purchase and use Microsoft Defender for Identity or add EMS E5 to their E-suite license below E5. In addition to the license requirements, organizations must also ensure that they have the necessary permissions to deploy and configure Microsoft Defender for Identity. This includes permissions to create and manage Microsoft Entra ID applications, configure network settings, and manage user accounts and permissions.

Configuring Microsoft Defender for Identity

Configuring Microsoft Defender for Identity is a crucial step in ensuring that the solution is effectively protecting an organization's on-premises AD environment. In this section, we will discuss the steps involved in configuring Microsoft Defender for Identity.

Important note

Before starting to configure Microsoft Defender for Identity, please use the official **Microsoft Sizing Tool** for Microsoft Defender for Identity. The Microsoft Sizing Tool for Microsoft Defender for Identity is a tool designed to help organizations determine the hardware and software requirements needed to deploy Microsoft Defender for Identity in their environment. The Sizing Tool helps organizations plan for the deployment of Microsoft Defender for Identity by collecting information about their AD environment, such as the number of DCs, the size of their domain, and the number of users and devices. Based on this information, the tool provides recommendations for the number of sensors and storage required to support the deployment. The tool also helps organizations estimate the network traffic generated by Microsoft Defender for Identity and provides guidance on network bandwidth requirements. This helps ensure that the organization's network can handle the traffic generated by Microsoft Defender for Identity without impacting other applications or services.

Before diving into the configuration details, ensure a seamless integration with Microsoft Defender for Identity by checking your network firewall settings, examining the specified ports, and verifying internet access. Additionally, review your Group Policy settings related to Windows events that will be forwarded to Microsoft Defender for Identity.

Check your network firewall for the following ports and internet access as well as your Group Policy regarding Windows events that will be sent to Microsoft Defender for Identity:

Protocol	Port	Transport	Destination: FROM	Destination: TO
DNS	445	TCP/UDP	Defender for Identity sensor	DNS server
RADIUS	1813	UDP	RADIUS	Defender for Identity sensor
SSL	443	TCP/UDP	Defender for Identity sensor	Defender for Identity cloud service
(*_atp.azure.com)				
Netlogon	445	TCP/UDP	Defender for Identity sensor	All devices
RDP	3389	TCP	Defender for Identity sensor	All devices
NetBIOS	137	UDP	Defender for Identity sensor	All devices
NTLM over RPC	135	TCP	Defender for Identity sensor	All devices

Table 8.2 – List of network ports

To collect Windows events for Microsoft Defender for Identity, you need to enable auditing for certain events on the relevant Windows servers or workstations. Here are recommended events to collect:

- Account logon events (event IDs 4624 and 4634)
- Account management events (event IDs 4720, 4722, 4723, 4724, 4725, 4726, 4727, 4728, 4729, 4730, 4731, 4732, 4733, 4734, 4735, 4737, 4740, and 4765)
- Directory service access events (event IDs 4662, 4663, and 4664)
- Logon events (event IDs 4624 and 4634)
- Object access events (event IDs 4656, 4658, and 4660)
- Policy changes events (event IDs 4719, 4902, and 4904)
- Process tracking events (event IDs 4688 and 4689)
- System events (event IDs 1102, 4616, and 4621)

Important note

It's important to keep in mind that the list of Windows events needed to be collected and sent to Microsoft Defender for Identity may vary depending on the specific needs and configurations of each organization. The examples provided earlier are just a starting point for identifying the events that may be relevant to your organization's security posture. Therefore, it's crucial to assess your organization's unique requirements and consult with your security team to determine the most appropriate events to collect and monitor.

Collecting these events can help you detect suspicious activity such as attempts to log on with stolen credentials, changes to user accounts or group memberships, and attempts to modify critical system files or registry keys.

The first step in configuring Microsoft Defender for Identity is to onboard the solution. To enable Microsoft Defender for Identity, go to the **Security Portal**, access **Settings**, and choose the **Identities** option:

Figure 8.1 – Microsoft Defender for Identity portal

Important note

If you get the message `Something went wrong. Your instance was not created because a security group with the same name already exists in Microsoft Entra ID. Delete the existing security groups and try again.`, go to your Microsoft Entra ID, and under **Groups**, search for and delete all three **Azure Advanced Threat Protection** (AATP) groups (**Azure ATP Administrators**, **Azure ATP Users**, and **Azure ATP Viewers**).

Configuring sensors for Microsoft Defender for Identity

Microsoft Defender for Identity (formerly known as AATP) uses sensors to collect information about user and device activities within an organization's network.

A sensor is a lightweight software component that is installed on DCs and other types of servers to monitor and collect security-related events, such as authentication attempts, privilege escalation, and lateral movement. The sensors collect data from the security logs of servers and send it to the Microsoft Defender for Identity cloud service for analysis and correlation with other data sources. The Microsoft Defender for Identity sensor provides visibility into the activities of users and devices, detects anomalies and suspicious behavior, and provides insights and recommendations to help organizations improve their security posture. By using sensors, Microsoft Defender for Identity can detect threats and attacks that might otherwise go unnoticed, enabling organizations to respond quickly and effectively to protect their sensitive data and assets.

Configuring the Microsoft Defender for Identity sensor involves several steps, including preparing the environment, deploying the sensor, and configuring the sensor settings. Here's a general overview of the process:

1. **Prepare the environment**: Make sure your environment meets the requirements for deploying the sensor, which includes having a Microsoft Entra ID tenant and appropriate permissions, DCs, and other servers to monitor, and a supported operating system and network configuration:

   I. On the **Microsoft Defender for Identity** portal, under **General**, click **Sensors** and press **Add sensor**:

Figure 8.2 – Configuring sensor for Microsoft Defender for Identity

II. On **Add a new sensor**, click on **Download installer** and copy the access key to a safe place or regenerate a new key:

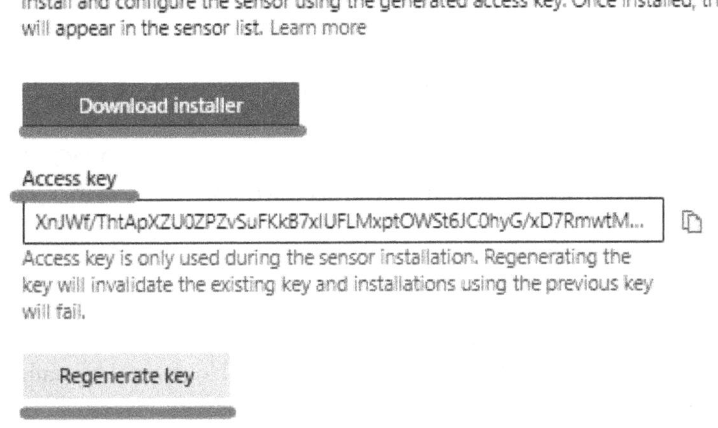

Figure 8.3 – Adding a new sensor

III. After successful sensor installation on the DC, press **Refresh** on Microsoft Defender for Identity to check the connectivity and visibility of the DC.

2. **Deploy the sensor**: You can deploy the sensor using various methods, such as Group Policy, **System Center Configuration Manager** (**SCCM**), or manually installing it on each server. Make sure you use the correct version of the sensor for your environment and follow the deployment instructions carefully.

3. **Configure the sensor settings**: Once the sensor is deployed, you can configure its settings using the Microsoft Defender for Identity portal. This includes enabling/disabling specific sensors, configuring data collection, setting up notifications, and configuring integration with other security solutions.
4. When you finish with sensor deployment and configuration, add **Directory Services accounts (DSAs)** through the Microsoft Defender for Identity portal:

   A. Click on **Directory services accounts**, choose the **Add Credentials** option, and define the following:

   - **Account name**
   - **Domain**
   - **Password**

Figure 8.4 – Adding credentials

In Microsoft Defender for Identity, DSAs are used to manage and monitor AD DCs. DSAs are privileged accounts that can access sensitive data and perform critical operations, such as modifying AD objects and group policies.

With Microsoft Defender for Identity, you can use DSAs to do the following:

- **Monitor DSA activity**: Microsoft Defender for Identity monitors and alerts on any suspicious or anomalous behavior related to DSA accounts, such as unusual login patterns, failed logins, or attempts to modify critical AD objects.
- **Identify high-risk accounts**: Microsoft Defender for Identity provides a risk assessment of each DSA, which helps administrators identify high-risk accounts and prioritize their monitoring efforts.
- **Investigate DSA-related incidents**: Microsoft Defender for Identity provides detailed information and context about any suspicious activity related to DSA accounts, including the account's name, domain, and group membership, as well as the specific activity performed by the account.

- **Detect anomalies**: Microsoft Defender for Identity uses ML to detect anomalies in the activity associated with each DSA. If an anomaly is detected, an alert is generated, and the administrator can investigate further.
- **Manage DSA permissions**: Microsoft Defender for Identity enables you to view and manage permissions assigned to DSA accounts, including user rights, security groups, and **Group Policy Objects (GPOs)** that the account has access to.
- **Secure DSA accounts**: Microsoft Defender for Identity helps you secure DSA accounts by providing recommendations for improving their security posture, such as enforcing strong passwords, implementing **multi-factor authentication** (**MFA**), or limiting DSA account access to specific computers or networks.
- **Mitigate risks**: Microsoft Defender for Identity provides guidance on how to mitigate the risks associated with each incident, such as disabling the compromised DSA, resetting the password associated with the DSA, or monitoring the affected user accounts.

If you wish to use a VPN, you can easily enable a RADIUS account through the **Microsoft Defender for Identity** portal. To enable RADIUS account monitoring in Microsoft Defender for Identity, you need to follow these steps:

1. **Open the Microsoft Defender for Identity portal**: Log in to the **Microsoft Defender for Identity** portal using your credentials.
2. **Navigate to the Configuration page**: Under **General**, click **VPN**:

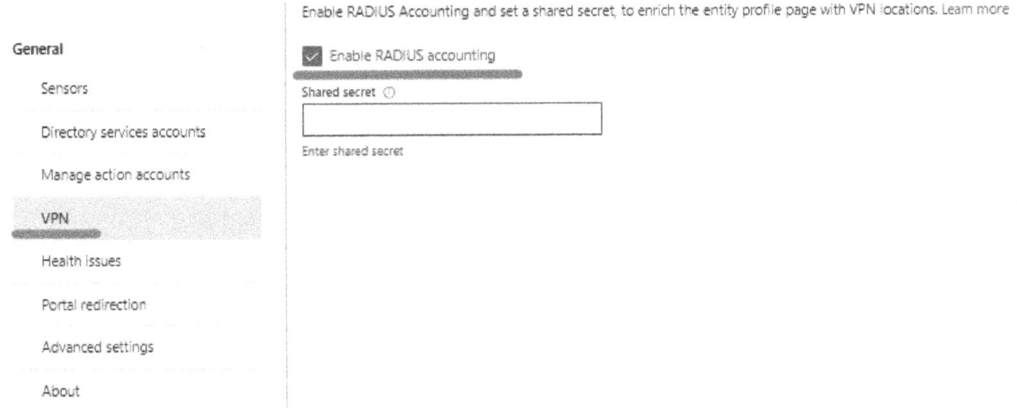

Figure 8.5 – Enabling RADIUS accounting

3. **Enable RADIUS monitoring**: Under the **Monitoring** section, toggle the **RADIUS monitoring** switch to the **On** position.

4. **Configure RADIUS settings**: Click the **Configure RADIUS** button and enter the settings for your RADIUS server, such as the RADIUS server name or IP address, the shared secret, and the UDP port number.
5. **Save the settings**: Click the **Save** button to save the RADIUS server settings.
6. **Verify the configuration**: Once you've saved the RADIUS settings, verify the configuration by clicking on the **Test Connection** button to confirm that the Defender for Identity service can connect to the RADIUS server.

With these steps, you have enabled RADIUS account monitoring in Microsoft Defender for Identity, allowing you to detect and investigate suspicious RADIUS authentication activity.

After configuring the sensor, you should test and verify that it's working correctly by reviewing the data in the Microsoft Defender for Identity portal, running simulated attacks or tests, and validating the results. All details about Microsoft Defender for Identity deployment can be found on the **About** portal. The **About** portal is located under **General** and contains all details about workspace, geolocation, system status, and so on:

Figure 8.6 – General options overview

Entity tags

Entity tags in Microsoft Defender for Identity are a way to group entities (users, devices, groups, and servers) that have similar characteristics or risk levels. Using entity tags can help you to manage your environment more efficiently and prioritize your security efforts.

Here's how to use entity tags in Microsoft Defender for Identity:

1. **Navigate to the Entity tags page**: Log in to the **Microsoft Defender for Identity** portal and navigate to the **Entity tags** page:

Figure 8.7 – Entity tags overview

2. **Under Sensitive, Honeytoken, and Exchange server, create a new entity tag**: Click on the **New entity tag** button to create a new entity tag:

   - Honeytoken entity tags in Microsoft Defender for Identity are a way to create fake accounts or resources that are designed to attract attackers and provide early warning of a potential breach. Honeytokens are essentially fake credentials or resources that are monitored by the Defender for Identity service, and when an attacker attempts to use them, the Defender for Identity service generates an alert. With Honeytokens, you can create a more proactive defense against attackers and get early warning of potential breaches. Honeytokens can be used to detect attacks such as credential theft or lateral movement and can help you act before an attacker is able to do significant damage:

Figure 8.8 – Honeytoken tags

3. **Define the criteria for the entity tag**: Choose criteria that will be used for **Users**, **Devices**, and **Groups** entities.
4. **Add entities to the entity tag**: Once you have defined the criteria for the entity tag, you can add entities to it manually or by using automatic tagging rules. For example, you could create a rule that automatically adds all devices running a certain operating system to a particular entity tag.
5. **Use entity tags to manage entities**: Once you have created entity tags and added entities to them, you can use them to manage your environment more efficiently. For example, you could use entity tags to do the following:
   - View the activity of entities with similar characteristics.
   - Create alerts or policies that apply to all entities in a particular tag.
   - Prioritize your investigation and response efforts based on the risk level of entities in a particular tag.

In the end, using entity tags in Microsoft Defender for Identity can help you streamline your security management efforts and improve your overall security posture.

Working with detection rules

In today's digital world, cybersecurity is becoming increasingly important for businesses of all sizes. Cybercriminals are always looking for new ways to exploit vulnerabilities in networks, endpoints, and identities to steal sensitive information, disrupt operations, or cause other forms of harm. Therefore, it is essential for organizations to have robust security solutions in place to protect against such threats. One of the key features of Microsoft Defender for Identity is detection rules. Let's explore detection rules in Microsoft Defender for Identity in more detail.

What are detection rules in Microsoft Defender for Identity?

Detection rules are predefined or custom conditions that are used to detect suspicious activities or behavior on the network, endpoints, or identity data. These rules are designed to help organizations identify potential security risks and take appropriate actions to mitigate them. Detection rules use a combination of advanced algorithms, ML models, and heuristics to analyze network traffic, endpoint logs, and identity data. They can detect a wide range of security threats, such as brute-force attacks, lateral movement, privilege escalation, suspicious logins, and more.

Microsoft Defender for Identity comes with a set of preconfigured detection rules that are based on best practices and industry standards. Currently, there are more than 50 preconfigured detection rules that you can use. Microsoft Defender for Identity provides several types of detection rules that can be used to detect different types of threats. These include the following:

- **Behavioral detection rules**: These rules use ML models to analyze user behavior and detect deviations from normal patterns. For example, if a user suddenly starts accessing resources that they have never accessed before or if a user is accessing resources from a location that is not typical for them, it may trigger a behavioral detection rule.
- **Anomaly detection rules**: These rules use statistical analysis to detect anomalies in network traffic or endpoint logs. For example, if there is a sudden increase in failed login attempts or if a device starts communicating with an IP address that is not recognized, it may trigger an anomaly detection rule.
- **Threat intelligence (TI) detection rules**: These rules use TI feeds to detect known malicious activities or **indicators of compromise** (**IoCs**). For example, if a user tries to execute known malware or if a device is communicating with a known **command-and-control** (**C2**) server, it may trigger a TI detection rule.

When a detection rule is triggered, Microsoft Defender for Identity generates an alert that includes information about the suspicious activity, the affected user or device, and recommended actions to mitigate the threat. The alert can be viewed in the Microsoft Defender for Identity portal, and can also be sent to other security tools, such as **security information and event management** (**SIEM**) solutions or ticketing systems, for further analysis or action.

Benefits of detection rules in Microsoft Defender for Identity include the following:

- **Proactive threat detection**: Detection rules in Microsoft Defender for Identity enable organizations to proactively detect potential security threats before they can cause significant damage. By analyzing network traffic, endpoint logs, and identity data in real time, detection rules can identify suspicious activities and alert security teams to act.
- **Customization**: Microsoft Defender for Identity allows organizations to create custom detection rules that are tailored to their specific security needs. This level of customization ensures that the organization's unique security risks are addressed.
- **Simplified security operations**: Detection rules in Microsoft Defender for Identity enable security teams to focus on the most critical security threats by providing automated alerts and recommended actions. This reduces the time and effort required to investigate security incidents and respond to them.

Detection rules in Microsoft Defender for Identity are a powerful tool for organizations looking to enhance their security posture. By proactively detecting potential security threats, organizations can mitigate risks and prevent significant damage. With the ability to create custom detection rules and automate alerting and response, Microsoft Defender for Identity can simplify security operations and help organizations stay ahead of emerging threats.

Detection rule examples

In this part of Microsoft Defender for Identity, we will try to explain a few preconfigured detection rules that you can use in your organization and configure as per your needs.

Detection rule: *Abnormal ADFS authentication using a suspicious certificate*

Abnormal ADFS authentication using a suspicious certificate is a type of cyber-attack where an attacker uses a forged or stolen digital certificate to authenticate with the ADFS server. This allows the attacker to bypass authentication controls and gain unauthorized access to resources in the organization. To help organizations detect this type of attack, Microsoft Defender for Identity includes a preconfigured detection rule called *Abnormal ADFS authentication using a suspicious certificate*. This rule uses a combination of ML models and heuristics to analyze authentication traffic to the ADFS server and identify anomalies that may indicate the use of a suspicious certificate. The *Abnormal ADFS authentication using a suspicious certificate* detection rule works by analyzing several different characteristics of authentication traffic to the ADFS server. These characteristics include the following:

- **Certificate chain validation**: The rule checks whether the certificate presented during the authentication process is part of a valid certificate chain. If the certificate chain is invalid or does not match the expected chain, the rule triggers an alert.
- **Certificate revocation status**: The rule checks whether the certificate presented during the authentication process has been revoked. If the certificate has been revoked or has an unknown status, the rule triggers an alert.
- **Certificate attributes**: The rule checks the attributes of the certificate presented during the authentication process, such as the **certificate authority** (**CA**), key length, and expiration date. If the certificate attributes are suspicious or do not match the expected values, the rule triggers an alert.
- **Authentication context**: The rule checks the context of the authentication request, such as the user account, device information, and network location. If the context is suspicious or does not match the expected values, the rule triggers an alert.

Exclusion by detection rules in Microsoft Defender for Identity is a valuable feature that allows organizations to fine-tune their security alerts and focus on the most critical threats. These rules permit security administrators to specify criteria that, when met, exclude certain activities or entities from triggering alerts. Defining such exclusions helps reduce noise generated by false positives, ensuring that security teams can prioritize and investigate genuine threats more effectively. This capability empowers organizations to customize their threat detection mechanisms, enhancing the efficiency and accuracy of their security operations while minimizing unnecessary distractions from non-threatening events:

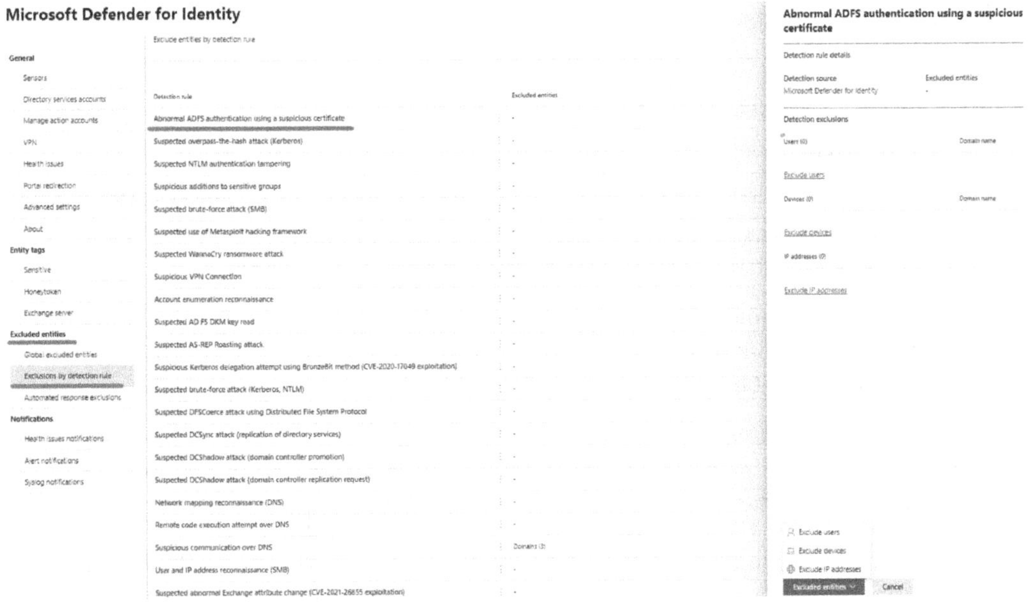

Figure 8.9 – Exclusion by detection rules

When the *Abnormal ADFS authentication using a suspicious certificate* detection rule is triggered, Microsoft Defender for Identity generates an alert that includes information about the suspicious activity, the affected user or device, and recommended actions to mitigate the threat. The alert can be viewed in the Microsoft Defender for Identity portal, and can also be sent to other security tools, such as SIEMs or ticketing systems, for further analysis or action.

Detection rule: *Suspected brute-force attack (SMB)*

A *Suspected brute-force attack (SMB)* detection rule is a security feature in Microsoft Defender for Identity that helps detect and mitigate brute-force attacks targeting the **Server Message Block** (**SMB**) protocol. Brute-force attacks are a type of cyber-attack that involves automated attempts to guess or crack login credentials, typically through trial-and-error methods.

The SMB protocol is a network protocol used for file sharing, printer sharing, and other networking tasks in Windows-based operating systems. As a result, it is a common target for cyber-attacks, including brute-force attacks. To help organizations protect against SMB brute-force attacks, Microsoft Defender for Identity includes a preconfigured detection rule called *Suspected brute-force attack (SMB)*. This rule analyzes authentication traffic to SMB servers and identifies patterns that indicate a brute-force attack may be underway.

The *Suspected brute-force attack (SMB)* detection rule works by analyzing several different characteristics of authentication traffic to SMB servers. These characteristics include the following:

- **Failed login attempts**: The rule looks for a high number of failed login attempts to SMB servers from a single source IP address. This may indicate that an attacker is using a brute-force method to guess login credentials.
- **Account lockouts**: The rule checks for a high number of account lockouts on SMB servers. Account lockouts occur when a user exceeds the maximum number of allowed failed login attempts, indicating that an attacker may be attempting to guess credentials.
- **Login attempts from unusual locations**: The rule checks for login attempts from unusual or unexpected network locations. This may indicate that an attacker is attempting to use a compromised account to access resources from a different location.
- **Login attempts at unusual times**: The rule checks for login attempts outside of normal business hours or during other unusual times. This may indicate that an attacker is attempting to gain access to resources when the organization's security defenses are likely to be weaker.

When the *Suspected brute-force attack (SMB)* detection rule is triggered, Microsoft Defender for Identity generates an alert that includes information about the suspicious activity, the affected user or device, and recommended actions to mitigate the threat. The alert can be viewed in the Microsoft Defender for Identity portal and can also be sent to other security tools, such as SIEMs or ticketing systems, for further analysis or action. If you want, you can exclude specific devices and IP addresses from this detection rule:

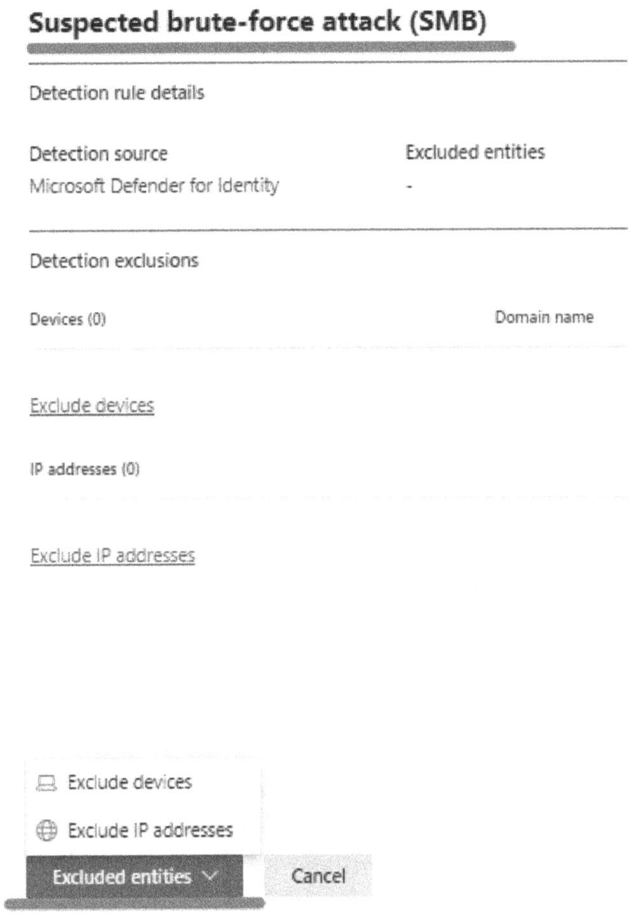

Suspected brute-force attack (SMB)

Detection rule details

Detection source
Microsoft Defender for Identity

Excluded entities
-

Detection exclusions

Devices (0) Domain name

Exclude devices

IP addresses (0)

Exclude IP addresses

Exclude devices

Exclude IP addresses

Excluded entities

Cancel

Figure 8.10 – Suspected brute-force attack (SMB) detection rule

In addition to the *Suspected brute-force attack (SMB)* detection rule, Microsoft Defender for Identity includes other preconfigured rules that help organizations detect and mitigate a wide range of security threats, such as lateral movement, privilege escalation, suspicious logins, and more. These rules are constantly updated by Microsoft to reflect the latest TI and to improve the accuracy of detections. The *Suspected brute-force attack (SMB)* detection rule is an important tool for organizations to detect and mitigate the risk of SMB brute-force attacks.

Detection rule: *Suspected NTLM relay attack (Exchange Server account)*

The *Suspected NTLM relay attack (Exchange Server account)* detection rule is a security feature in Microsoft Defender for Identity that helps organizations detect and mitigate **NT LAN Manager** (**NTLM**) relay attacks targeting Exchange Server accounts. NTLM relay attacks are a type of cyber-attack that exploits weaknesses in the authentication process to gain unauthorized access to sensitive information.

Exchange Server is a popular email and messaging platform used by many organizations. As a result, it is a common target for cyber attackers seeking to steal sensitive information, such as email messages, contact lists, and other confidential data. To help organizations protect against NTLM relay attacks targeting Exchange Server accounts, Microsoft Defender for Identity includes a preconfigured detection rule called *Suspected NTLM relay attack (Exchange Server account)*. This rule analyzes authentication traffic to Exchange Server accounts and identifies patterns that indicate an NTLM relay attack may be underway.

The *Suspected NTLM relay attack (Exchange Server account)* detection rule works by analyzing several different characteristics of authentication traffic to Exchange Server accounts. These characteristics include the following:

- **Authentication requests from unknown devices**: The rule looks for authentication requests from devices that have not been previously seen or authenticated by Microsoft Defender for Identity. This may indicate that an attacker is attempting to use a rogue device to relay authentication requests and gain access to the target account.
- **Authentication requests from multiple devices**: The rule checks for authentication requests from multiple devices within a short period of time. This may indicate that an attacker is attempting to relay authentication requests to multiple devices to gain access to the target account.
- **Authentication requests from different locations**: The rule looks for authentication requests from different geographic locations. This may indicate that an attacker is attempting to use a compromised device to relay authentication requests from a different location.
- **Authentication requests at unusual times**: The rule checks for authentication requests outside of normal business hours or during other unusual times. This may indicate that an attacker is attempting to gain access to resources when the organization's security defenses are likely to be weaker.

When the *Suspected NTLM relay attack (Exchange Server account)* detection rule is triggered, Microsoft Defender for Identity generates an alert that includes information about the suspicious activity, the affected user or device, and recommended actions to mitigate the threat. The alert can be viewed in the Microsoft Defender for Identity portal and can also be sent to other security tools, such as SIEMs or ticketing systems, for further analysis or action.

Configuring Microsoft Defender for Identity and Microsoft Sentinel

Before we start to explain the configuration between these two security solutions, we need to explain what Microsoft Sentinel is.

In short, Microsoft Sentinel is a cloud-native SIEM solution that helps organizations collect, analyze, and respond to security incidents across their entire IT environment. Built on top of the Microsoft Azure cloud platform, Sentinel provides a unified view of security events and alerts from various sources, including Azure, Office 365, third-party solutions (such as Cisco, Barracuda, and Fortinet), and on-premises infrastructure. Sentinel leverages advanced ML algorithms and **artificial intelligence** (**AI**) to detect and respond to security threats in real time. It uses a combination of rule-based and anomaly-based detection methods to identify suspicious behavior and provides a central dashboard for security analysts to investigate and remediate security incidents.

One of the key benefits of Microsoft Sentinel is its integration with other Microsoft security solutions, including Microsoft Defender for Endpoint, Microsoft Defender for Identity, and Microsoft Cloud App Security. This allows organizations to benefit from a seamless and integrated security ecosystem, with a unified view of security events across different services.

Another advantage of Sentinel is its scalability and flexibility. Because it is a cloud-native solution, organizations can quickly and easily scale up or down as their security needs change, without the need for additional hardware or infrastructure. Additionally, Sentinel provides a wide range of connectors and APIs that allow organizations to easily integrate with third-party security solutions and customize the platform to their specific needs. In the current Microsoft Sentinel version, you have more than 100 different non-Microsoft connectors to configure (Cisco, IBM, Palo Alto, Barracuda, Fortinet, and so on).

In a short time, Microsoft Sentinel became a very important player in the SIEM world. Overall, Microsoft Sentinel is a powerful and flexible SIEM solution that helps organizations improve their security posture and respond to security incidents in a timely and effective manner. With its advanced ML capabilities, integration with other Microsoft security solutions, and cloud-native architecture, Sentinel is well suited for organizations of all sizes and industries.

So, how can you connect Microsoft Defender for Identity and Microsoft Sentinel? First, for Microsoft Sentinel, you need to have a valid Azure subscription and configure Microsoft Sentinel services in Azure. Configuring Microsoft Sentinel is not a part of this book, so we will focus on configuring the two solutions and making them work together.

To connect Microsoft Defender for Identity and Microsoft Sentinel, follow these steps:

1. Log in to Azure with your Azure admin account.
2. Open the **Microsoft Sentinel** portal (if you cannot see the portal, type `Microsoft Sentinel` in search).
3. In the **Microsoft Sentinel** portal, go to **Data connectors**, and in search, type `Microsoft 365 Defender`:

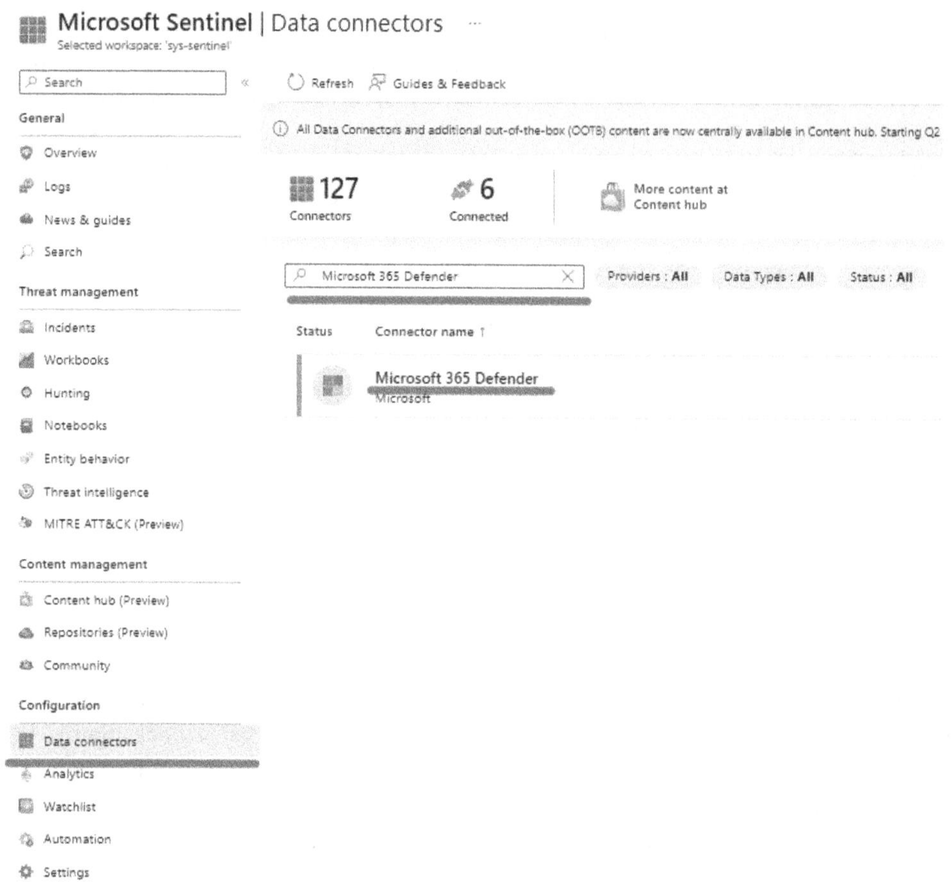

Figure 8.11 – Data connectors

Important note

Microsoft Sentinel can accept logs from all Microsoft 365 Defender suite solutions:

- Microsoft Defender for Office 365
- Microsoft Defender for Cloud Apps
- Microsoft Defender for Identity
- Microsoft Defender for Endpoint
- Alerts
- Microsoft Defender Vulnerability Management
- Microsoft Entra ID Protection
- Microsoft Purview **Data Loss Prevention** (**DLP**)

4. In the open window, click on **Open connector page**: On this page, you will see that the selected data connector contains 2 workbooks, 4 queries, and 72 predefined analytics rules.
5. Check **Prerequisites** for proper integration:
    - Check **Workspace**
    - Check **Connector Access Control**
    - Check **Tenant Permissions**

Figure 8.12 – Prerequisites for proper integration

6. Under the **Configuration** section, check the **Turn off all Microsoft incident creation rules for these products. Recommended.** option:

> **Important note**
>
> Microsoft 365 Defender automatically groups alerts from Microsoft Defender for Endpoint, Microsoft Defender for Identity, Microsoft Defender for Office 365, Microsoft Defender for Cloud Apps, and Microsoft Entra ID Identity Protection into incidents. To avoid duplications in the incidents queue, it is recommended to turn off incident creation rules for those products. Note that if you have any filters in your incident creation rules, they will not be considered in the direct incident integration.

Figure 8.13 – Connecting incidents and alerts

7. Under **Connect entities**, click on **Go the UEBA configuration page**:

    - **Microsoft Sentinel User and Entity Behavior Analytics** (**UEBA**) is a feature within Microsoft Sentinel, a cloud-native SIEM solution. UEBA uses ML algorithms to detect anomalies in user and entity behavior by analyzing patterns of activities, such as login attempts, file access, and network traffic. It helps identify potential insider threats, compromised accounts, and other suspicious activities that may pose a security risk to an organization. With the help of UEBA, security teams can investigate security incidents more efficiently and take proactive measures to prevent potential threats before they cause harm.

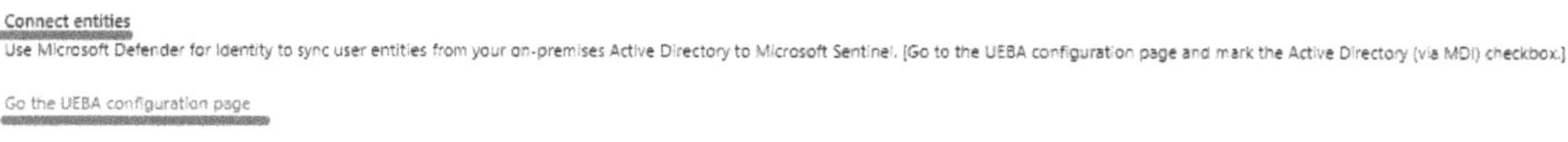

Figure 8.14 – Connecting entities

8. Configure options on the UEBA portal, connect your Microsoft Sentinel with your Microsoft Entra ID and/or AD, and select which data sources you want to send to Microsoft Sentinel:

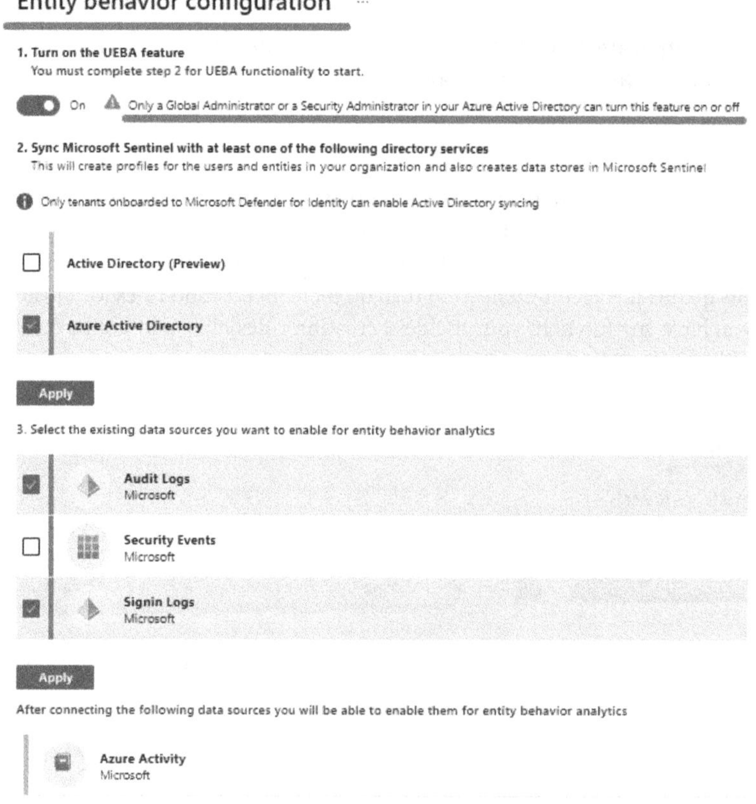

Figure 8.15 – Entity behavior configuration

9. Under **Connect events**, select which logs will be sent from Microsoft Defender for Identity to Microsoft Sentinel:

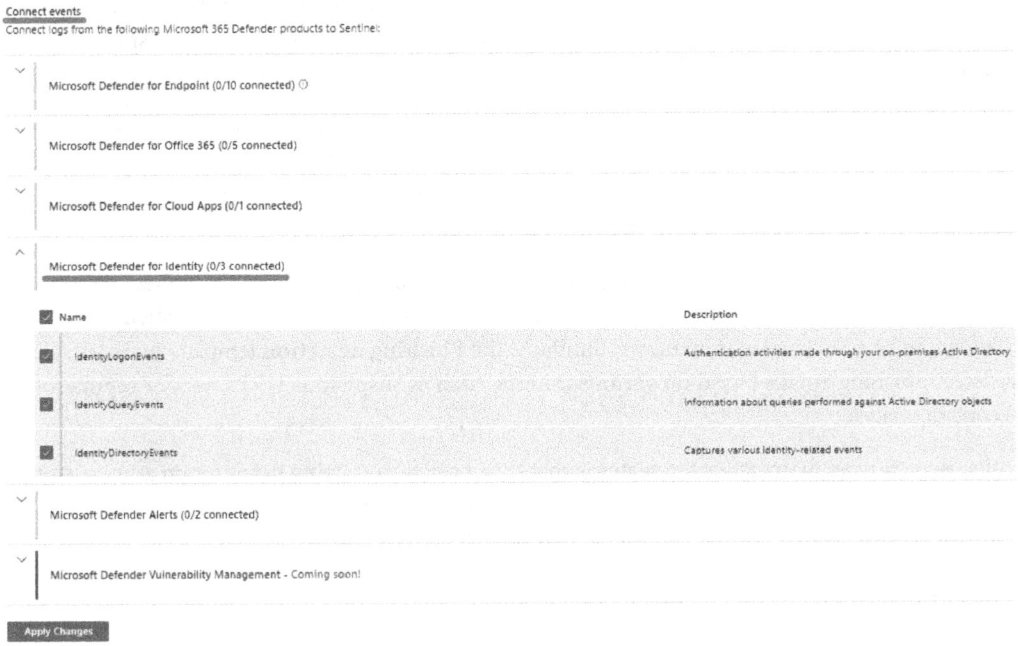

Figure 8.16 – Connecting events

We'll now navigate through the world of analytics rules in Microsoft Sentinel, unveiling how these rules play a pivotal role in identifying and responding to security threats across your organization's data landscape. Analytics rules in Microsoft Sentinel are the backbone of proactive **threat detection and response** (**TDR**) within the Microsoft Sentinel platform. These rules serve as the intelligence behind identifying suspicious activities, security anomalies, and potential threats across an organization's data sources. By customizing and deploying analytics rules, security teams can create tailored detection scenarios, allowing them to promptly identify and respond to security incidents. These rules enable organizations to stay one step ahead of cyber threats, ensuring the protection of their digital assets and the integrity of their systems.

Analytics rules in Microsoft Sentinel

Analytics rules templates are preconfigured rule templates that help security teams detect common threats and suspicious activities in their Microsoft 365 environment. These templates are designed to work with data sources such as Microsoft Defender for Office 365, Microsoft Defender for Endpoint, Microsoft Defender for Identity, and Microsoft Entra ID Protection.

Using analytics rules templates, security teams can quickly set up and customize security monitoring for their Microsoft 365 environment. They can also create new rules based on the templates or modify existing ones to better suit their specific needs. This approach helps teams save time and effort in creating security rules from scratch and enables them to focus on identifying and responding to potential threats more efficiently.

One of the key benefits of analytics rules templates is that they cover a range of security scenarios, such as malware detection, phishing attacks, suspicious logins, and data exfiltration. Each template consists of predefined rules that use advanced analytics techniques, such as ML, to analyze data from multiple sources and detect anomalies and potential security threats.

For example, the **Malware detection** template includes preconfigured rules that detect common malware behavior, such as attempts to install or execute malware on endpoints, or the downloading of files known to be associated with malware. Similarly, the **Phishing detection** template includes rules that detect phishing emails based on various criteria, such as suspicious URLs, sender reputation, and content analysis.

Another benefit of analytics rules templates is that they provide a starting point for creating custom rules that meet specific organizational needs. Security teams can use the templates as a foundation and modify the rules to better suit their unique environment and security posture. They can also create new rules based on the templates, using the same advanced analytics techniques to detect potential threats and anomalies.

Custom rules can be created in a variety of ways. For example, teams can create a custom rule based on a pre-existing template by modifying the rule parameters or logic to better fit their specific environment. Alternatively, they can create a custom rule from scratch using the same advanced analytics techniques and data sources used in the analytics rules templates.

For a quick overview of incidents and events in data connectors for Microsoft 365 Defender, you can simply choose one of the following data types:

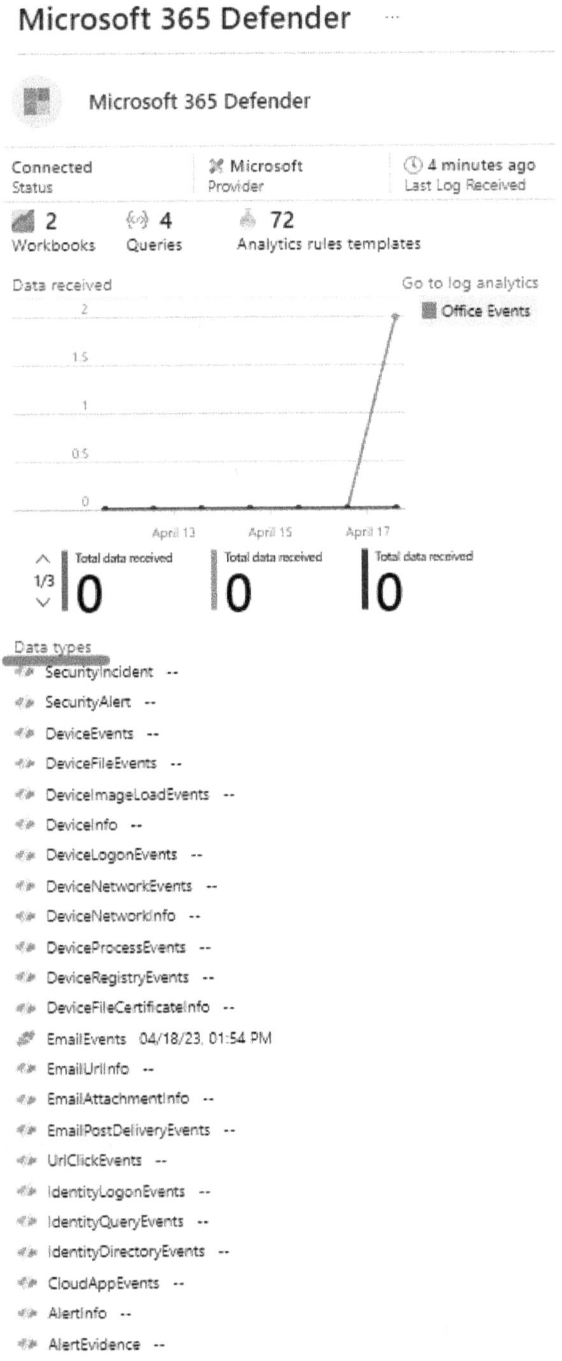

Figure 8.17 – Microsoft 365 Defender in Microsoft Sentinel

Microsoft Defender for Identity data types include the following:

- `IdentityLogonEvents`
- `IdentityQueryEvents`
- `IdentityDirectionEvents`

Here are a few examples of **Kusto Query Language** (**KQL**) code for searching `IdentityLogonEvents`:

```
IdentityLogonEvents
| where TimeGenerated >= ago (7d)
| where UserPrincipalName == "user name@domain"
```

Also, here's an example KQL query that searches for all failed logon events in AD within Microsoft Sentinel:

```
SecurityEvent
| where TimeGenerated >= ago(24h)
| where EventID == 4625
| where AccountType == 'User'
| where Status == '0xc000006d' or Status == '0xc000006e' or Status ==
'0xc000006f' or Status == '0xc0000070'
```

This query looks for events in the `SecurityEvent` table within the last 24 hours (`ago(24h)`). It filters for event ID 4625, which indicates a failed login attempt. It also filters for an `AccountType` value of `'User'`, as we're interested in failed user logins. Finally, it filters for specific failure status codes (`'0xc000006d'`, `'0xc000006e'`, `'0xc000006f'`, or `'0xc0000070'`) that correspond to various types of failed login attempts.

This is an example of searching for locked user accounts:

```
SecurityEvent
| where TimeGenerated >= ago(30d)
| where EventID == 4740
| where AccountType == 'User'
| where EventData contains "%%2313" // this is the code for "Account
Lockout"
```

This query looks for events in the `SecurityEvent` table within the last 30 days (`ago(30d)`). It filters for event ID 4740, which indicates an account was locked out. It also filters for an `AccountType` value of `'User'`, as we're interested in user accounts being locked out. Finally, it searches for the `"%%2313"` string in the `EventData` field, which is the code for `"Account Lockout"` in Windows event logs.

> **Important note**
>
> For proper searching of events in Microsoft Sentinel, as well as Microsoft Defender for Identity, it is important to have configured GPOs in your AD environment.

You can modify the time range as needed and adjust the filter conditions to search for specific users or computers if necessary.

In addition to providing a starting point for creating custom rules, analytics rules templates also provide a way to keep security monitoring up to date with the latest threats and attack methods. Microsoft continually updates the templates to include new rules and scenarios based on the latest TI and security research. As a result, security teams can be confident that their security monitoring is keeping pace with the ever-evolving threat landscape.

To get the most out of analytics rules templates, it is important to understand the different types of rules that are included in the templates. There are three main types of rules:

- **Detection rules**: These rules use advanced analytics techniques to detect potential threats and anomalies based on data from multiple sources. For example, a detection rule might analyze logins from a specific IP address and identify suspicious activity based on factors such as the number of login attempts, time of day, and location.
- **Response rules**: These rules define actions that should be taken when a potential threat or anomaly is detected. For example, a response rule might trigger an automated email to a security analyst when a potential phishing email is detected.
- **Data enrichment rules**: These rules provide additional context and information about an event or activity, which can help security analysts better understand the potential threat and respond more effectively. For example, a data enrichment rule might retrieve additional information about a user's behavior or device configuration.

Analytics rules templates in Microsoft Sentinel for Microsoft 365 Defender provide security teams with a powerful tool for monitoring and detecting potential threats in their Microsoft 365 environment. The preconfigured rules and advanced analytics techniques enable security teams to quickly set up and customize security monitoring without requiring extensive knowledge of data analysis or security best practices. While false positives can be a potential challenge, the templates are regularly updated to ensure that security monitoring remains effective and efficient.

Summary

Throughout this chapter, we've taken you on a journey to uncover the multifaceted world of configuring Microsoft Defender for Identity, a vital component of an organization's cybersecurity arsenal. With each step, you've had the opportunity to delve into this robust security solution, discovering how to harness its full potential for safeguarding your digital environment. This chapter serves as a comprehensive guide, equipping you with the knowledge and tools necessary to configure Microsoft Defender for Identity effectively.

After activating the service, we delved into the world of configuration settings. One of the compelling features of Microsoft Defender for Identity is its adaptability, allowing you to align its settings with your organization's specific security policies, threat detection thresholds, and compliance requirements. The depth of this configurability provides you with the means to optimize the service's performance, ensuring it aligns with your organization's unique security objectives.

In conclusion, this chapter has been a deep dive into the world of configuring Microsoft Defender for Identity. From service activation to fine-tuning settings, connectors, and sensors, you are now well equipped with the knowledge and skills needed to unlock the full potential of this robust security solution. Implementing these configurations effectively will not only fortify your organization's security posture but also enable you to proactively identify and mitigate identity-based threats, ensuring a safer and more secure digital environment. As we continue this journey, you'll find yourself better prepared to navigate the ever-evolving landscape of cybersecurity.

We will take a dive into the world of improved data governance with the next chapter on Microsoft Purview Insider Risk Management. We will see how this state-of-the-art solution gives organizations the power to spot and address insider risks in their data networks ahead of time. We will explore everything from advanced threat detection to a thorough risk assessment, and witness the capabilities that redefine how we safeguard data in the digital age.

Part 3: Microsoft 365 Governance and Compliance

In this third part, we will discuss products and features responsible for governance and compliance in Microsoft 365. We will include Microsoft Purview Insider Risk Management with Insider Risk Management, Information Barriers, and Communication Compliance, and Microsoft Purview Information Protection, labeling, and classification capabilities. To wrap it up, we will address auditing and records life cycle management in Microsoft 365.

This part has the following chapters:

- *Chapter 9, Microsoft Purview Insider Risk Management*
- *Chapter 10, Microsoft Purview Information Protection*
- *Chapter 11, Understanding the Lifecycle of Auditing and Records*

9

Microsoft Purview Insider Risk Management

In a conversation about computer security, cloud security, cyber threats, cyber-attacks, attacks on computer systems, the ways companies and individuals become victims of attacks and lose their data, and how the data is stolen, people usually immediately think about hackers and how external attacks are the reason for data breaches and data loss.

Undoubtedly, hackers and external attacks still pose a threat to company data but as companies and their computer and cloud infrastructure get progressively better protection, attackers increasingly turn to the ones with direct contact with valuable company data.

People with direct contact with the data – employees – are becoming the major threat and concern among businesses of all sizes. Insider threat statistics are scary, and the numbers have been rising constantly. According to various statistics, around 65% of data breaches are caused by insider threats, while more than 70% of organizations report that insider attacks have increased constantly over the last 2 years. More than half of companies have had an insider attack in the last 12 months, and the number of incidents due to insider threats has increased by over 50% in 2 years.

Obviously, the major threat to company data is privileged users such as administrators and C-level executives because they have access to the most sensitive data, but essentially, every user is a potential threat if they have access to the data that attackers want.

According to Eleanor Thompson's "*The Insider Threat – Assessment and Mitigation of Risks*," there are four types of malicious insiders or insider threats – the malevolent insider, the vengeful insider, the wicked insider, and the virtuous insider. A malevolent insider deliberately harms a system for their personal gain, a vengeful insider retaliates against the organization and its leadership, a wicked insider knows what the rules are but disobeys them either for personal interest or because of some other intentions, while the virtuous insider is an employee that is usually well intended but places organizations at high risk through their risky behavior.

There is no single guaranteed tool to prevent insider threats, but a multitude of tools and a sound, holistic approach is what organizations need to reduce insider threats: privileged access management; just-in-time access; access control lists; incident response management; employee monitoring; security incident, data loss prevention, and event management systems such as **Security Information and Event Management** (**SIEM**); and others.

Fortunately, Microsoft Purview's comprehensive insider risk prevention features will significantly increase organizations' capability to mitigate these types of security and compliance concerns.

In this chapter, we are going to cover the following main topics:

- Insider risk management
- Information barriers
- Communication compliance

In this chapter, you will learn about comprehensive insider risk capabilities in Microsoft 365, information barriers, and communication compliance abilities, including relevant alerting, reporting, and auditing.

Technical requirements

To be able to use Microsoft 365 Purview Insider risk management, you must have one of the Microsoft 365 E5, A5, F5, or G5 subscriptions. Alternatively, Microsoft 365 E3, A3, F3, and G3 subscriptions will work too, together with either compliance or insider risk management add-ons.

Ultimately, an Office 365 E3 subscription paired with Enterprise Mobility and Security E3 paired with a compliance add-on will provide you with sufficient rights to work with Insider Risk Management.

Insider Risk Management

Microsoft Purview **Insider Risk Management** (**IRM**) is just one product in the palette of risk and compliance solutions available in Microsoft Purview that works together with communication compliance, information barriers, and privileged access management to help organizations successfully mitigate insider threats.

The potential dangers posed by insider threats, emerging from activities that are illegal, inappropriate, unauthorized, or unethical, constitute a significant concern for all companies. These risks can often remain unnoticed until it's too late. Whether it involves intellectual property theft, data breaches, or other potential scenarios, safeguarding an organization's data from both unintentional and malicious actions is of utmost importance. While it is harder to stop an intentional data exfiltration action than an unintentional action, IRM provides an additional layer of protection against data leakage and exfiltration. Microsoft provides solutions that assist organizations in achieving the right, appropriate balance between safeguarding their data and maintaining productivity among an organization's employees.

Insider Risk Management will help you mitigate regulatory compliance violations, leaks of sensitive data, policy and confidentiality violations, IP theft, fraud, and different types of data loss.

Initial setup

Before proceeding with the technical implementation of insider risk management, organizations should start the onboarding process with planning activities that will thoroughly assess and determine desirable and required compliance regulations, procedures, and requirements. This task requires the involvement of various departments besides the information technology department, and the involvement of different stakeholders such as privacy, human resources, legal, security, and compliance stakeholders.

Implementing and enabling Insider Risk Management in production should not be different than what the standard practice describes when implementing any potentially disrupting procedures, products, or features. You should test insider risk policies on a small subset of users in a test environment to determine privacy, compliance, or legal issues in your organization, and fine-tune the policies to meet all necessary requirements. The alternative is to test insider risk policies in the production environment, but also on a small subset of users to minimize any potentially negative impact on your production environment.

To get started with Insider Risk Management, log in to `https://compliance.microsoft.com` and select the **Insider Risk Management** option on the left-side menu.

To have access to the **Insider Risk Management** menu option on the left, you must be assigned at least one of the following roles:

- Microsoft Entra ID Global Administrator
- Microsoft Entra ID Compliance Administrator

You also need to be a member of at least one of the following role groups:

- Microsoft Purview Organization Management
- Microsoft Purview Compliance Administrator
- Insider Risk Management
- Insider Risk Management Admins

To work with Insider Risk Management, the well-known principle of least privilege should be on the top of the list of priorities, and for that, there are the following role groups in IRM:

- Insider Risk Management
- Insider Risk Management Admins
- Insider Risk Management Analysts
- Insider Risk Management Investigators
- Insider Risk Management Auditors
- Insider Risk Management Approvers

> **Note**
>
> For the complete list of IRM role group options and solutions, visit `https://learn.microsoft.com/en-us/purview/insider-risk-management-configure`.

Before going deeper into the IRM workflow, you need to consider completing the following initial and desirable steps, and a high-level summary is very conveniently available on the **Overview** page.

The following initial steps are not the only steps you should perform, of course; they are instead a handful of recommended actions only. Selecting **All recommended actions** will bring up a somewhat expanded list of recommendations that provide an excellent starting point for configuring Insider Risk Management. These options are available from the IRM settings anyway, but following this advice will save you some time in configuring IRM while focusing on the most important configuration settings. To access the **Recommended actions** pane, select **All recommended actions** on the **Overview** page, or click on the wrench icon in the upper-right corner of the **Overview** page:

Insider risk management > Recommended actions

Recommended actions

Whether you're just getting started or actively detecting and reviewing user activity, complete these recommended actions to get the most out of insider risk management capabilities.

Not started 6 | Completed 2

Show completed actions

Setup actions

Action	Status	Required or optional	Time to complete	Tutorial
Turn on analytics to scan for potential risks Scans run daily and provide real-time insights to help detect activity that matters most.	Completed	Optional	48 hours	Includes video tutorial
Get to know insider risk management Learn about the solution...what it is, best practices, common terms, and more.	Not started	Optional	10 min	
Configure insider risk settings Define settings that apply to all insider risk features and workflows.	Not started	Required	10 min	Includes video tutorial
Create your first policy Use predefined templates to detect risk activities, such as data theft.	Completed	Required	5 min	
Make sure your team can get their jobs done Assign permissions by adding other admins to insider risk management role groups.	Not started	Required	10 min	Includes video tutorial

Investigation actions

Action	Status	Required or optional	Time to complete	Tutorial
Review users whose activity is being scored See which users are having their activity scored by your policies.	Not started	Optional	5 min	
Review alerts Review alerts generated by policies to decide if further investigation is needed.	Not started	Optional	5 min	
Investigate a case Deeply investigate a user's activities to identify and take action on potential risks.	Not started	Optional	10 min	

Figure 9.1 – Insider Risk Management recommended actions

The recommended setup actions or initial steps to get started and configure IRM are in fact the list of actions you should do first when setting up IRM:

- Turn on auditing to record user and admin activity
- Set up the right permissions by assigning users to the correct groups
- Choose policy indicators, that is, risk management activities you want to detect
- Create a policy to start receiving alerts
- Assign permissions to other users, to delegate access

The first thing you should do is turn on analytics to scan for potential risks. Analytics scans different areas for user activity, such as Microsoft 365 audit logs, Microsoft Entra ID activities, Exchange Online activities, and, if configured, Microsoft 365 HR data connector activities. The first analytics scan usually takes 48 hours to complete while analytics scans after that are completed daily. Analytics settings can be found on the Insider Risk Management settings page and turned on there later if needed. The recommended setting is to turn analytics on so Microsoft 365 can scan sources in organization logs to detect activities using insider risk policies. These scans run daily and can be used later to set up insider risk policies:

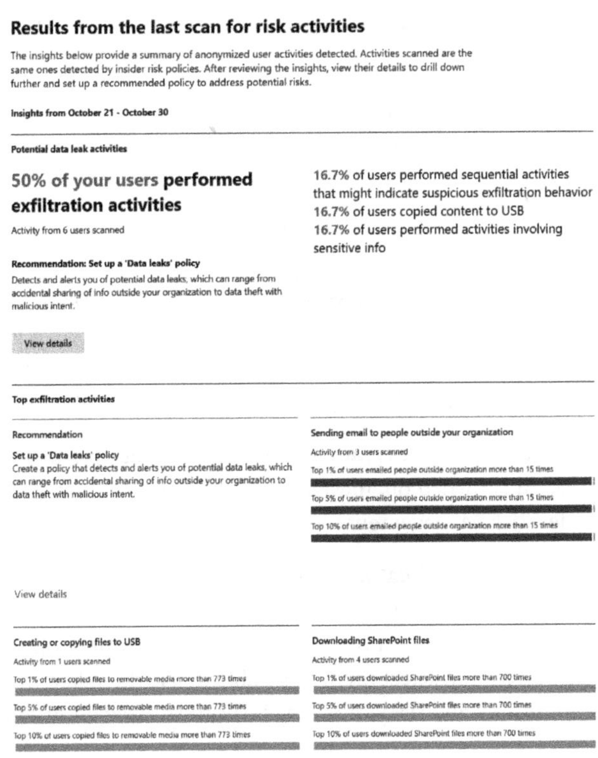

Figure 9.2 – Analytics results summary from the last scan for risky activities

After the initial analytics scan finishes, the analytics report will include insights for any potential data leaks, data theft, and exfiltration attempts. The report will show details about detected activities and recommendations for creating policies that will detect alerts and prevent such activities.

The **Configure insider risk settings** recommended action contains **Privacy**, **Policy indicators**, and **Admin email notifications** recommended settings that will apply to the entire Insider Risk Management product:

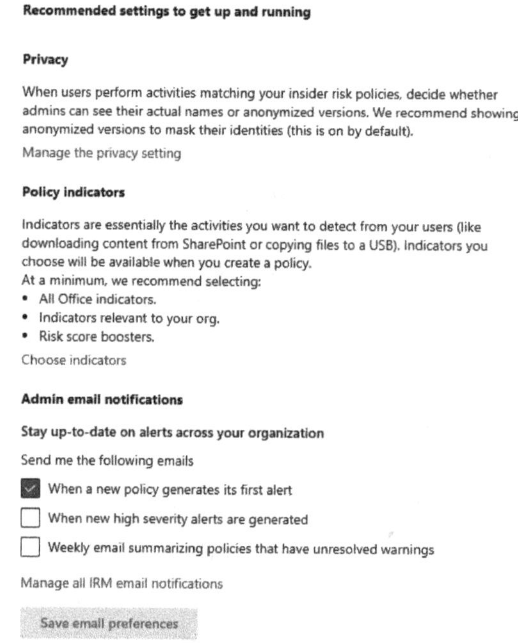

Figure 9.3 – Recommended settings to get started with IRM

All three recommended settings to get up and running are a part of the Insider Risk Management settings, which can be easily accessed by selecting the cog in the upper-right corner.

Select **Manage the privacy settings** (or **Privacy** in **Settings**) to set up a display of anonymized usernames, where if this option is turned on, masked versions of usernames will be used instead of real usernames across Insider Risk Management.

Select **Choose indicators** (or **Policy Indicators** in **Settings**) to select different types of built-in or custom indicators that will be included in policy templates. Indicators are descriptions of user activities that will trigger alerts when enabled. Not all the indicators are on by default, so you must look at what indicators are relevant to you and select them to be able to use them later in the policies. Some indicators, such as device indicators and risky browsing indicators, need additional setups to be able to select them.

The available built-in indicators are as follows:

- Office indicators
- Device indicators
- Microsoft Defender for Endpoint indicators
- Risky browsing indicators
- Microsoft Defender for Cloud Apps indicators
- Health record access indicators
- Cumulative exfiltration detection indicators
- Risk score booster indicators

Admin email notifications (or **Admin notifications** in **Settings**) allows you to quickly configure administrative notifications for normal and high-severity alerts, warnings, and summaries, for different IRM role groups.

The last two recommended actions are **Create your first policy** and **Make sure your team can get their jobs done**, which are the next logical steps to finish the initial configuration of the IRM. The first recommendation is to create risk management policies, and we will devote more time to that later in the chapter. The next recommended step is to create the required Insider Risk Management role groups.

> NOTE
>
> Please visit the following link for the Insider Risk Management role groups and permissions comparison table: `https://learn.microsoft.com/en-us/purview/insider-risk-management-configure#step-1-required-enable-permissions-for-insider-risk-management`.

There are also three recommendations for investigation actions, but you will have to return to these later because you will need some user activities and alerts to investigate a case.

On the **Insider risk management** start page, click the cog icon in the top-right corner to display the IRM settings page. As you already visited it and set a few of the initial settings, such as a privacy policy, indicators, and admin notifications, you also need to set the policy time frames that will determine the time periods that IRM will take into account when determining a period to trigger a match for an insider risk policy. Policy frames have two settings: **Activation window**, which is the number of days that the policy will use to detect user activities, and **Past activity detection**, which sets how far back a policy will look to detect user activities.

On the **Insider risk management** page, click on the clipboard icon in the top-right corner to open the **Insider risk audit log** page:

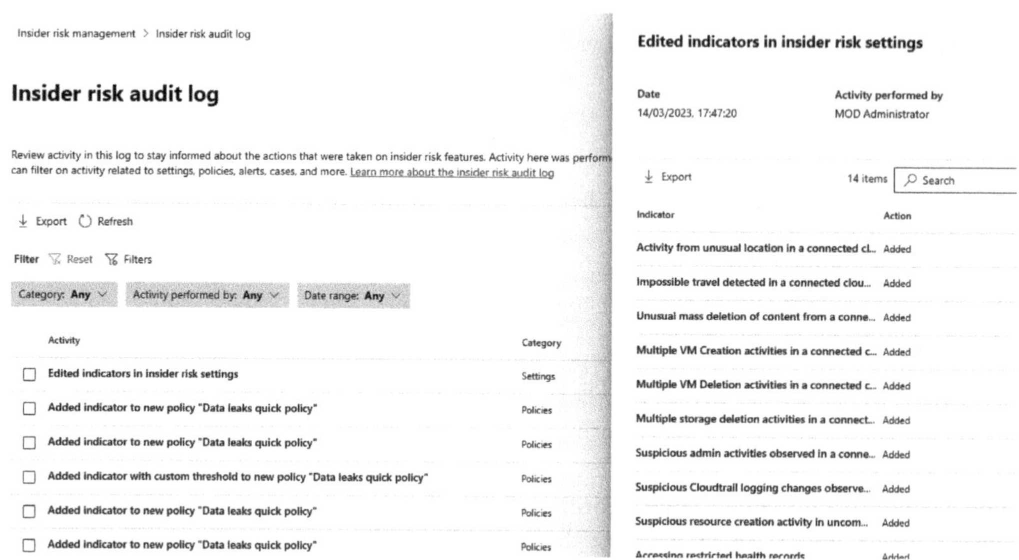

Figure 9.4 – Insider risk audit log

One of the important activities to keep in mind is reviewing the **Insider risk audit log** page regularly, where a few columns are available: **Activity**, **Category**, **Activity Performed by**, and **Date**. Selecting a log activity entry will display additional details about the activity, which of course will be specific to a log activity, but can include policy template details, actions, membership information, and more.

Some of the most important Insider Risk Management settings are as follows:

- **Policy timeframes**: Here, you can set **activation window** and **past activity detection timeframe** settings. Activation window settings determine how long a policy will detect user activity once a policy setting is matched. Past activity detection timeframe settings configure how far back in the past the policy will detect user activity after a policy is triggered.
- **Intelligent detections**: These settings influence the way the policy detects user activity. You can set different types of exclusions (file types, file paths, sensitive info types, trainable classifiers, sites, keywords), alert volume settings, and allowed and unallowed domains.
- **Export alerts**: It is possible to turn Office 365 management activity APIs on, to export insider risk alert details to an external event management service. However, alerts that are exported do not support the anonymization of usernames.
- **Priority user groups**: If there are user groups that contain users whose risk level is typically higher than other users, you can prioritize these groups to have more sensitive risk scoring and prioritized inspection and detection.

There are, of course, more configuration settings available, and at the time of writing, many of them are in the preview phase.

After reviewing alerts, incidents, and user actions, you should have gathered enough information to decide whether such activities are indeed actions that need to be investigated because these might indicate true positive user behavior and it's a good time to create and assign an Insider Risk Management case.

Resolving insider risk cases

To be able to create alerts, Insider Risk Management needs to scan user activity and match these activities to active policies. You have already turned analytics on, as a part of the initial Insider Risk Management setup; now you need to create and activate policies that will generate alerts if a match is found. After that, one or more alerts can be assigned to a user, as an **Insider Risk Management case**, or just a **case** for short, which will be used as a boundary to resolve assigned alerts.

Resolving insider risk cases involves the following flow:

1. Define and create Insider Risk Management policies.
2. Alerts are created based on matched conditions in policies.
3. Triage user activities.
4. Investigate user activities.
5. Act to resolve cases.

Defining and creating Insider Risk Management policies

To define and create an Insider Risk Management policy, open the **Insider risk management** blade at `https://compliance.microsoft.com`, and select **Policies** from the top menu:

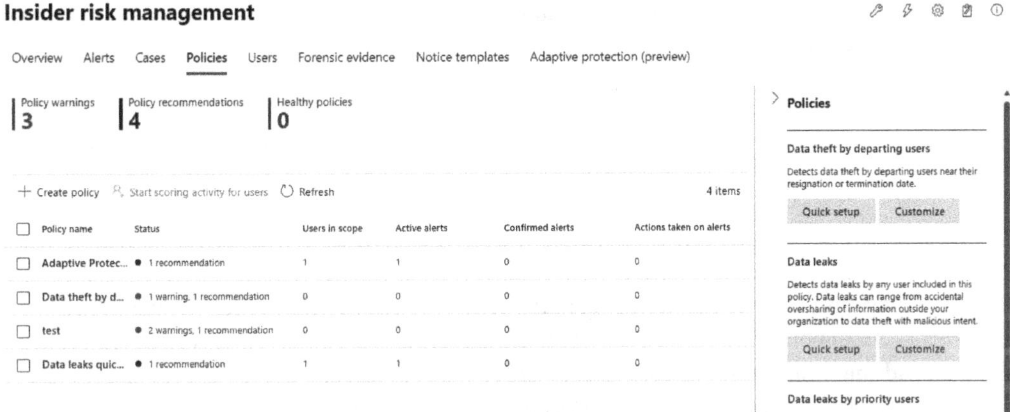

Figure 9.5 – Insider Risk Management policies

This opens the **Policies** dashboard, which gives an overview of defined policies, their status, active and confirmed alerts, actions taken on alerts, and policy alert effectiveness.

The quicker way to create an Insider Risk Management policy is to click on an arrow on the right side of the blade, which will open the **Policies** menu on the side. Some policies have a quick setup button that allows you to create a policy quickly, with preset or predefined settings. You can always choose the **Customize** button to modify a policy and granularly set it up to better suit your needs.

To create a policy from scratch, click on the **+Create policy** option. There are several policy template categories to choose policies from: **Data theft**, **Data leaks**, **Security policy violations**, **Health record misuse**, and **Risky browser usage**:

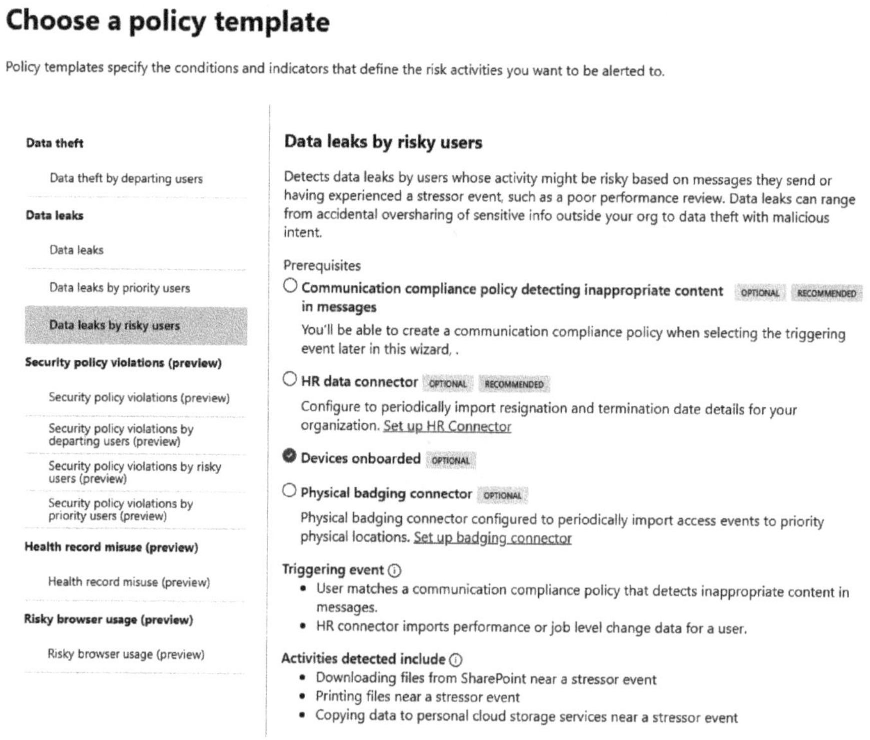

Choose a policy template

Policy templates specify the conditions and indicators that define the risk activities you want to be alerted to.

Data theft

Data theft by departing users

Data leaks

Data leaks

Data leaks by priority users

Data leaks by risky users

Security policy violations (preview)

Security policy violations (preview)

Security policy violations by departing users (preview)

Security policy violations by risky users (preview)

Security policy violations by priority users (preview)

Health record misuse (preview)

Health record misuse (preview)

Risky browser usage (preview)

Risky browser usage (preview)

Data leaks by risky users

Detects data leaks by users whose activity might be risky based on messages they send or having experienced a stressor event, such as a poor performance review. Data leaks can range from accidental oversharing of sensitive info outside your org to data theft with malicious intent.

Prerequisites

Communication compliance policy detecting inappropriate content in messages OPTIONAL RECOMMENDED

You'll be able to create a communication compliance policy when selecting the triggering event later in this wizard, .

HR data connector OPTIONAL RECOMMENDED

Configure to periodically import resignation and termination date details for your organization. Set up HR Connector

Devices onboarded OPTIONAL

Physical badging connector OPTIONAL

Physical badging connector configured to periodically import access events to priority physical locations. Set up badging connector

Triggering event

- User matches a communication compliance policy that detects inappropriate content in messages.
- HR connector imports performance or job level change data for a user.

Activities detected include

- Downloading files from SharePoint near a stressor event
- Printing files near a stressor event
- Copying data to personal cloud storage services near a stressor event

Figure 9.6 – Insider risk policy settings

Not every policy template has the same requirements or prerequisites, but they all share the same characteristics. Each policy has prerequisites that are specific to the policy you are configuring, such as **Physical badging connector**, **HR data connector**, a Microsoft Defender for Endpoint subscription, a DLP policy, devices onboarded, or a previously defined priority user group, for example.

Next, a policy needs a triggering event, which will determine how the policy assigns a risk score to a user activity. An example of such an event might be a user account being deleted from Microsoft Entra ID, a user having exfiltrated data and exceeded the defined thresholds, or a user activity triggering and matching a specific DLP policy.

Lastly, the policy will be triggered if specified user activities are detected, and each policy uses specific indicators to detect user activities to detect anomalous user behavior. After an event is triggered, a user's activity is assigned a risk score. Such activities might include printing files and copying data to third-party cloud storage, mass downloading files from SharePoint or OneDrive, installing malware, tampering with security features, or browsing websites that aren't allowed.

Name your policy concisely, and do not forget to enter a description for a policy as well. Generally, and not just related to Insider Risk Management policies, you should always write a clear and concise description of a policy, setting, or feature wherever possible, that is, where a **Description** text field is available. Doing so will greatly help you and other administrators in the future.

After you choose and include specific users and groups that this policy will apply to, you must decide whether to prioritize content from SharePoint sites, sensitivity labels, sensitive info types, file extensions, or trainable classifiers. Any activity associated with any chosen object, such as labels, file extensions, or sites, will be assigned a higher risk score. The scoring of risks can be applied to all activities defined in this policy or to activities that include priority content only.

Additionally, you must choose a triggering event for the policy, which will determine activities after which the policy will begin assigning risk scores:

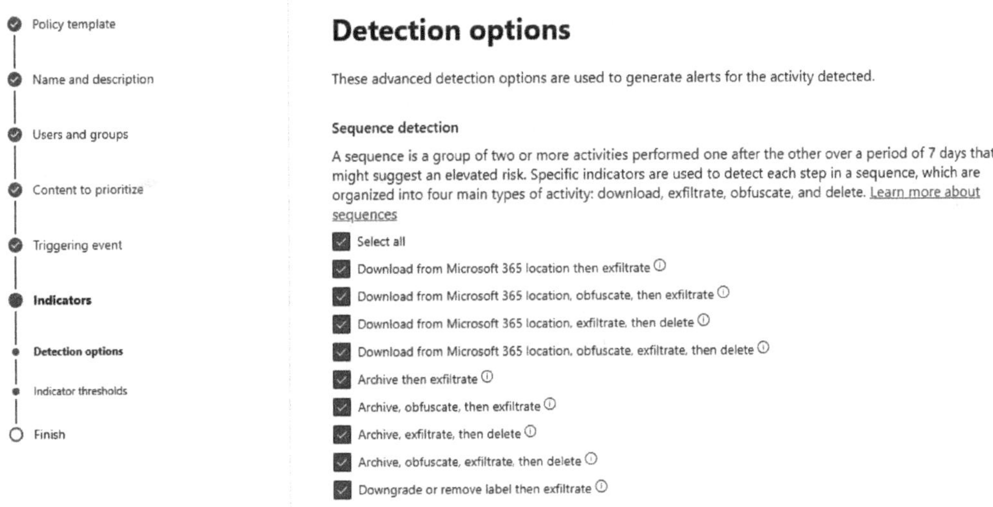

Figure 9.7 – Insider risk policy detection options

In the last step, you must choose indicators that will be used to generate alerts for the activities that the policy defined. You can choose any indicator available from the categories of **Office indicators**, **Device indicators**, **Physical access indicators**, and **Microsoft Defender for Cloud Apps indicators**. Additionally, choose any sequence detection options, as well as cumulative exfiltration detection options, that might suggest an elevated risk based on specific steps taken in sequence, while detecting out-of-the-baseline exfiltration types of activities.

The last policy setting allows you to use default indicator thresholds or to fine-tune your own custom indicator thresholds. At this point, I suggest that you use default thresholds for all indicators that you have selected in the policy. You can always fine-tune and choose your own thresholds after the policy has been in effect for a few days or weeks when you investigate triggered alerts and determine whether the policy behavior is as expected or needs additional adjustments.

As you review the policy settings, click the **Submit** button to finish creating the policy. The policy will go into effect immediately, but it may take up to 24 hours for a policy to start generating alerts.

Triaging and investigating alerts

After policies generate alerts, the alert information is displayed on the **Alerts** tab. It displays a graph displaying the total number of alerts that need to be reviewed, information about your responsiveness in resolving alerts – that is, the average time it took to resolve alerts – as well a summary or list of alerts containing important alert details: its unique ID and any user that triggered the alert, the policy that generated an alert, the severity, the time when an alert was triggered, details about the case, and the assigned user. The status of the alert will show a summary of confirmed and resolved alerts, as well as dismissed alerts or how many of them still need to be reviewed.

As you select an alert, the details of the alert – or, we could also say that these are the details of an alert policy – are opened and displayed on a dedicated page.

The details page of an alert – or, we could also say that these are the details of a triggered policy event – contains all details of the alert, organized into two main parts. Along with the alert details already available on the alert page, the top part shows more information about the activities that triggered the alert, describing similar events that occurred close to that timeframe, details of the user involved in the event, as well as the user alert history.

All relevant information is synthesized on the page, allowing an analyst to obtain additional, detailed information with just a click.

The lower part hosts three tabs, each containing abundant and thorough information about the risk factors involved, activities that led to triggering the alert, as well as relevant user activities:

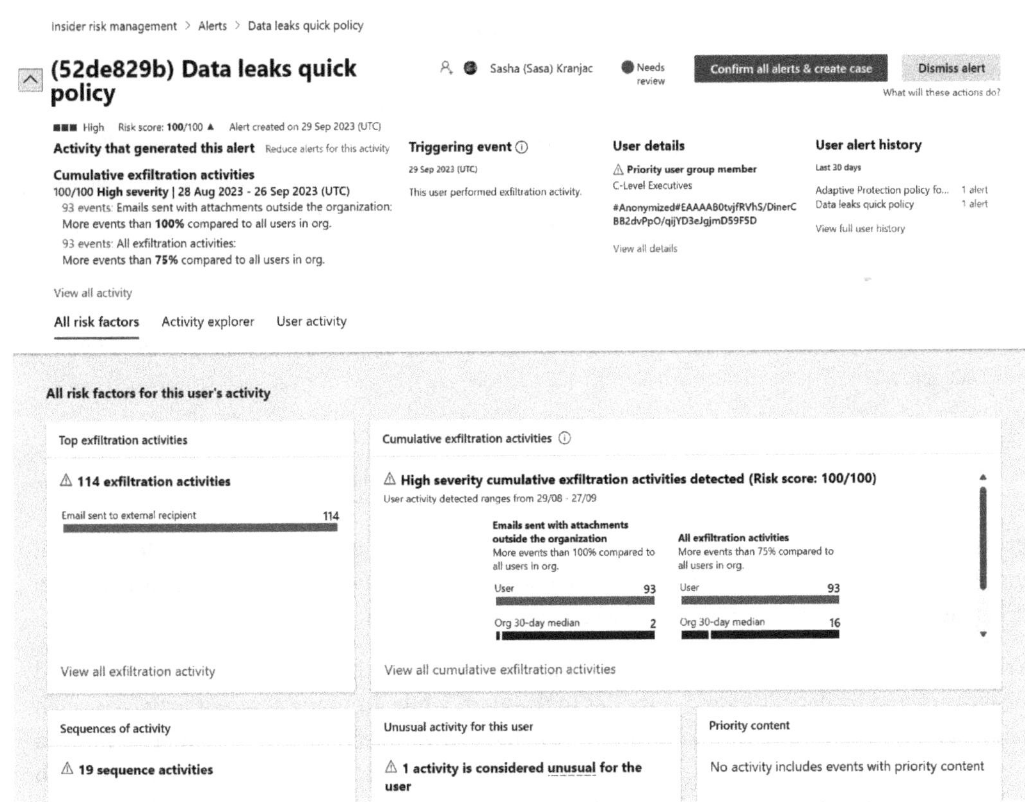

Figure 9.8 – Insider risk policy overview page – All risk factors information tab

The **All risk factors** tab is the home of all risk factors for this user's activities, and content detected, presented in convenient, graphical information, paired with clickable links that lead to further exploration of detailed information connected to the specific activity. The information presented might include but is not limited to top exfiltration activities, cumulative exfiltration activities, activities performed in a sequence, and any unusual activities detected for a user.

The **Activity explorer** tab contains two lists of activities, separated vertically. The list on the right side is the detailed list of activities that a user has performed, including the timestamp, activity, filename and type, object identifier including URL, and the workload (service or application) that performed the activity.

Export   1 of 2094 selected   Reset columns   Customize columns   Save this view   View

Date (UTC)	Activity	File name	Item type	Object ID	Workload
10 Oct 2023 07:40	Email sent to external recipient	image001.png,image0...	Email	<VI1P193MB06728A5D90736E4A9B...	IrmHygiene
10 Oct 2023 07:40	Email sent to external recipient	image001.png,image0...	Email	<VI1P193MB06727B0C5CCE104128...	IrmHygiene
10 Oct 2023 07:40	Email sent to external recipient	image001.png,image0...	Email	<VI1P193MB0672C2BB984ADCA42A...	IrmHygiene
10 Oct 2023 07:40	Email sent to external recipient	image001.png,image0...	Email	<VI1P193MB067289FA08774F0B0C8...	IrmHygiene
10 Oct 2023 07:40	Email sent to external recipient	image001.png,image0...	Email	<VI1P193MB067289FA08774F0B0C8...	IrmHygiene
10 Oct 2023 07:40	Email sent to external recipient	image001.png,image0...	Email	<VI1P193MB0672C2BB984ADCA42A...	IrmHygiene
10 Oct 2023 07:40	Email sent to external recipient	image001.png,image0...	Email	<VI1P193MB067272F900ADA0B6D7...	IrmHygiene
10 Oct 2023 07:40	Email sent to external recipient	image001.png,image0...	Email	<VI1P193MB067272F900ADA0B6D7...	IrmHygiene
10 Oct 2023 07:40	Email sent to external recipient	image001.png,image0...	Email	<VI1P193MB0672F7BC9B027EF206A...	IrmHygiene

Figure 9.9 – Insider risk policy activity explorer

Selecting an activity reveals a lot about the activity itself – location details such as the site URL and client IP; device details such as the device's full name, platform, and whether the device is managed; item details such as the item type and its URL, filename and extension, and a unique object ID.

The right-side activity list contains the list of activities that the policy triggered, which can be categorized as suspicious, and by default scored activities in the alert, while grouping adjacent activities, such as ones that have been performed sequentially. The following screen clip shows examples of only a few of the activities that have been performed, and have triggered the policy, such as **Emails with attachments sent outside the organization** and **Files downloaded from OneDrive while syncing**. These activities have been conveniently grouped together under the **(2) SEQUENCE: Files collected and exfiltrated**, where **(2)** denotes the number of activities a sequence contains:

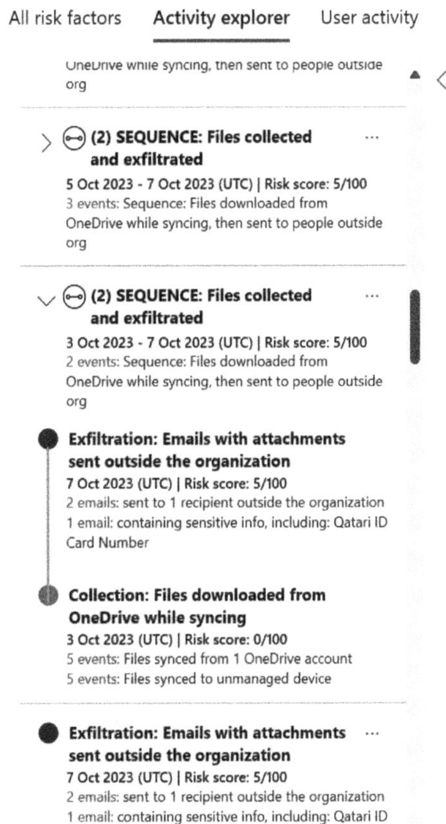

Figure 9.10 – Insider risk policies user activity sequence

Each suspicious activity handily contains links to entities involved in the activity, such as emails, files, and events. These activities might include events that are excluded from scoring as *risky activity* if a sequence includes activities and steps that are considered to be risky behavior.

The **User activity** tab contains some of the most important information in the insider risk analysis process. The left side contains a list of risk alerts in chronological order, including the details of the alert, timestamp, risk score, and information about actions and entities included, such as emails and events.

The right side contains time filters where you can filter the scatter plot chart by selecting different time ranges, for example, one-month, three-month, and six-month time ranges to display activities. Risk activity details are displayed as colored bubbles or circles, where each color represents a different risk category: access, deletion, collection, exfiltration, obfuscation, infiltration, security, custom indicator, sequence, cumulative exfiltration activities, and an exfiltration charts bubble:

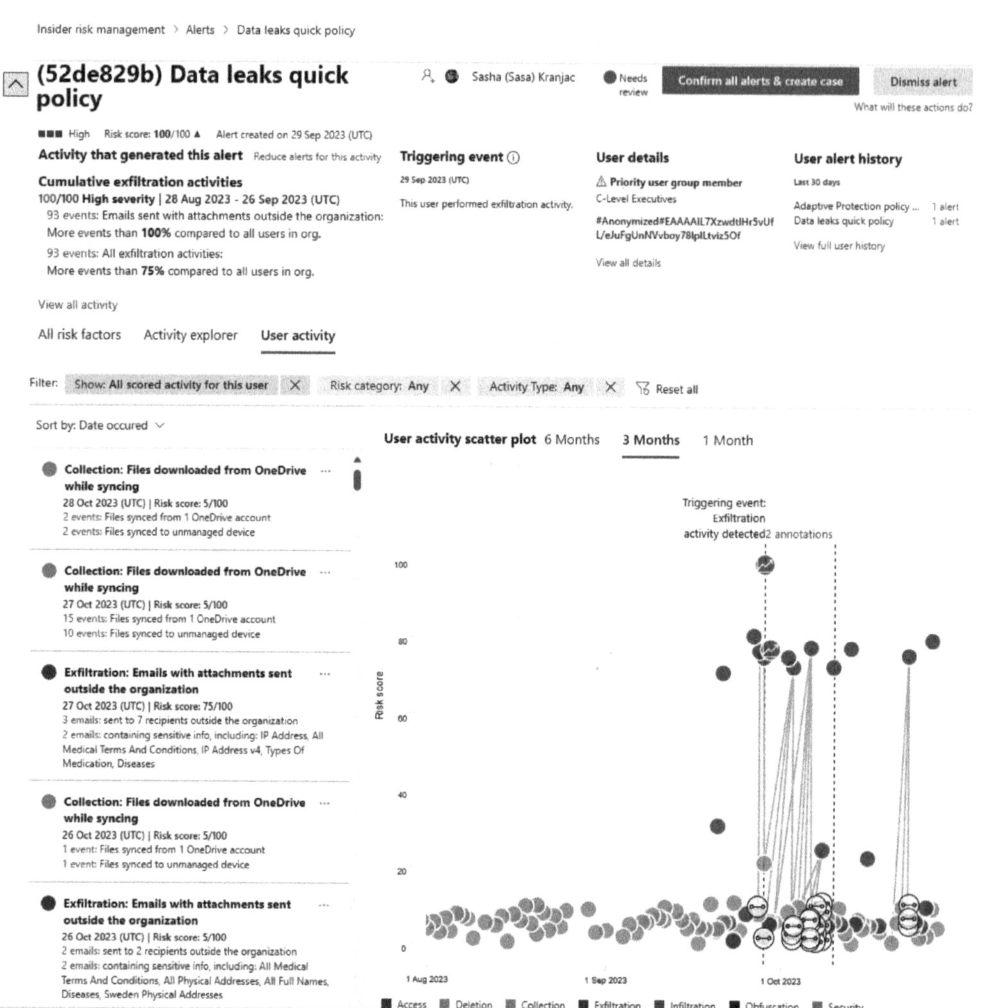

Figure 9.11 – Insider risk policy user activity

The **Activity explorer** and **User activity** lists together present a complex yet complete overview and insight into users' behavior. Using **User activity**, you will have a view that will help you find potentially hazardous actions and observe related activities that unfold in sequences. It is designed to facilitate a swift examination of a case, offering a chronological record of all activities, specific details about each activity, the current risk assessment for the user in question, the sequence of risky events, and filtering options to aid in investigative endeavors. A window into users' activities, the **Activity explorer** tab offers risk investigators extensive analytics capabilities that give in-depth insights into activities. Through **Activity explorer**, you can promptly assess a timeline of identified risky behavior and pinpoint and filter all potentially hazardous activities linked to alerts.

Resolving cases

To create a case, in the upper-right corner, click the **Confirm all alerts & create case** button. Enter the case name and comments and select the **Create case** button to finish creating a case. Now that you have created a case, return to the **Overview** tab of the **Insider Risk Management** blade, and select the **Cases** tab at the top of the screen. Here, you can see the list of all active and closed cases, their status (whether a case is active or closed), the date and time when a case was opened, and to whom it has been assigned. To see more details about a case and to continue working on resolving a case, click or select the case.

There are several tabs on a case page. Some of them contain the same information as the alert tabs but there are some more tabs specific to the Insider Risk Management case, such as **Alerts**, **Content explorer**, **Case notes**, and **Contributors**.

While the case overview has general information about the case, the **Alerts** tab contains a list of all alerts associated with the incident, and with the case.

The **Activity Explorer** tab contains a list of all users' activities, with detailed information about an activity, location, and device details, as well as further information such as an activity object ID, file path, relative URL, and more.

The **Content Explorer** tab includes a list of all files and emails captured by the policies included in the case. It takes an hour, on average, for files and emails to appear on the list, while it will take significantly longer if you have more alerts and more entities involved in an incident. To preview an email or a file, simply select the desired content to display it.

To keep track of the case investigation, you can use the **Case notes** tab, whereas the **Contributors** tab is useful if you want to include additional collaborators to assist you with a case investigation.

A **Case actions** button is available above the **Cases** tabs, to assist you with a case during an investigation, with additional actions such as sending an email to a user included in a case; escalating it for investigation creating an eDiscovery (Premium) case for this user, and at the same time notifying the eDiscovery Administrator and eDiscovery Manager about the case; creating Power Automate flows, which can be very useful to manage risk management processes automatically, creating a record for an insider risk case in ServiceNow, for example; copying and sharing a case link via email; and managing the pseudonymize option to show anonymized versions of usernames, to preserve user-level privacy.

After an investigation is concluded, a case can be closed by selecting the **Resolve case** button. A case can be resolved as **Benign** where case alerts have been observed as non-risky, or as false positives for example, or as **Confirmed policy violation** if investigation has shown case alerts have indeed been confirmed as having malicious or risky intent. You are required to enter information about and describe actions taken and optionally can delete the case and case content immediately.

Microsoft Purview Insider Risk Management is a compliance tool designed to mitigate internal risks by detecting, investigating, and addressing both intentional and unintentional misconduct within your organization. It allows you to establish insider risk policies to specify the kinds of risks you want to monitor and provides the option to escalate cases to Microsoft eDiscovery (Premium) if necessary. Risk analysts can swiftly take appropriate steps to ensure users adhere to your organization's compliance standards.

This system utilizes a range of signals to pinpoint potential insider risks, such as intellectual property theft, data leaks, and security breaches. It empowers customers to establish policies for handling security and compliance. Importantly, it's designed with privacy in mind, as user identities are anonymized by default. Additionally, role-based access controls and audit logs are in place to safeguard individual privacy.

Information barriers and access management

Microsoft 365 streamlines communication and collaboration across teams and organizations, offering tools to set boundaries when needed. This could mean limiting interactions between specific groups to prevent conflicts of interest or safeguard sensitive information.

Microsoft Purview **Information Barriers (IB)** is seamlessly integrated into Microsoft Teams, SharePoint Online, and OneDrive for Business. Administrators have the power to establish policies regulating communication between defined boundaries within an organization. This feature comes in handy for scenarios such as restricting finance personnel handling confidential company data from communicating or sharing files with specific groups within their organization or securing internal teams with sensitive trade secrets, preventing them from calling or chatting online with users in specific groups.

Microsoft Purview IB is a two-way communication and collaboration compliance tool, allowing you to impose communication restrictions between users in Microsoft SharePoint, Teams, and OneDrive.

Microsoft Purview IB requirements

To work with Microsoft Purview IB, you must have at least one of the following licenses: Microsoft 365 E5, E5 Compliance, Office 365 E5, F5, or F5 Compliance. Additionally, you must be assigned one of the following roles: Microsoft 365 Global Administrator, Office 365 Global Administrator, Compliance Administrator, or Information Barrier Compliance Administrator.

Microsoft Purview IB comprises several parts and terms:

- **IB policies**: The rules that define communication boundaries or limits. There are two types of IP policies:
    - **Block** policies prevent one segment from interacting with another segment.
    - **Allow** policies grant one segment the ability to communicate solely with specific other segments.
- **Segments** are essentially collections of groups or users, defined either in the compliance portal or through PowerShell, utilizing selected group or user account attributes. Each organization can create up to 5,000 segments, and users can be associated with a maximum of 10 segments.

- **User account attributes** are present in Microsoft Entra ID, encompassing details such as department, job title, location, and team name, providing a comprehensive job profile. Microsoft Purview IB will use these attributes to link users or groups to specific segments.
- **Policy application** occurs after all IB policies are defined and ready for implementation.

In OneDrive, information barriers serve to identify and block the following unauthorized collaborations:

- Accessing OneDrive or its stored content
- Sharing OneDrive or its stored content with other users

In Microsoft Teams, information barriers are in place to identify and prevent the following unauthorized collaboration types:

- Adding a user to a team or channel
- Accessing content within a team or channel
- Accessing 1:1 and group chats
- Accessing meetings
- Disabling lookups and discovery, rendering users invisible in the people picker

In SharePoint, information barriers are deployed to identify and prevent the following unauthorized collaborations:

- Adding a user to a site
- Accessing a site or its content
- Sharing a site or its content with other users

> **Note**
>
> At present, IB policies do not offer the capability to limit communication and collaboration between groups and users in email messages but are only supported in Exchange Online. If you require the ability to restrict email communications, it is recommended to utilize Exchange mail flow rules instead.

The typical workflow to configure and implement Microsoft Purview IB would consist of the following steps:

1. **Ensure that requirements are satisfied**: Ensure that your organization's hierarchy is accurately represented in the directory data. This involves verifying that user account attributes such as group membership and department name are correctly filled in within Microsoft Entra ID. Additionally, audit logging must be turned on in Microsoft 365.

2. **Create organizational segments**: Tailor IB policies to suit your organization's requirements. Categorize your policies into two types: **Block** policies restrict one group's communication with another, while **Allow** policies permit a group to communicate exclusively with specific groups. Once you've determined and outlined your required groups and policies, move on to identifying the segments needed for implementing IB policies.

Figure 9.12 – Information Barriers Segments definition

3. **Create Information Barriers policies**: Before defining your IB policies, assess whether you need to either restrict communications between specific segments or confine them to particular segments. It's advisable to employ the fewest IB policies necessary to meet industry compliance standards, as well as any internal or legal policies or regulations. You have the option to create and enforce IB policies through either the compliance portal or PowerShell.

Figure 9.13 – Configuring communication and collaboration options in Information Barriers

4. **Apply Information Barriers policies**: On the **Information barriers** page, select **Policy application**. Select **Apply all policies** to apply all IB policies. The application of policies starts, but it can take 30 minutes for policies to go into effect. As the policies are applied by the user, it

may take significantly longer to process all users in large organizations. IB policies are applied to approximately 5,000 user accounts per hour.

Microsoft Purview IB is a compliance tool that enforces restrictions on two-way communication and collaboration within Microsoft Teams, SharePoint, and OneDrive. Primarily utilized in heavily regulated sectors, IB serves to prevent conflicts of interest and protect sensitive internal information among users and different parts of the organization.

Once IB policies are implemented, users who should not interact or exchange files with specific others will be unable to locate, select, chat, or call those individuals. These policies establish automatic safeguards to identify and prevent unauthorized communication and collaboration within designated groups and users.

Communication Compliance

Microsoft Purview Communication Compliance is an insider risk solution designed to identify, capture, and respond to inappropriate messages that may pose a risk to data security or compliance within your organization. It assesses both text- and image-based messages across various platforms such as Microsoft Teams, Viva Engage, Outlook, and more. This includes monitoring for policy breaches such as improper sharing of sensitive information, the use of threatening or harassing language, and potential violations of regulatory standards. Communication Compliance employs machine learning models and keyword matching to flag messages that may contain potential breaches of business conduct or regulatory policies. These flagged messages are then subsequently reviewed by a Communication Compliance investigator.

Some examples of Communication Compliance uses are to serve the purpose of enabling organizations to identify, assess, and address communications that may potentially breach business conduct or regulatory compliance standards. Similar to other Microsoft Purview features or products, Communication Compliance uses predefined policy templates, powered and helped by machine learning classifiers for uses covering areas such as the following:

- **Business conduct**: Discrimination, profanity, threat, and targeted harassment classifiers
- **Regulatory compliance**: Corporate sabotage, customer complaints, gifts and entertainment, money laundering, regulatory collusion, stock manipulation, unauthorized disclosure classifiers

Communication Compliance can flag risk indicators found in messages to be used in Insider Risk Management policies for potentially risky users. By employing a specialized policy that detects inappropriate text with Communication Compliance, it is possible to have the option to incorporate this policy into **Data leaks by risky employees** or **Security policy violations by risky employees** policies found in Insider Risk management. Any risky users identified in messages through the communication Compliance policy can serve as a triggering event, bringing them under consideration for Insider Risk Management policies.

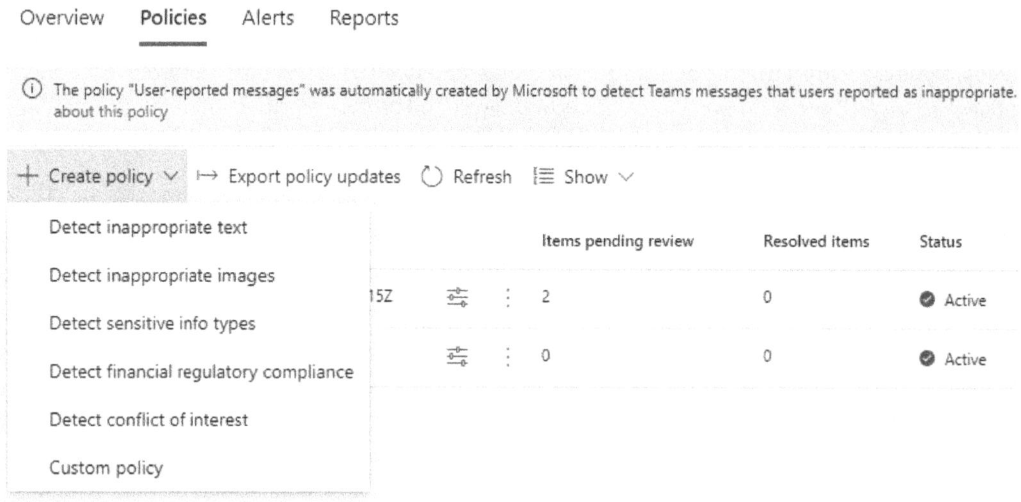

Figure 9.14 – Communication Compliance policies

Several Communication Compliance policies exist now, enabling you to detect many different unwanted ways of communication, such as the following:

- Sending inappropriate text: targeted harassment, threat, discrimination
- Inappropriate images: adult or racy images
- Sensitive information types
- Conflict of interest
- Financial regulatory compliance communication breaches: customer complaints, regulatory collusion, stock manipulation, gifts and entertainment, unauthorized disclosure, money laundering

Creating custom policies is also supported, where you can do the following:

- Include different users and groups
- Select reviewers
- Choose locations to detect communications: Exchange, Teams, Viva Engage
- Select communication direction: inbound, outbound, internal
- Include OCR content: extracted printed and handwritten text from embedded or attached images in email and Teams chat messages are analyzed for inappropriate content

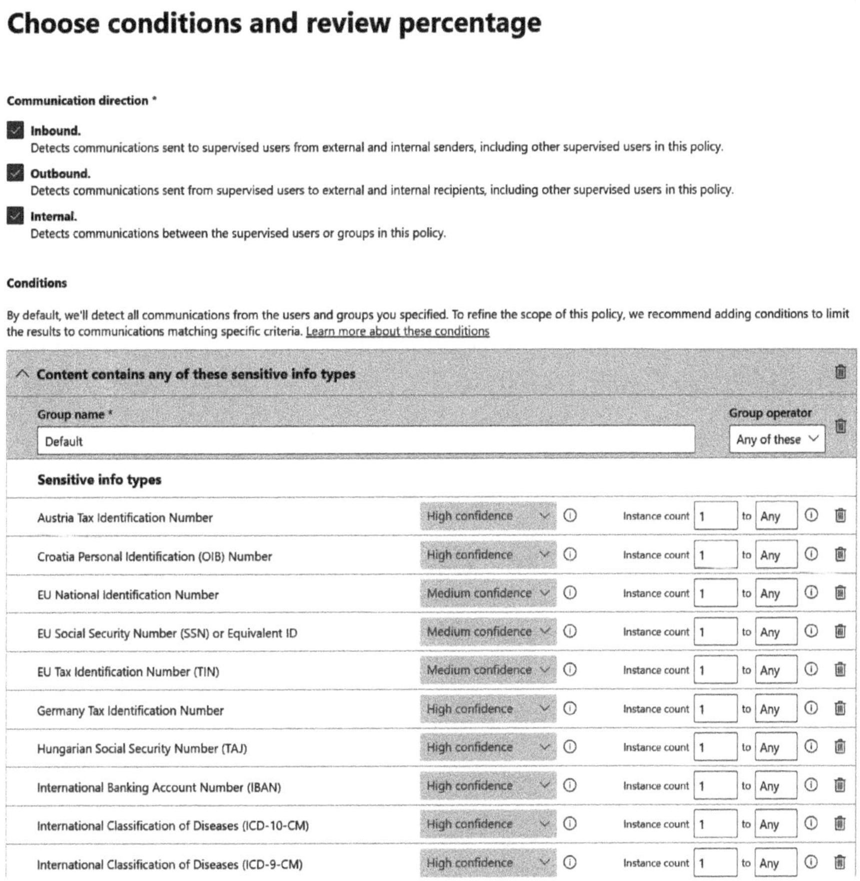

Choose conditions and review percentage

Communication direction *

☑ **Inbound.**
Detects communications sent to supervised users from external and internal senders, including other supervised users in this policy.

☑ **Outbound.**
Detects communications sent from supervised users to external and internal recipients, including other supervised users in this policy.

☑ **Internal.**
Detects communications between the supervised users or groups in this policy.

Conditions

By default, we'll detect all communications from the users and groups you specified. To refine the scope of this policy, we recommend adding conditions to limit the results to communications matching specific criteria. Learn more about these conditions

Content contains any of these sensitive info types

Group name * : Default — Group operator: Any of these

Sensitive info types

Sensitive info type	Confidence	Instance count	to
Austria Tax Identification Number	High confidence	1	Any
Croatia Personal Identification (OIB) Number	High confidence	1	Any
EU National Identification Number	Medium confidence	1	Any
EU Social Security Number (SSN) or Equivalent ID	Medium confidence	1	Any
EU Tax Identification Number (TIN)	Medium confidence	1	Any
Germany Tax Identification Number	High confidence	1	Any
Hungarian Social Security Number (TAJ)	High confidence	1	Any
International Banking Account Number (IBAN)	High confidence	1	Any
International Classification of Diseases (ICD-10-CM)	High confidence	1	Any
International Classification of Diseases (ICD-9-CM)	High confidence	1	Any

Figure 9.15 – Communication Compliance policy condition definition

In a policy, you can refine the scope of the policy by choosing and fine-tuning policy conditions: content matches, attachments, and message characteristics. After creating or updating a policy, it might take up to one hour to activate it. Subsequent policy scans are processed every 24 hours from the time the policy was created or updated.

Once you've established a Communication Compliance policy, you have the option to temporarily halt its operation if necessary. This pause can be useful for conducting tests, addressing policy matching issues, or refining the policy's criteria. Opting to pause rather than delete a policy ensures that any existing policy alerts and messages are retained for ongoing examination and evaluations. While a policy is in a paused state, it suspends the examination and alerting process for all user message conditions defined and specified in the policy. To initiate or lift a policy pause, a user must hold membership of the Communication Compliance Admins role group.

To investigate issues flagged by your policies, the initial step is to examine policy matches and alerts. Within the Communication Compliance section, there are distinct areas designed to expedite this process:

- **Policies**: This page is accessible by signing into Microsoft Purview with administrative credentials. Navigate to Communication Compliance and select the **Policies** page. Here, you will find a list of Communication Compliance policies set up for your Microsoft 365 organization. It also provides links to recommended policy templates. Each listed policy includes information such as the count of pending policy matches (found in the **Items pending review** column), the number of escalated and resolved items, the policy status, and the date and **Coordinated Universal Time** (**UTC**) of the last policy modification, along with the UTC for the last policy scan. To initiate remediation actions, select the policy linked to the alert, which will direct you to the **Policy details** page. From there, you can review an overview of activities, examine and address any pending policy matches on the **Pending** tab, or review the history of resolved policy matches on the **Resolved** tab.
- **Alerts**: Head to Communication Compliance, and click **Alerts** to view alerts from the past 30 days, categorized by policy matches. This layout allows you to do a swift assessment of which Communication Compliance policies are generating the highest number of alerts, sorted by severity. It's important to note that an alert encompasses multiple policy matches, rather than just one. Once the requisite number of policy matches triggers a specific alert, an email notification is dispatched to the designated recipient.

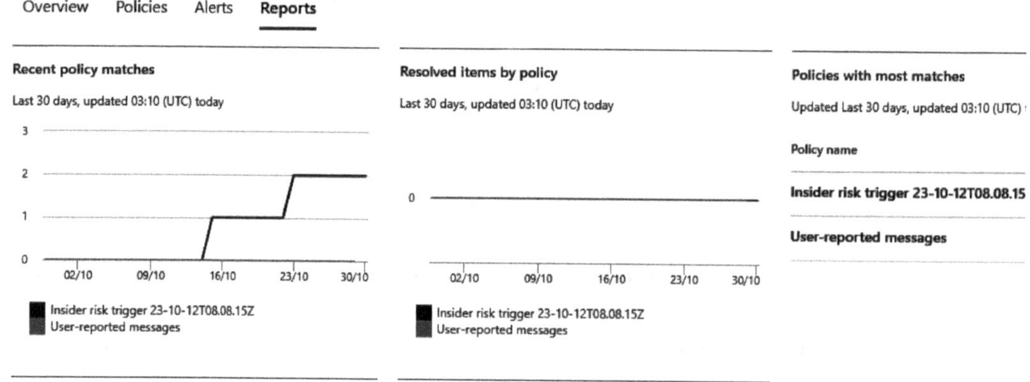

Figure 9.16 – Communication Compliance reporting

- **Reports**: Visit Communication Compliance, then click on the **Reports** tab to access Communication Compliance report widgets and graphs. Each widget offers an overview of Communication Compliance activities and statuses. It also provides access to more detailed insights regarding policy matches and subsequent remediation actions.

Summary

An important part of any organization is to stay compliant with standards, regulations, and laws, whether small, medium, or enterprise-sized. In today's digital landscape, safeguarding sensitive information and ensuring compliance with internal policies is paramount for any organization. Microsoft 365 offers a comprehensive suite of tools designed to address these concerns: Insider Risk Management, Information Barriers, and Communication Compliance capabilities. Together, they form a robust defense against potential risks and compliance breaches.

These capabilities collectively empower an organization to fortify its security and compliance efforts. By utilizing advanced technology and machine learning, these tools offer a proactive defense against potential threats and breaches. As organizations navigate an increasingly digital landscape, having a comprehensive suite of compliance solutions is not just an advantage – it's a necessity. Microsoft 365 provides the robust framework needed to ensure secure collaboration and maintain regulatory compliance, ultimately safeguarding the integrity of organizations in today's fast-paced, interconnected world.

Further readings

There are many reports and research that show various cybersecurity-related statistics and, while there are numerous important publishers and institutions, here are some links to help you get started.

- ISACA State of Cybersecurity 2023 report: `https://www.isaca.org/resources/reports/state-of-cybersecurity-2023`
- The ENISA Threat Landscape (ETL) report: `https://www.enisa.europa.eu/topics/cyber-threats/threats-and-trends`
- CompTIA State of Cybersecurity 2024: `https://www.comptia.org/content/research/cybersecurity-trends-research`
- CompTIA IT Industry outlook: `https://connect.comptia.org/content/research/`
- Microsoft Digital Defense Report: `https://www.microsoft.com/en-us/security/business/security-intelligence-report`

10

Microsoft Purview Information Protection

In the modern business landscape, information plays a pivotal role in shaping organizations' success. It includes a wide range of data, including proprietary knowledge, customer details, financial records, strategic plans, and intellectual property. Given the ever-increasing reliance on technology and the importance of safeguarding, this information has become very important.

Information can be defined as data that has been processed, organized, or structured in a meaningful way, providing insights, knowledge, or context to the user. It is the lifeblood of modern organizations, enabling informed decision-making, efficient operations, competitive advantages, and innovation. Information can exist in various formats, such as digital documents, databases, emails, or physical records.

In this chapter, we will learn about the following:

- Microsoft Purview Information Protection (formerly known as Microsoft Information Protection)
- Configuring Information Protection

About Microsoft Purview Information Protection

The Information Protection service in Microsoft Purview is designed to help organizations identify, classify, and protect sensitive information throughout its lifecycle. It enables businesses to gain visibility into their data landscape and establish robust data protection policies. With this service, organizations can effectively mitigate risks associated with data breaches, unauthorized access, and non-compliance.

The Information Protection service delivers the following advantages to businesses:

- **Confidentiality**: Businesses handle sensitive information, including trade secrets, proprietary formulas, and customer data. Unauthorized access or disclosure of such information can lead to severe consequences, such as the loss of competitive advantage, reputational damage, or legal liabilities. Robust information protection measures ensure the confidentiality of valuable assets.

- **Competitive advantage**: Businesses that can effectively protect their information gain a competitive edge. Safeguarding strategic plans, research and development initiatives, and intellectual property prevents competitors from gaining insights into key differentiators. This protection fosters innovation, allowing organizations to maintain their market position and stay ahead of rivals.
- **Compliance**: Is it enough to mention GDPR compliance? In today's regulatory landscape, companies are subject to numerous data protection and privacy laws. Failing to comply with these regulations can result in substantial penalties, loss of public trust, and even business closure. By implementing strong information protection practices, businesses can demonstrate their commitment to data privacy and regulatory compliance.
- **Business continuity**: Information is crucial for the smooth functioning of business operations. In today's interconnected world, disruptions or loss of critical information can paralyze organizations, leading to financial losses, operational inefficiencies, and missed opportunities. Robust information protection measures including data backups, disaster recovery plans, and cybersecurity protocols ensure operational continuity and mitigate risks.

In the present business landscape, information is a strategic asset that requires higher protection. Safeguarding information ensures confidentiality, maintains competitive advantages, aids regulatory compliance, fosters trust, and enables operational continuity. As the reliance on technology continues to grow, organizations must prioritize robust information protection measures to mitigate risks, preserve their reputation, and thrive in an increasingly competitive environment.

To fully utilize **Microsoft Purview Information Protection** and its features, certain licenses are required. The specific licenses needed may vary depending on the Microsoft 365 subscription plan and the level of functionality required. Here are some licenses commonly associated with Microsoft Purview Information Protection:

- **Microsoft 365 E3/E5**: Microsoft 365 Enterprise plans such as E3 and E5 include the necessary licenses for MIP. These plans offer comprehensive security and compliance features, including sensitivity labels, **data loss prevention** (**DLP**), and encryption capabilities.
- **Microsoft 365 E5 Compliance**: This license includes advanced compliance features, making it suitable for organizations with stringent regulatory requirements. It provides enhanced capabilities for information protection and governance, including advanced data loss prevention, eDiscovery, and communication compliance.
- **Office 365 E3/E5**: Office 365 Enterprise plans such as E3 and E5 also include basic MIP functionality. They provide sensitivity labels, encryption options, and some data loss prevention capabilities. However, advanced features such as auto-labeling may require additional licenses.
- **Microsoft 365 E5 Information Protection and Governance**: This license is specifically designed to meet the data protection and governance needs of organizations. It includes features such as sensitivity labels, data classification, auto-labeling, and data loss prevention policies.

- **Azure Information Protection** (**AIP**) Premium P1/P2: AIP is a standalone solution that offers advanced information protection features. It can be used in conjunction with Microsoft 365 plans to enhance data classification, labeling, and protection. AIP Premium P2 provides additional capabilities such as automatic labeling and integration with on-premises solutions. In the following table, you'll find all the information you need about the various Microsoft Purview Information Protection options. These options correspond to different subscription plans, so you can make a well-informed decision:

Features	Microsoft 365 E3	Microsoft 365 E5	Microsoft 365 E3 Security	Microsoft 365 E5 Security
Information Protection Plan 1	•			
Information Protection Plan 2		•		•
Manual, default, and mandatory sensitivity labeling	•	•		
Automatic sensitivity labeling		•		•
Automatic sensitivity labels in Exchange, SharePoint, and OneDrive		•		•
Sensitivity labels based on machine learning/trainable classifiers/exact data match		•		•
Basic message encryption	•	•		
Advanced message encryption		•		

Table 10.1 – Information protection plans overview

It's important to refer to the official Microsoft documentation to determine the precise licensing requirements for MIP based on your organization's needs. Licensing models and options may change over time.

The list of supported file types is as follows:

`.dng`, `.doc`, `.docm`, `.docx`, `.dot`, `.dotm`, `.dotx`, `.mmp`, `.mpt`, `.oxps`, `.pdf`, `.potm`, `.potx`, `.pps`, `.ppsm`, `.ppsx`, `.ppt`, `.pptm`, `.pptx`, `.psd`, `.pub`, `.vdw`, `.vsd`, `.vsdm`, `.vsdx`, `.vss`, `.vssm`, `.vst`, `.vstm`, `.vssx`, `.vstx`, `.xls`, `.xlsb`, `.xlt`, `.xlsm`, `.xlsx`, `.xltm`, `.xltx`, and `.xps`

Supported image file types: `.jpg`, `.jpe`, `.jpeg`, `.jif`, `.jfif`, `.jfi`, `.png`, `.tif`, and `.tiff`

Unsupported file types: `.lnk`, `.exe`, `.com`, `.cmd`, `.bat`, `.dll`, `.ini`, `.pst`, `.sca`, `.drm`, `.sys`, `.cpl`, `.inf`, `.drv`, `.dat`, `.tmp`, `.msp`, `.msi`, `.pdb`, and `.jar`

To effectively manage and configure Microsoft 365 Information Protection (formerly known as Azure Information Protection), the following permissions are typically required:

- **Global Administrator**: The Global Administrator role has the highest level of administrative privileges in Microsoft 365. This role can perform all administrative tasks related to Microsoft 365 Information Protection, including configuring labels, protection policies, and **Data Loss Prevention** (**DLP**) settings.
- **Security Administrator**: The Security Administrator role focuses on managing security-related features and settings within Microsoft 365. This role often includes permissions necessary to configure and manage Information Protection, such as creating and modifying sensitivity labels, configuring protection policies, and managing DLP policies.
- **Compliance Administrator**: The Compliance Administrator role is responsible for managing compliance-related features and settings within Microsoft 365. This role typical policies and permissions to configure sensitivity labels, create and manage retention policies, and perform compliance-related tasks such as eDiscovery and data retention.
- **Information Protection Administrator**: The Information Protection Administrator role is specifically designed to manage Information Protection features in Microsoft 365. This role has permission to configure sensitivity labels, protection policies, and other settings related to data classification and protection.
- **SharePoint Administrator**: SharePoint Administrators have permission to manage SharePoint sites and settings. They may require additional permissions to configure Information Protection features specific to SharePoint, such as applying sensitivity labels to SharePoint sites, libraries, or lists.

It's important to note that the specific permissions required may vary depending on the complexity of the Information Protection configuration and the level of administrative control needed. It is recommended to review the official Microsoft documentation and consult with your organization's IT administrators to determine the precise permissions required for Microsoft 365 Information Protection based on your organization's needs and security requirements.

Data classification

One of the key features of the Information Protection service is data classification. It enables users to automatically or manually classify data assets based on sensitivity levels, such as **personally identifiable information** (**PII**), financial data, or intellectual property. Purview leverages powerful machine-learning capabilities to analyze data patterns, identify sensitive information, and apply appropriate labels and classifications. This enables organizations to prioritize their efforts and focus on securing critical data assets.

In addition to classification, the Information Protection service facilitates data protection through access controls and encryption. Purview integrates with **Microsoft Entra ID** (former **Azure AD**), allowing organizations to define fine-grained access policies and permissions for data assets. Administrators can ensure that only authorized users and applications have access to sensitive information, thereby minimizing the risk of data breaches and unauthorized disclosures.

The Information Protection service also assists organizations in achieving compliance with regulatory requirements. Purview provides built-in connectors and integrations with various data sources and systems, enabling organizations to discover and classify data residing in disparate locations. This facilitates compliance efforts by ensuring that sensitive data is properly identified, protected, and audited, reducing the risk of non-compliance penalties.

Furthermore, Purview supports encryption both at rest and in transit. Data assets stored within Purview are encrypted using industry-standard encryption algorithms, providing an additional layer of protection against unauthorized access. When data is transmitted between Purview and other systems, secure communication protocols, such as HTTPS, are utilized to maintain data integrity and confidentiality.

Moreover, Purview offers advanced auditing and monitoring capabilities through its Information Protection service. Organizations can track data access, modifications, and data protection activities to gain insights into potential security incidents or policy violations. These auditing features help in maintaining an audit trail and demonstrate compliance with regulatory obligations.

In Microsoft Purview, DLP and Information Protection are two distinct but interconnected concepts that work together to enhance data security and privacy. DLP in Microsoft Purview focuses on preventing the unauthorized disclosure or leakage of sensitive data, whereas Information Protection encompasses a wider range of measures aimed at protecting data throughout its lifecycle. DLP primarily deals with detecting and preventing data leakage, while Information Protection includes additional security controls such as encryption, access controls, and data classification to ensure data confidentiality, integrity, and availability.

Overall, the Information Protection service in Microsoft Purview offers a comprehensive suite of tools and features to protect sensitive information, establish data governance policies, and comply with privacy regulations. By leveraging data classification, access controls, encryption, and auditing capabilities, organizations can strengthen their data protection posture, mitigate risks, and ensure the confidentiality, integrity, and availability of their valuable data assets.

Labeling is an important aspect of data management and protection in Microsoft Purview. Here are a few reasons why labeling is crucial in this context:

- **Data classification**: Labels provide a systematic way to classify and categorize data based on its sensitivity, importance, or regulatory requirements. By applying labels to data assets, organizations gain a clear understanding of the types of data they possess and can prioritize their protection efforts accordingly. This classification enables more efficient data governance, security, and compliance management.
- **Risk mitigation**: Labels help identify and mitigate potential risks associated with data handling. By assigning labels that reflect the sensitivity of the information, organizations can enforce appropriate security controls and access permissions. This helps prevent unauthorized access, data breaches, or accidental exposure of sensitive data, reducing the risk of financial, reputational, or regulatory consequences.
- **Compliance and regulatory requirements**: Many industries and regions have specific data protection regulations and compliance requirements. Labels enable organizations to align their data management practices with these regulations by applying the necessary protection measures to labeled data. Labels help track and enforce compliance requirements, ensuring that sensitive data is handled and stored in accordance with legal obligations and industry standards.
- **Data protection policies**: Labels facilitate the implementation and enforcement of data protection policies. By associating policies with specific labels, organizations can define rules and controls that govern the handling, storage, sharing, and retention of labeled data. This enables consistent and automated application of security measures, such as encryption, access controls, and data loss prevention, based on the sensitivity level indicated by the label.
- **Advanced data discovery and search**: Labels enhance data discovery and search capabilities within Microsoft Purview. With labeled data, users can easily search for and locate relevant information based on its classification. This streamlines data retrieval processes, enhances productivity, and promotes efficient data utilization across the organization.
- **Data lifecycle management**: Labels play a crucial role in managing the lifecycle of data. By assigning labels that define retention periods or disposition instructions, organizations can automate data archival or deletion processes. This helps ensure compliance with data retention policies and reduces the risk of retaining unnecessary or obsolete data.

Labeling in Microsoft Purview is essential for effective data management, security, and compliance. It enables data classification, risk mitigation, compliance management, policy enforcement, improved data discovery, and streamlined data lifecycle management. By utilizing labels, organizations can enhance their data protection strategies, mitigate risks, and ensure proper governance of their data assets.

> **Important note**
>
> Data classification is a crucial aspect of data management and protection. It involves categorizing data based on its sensitivity, value, and importance to the organization. This process is vital for data security, risk management, compliance, effective data governance, incident response, resource allocation, and facilitating collaboration. It provides the foundation for implementing appropriate security measures, minimizing risks, and ensuring that data is handled and protected in a manner consistent with its value and sensitivity.

Configuring Information Protection

As we prepare to take on the journey of configuring Microsoft Purview Information Protection in the upcoming sections, it's crucial to begin with a solid foundation. By gaining a clear understanding of the key components and concepts we'll be delving into, you'll be well-equipped to effectively navigate the world of information protection within the Microsoft ecosystem.

Information Protection

Before you start configuring labels, go to **Overview** and check the recommended information protection features:

1. Log in to the **Microsoft 365 Purview admin center**, and in the left menu under **Information protection**, click on **Overview**.
2. Click on **Choose what to set up**, as shown in the following screenshot:

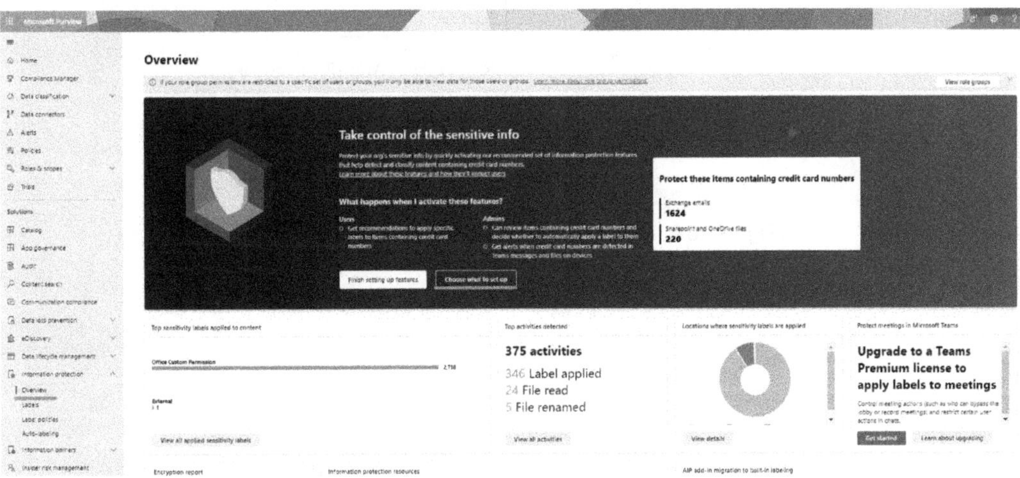

Figure 10.1 – Information Protection Overview dashboard

3. Check **Create and publish sensitivity labels** for recommendations. (Checked option **Set up in-app labeling suggestion for my labels** is optional and if you select, you can choose additional labeling protection for newly created sensitivity label.):

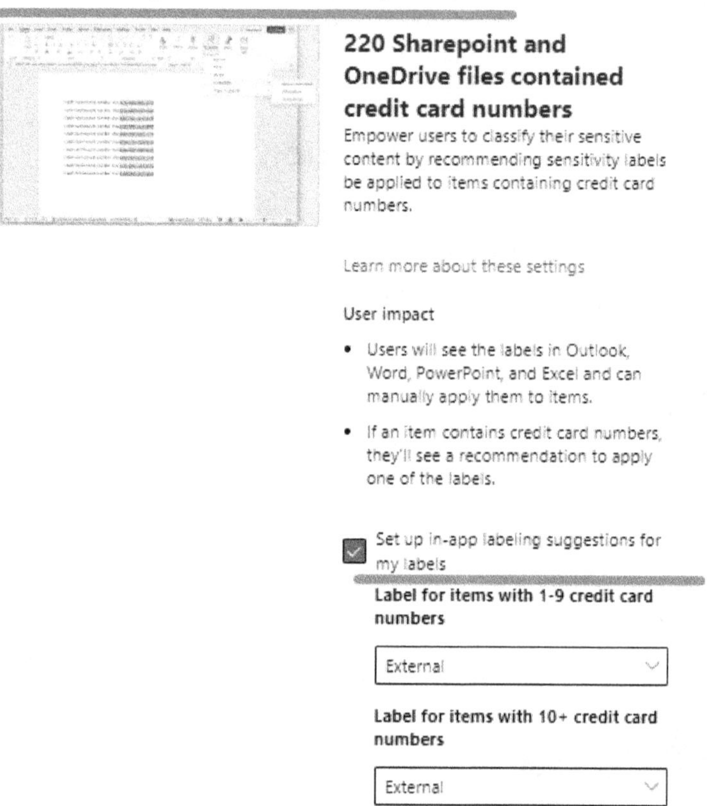

Figure 10.2 – Create and publish sensitivity labels

4. Check **Create auto-labeling policy** for recommendations. (The following screenshot shows some examples of these recommendations. See the checked options):

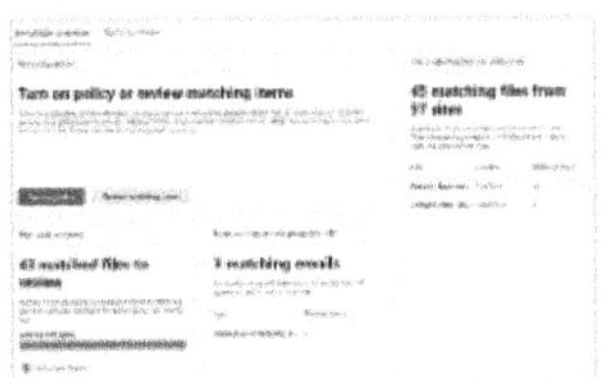

Figure 10.3 – Create auto-labeling policy

5. Check **Create data loss prevention (DLP) policies** (The following screenshot shows some examples of these recommendations. See the checked options.):

Figure 10.4 – Create DLP policies

6. If you choose to apply any of the recommendations, press **Activate recommended features**.

Here's a general overview of the steps to create information protection labels using the Microsoft 365 Purview admin portal:

1. Log in to the **Microsoft 365 Purview admin center** and in the left menu under **Information protection**, click on **Labels**:

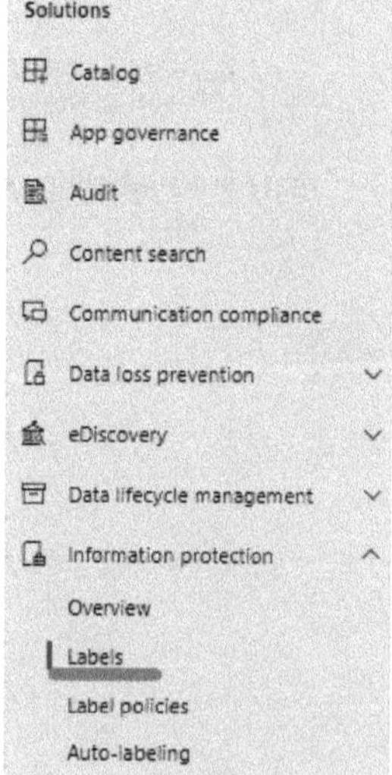

Figure 10.5 – Labels dashboard

2. Now we need to define some sensitivity labels. Click on + **Create a label** and fill in the fields under the **Name and tooltip** section. Use commonly used names, descriptions, and colors for different labels:

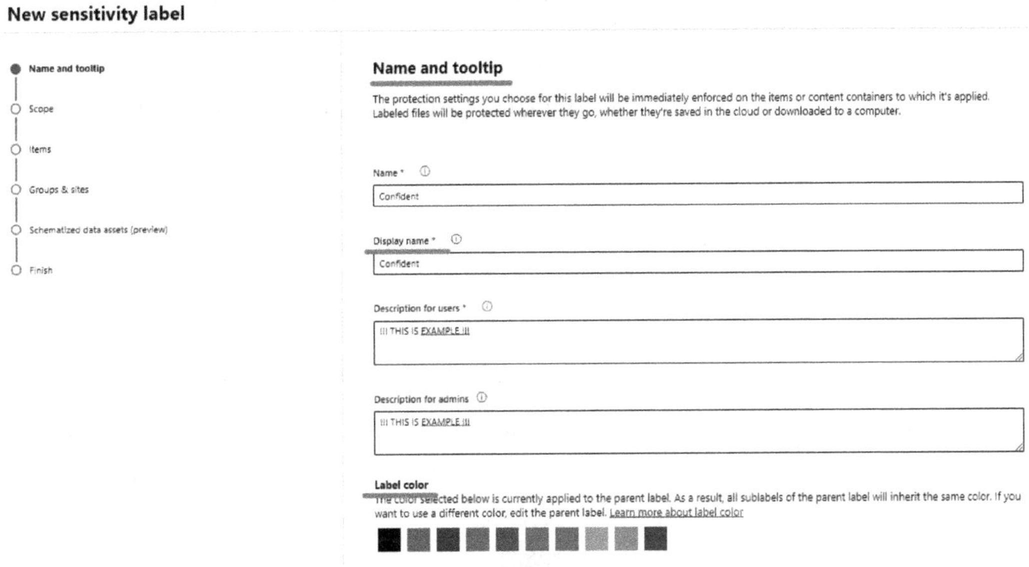

New sensitivity label

Name and tooltip
Scope
Items
Groups & sites
Schematized data assets (preview)
Finish

Name and tooltip

The protection settings you choose for this label will be immediately enforced on the items or content containers to which it's applied. Labeled files will be protected wherever they go, whether they're saved in the cloud or downloaded to a computer.

Name *
Confident

Display name *
Confident

Description for users *
!!! THIS IS EXAMPLE !!!

Description for admins
!!! THIS IS EXAMPLE !!!

Label color
The color selected below is currently applied to the parent label. As a result, all sublabels of the parent label will inherit the same color. If you want to use a different color, edit the parent label. Learn more about label color

Figure 10.6 – Creating a sensitivity label

Important note

When creating labels in Microsoft Purview, it is important to use easily available names that clearly indicate the purpose or sensitivity of the data being labeled. Additionally, it is beneficial to define descriptions for each label to provide users with more detailed information about its intended use and implications. Using common names for labels helps promote clarity and understanding among users. It allows them to quickly identify and comprehend the purpose or sensitivity level associated with a particular label. For example, using names such as **Confidential**, **Internal Use Only**, or **Public** can help users make informed decisions about handling and sharing data.

Including **descriptions** for labels provides additional context and clarification. Descriptions can explain the criteria for applying the label, provide guidance on handling the labeled data, or highlight any compliance requirements associated with it. These descriptions serve as valuable resources for users, helping them make informed decisions and reinforcing best practices for data protection.

> The choice of **label colors** is another crucial consideration. Labels should have distinct and easily recognizable colors to avoid confusion. Each color should be assigned to a specific label, ensuring consistency and clarity across the labeling system. For instance, using red for **Confidential**, yellow for **Internal Use Only**, and green for **Public** establishes a visual association that reinforces the intended meaning of each label.

3. Next, we configure label settings. Define the scope for the label as **Files**, **Emails**, and **Meetings**:

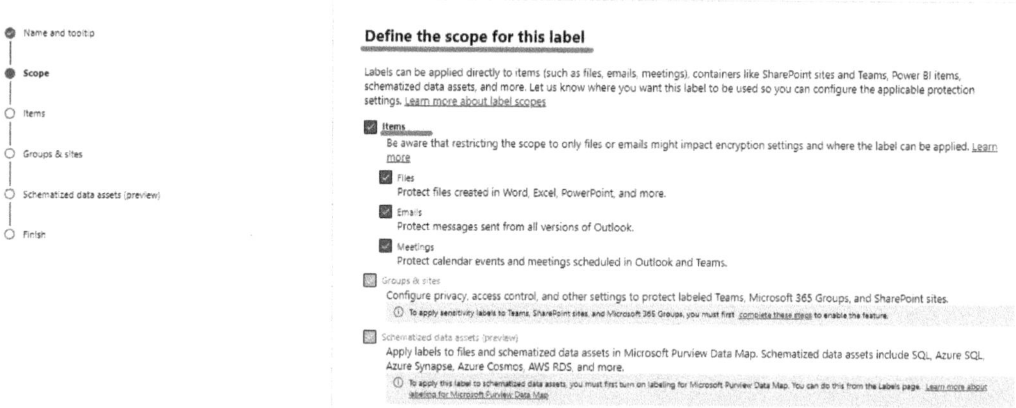

Figure 10.7 – Defining the scope for the new sensitivity label

4. **Choose protection settings for label items**: Add custom header, footer, watermarks, and control who can access protected documents (define when access will expire, offline/online access, etc.):

Figure 10.8 – Selecting protection for new label

Once you've established the protection criteria for the new label, the next step is to define encryption and apply it to the sensitivity label:

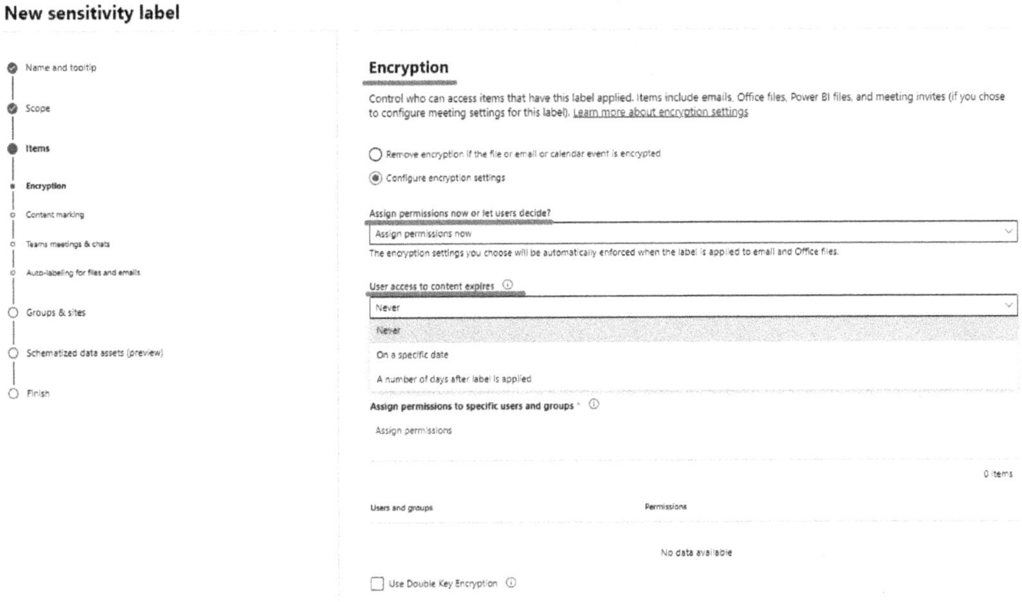

Figure 10.9 – Defining encryption for new sensitivity label

5. Assign permission for users and groups:

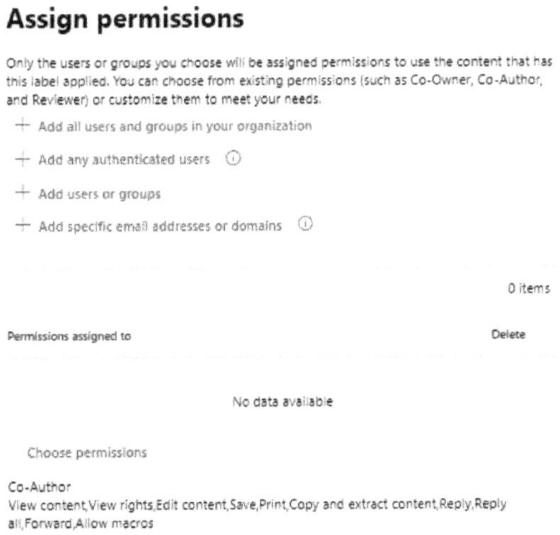

Figure 10.10 – Assigning permissions

6. Define a header, footer, and watermark.

Figure 10.11 – Defining content marking

7. Configure label settings for Teams meetings and chats:

Figure 10.12 – Configuring settings for Teams meetings and chats

8. Leave auto-labeling off. (More about auto-labeling follows shortly.)
9. Review, submit, and publish the new label.

Another way of creating labels is by creating an auto-labeling policy. Auto-labeling refers to the process of automatically assigning labels or tags to data based on predefined rules, machine learning algorithms, or other techniques. This approach can help categorize and organize large volumes of data more efficiently. Auto labeling can be particularly useful in data management and data governance scenarios, allowing organizations to streamline data classification and improve data discovery.

To create an auto-labeling policy in Microsoft Purview, follow these general steps:

1. Access the **Microsoft Purview admin center**, and in the menu on the left under **Information protection**, click on **Auto-labeling**. Click on + **Create auto-labeling policy**:

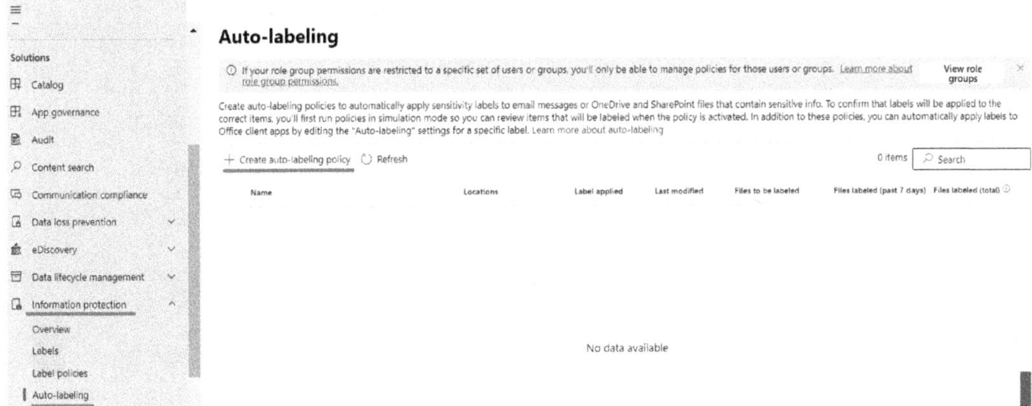

Figure 10.13 – Creating auto-labeling policy

2. Choose the information and categories to which you want to apply the auto-labeling policy:

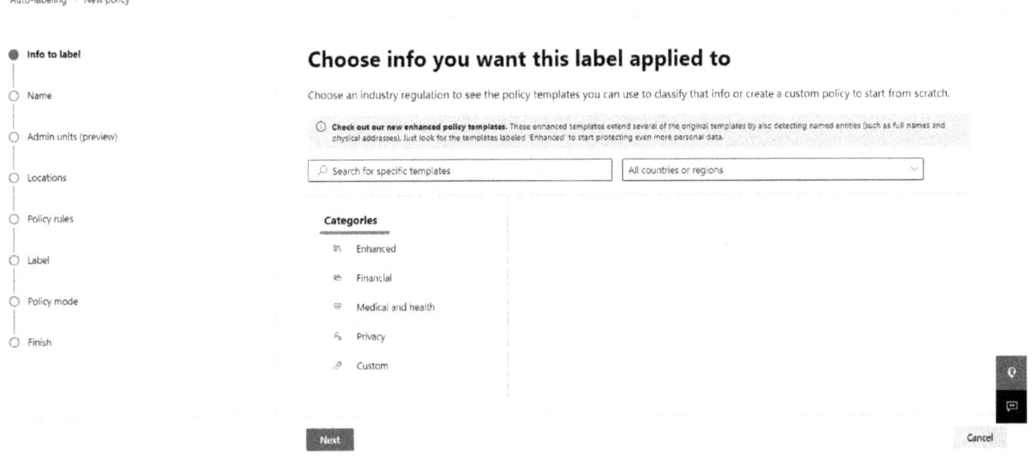

Figure 10.14 – Selecting information to whichi to apply the auto-labeling policy

3. Define the auto-labeling policy by providing the necessary details for your auto-labeling policy, including the name, description, and scope of the policy, and assign admin units.

4. Choose the locations where the auto-labeling policy will be applied (the Exchange Online location toggled on in the following screenshot is just an example):

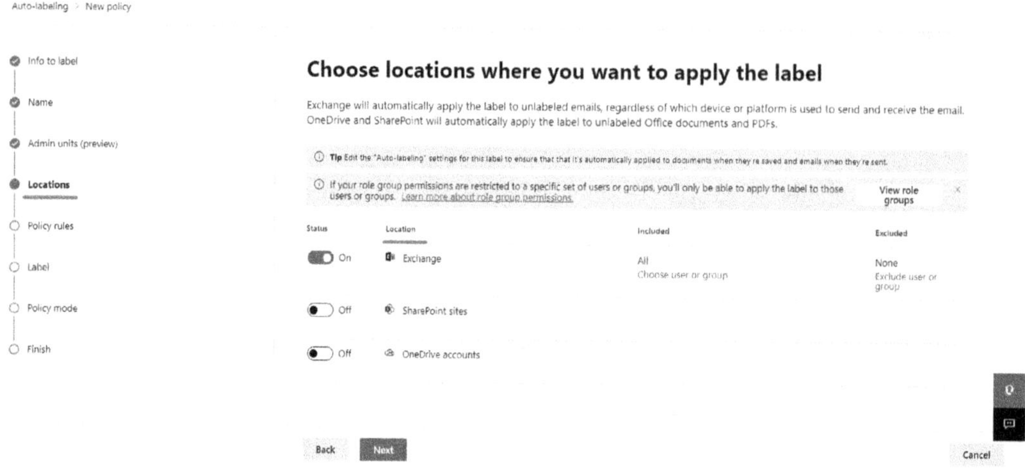

Figure 10.15 – Selecting locations for the auto-labeling policy

5. Next, configure general or advanced rules for your auto-labeling policy. Here you can create new rules based on your business needs. The following screenshot presents examples of the advanced rules you can create for your auto-labeling policy.

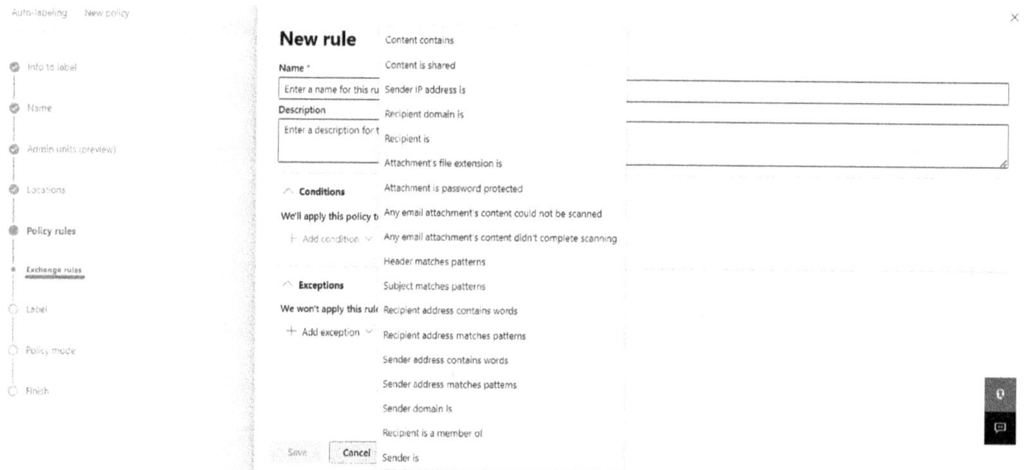

Figure 10.16 – Defining rules for your auto-labeling policy

Defining rules for content across all locations within Microsoft Purview Information Protection is a pivotal step in ensuring comprehensive data security and compliance.

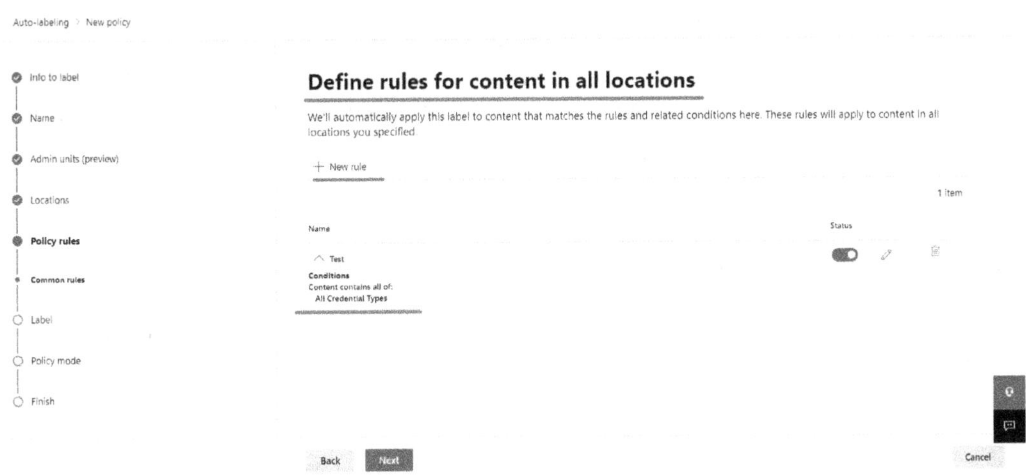

Figure 10.17 – Defining rules for content

Select the label to be applied by the auto-labeling policy.

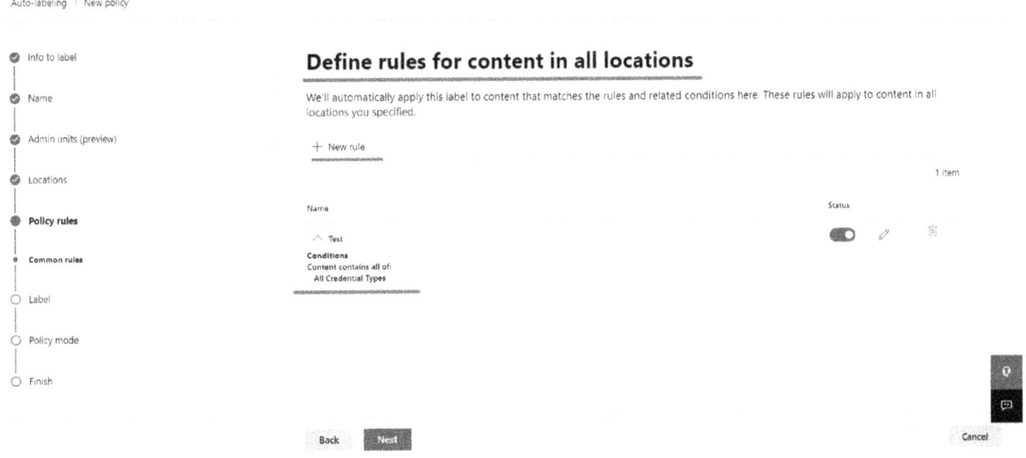

Figure 10.18 – Choosing a sensitivity label

Check **Additional Settings**. There are two additional settings which you can select:

- **Automatically replace existing label that have the same or lower priority**: If chosen, this label will replace existing labels with equal or lower priority, irrespective of whether the existing label was applied automatically or manually.

- **Apply encyption to email received from outside your organization**: The chosen label includes encryption settings. Upon application to messages originating from external sources, encryption will be activated. This occurs when you assign a Rights Management owner from within your organization. This process guarantees that authorized personnel possess the necessary permissions to decrypt the content when necessary.

It's recommended to test your newly created auto-labeling policy before applying it more broadly. To do this, click on **Run policy in simulation mode**, as shown in the following screenshot:

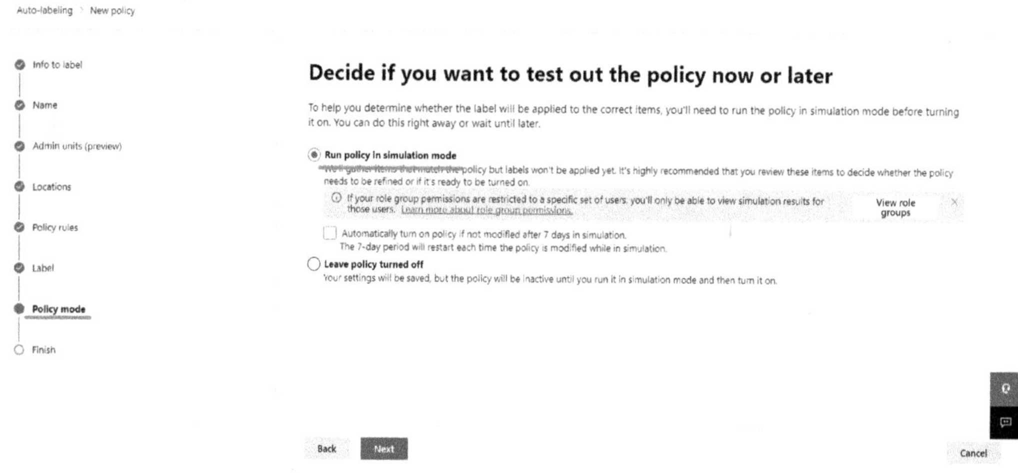

Figure 10.19 – Test created policy

Review the details and click **Next** to create your auto labeling policy.

With this, you have created an auto-labeling policy. Auto-labeling policies hold a vital role within Microsoft Purview as they significantly contribute to effective data governance and management.

After creating a new sensitivity policy, the next step is to understand how to effectively publish this policy. This is a crucial process in ensuring that the policy's rules and protections are enforced throughout your organization. Let's explore the steps involved in publishing your newly created sensitivity policy.

Publishing label policies

Publishing labels in MIP allows organizations to classify and protect their sensitive data. Labels define the properties of the data and specify the actions to be taken based on those properties. By applying the following steps, you can easily publish labels in Microsoft Purview Information Protection:

1. **Understand your labeling requirements**: Before publishing labels, it's important to have a clear understanding of your organization's data classification and protection requirements. Identify the types of sensitive data that need to be labeled, the desired classification levels, and the corresponding protection policies.

2. **Configure Microsoft Purview Information Protection**: Ensure that you have the necessary permissions to configure Information Protection in your organization's Microsoft 365 environment. Access the MIP settings and make sure the required features are enabled, such as sensitivity labels, protection settings, and retention policies.
3. **Define label names and descriptions**: Create a list of label names that accurately represent the different types of sensitive data within your organization. Include a brief description for each label to help users understand the purpose and implications of applying the label.
4. **Specify label properties**: Define the properties associated with each label. These properties may include classification levels (e.g., Public, Confidential, Highly Confidential), visual markings (e.g., watermarks, headers, or footers), protection settings (e.g., encryption or rights management), and retention policies (e.g., a specified data retention duration).
5. **Configure label settings**: Access the label settings in MIP and configure the properties defined in the previous step. Specify the visual markings, protection options, and retention policies for each label. You can also customize the behavior of each label, such as whether it's auto-applied or requires user confirmation.
6. **Test the labels**: Before publishing the labels to the entire organization, it's crucial to thoroughly test them. Apply the labels to different types of files and validate if the expected visual markings, protection, and retention settings are applied correctly. Engage with a select group of users to gather feedback and address any potential issues.
7. **Publish the labels**: Once the labels have been tested and refined, it's time to publish them to the organization. Use the Microsoft 365 Security & Compliance Center or the Azure portal to distribute the labels. Ensure that the labels are made available to all users or targeted to specific departments or user groups as required.
8. **Educate users**: It is extremely important, to ensure successful adoption, that you educate your users about the newly published labels. Conduct training sessions, create documentation, and provide clear instructions on how to apply the labels to different types of data. Help users understand the importance of data classification and the role they play in protecting sensitive information.
9. **Maintain and update labels**: Data classification and protection requirements may evolve over time, so it's essential to review and update the labels periodically. Stay updated with the latest features and enhancements in Microsoft Purview Information Protection to leverage new capabilities and improve the overall data protection posture of your organization.

By following these steps, you can successfully publish labels in Microsoft Purview Information Protection, enabling effective data classification and protection within your organization.

Once the labels have been successfully published, the next stage involves configuring the Information Protection scanner. Let's dive into the process of setting up this scanner to enhance your data protection and security measures.

Information Protection scanner

In an era where data breaches and information leaks constitute significant risks to organizations, protecting sensitive information has become a very important concern. Microsoft has developed an innovative solution called the **Information Protection scanner** to help businesses protect their data and ensure compliance with regulatory standards. The MIP scanner is a comprehensive tool that empowers organizations to identify, classify, and protect sensitive data, minimizing the potential for data loss or unauthorized access. In this section, we will explore the features and benefits of the Microsoft Purview Information Protection scanner and its crucial role in bolstering data security.

The Microsoft Purview Information Protection scanner is an advanced security tool that works by continuously scanning on-premises and cloud repositories, identifying sensitive data, and applying appropriate protective measures. Let's delve into the key features that make the MIP scanner an invaluable asset for organizations:

- **Data discovery and classification**: The MIP scanner employs powerful machine learning algorithms to analyze files and identify sensitive information across various data repositories. It can detect sensitive data such as PII, financial records, intellectual property, and more. Additionally, the MIP scanner offers predefined and customizable data classification labels, enabling organizations to categorize their data based on sensitivity levels and compliance requirements.
- **Automatic and manual labeling**: Once sensitive data is identified, the MIP scanner can automatically apply classification labels and protection policies based on predefined rules or organizational guidelines. These labels can be used to track and control access to sensitive data, ensuring that the right users have appropriate permissions. Furthermore, organizations can also utilize manual labeling options to review and assign labels to files based on their unique context.
- **Integration and collaboration**: The Microsoft Purview Information Protection scanner seamlessly integrates with Microsoft 365 services, enabling organizations to enforce data protection policies across multiple platforms. This integration facilitates collaboration and secure information sharing within and outside the organization. The MIP scanner's unified dashboard provides a centralized view of data protection activities, allowing administrators to monitor and manage data security effectively.
- **Compliance and reporting**: The MIP scanner plays a vital role in helping organizations meet regulatory compliance requirements. It provides comprehensive auditing and reporting capabilities, offering detailed insights into data usage, access controls, and policy violations. This feature is particularly crucial for industries such as healthcare, finance, and legal sectors that deal with sensitive information and have stringent compliance obligations.

Implementing the Microsoft Purview Information Protection scanner can bring numerous benefits to organizations:

- **Enhanced data security**: By continuously scanning and identifying sensitive data, the MIP scanner helps organizations stay one step ahead of potential threats and vulnerabilities. It enables proactive measures to safeguard critical information, reducing the risk of data breaches and unauthorized access.
- **Compliance**: The MIP scanner assists organizations in adhering to various regulatory frameworks, including GDPR, HIPAA, and CCPA. By automating data classification, labeling, and protection, it ensures compliance with data protection regulations, avoiding potential legal consequences and reputational damage.
- **Increased productivity and collaboration**: With the MIP scanner, employees can confidently share and collaborate on sensitive data, knowing that appropriate security measures are in place. This promotes productivity and teamwork while maintaining the necessary data protection controls.
- **Simplified data governance**: The MIP scanner simplifies the management and governance of sensitive data by providing a unified platform for data discovery, classification, and protection. Organizations control any track data usage, monitor access controls, and respond swiftly to any policy violations.

Configuring the Microsoft Purview Information Protection scanner involves several steps to ensure the effective implementation and protection of sensitive data. Here is a general guide to help you get started:

1. Assess your requirements and objectives:
   - Identify the sensitive data that needs protection and determine the specific compliance requirements applicable to your organization
   - Define the goals and objectives you aim to achieve through the implementation of the Microsoft Purview Information Protection scanner
2. Prepare the environment:
   - Ensure that your organization has the necessary infrastructure. Your server must meet the following minimum requirements: a quad-core processor, 8 GB of RAM, and a 64-bit version of Windows Server, with compatibility extending to at least Windows Server 2012R2. (Supported versions also include Windows Server 2016, 2019, and 2022.) Your organization also needs to meet the licensing requirements for Microsoft Purview Information Protection.
   - Verify that your systems meet the minimum hardware and software requirements for the MIP scanner.

3. Install and configure the Microsoft Purview Information Protection scanner:

   - Open the Microsoft Purview admin center and click on **Settings**.

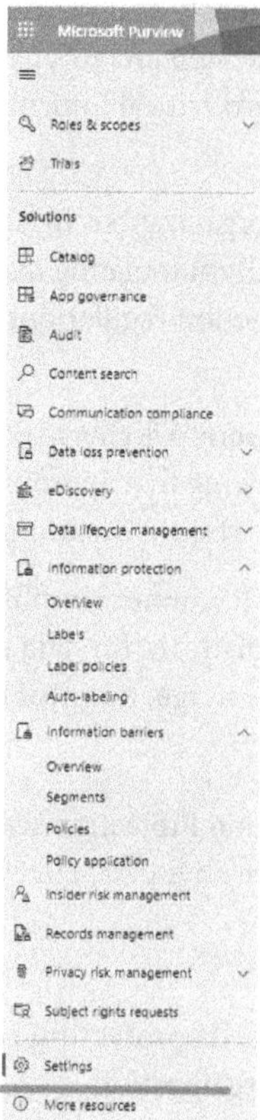

Figure 10.20 – Open the settings for the information protection scanner

   - Select **Information protection scanner**.

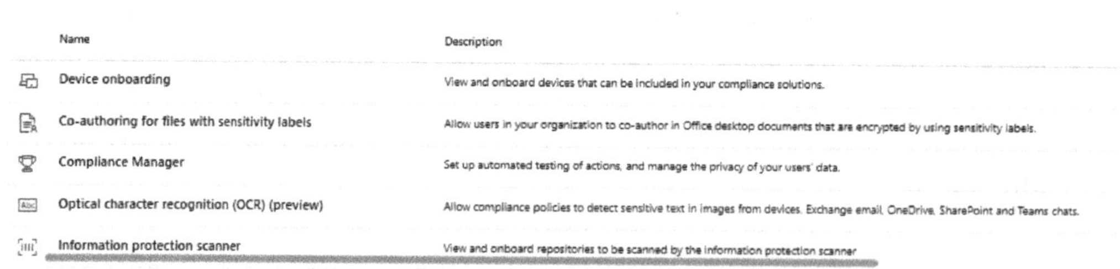

Settings

Name	Description
Device onboarding	View and onboard devices that can be included in your compliance solutions.
Co-authoring for files with sensitivity labels	Allow users in your organization to co-author in Office desktop documents that are encrypted by using sensitivity labels.
Compliance Manager	Set up automated testing of actions, and manage the privacy of your users' data.
Optical character recognition (OCR) (preview)	Allow compliance policies to detect sensitive text in images from devices, Exchange email, OneDrive, SharePoint and Teams chats.
Information protection scanner	View and onboard repositories to be scanned by the information protection scanner

Figure 10.21 – Information protection scanner settings

4. Create a cluster (the cluster name serves as an identifier for the scanner's configurations and repositories. For instance, you may input any name to denote the geographical locations of the data repositories you intend to scan. Later, you will utilize this name to specify the installation or upgrade location for your scanner):

   - Click on + **Add** to create a new cluster:

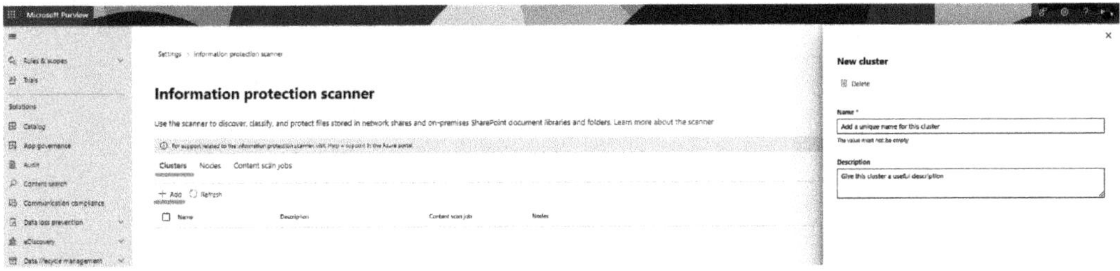

Figure 10.22 – Setting up the information protection scanner

   - Configure the necessary connections within the MIP scanner to establish communication.

5. Define and customize the scanner:

   - Create content scan jobs by clicking on + **Add**, as shown in the following screenshot:

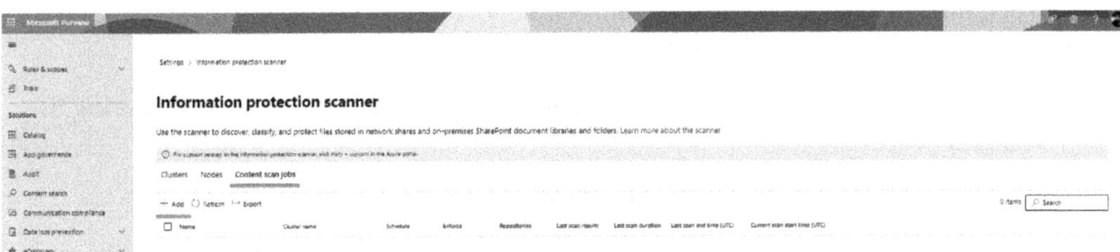

Figure 10.23 – Creating content scan job

- Edit the content scan job and assign your created cluster.

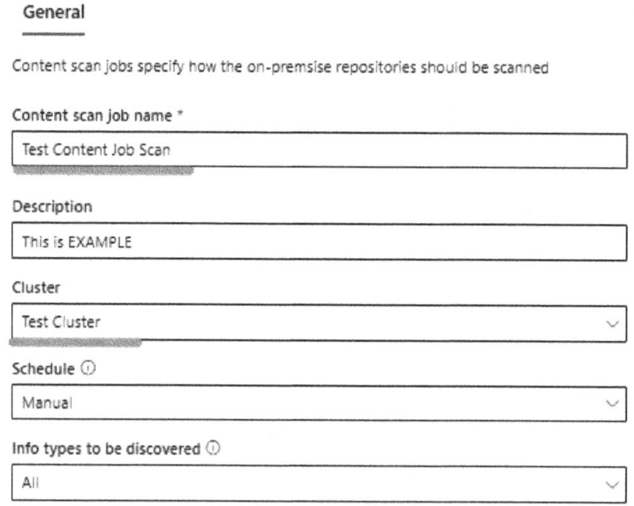

Figure 10.24 – Assigning a cluster to the information protection scanner

6. Configure scanning rules and policies:

   - Define the scanning rules and policies that the MIP scanner should enforce during the scanning process.
   - Specify criteria for identifying sensitive data.
   - Configure actions to be taken upon detecting sensitive data, such as applying classification labels, protecting files, or generating alerts. (The settings in the following screenshot are just examples.):

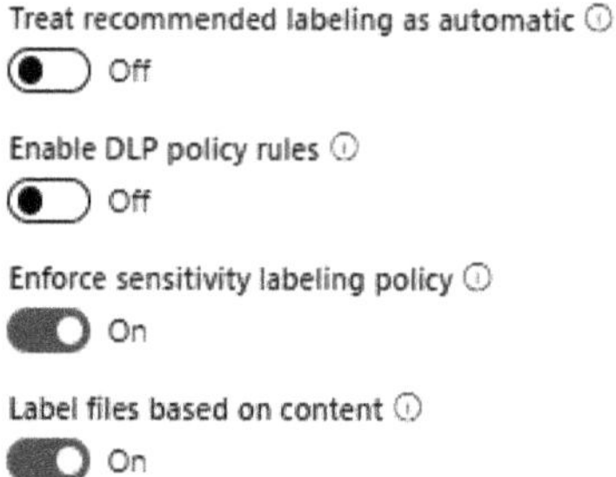

Figure 10.25 – Configuring scanning rules

7. Schedule and run your scans:

    - Set up a scanning schedule that aligns with your organization's needs and resource availability
    - Configure scan parameters, such as scanning frequency, scan depth, and exclusions for specific file types or directories
    - Initiate the scanning process and monitor the progress and results

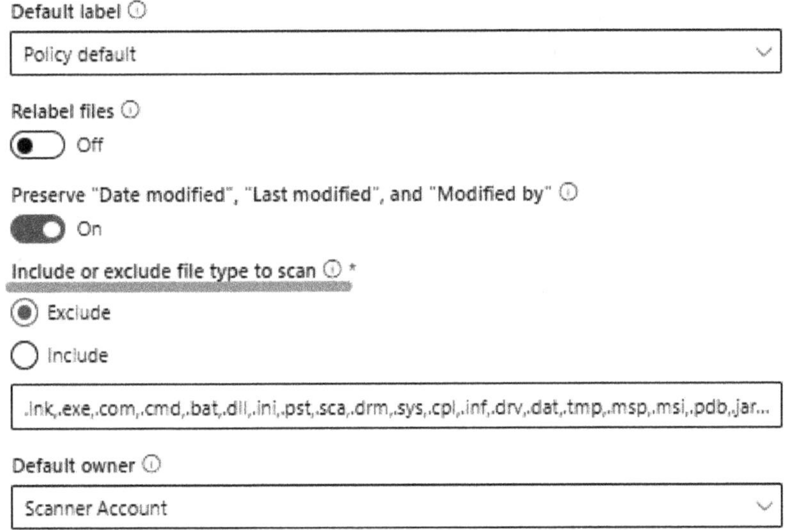

Figure 10.26 – Configuring file type to scan

8. Define **Universal Naming Convention** (**UNC**) paths and SharePoint Server sites for SharePoint on-premises:

    - Click on the created content scan job and select **Repositories**.
    - Define SharePoint URLs.

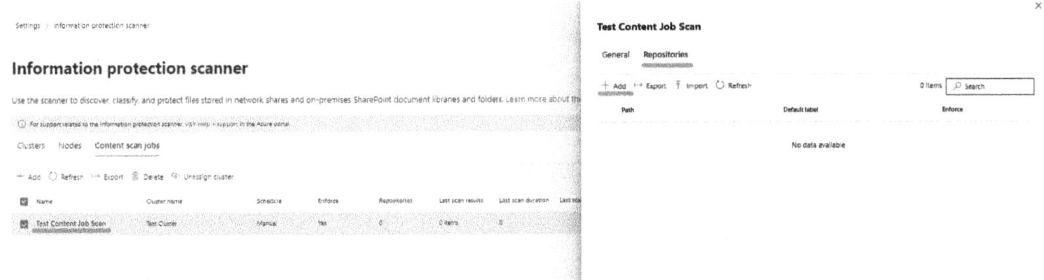

Figure 10.27 – Testing your content scan job

- Use the following path format:
  - For a network share, use `\\Server\Folder`:
  - For a SharePoint library, use `http://sharepointonline.sitename.com/Shared%20Documents/Folder`.
  - For a local path: `C:\Folder`

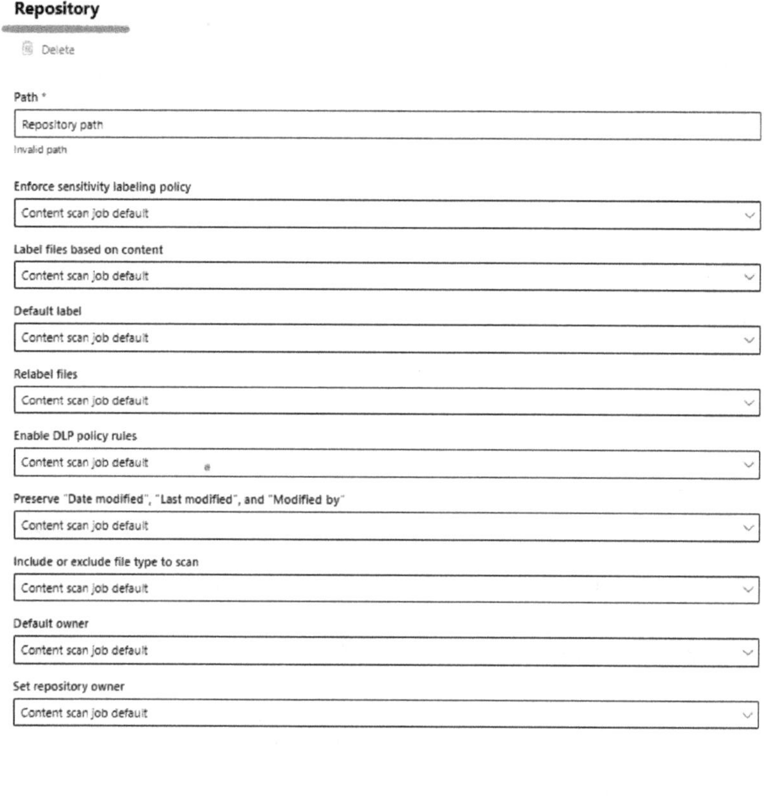

Figure 10.28 – Configuring repository

Remember, the specific configuration steps may vary based on your organization's requirements and the Microsoft 365 services you are utilizing. It is recommended to prepare a detailed plan for the implementation of Microsoft Purview Information Protection, if needed to ensure a smooth and effective configuration process.

Installing the Microsoft Purview Information Protection scanner

> **Important note**
>
> Please be aware that the installation of the Microsoft Purview Information Protection scanner is performed through PowerShell. Additionally, it is essential to have access to Microsoft Entra ID and create the necessary AD token to proceed with the installation.

1. Sign in to the server where you want to run the information protection scanner.
2. From the Microsoft website, install the latest version of the **Azure Information Protection** (**AIP**) unified labeling client (use any internet browser and search for the last AIP URL, then download and run `AzInfoProtection_UL.exe`).
3. Search for and open Windows PowerShell as an admin.
4. Run the following command: `Install-AIPScanner -SqlServerInstance <name> -Cluster <cluster name>` where `-SqlServerInstance` is your local SQL Server instance with a database created for the MIP scanner and where `-Cluster` is the name of the cluster you created in your Microsoft Purview Information Protection portal
5. Enter your Active Directory username and password.
6. Check the status of the Microsoft Purview Information Protection scanner under **Services**.
7. Get a Microsoft Entra ID token for the created service to run unattended.

   When we say that the scanner can run unattended, it means that the Microsoft Purview Information Protection scanner can operate without the need for manual intervention or user interaction. This capability allows the scanner to perform its scanning and protection tasks automatically, following predefined rules and policies, without requiring constant supervision or input from an administrator or user. By running unattended, the scanner can perform scheduled scans, continuously monitor data repositories for sensitive information, apply classification labels, and enforce protection policies as configured. This unattended operation ensures that data security measures are consistently applied, even in the absence of direct human involvement.

Summary

In this chapter of the book, we took on a journey to explore the rich landscape of Microsoft Purview, a powerful service designed to empower organizations in their data governance and management endeavors. Recognizing the vastness and complexity of Purview, we carefully curated our discussion of a selection of key components, aiming to provide you with valuable insights into its essential elements and highlight the most important services that you can configure.

We covered the importance of data classification and labeling within Purview. With an ever-increasing volume of data, automating the process of assigning labels and tags is imperative. We examined how Purview employs machine learning algorithms and predefined rules to streamline data categorization, leading to improved efficiency and accuracy in data organization and management.

It is important to mention that Microsoft Purview is an evolving ecosystem. As new features and services are introduced, it is essential to stay up to date with the latest developments and innovations within the platform. Our intention is to equip you with a solid foundation, empowering you to adapt and explore the possibilities that Purview holds. While acknowledging the impossibility of covering every part of the Purview service (such as eDiscovery, LegalHold, information barriers, etc.), we hope we have ignited your curiosity and have shown you directions in which to explore and discover Microsoft Purview Information Protection further. In the next chapter, we will try to understand auditing lifecycle and records.

11

Understanding the Lifecycle of Auditing and Records

In today's digital age, data is the lifeblood of organizations. It holds sensitive information, intellectual property, and other critical assets. As a result, maintaining security, integrity, and compliance in terms of data is of paramount importance. Microsoft 365, a comprehensive suite of cloud-based productivity and collaboration tools, offers a range of features to help organizations manage their data effectively. Among these features, the lifecycle of auditing and record management represent key components for ensuring data security, compliance, and overall governance. We will delve into the concepts of auditing and records in terms of their lifecycle in Microsoft 365, exploring their significance and best practices.

We'll cover the following topics in this chapter:

- Getting started with the lifecycle of auditing and records
- Microsoft data lifecycle management
- Records management
- eDiscovery and data holds
- Auditing and alerts

Getting started with the lifecycle of auditing and records

Getting started with the lifecycle of **auditing** and **managing records** is a critical step in maintaining data security and compliance. To begin, organizations should define their auditing objectives and decide what aspects of data access and usage they want to monitor. Next, configuring audit policies within tools such Security and Compliance Center in Microsoft 365 is essential to tailor the auditing process to specific needs.

As for the lifecycle of records, organizations must establish retention policies to determine how long data should be kept and when they should be disposed of. This ensures compliance with regulatory requirements and facilitates efficient data management. Training employees on the importance of following record-keeping and disposal procedures is also crucial to maintaining an organized and secure data environment. In this digital age, getting started with the lifecycle of auditing and record management is a fundamental aspect of modern data governance.

The lifecycle of audits and records in Microsoft 365

Auditing is the process of tracking and recording activities related to data access, usage, and changes within Microsoft 365. This functionality is vital for organizations, as it helps in understanding who is accessing data, what they are doing with it, and when these actions occur. In Microsoft 365, auditing provides a comprehensive set of tools to monitor and analyze data-related activities. The key aspects of auditing in Microsoft 365 include the following:

- **Audit logs**: Microsoft 365 maintains detailed audit logs that record activities across various services such as SharePoint, OneDrive, Exchange, and more. These logs capture user actions, including file access, sharing, modification, and even administrative changes, such as adding or deleting users.
- **Security and Compliance Center**: This central hub in Microsoft 365 offers a user-friendly interface for managing auditing. It allows administrators to configure audit policies, review audit reports, and set up alerts for specific events, ensuring they stay informed about critical activities in their environment.
- **Data retention policies**: Auditing data can accumulate quickly, making it essential to manage its retention. Microsoft 365 provides retention policies that allow organizations to specify how long audit logs should be kept. This is crucial for compliance purposes and can help in forensic investigations.
- **Advanced threat protection**: Microsoft 365's advanced threat protection features, such as threat intelligence and advanced security management, complement auditing by helping to identify and respond to security threats and vulnerabilities effectively.

Record lifecycle management is a systematic approach to managing documents, emails, and other digital assets throughout their entire lifecycle. In Microsoft 365, the records management feature plays a crucial role in ensuring that data are retained, archived, and disposed of in accordance with legal, regulatory, and business requirements. The records lifecycle typically consists of the following stages:

- **Creation and capture**: This is the initial phase, where records are created, whether through emails, documents, or other forms of data. In Microsoft 365, records can be automatically classified and tagged during this stage, making it easier to manage them throughout their lifecycle.
- **Retention and archiving**: Microsoft 365 allows organizations to define retention policies and labels. These policies specify how long data should be retained, and labels help classify records accordingly. Data that needs to be retained for legal or compliance reasons can be archived to ensure their preservation.

- **Disposition and deletion**: Records that have reached the end of their useful life or those that are no longer needed can be disposed of in a controlled manner. Microsoft 365 offers disposition policies that automatically delete or archive records when their retention period expires.
- **Legal hold and litigation support**: In case of legal investigations or disputes, Microsoft 365 provides the ability to place content on legal hold. This ensures that potentially relevant records are preserved and cannot be altered or deleted during the litigation process.
- **Audit and reporting**: Throughout the records lifecycle, organizations can audit and report on the management of records. This includes tracking who accessed, modified, or deleted records, which is essential for compliance and transparency.

Microsoft Purview Records Management

Microsoft Purview Records Management is a component of the Microsoft Purview data governance service designed to help organizations effectively manage their records throughout their lifecycle. This feature offers capabilities for defining, classifying, and managing records, ensuring that sensitive and valuable data are appropriately retained, archived, and disposed of in compliance with regulatory requirements and organizational policies. Purview Records Management provides a structured approach to record declaration, retention policies, and disposition workflows, making it easier for businesses to maintain compliance, reduce legal risks, and ensure the integrity and security of their critical records. This feature is particularly valuable for organizations in highly regulated industries and those seeking robust data governance solutions.

Licensing for Microsoft Purview Data Lifecycle Management is an essential consideration for organizations seeking to govern and manage their data assets effectively. Microsoft typically offers licensing options tailored to specific services within the Microsoft 365 Purview ecosystem, such as Retention and DLP. These licenses enable administrators to access features such as data discovery, data classification, and metadata management. Additionally, organizations may need to explore Microsoft 365 compliance and security licenses if they plan to integrate Purview with Microsoft 365 for enhanced data governance and regulatory compliance. Accurate and up-to-date information on licensing options should be obtained directly from Microsoft to align with an organization's specific needs and objectives.

Permissions for Microsoft 365 auditing and records lifecycle management are crucial for ensuring the security, compliance, and effective management of an organization's data. In Microsoft 365, administrators can configure permissions to control who can access and modify audit logs, set retention policies, and manage records. This granular control allows organizations to restrict access to sensitive data and compliance-related functions to authorized personnel. Properly configured permissions help safeguard critical data, maintain regulatory compliance, and promote efficient record management while preventing unauthorized access and potential data breaches. The regular auditing and monitoring of permissions ensures that access rights align with organizational policies and security best practices.

The Microsoft Purview compliance portal empowers administrators to oversee and control user permissions for performing compliance-related tasks directly within Microsoft 365. Through the newly introduced Permissions page in the compliance portal, you gain the ability to finely tune user access to a range of critical compliance features, including device management, Microsoft Purview Data Loss Prevention, eDiscovery, insider risk management, retention, and more. Users are only able to engage in compliance tasks that have been explicitly authorized.

Access to the **Permissions** tab within the compliance portal is contingent on user roles. Users must hold the position of a Global Administrator or be assigned the Role Management role (which is exclusively designated to the Organization Management role group). The Role Management role endows users with the capabilities to view, create, and adjust role groups, thus ensuring the precise management of permissions.

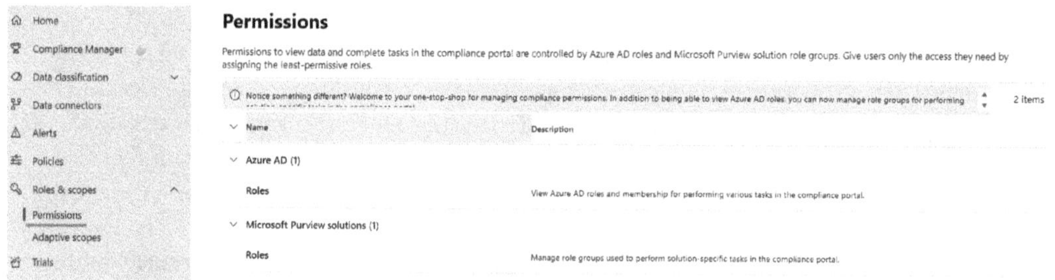

Figure 11.1 – Permission portal in Microsoft Purview

Within the compliance portal, permissions are governed by the well-established **role-based access control** (**RBAC**) permissions model. RBAC serves as the foundation for permissions across many Microsoft 365 services, making the process of granting permissions within the compliance portal akin to that in other services you may be familiar with. It's essential to bear in mind, however, that the permissions administered in the compliance portal are specific to its realm and do not encompass the entirety of permissions required for each individual service it interfaces with.

You have the capability to include users and groups within administrative units through the utilization of the following predefined role groups:

- Compliance administrator
- Compliance data administrators
- Information protection (admins, analysts, investigators, and readers)
- Organization management
- Records management
- Security administrator
- Security operator

- Security reader

Permissions > Role groups for Microsoft Purview solutions

Role groups for Microsoft Purview solutions

Admin roles give users permission to view data and complete tasks in the Microsoft Purview compliance portal. Give users only the access they need by assigning the least-permissive role. Learn more about role groups

+ Create role group ◯ Refresh 63 items Search

Name	Type	Description	Last modified
Attack Simulator Administrators	Built-in		-
Attack Simulator Payload Authors	Built-in		-
Organization Management	Built-in		-
Security Administrator	Built-in		-
Audit Manager	Built-in		-
Billing Administrator	Built-in		-
eDiscovery Manager	Built-in		-
Compliance Administrator	Built-in		-

Figure 11.2 – Built-in role groups in Microsoft Purview

When assigning role groups, you are presented with the flexibility to choose individual members or groups for inclusion. Additionally, you can leverage the **Assign admin units** option to specify and select administrative units previously established within Microsoft Entra ID. This approach empowers you to finely tune the access control and responsibilities of users and groups in alignment with your organizational structure and objectives:

Organization Management

Figure 11.3 – Assign admin units

Creating **Administrative Units** in **Microsoft Entra ID** allows you to segment your directory into smaller, more manageable units for the delegation of administrative tasks. Here are the steps to create **Administrative Units**:

1. Go to the **Azure Portal** (`https://portal.azure.com`) and sign in with your Microsoft Entra ID global administrator or privileged role account.
2. In the left-hand navigation pane, click on **Microsoft Entra ID** (formerly Azure Active Directory).
3. Within the **Microsoft Entra ID** section, select **Administrative units**.

4. Add a new **Administrative unit**.
5. Click on the + **Add** button to create a new **Administrative unit**.

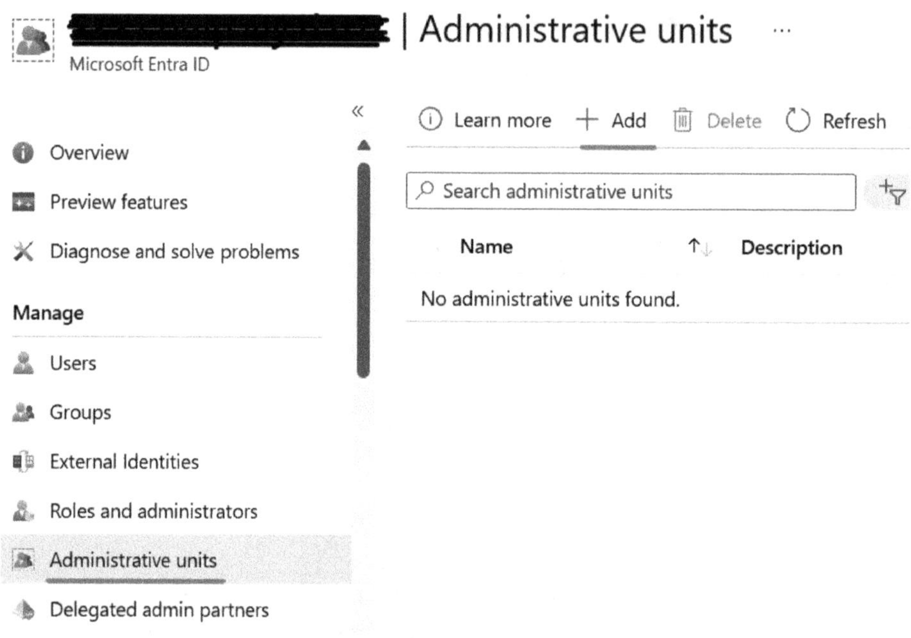

Figure 11.4 – Create administrative units in Microsoft Entra ID

6. Configure the administrative unit details (you will need to provide a display name and a description for the administrative unit you're creating).
7. Select **Administrative Role** and add members (click on the **Members** tab to add users or groups to the administrative unit. You can select the users or groups that you want to associate with this administrative unit. These members will have delegated administrative privileges for the objects within this unit).

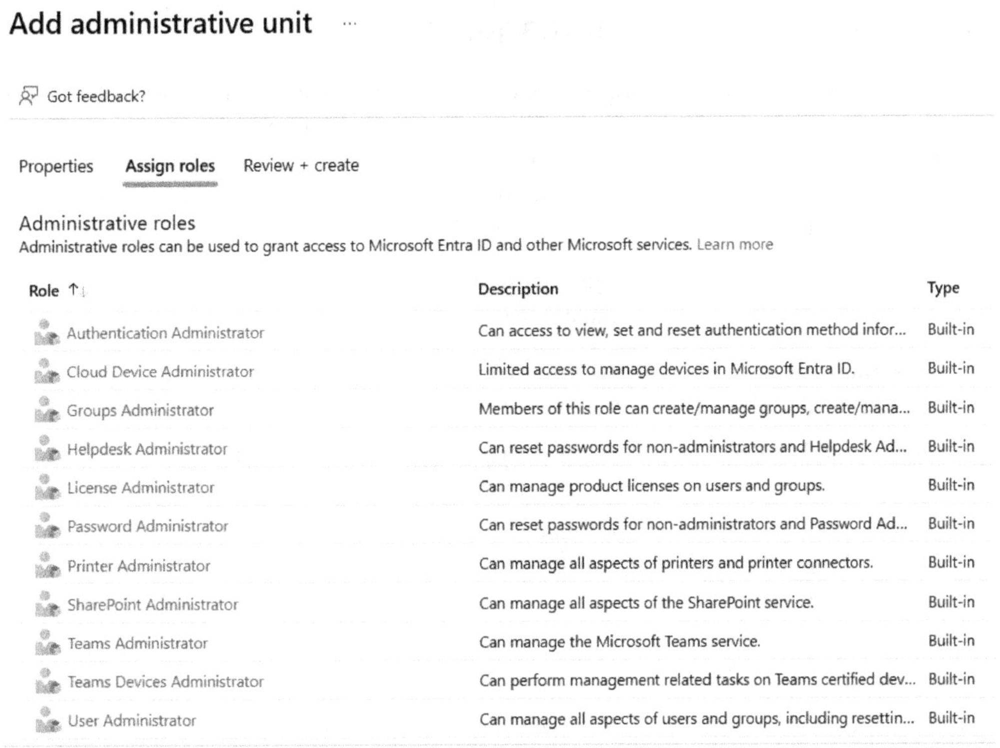

Add administrative unit ...

Got feedback?

Properties Assign roles Review + create

Administrative roles

Administrative roles can be used to grant access to Microsoft Entra ID and other Microsoft services. Learn more

Role ↑↓	Description	Type
Authentication Administrator	Can access to view, set and reset authentication method infor...	Built-in
Cloud Device Administrator	Limited access to manage devices in Microsoft Entra ID.	Built-in
Groups Administrator	Members of this role can create/manage groups, create/mana...	Built-in
Helpdesk Administrator	Can reset passwords for non-administrators and Helpdesk Ad...	Built-in
License Administrator	Can manage product licenses on users and groups.	Built-in
Password Administrator	Can reset passwords for non-administrators and Password Ad...	Built-in
Printer Administrator	Can manage all aspects of printers and printer connectors.	Built-in
SharePoint Administrator	Can manage all aspects of the SharePoint service.	Built-in
Teams Administrator	Can manage the Microsoft Teams service.	Built-in
Teams Devices Administrator	Can perform management related tasks on Teams certified dev...	Built-in
User Administrator	Can manage all aspects of users and groups, including resettin...	Built-in

Figure 11.5 – Assign roles and members for the administrative unit

8. After setting up the details, members, and roles, review your settings to ensure they are accurate. Then, click the **Create** button to create the administrative unit.

Administrative units are particularly useful for delegating tasks and responsibilities within Microsoft Entra ID. The users or groups added to an administrative unit will be able to manage objects within that unit, making it easier to manage access control in a structured way.

Please note that the ability to create administrative units might be subject to licensing and role requirements, and Microsoft Entra ID capabilities and features can change over time, so it's a good practice to refer to the most current Microsoft documentation or consult with your Microsoft Entra ID administrator for precise guidance.

Microsoft data lifecycle management

Data lifecycle management is a critical aspect of modern business operations, and Microsoft offers a comprehensive suite of tools and services to assist organizations in managing their data throughout its entire lifecycle. Whether it's about retaining critical business information, safeguarding sensitive data, or ensuring compliance with regulatory requirements, Microsoft's Data Lifecycle Management solutions are designed to meet the needs of businesses of all sizes.

The data lifecycle encompasses the entire journey of data within an organization, from its creation and capture to its disposal. It typically includes the following stages:

1. **Data creation and ingestion**: This is where data is initially created or ingested into the organization's systems. It could be through customer interactions, internal processes, or external data sources.
2. **Data usage and analysis**: Once data is captured, it is put to use for various purposes, such as analytics, reporting, decision-making, and more.
3. **Data retention**: Some data must be retained for specific periods due to legal, compliance, or business requirements. This stage involves defining retention policies and ensuring data is preserved accordingly.
4. **Data archiving**: Data that is no longer actively used but needs to be retained is typically archived. Archiving reduces the load on active systems while ensuring data is still accessible.
5. **Data disposal**: At the end of its useful life, data are disposed of in a secure and compliant manner to minimize risks and legal liabilities.

Microsoft's Data Lifecycle Management solutions address each of these stages to help organizations streamline their data management processes. In summary, Microsoft offers a robust set of solutions for data lifecycle management, encompassing data retention, archiving, disposal, and compliance. By adopting best practices and utilizing Microsoft's tools, organizations can efficiently manage their data from creation to destruction while staying in line with regulatory and business requirements. Data lifecycle management not only reduces risks but also contributes to the overall efficiency and security of an organization's data assets:

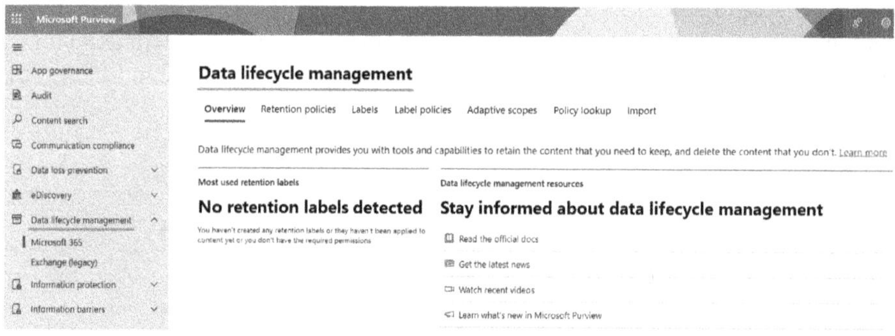

Figure 11.6 – Data lifecycle management portal

Retention policies serve as the foundation of data lifecycle management within Microsoft 365, covering a range of critical workloads, including Exchange, SharePoint, OneDrive for Business, and Teams, among other services. With these policies, you have the flexibility to define whether content should be retained indefinitely, for a specific duration, or be automatically and permanently deleted after a set period, especially if no user action prompts its deletion. A common configuration involves a combination of both retention and deletion actions, such as retaining emails for three years and subsequently deleting them.

These retention policies can be applied universally across your organization, including all instances such as mailboxes and SharePoint sites, or selectively, targeting specific departments, regions, or chosen SharePoint sites.

In cases where you require special treatment, such as extending how long legal documents are kept, Microsoft 365 has you covered with retention labels. These labels can be shared with your applications, giving users the ability to apply them either by hand or automatically based on the content they're working with. This way, you can ensure that data receive the precise handling they need within your data lifecycle management setup.

Creating retention policies

Creating a retention policy in Microsoft 365 involves defining how long you want to retain certain types of content and what should happen to that content when the retention period expires.

To create a retention policy, you need to be assigned a **Compliance Administrator** role or a **Retention Management** role. To have read-only rights for a retention policy, use **View-Only Retention Management** rights.

Here's a step-by-step guide on how to create a retention policy:

1. Sign in to Microsoft 365 Purview Center using an account that has the necessary administrative permissions, such as a Global Administrator or Compliance Administrator account.
2. In **Purview Center**, navigate to **Data Lifecycle Management|Microsoft 365**. Then, select **Retention policies**.

3. Click on the **New retention policy** button or a similar option to initiate the creation of a new retention policy:

Data lifecycle management

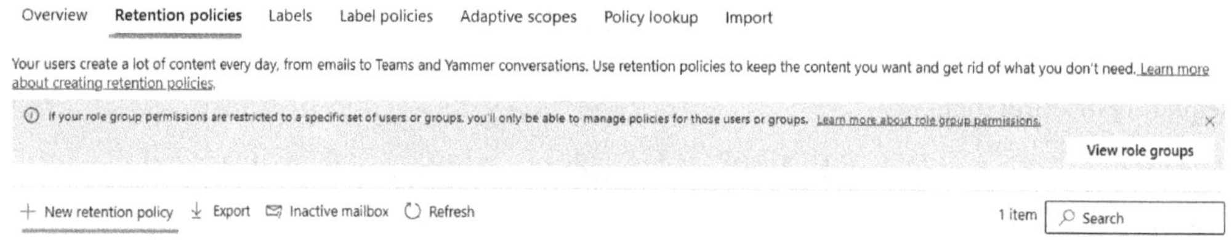

Figure 11.7 – Create retention policy

4. Give your retention policy a descriptive name and, if needed, add a meaningful description to help you and other administrators understand its purpose.
5. Configure **Retention settings**: Define the type of retention policy to create. Choose between the **Adaptive** or **Static** options.

   Policies come in two flavors: adaptive and static. The beauty of an adaptive policy lies in its ability to self-adjust its application based on the attributes or properties you set. It's like having a policy that stays in sync with your changing needs. In contrast, a static policy remains rooted in a specific set of locations, requiring manual updates if those locations ever change. In the adaptability contest, the adaptive policy takes the crown, making your life easier by automatically evolving with your requirements:

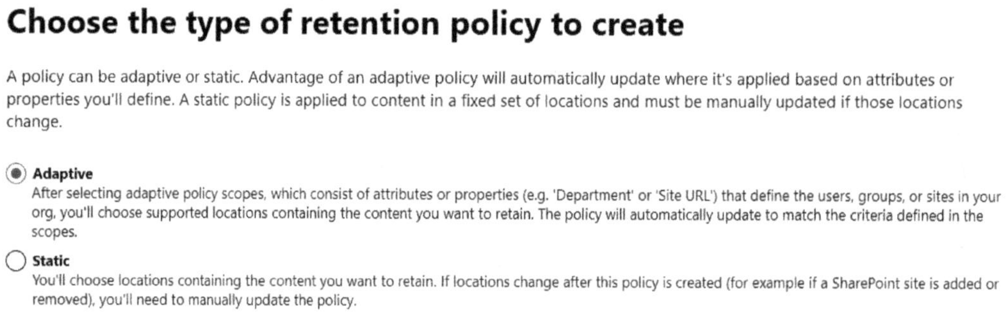

Choose the type of retention policy to create

A policy can be adaptive or static. Advantage of an adaptive policy will automatically update where it's applied based on attributes or properties you'll define. A static policy is applied to content in a fixed set of locations and must be manually updated if those locations change.

(●) **Adaptive**
After selecting adaptive policy scopes, which consist of attributes or properties (e.g. 'Department' or 'Site URL') that define the users, groups, or sites in your org, you'll choose supported locations containing the content you want to retain. The policy will automatically update to match the criteria defined in the scopes.

( ) **Static**
You'll choose locations containing the content you want to retain. If locations change after this policy is created (for example if a SharePoint site is added or removed), you'll need to manually update the policy.

Figure 11.8 – Choose the type of retention policy

6. Choose where to apply the policy:

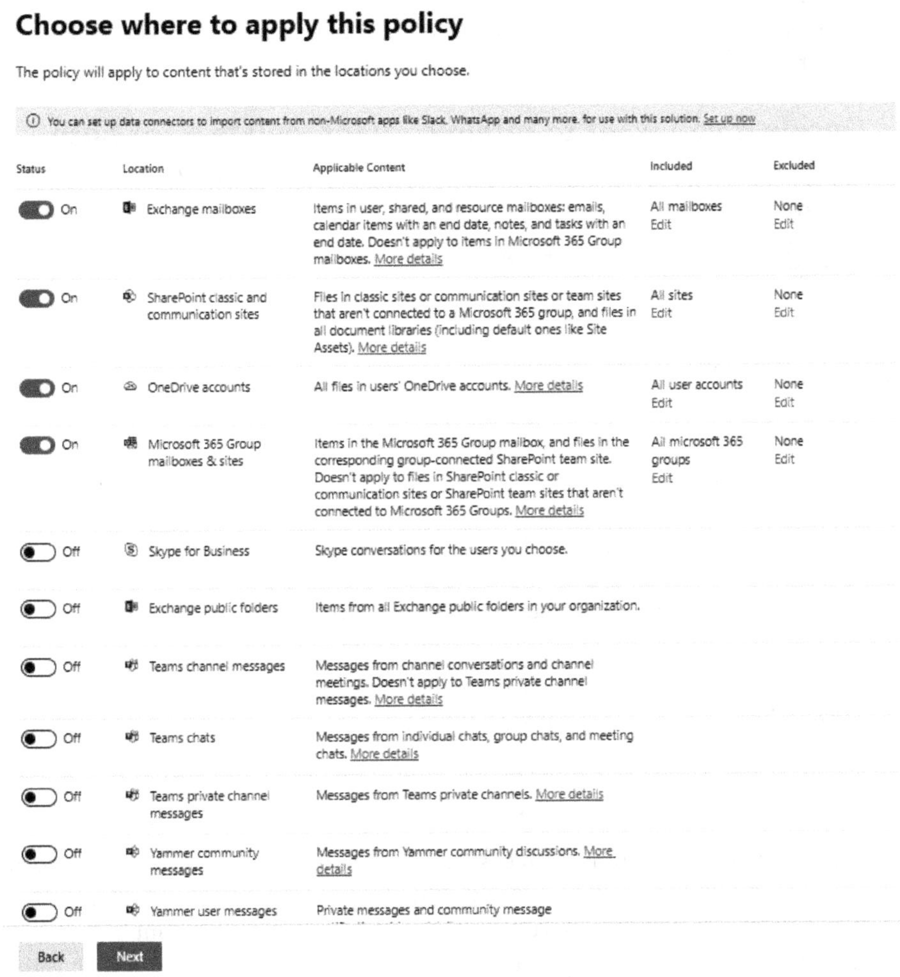

Choose where to apply this policy

The policy will apply to content that's stored in the locations you choose.

ⓘ You can set up data connectors to import content from non-Microsoft apps like Slack, WhatsApp and many more, for use with this solution. Set up now

Status	Location	Applicable Content	Included	Excluded
On	Exchange mailboxes	Items in user, shared, and resource mailboxes: emails, calendar items with an end date, notes, and tasks with an end date. Doesn't apply to items in Microsoft 365 Group mailboxes. More details	All mailboxes Edit	None Edit
On	SharePoint classic and communication sites	Files in classic sites or communication sites or team sites that aren't connected to a Microsoft 365 group, and files in all document libraries (including default ones like Site Assets). More details	All sites Edit	None Edit
On	OneDrive accounts	All files in users' OneDrive accounts. More details	All user accounts Edit	None Edit
On	Microsoft 365 Group mailboxes & sites	Items in the Microsoft 365 Group mailbox, and files in the corresponding group-connected SharePoint team site. Doesn't apply to files in SharePoint classic or communication sites or SharePoint team sites that aren't connected to Microsoft 365 Groups. More details	All microsoft 365 groups Edit	None Edit
Off	Skype for Business	Skype conversations for the users you choose.		
Off	Exchange public folders	Items from all Exchange public folders in your organization.		
Off	Teams channel messages	Messages from channel conversations and channel meetings. Doesn't apply to Teams private channel messages. More details		
Off	Teams chats	Messages from individual chats, group chats, and meeting chats. More details		
Off	Teams private channel messages	Messages from Teams private channels. More details		
Off	Yammer community messages	Messages from Yammer community discussions. More details		
Off	Yammer user messages	Private messages and community message		

Back Next

Figure 11.9 – Choose where to apply policy

7. Specify how long content should be retained by defining a retention period. You can choose to retain content indefinitely, retain it for a specific duration (e.g., 7 years), or specify custom retention settings. Decide what should happen when the retention period expires. You can either delete the content automatically or keep it forever:

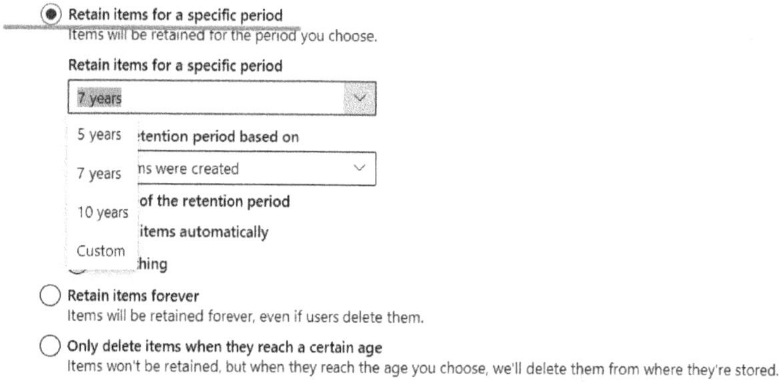

Figure 11.10 – Define the retention period

8. Review the policy details to ensure they match your requirements. Once you are satisfied, click the **Create** or **Save** button to create the retention policy.

After the policy is created, it may take some time for it to be applied to the specified locations and content. Be patient while the policy takes effect.

Regularly monitor the policy's application to ensure it is working as intended. You can also adjust or delete policies as needed to accommodate changes in your organization's requirements. Creating retention policies in Microsoft 365 is crucial for effective data management, compliance, and data security. Ensure you thoroughly understand your organization's requirements and consult with legal and compliance teams to establish appropriate retention policies.

Creating and publishing labels

Generate labels within your retention policies for content that requires special treatment. These exceptions might involve extending the retention period for documents or safeguarding select emails from permanent deletion, as needed. You can create a label in the following way:

1. Log on to the **Microsoft Purview** portal and select **Data Lifecycle Management|Microsoft 365**

2. Select the option **Label** and click on **Create a Label**:

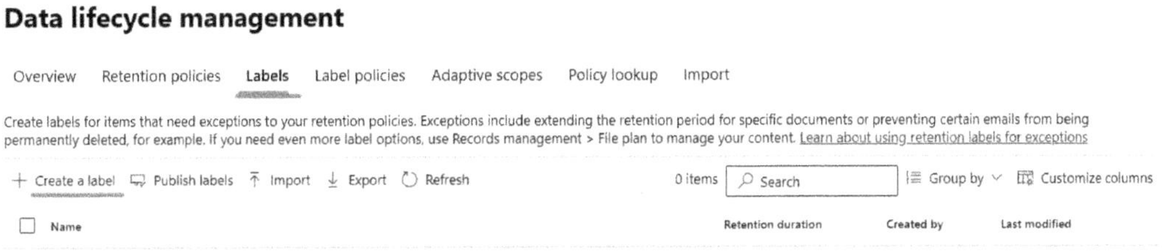

Data lifecycle management

Overview Retention policies **Labels** Label policies Adaptive scopes Policy lookup Import

Create labels for items that need exceptions to your retention policies. Exceptions include extending the retention period for specific documents or preventing certain emails from being permanently deleted, for example. If you need even more label options, use Records management > File plan to manage your content. Learn about using retention labels for exceptions

+ Create a label Publish labels Import Export Refresh 0 items Search Group by Customize columns

Name Retention duration Created by Last modified

Figure 11.11 – Create a label

3. Define the label settings and choose from the three options available, shown as follows:

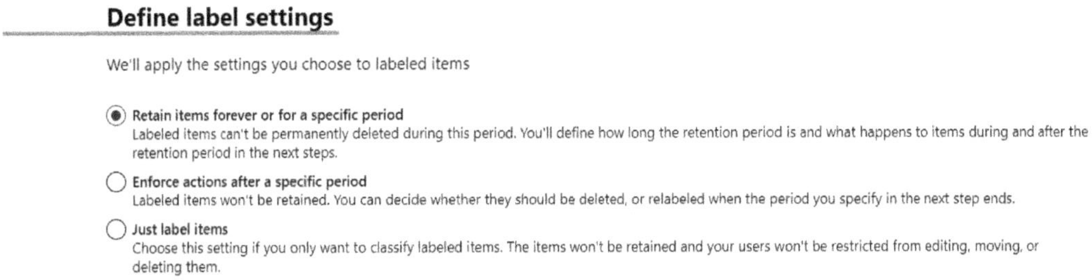

Define label settings

We'll apply the settings you choose to labeled items

- (●) **Retain items forever or for a specific period**
  Labeled items can't be permanently deleted during this period. You'll define how long the retention period is and what happens to items during and after the retention period in the next steps.
- ( ) **Enforce actions after a specific period**
  Labeled items won't be retained. You can decide whether they should be deleted, or relabeled when the period you specify in the next step ends.
- ( ) **Just label items**
  Choose this setting if you only want to classify labeled items. The items won't be retained and your users won't be restricted from editing, moving, or deleting them.

Figure 11.12 – Define the label settings

4. Define the retain period and retention periods based on different conditions:

Define the retention period

Specify how long the retention period should be.

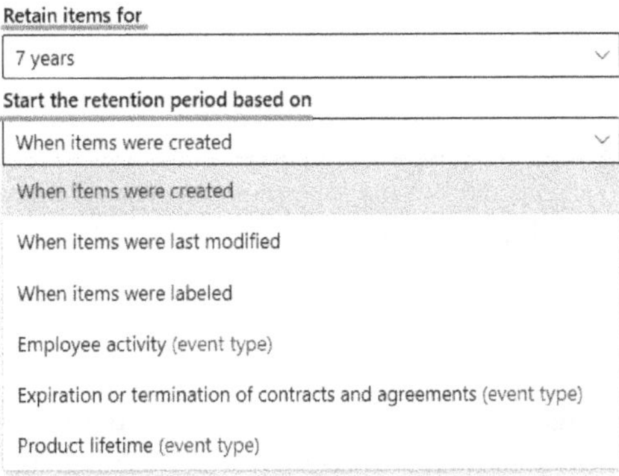

Figure 11.13 – Select retention period

5. Choose what happens after the retention period:

Choose what happens after the retention period

These settings determine what happens to items when the retention period ends.

- (●) **Delete items automatically**
  We'll permanently remove labeled items from wherever they're stored.
- ( ) **Start a disposition review**
  Let the disposition reviewers you assign in the next step decide if items can be safely deleted or whether other actions (such as changing the retention period) should be taken. Learn more
- ( ) **Change the label**
  You can extend the period by choosing an existing label to replace this one with. Learn more about relabeling items
- ( ) **Run a Power Automate flow**
  Customize what happens to labeled items with a Power Automate flow. You can run a flow to meet a specific business need, such as moving labeled items to a certain location or sending email notifications.
  Learn more about running a Power Automate flow
- ( ) **Deactivate retention settings**
  Labeled items won't be retained or deleted when their retention settings are deactivated. You'll have to manually remove any items that you want deleted.

Figure 11.14 – Select settings for after the retention period

6. Review the configuration of the label and press **Create**.
7. If you're satisfied with the label you've created, simply choose **Publish Label** to complete the process.

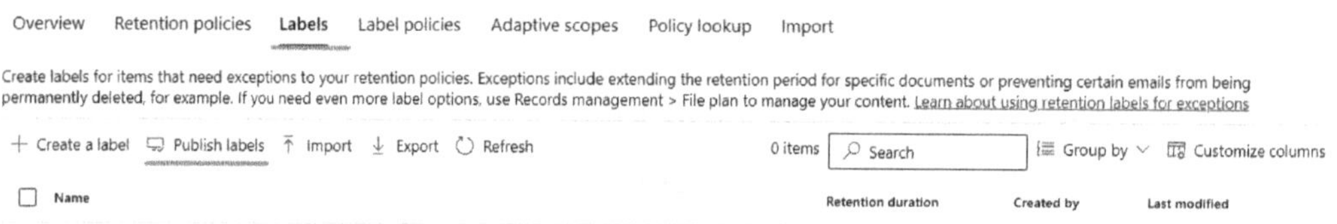

Figure 11.15 – Publish label

In having covered the fundamentals of data lifecycle management, it's time to shift our focus to understanding the workings of Microsoft record management within the broader context of the Microsoft 365 ecosystem. Let's explore how this aspect of data governance can help organizations efficiently manage their records and stay compliant.

Records management

Microsoft Purview's record management system provides organizations with a centralized and user-friendly platform to not only meet their legal obligations but also to maintain a defensible compliance posture. This entails creating and implementing robust retention policies, ensuring that records are disposed of in accordance with regulatory requirements, and streamlining the overall management of crucial information assets. By doing so, organizations can improve data governance, reduce compliance risks, and optimize the allocation of resources, all while aligning with evolving regulatory landscapes. A systematic approach ensures that organizations maintain a well-organized and compliant repository of their records, reducing the risks associated with non-compliance, data breaches, and legal disputes.

Within the records management solution in the Microsoft Purview compliance portal, when you create a retention label, you're given the flexibility to designate items as records, signifying their importance and need for special handling. Alternatively, if you've previously executed the PowerShell command, you can also choose to classify items as regulatory records. This distinction is particularly significant, as regulatory records carry specific legal and compliance implications, requiring careful handling to ensure full adherence to regulatory standards. By providing these options, Microsoft Purview empowers organizations to manage both their general records and regulatory records effectively, contributing to a comprehensive records management strategy that encompasses all facets of data governance and compliance.

When utilizing retention labels to mark items as records in SharePoint and OneDrive, it's important to consider whether adjustments to the default tenant setting are needed. Specifically, you should evaluate whether users should have the capability to modify the properties of a locked record when dealing with files larger than 0 bytes. This decision can significantly impact how your organization manages and maintains the integrity of critical records within these platforms. The following steps show how to change default settings:

1. Log on to the **Microsoft Purview** portal and select **Data lifecycle management|Records management**
2. Select **Record management settings**:

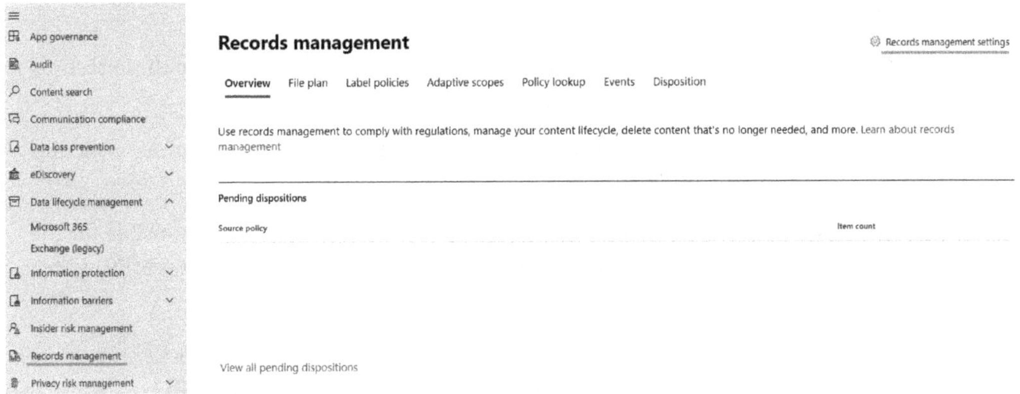

Figure 11.16 – Record management settings

3. In new windows, enable the following settings:
   - **Enable records versioning**
   - **Allow users to edit record properties**

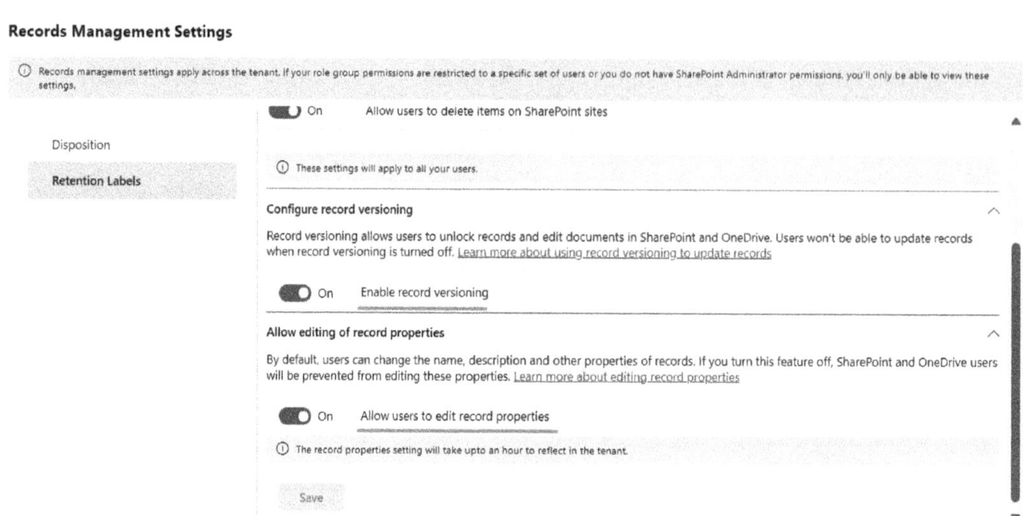

Figure 11.17 – Configure records management settings

File plan serves as SharePoint's central records management blueprint. While its specifics may vary from one organization to another, a typical file plan encompasses the following:

- **Record identification**: Identifying the specific types of items recognized as records within the organization
- **Categorization**: Grouping these items into broader categories to facilitate efficient organization and retrieval
- **Storage locations**: Specifying the designated repositories or locations where these records are stored
- **Retention timelines**: Defining the duration for which records should be retained, whether permanently or for specific periods
- **Responsibility assignments**: Clearly delineating the individuals or roles responsible for the management of distinct types of records, ensuring accountability throughout their lifecycle

You can create a file plan in the following way:

1. Log on to the **Microsoft Purview** portal and select **Data lifecycle management** | **Records management**

2. Select **File plan** and click on **Create a label**:

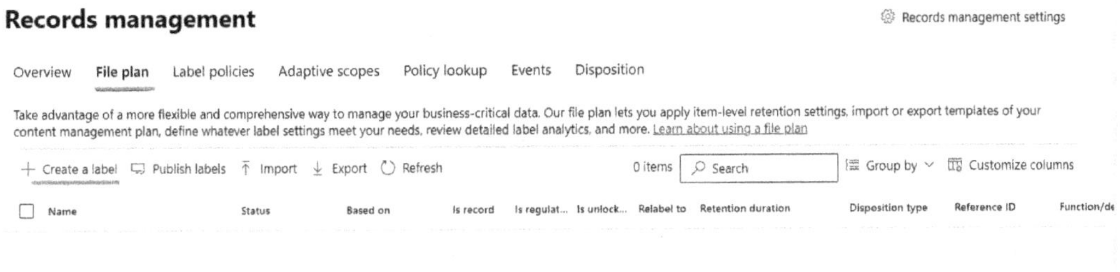

Records management

Records management settings

Overview File plan Label policies Adaptive scopes Policy lookup Events Disposition

Take advantage of a more flexible and comprehensive way to manage your business-critical data. Our file plan lets you apply item-level retention settings, import or export templates of your content management plan, define whatever label settings meet your needs, review detailed label analytics, and more. Learn about using a file plan

+ Create a label Publish labels Import Export Refresh 0 items Search Group by Customize columns

Name Status Based on Is record Is regulat... Is unlock... Relabel to Retention duration Disposition type Reference ID Function/de

Figure 11.18 – Create a label for a file plan

3. Define the following settings:
   - Business function/department
   - Category
   - Authority type
   - Provision/Citation

   For any of the settings above, you can create your own records. Select the **Choose** options:

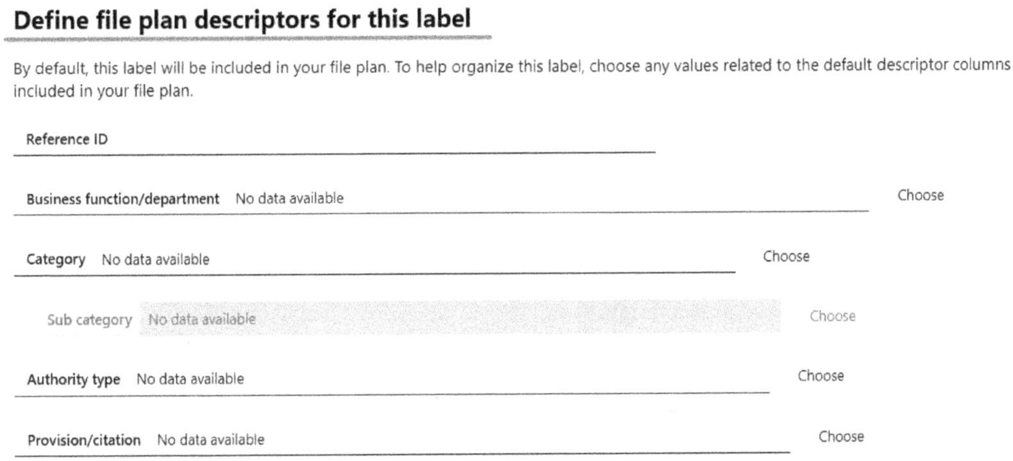

Define file plan descriptors for this label

By default, this label will be included in your file plan. To help organize this label, choose any values related to the default descriptor columns included in your file plan.

Reference ID

Business function/department No data available Choose

Category No data available Choose

Sub category No data available Choose

Authority type No data available Choose

Provision/citation No data available Choose

Figure 11.19 – Define the file plan

4. Define **Label settings** and **Period for File Plan**
5. Review and save

In conclusion, record management within the Microsoft Compliance ecosystem stands as a crucial pillar of data governance, compliance, and efficient organizational operations. By adopting Microsoft's robust record management solutions, organizations can systematically organize, classify, and control their records throughout their lifecycle. This ensures adherence to legal and regulatory obligations, reduces the risk of data breaches, and enhances operational efficiency. The ability to define and enforce retention policies, establish comprehensive file plans, and classify records with retention labels empowers organizations to maintain an organized and secure repository of records.

eDiscovery and data holds

eDiscovery, short for electronic discovery, has become a critical aspect of legal and compliance processes for organizations. It involves identifying, preserving, collecting, and analyzing electronic information, typically in the form of emails, documents, and other digital records, as part of a legal or regulatory investigation. Microsoft offers a robust eDiscovery service within its Compliance suite, designed to help organizations efficiently manage and respond to eDiscovery requests. In this overview, we'll delve into the key features, benefits, and best practices for eDiscovery in Microsoft Purview.

The Microsoft Purview eDiscovery service is a component of the broader Microsoft 365 Purview Center. It provides organizations with the tools and capabilities required to manage the discovery process efficiently and in compliance with legal and regulatory requirements. The service empowers organizations to do the following:

- Identify and preserve relevant data
- Collect and review electronic records
- Apply legal holds to prevent data deletion
- Export data for legal review and production

The key features and benefits of eDiscovery are as follows:

- **Data identification and preservation**: eDiscovery in Microsoft Compliance allows organizations to identify and preserve relevant data across Microsoft 365 services, including Exchange Online, SharePoint, OneDrive, and Microsoft Teams. This ensures that potentially critical information is retained, preventing accidental data loss.
- **Legal holds**: Organizations can apply legal holds to specific data, ensuring that it cannot be deleted or modified. Legal holds are crucial to maintaining data integrity during litigation or investigations.
- **Advanced search and filtering**: The service offers powerful search and filtering capabilities, allowing users to pinpoint specific documents, emails, or other electronic records. It helps streamline the identification process, reducing the volume of data that needs to be reviewed.

- **Review and export tools**: eDiscovery includes built-in review and export tools to facilitate legal reviews. Users can collaboratively review and tag documents for relevance or privilege. The service supports exporting data in various formats for use in legal proceedings.
- **Integration with Microsoft 365**: eDiscovery seamlessly integrates with Microsoft 365 services, making it easier to manage and discover data within the Microsoft ecosystem. This integration ensures a consistent and comprehensive approach to eDiscovery.
- **Audit and reporting**: Robust auditing and reporting features enable organizations to track eDiscovery activities, ensuring compliance and transparency throughout the process.
- **Scalability and cost-efficiency**: Microsoft Compliance eDiscovery is scalable, making it suitable for organizations of all sizes. It also offers cost-efficiency by eliminating the need for third-party eDiscovery solutions.

While Microsoft Search is indeed a powerful tool, it understandably restricts the content it displays to what you have regular access to in your daily work. When conducting investigations that require delving into locations not typically accessible, such as multiple user mailboxes, additional tools and permissions become essential. This is precisely where the eDiscovery tools step in.

Within Microsoft 365, several tools cater to the needs of investigations, including the following:

- eDiscovery (Standard)
- eDiscovery Premium
- Content Search
- User Data Search
- Microsoft Priva Subject Rights Requests

Content Search serves as the foundation for every eDiscovery tool, functioning as the primary search interface. However, it's the standard eDiscovery and premium eDiscovery that truly shine, providing extra features that go beyond basic search capabilities. These enhancements make them invaluable resources when conducting comprehensive investigations.

The difference between eDiscovery Standard and Premium and their distinct features are shown in the following list:

- eDiscovery (Standard):
  - Search and export
  - Legal hold
  - Case management
  - Search for data (with Content Search)

- eDiscovery Premium (additional features to eDiscovery Standard):
    - Advanced indexing
    - Legal hold notification
    - Analytics
    - Custodian management
    - Predictive coding models
    - Tagging

To access eDiscovery services in Microsoft Purview, users must have one of the following licenses:

- Microsoft 365 E3 (for eDiscovery Standard)
- Microsoft 365 E5 (for eDiscovery Premium features)

To enable individuals to make the most of eDiscovery tools within the Microsoft Purview compliance portal, it's vital to grant them the necessary permissions. The most straightforward method is to include them in the relevant role groups on the Permissions page of the compliance portal. There are two administrator subgroups:

- **eDiscovery Manager**: Those belonging to the eDiscovery Manager subgroup are equipped to use eDiscovery search tools to search various content locations within the organization. They possess the ability to execute a range of search-related actions, including previewing and exporting search results. It's important to note that eDiscovery Managers are limited to accessing and managing only the cases they have personally created, with no access to cases originating from other eDiscovery Managers.
- **eDiscovery Administrator**: This role is a notch above the eDiscovery Manager, and the members of this group inherently possess the same content search and case management capabilities. They can access the full roster of cases listed on the eDiscovery (Standard) and eDiscovery Premium pages within the compliance portal. A noteworthy distinction is that only eDiscovery Administrators hold the authority to remove members from an eDiscovery case. This capability is exclusive to them, as users within the eDiscovery Manager subgroup lack this power, even if they initiated the case.

Add users to the eDiscovery Manager group in the following way:

1. Log on to **Microsoft Purview Admin Center**
2. Click on **Roles and scopes** and select **Permissions**

3. Under **Microsoft Role Group** for Microsoft Purview solutions, in the search field, type **eDiscovery** and select the **eDiscovery Manager** built-in group:

Figure 11.20 – eDiscovery built-in admin group

4. In the new open windows, click on **Edit:**

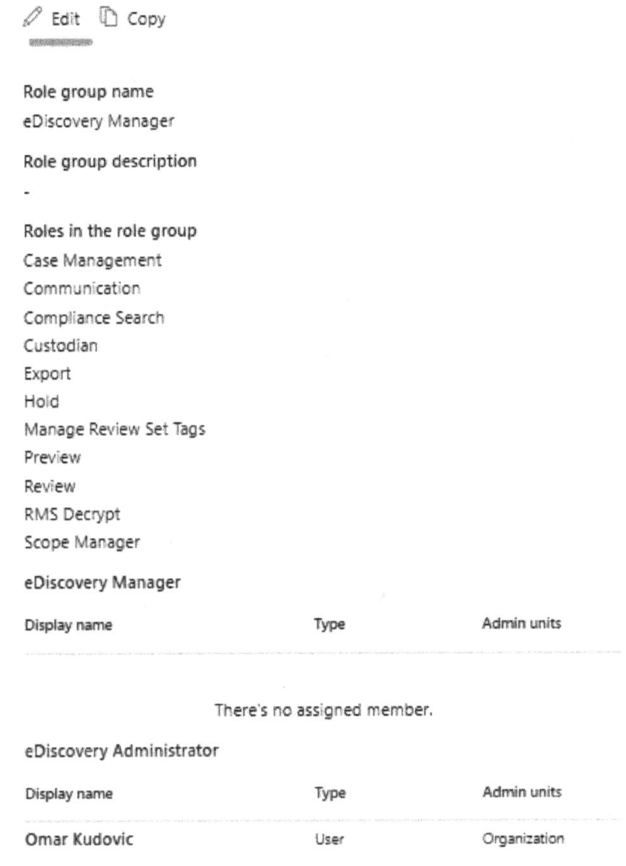

Figure 11.21 – Edit eDiscovery Manager group

5. Add users to **eDiscovery Manager** and the **eDiscovery Administrator** groups. Review and save:

eDiscovery Manager

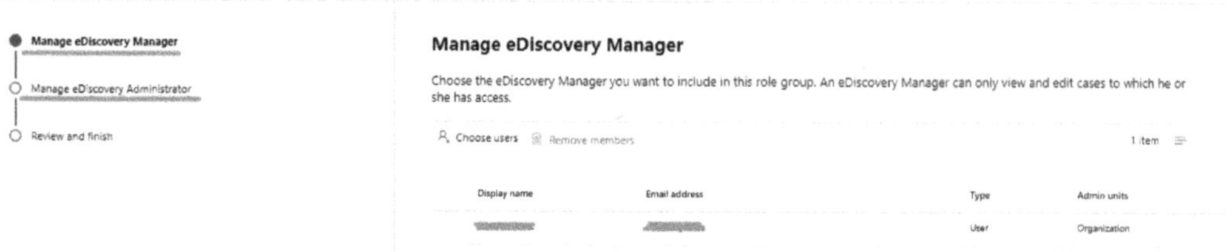

Figure 11.22 – Add users to eDiscovery groups

It's important to note that various administrator groups within Microsoft Purview come with distinct sets of options and capabilities. The following table offers a comprehensive overview of administrative rights within the realm of eDiscovery:

Role	eDiscovery Manager and Administrators	Compliance Administrators	Organization Administrator
Case Management	Yes	Yes	Yes
Export	Yes	No	No
Hold	Yes	Yes	Yes
Preview	Yes	No	No
Search and Purge	No	No	Yes
Compliance Search	Yes	Yes	Yes
Review	Yes	No	Yes
Custodian	Yes	No	No

Table 11.1 – eDiscovery roles

Once administrative permissions are defined and the necessary licenses are in place, let's explore the configuration process for both eDiscovery Standard and Premium services. This will enable organizations to harness these services to meet their specific eDiscovery and compliance needs effectively. These services play a pivotal role in enabling your organization to manage eDiscovery tasks and investigations efficiently, ensuring compliance and streamlined processes.

Configuring eDiscovery Standard and Premium

We'll begin our journey by creating and configuring an **eDiscovery Standard Hold** case in the Microsoft Purview Admin Center. This is a fundamental step in ensuring that your organization can effectively manage and retain data as part of the eDiscovery process. The process involves several key stages, including the following:

- **Case creation**: You'll initiate the process by creating a new eDiscovery Standard Hold case. This case will serve as the container for the data that need to be preserved during the investigation or legal matter.
- **Data identification**: Within the case, you'll define the criteria for identifying the data to be placed on legal hold. This could include specifying data sources, search terms, or other relevant parameters.
- **Legal hold implementation**: You'll implement legal holds on the identified data to ensure it cannot be altered or deleted. This is a critical step in preserving the integrity of the information throughout the eDiscovery process.
- **Case management**: The case itself will be managed within the eDiscovery Standard service, allowing for the efficient organization and tracking of the data associated with the specific investigation or legal matter.
- **Data review and export**: As part of the case management process, you'll configure workflows for reviewing and tagging data within the case. Once the necessary data have been identified and reviewed, you'll establish procedures for exporting these data for legal review and production.
- **Ongoing monitoring**: It's essential to set up mechanisms for ongoing monitoring and reporting within the eDiscovery Standard service. This ensures that the eDiscovery process remains compliant with legal and regulatory requirements and provides insights into the progress of the investigation.
- **Compliance updates**: Given the evolving nature of legal and regulatory standards, it's vital to continuously assess and update your eDiscovery Standard Hold case configuration to align with these changing requirements.

By taking a methodical and well-planned approach to creating and configuring your eDiscovery Standard Hold case, your organization can confidently address legal and compliance challenges, ensuring that data are preserved and managed appropriately throughout the eDiscovery process.

Perform the following steps for configuration:

1. Log on to the Microsoft Purview Admin portal and click on **eDiscovery**.

2. Select the **Standard** option:

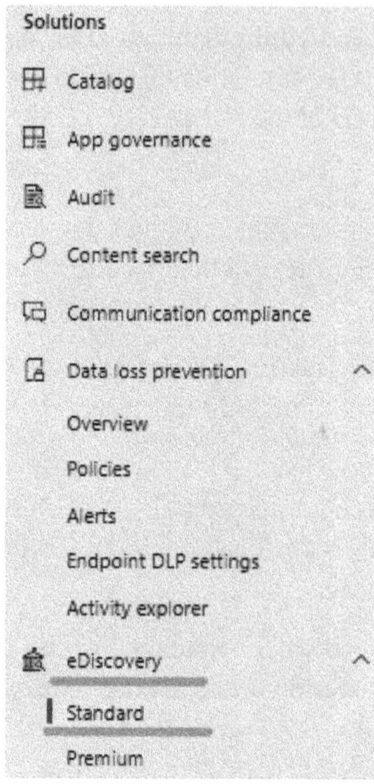

Figure 11.23 – eDiscovery portal

3. Click on **Create a case** and provide a name and description for a new case:

Figure 11.24 – Create a new eDiscovery case

4. Click on a newly created case in the portal and define the following options:

- Search
- Hold
- Exports
- Settings

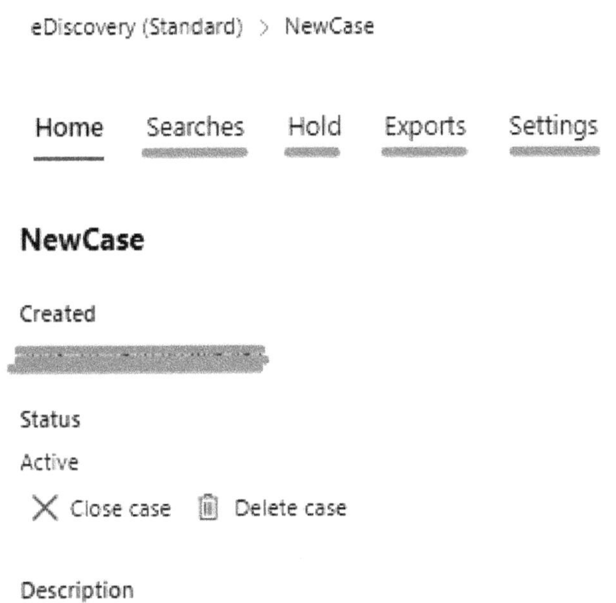

Figure 11.25 – New case setting

5. In the Search section, click on **New Search** and provide the **Name and destination**.
6. Define **Location** for search and users or group for a new case.

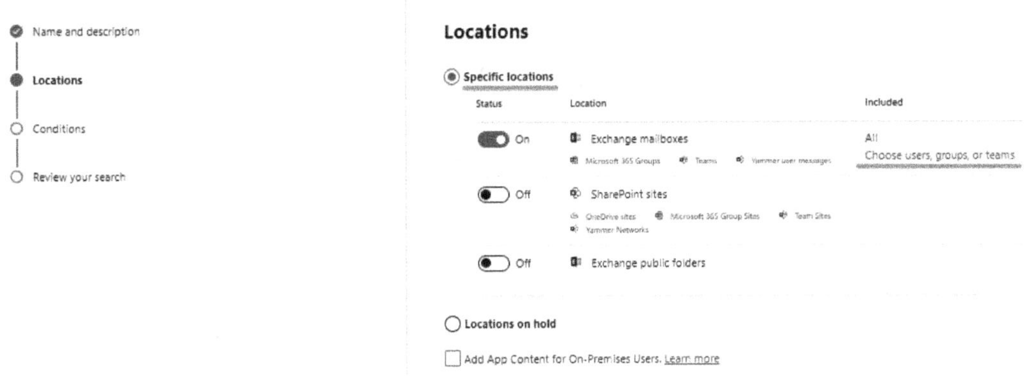

Figure 11.26 – Define the location in the search case

7. Define search conditions by using Query Builder or KQL editor and **Add condition**:

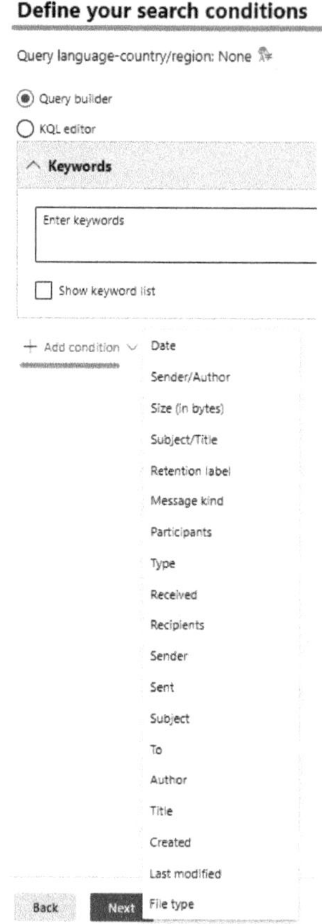

Figure 11.27 – Define search conditions

8. Review and create a **New Search**. After creating **New Search**, let's create **New Hold** for our case:
9. Click on the **Hold** option and select **Create**, provide a **Name** and **Description** for the new **Hold**:

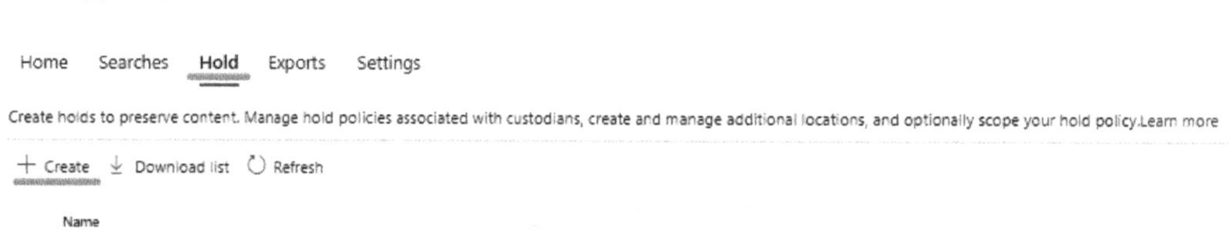

Figure 11.28 – Create a new Hold

10. Choose a location and define the **Query** for the **New Hold**:

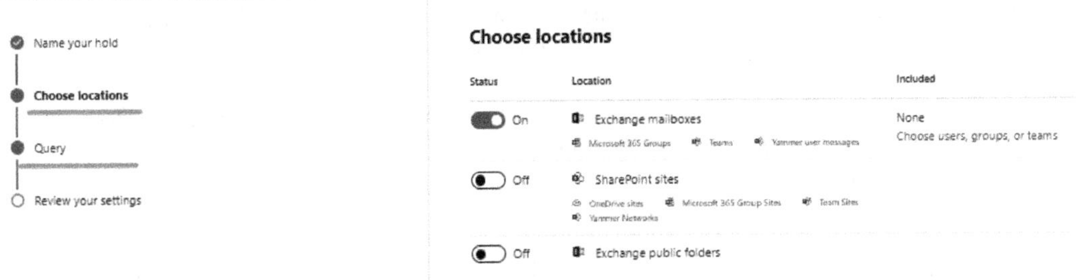

Figure 11.29 – Choose a location and define the query

11. Review and create.

If you want to select who can access your new case, click on **Settings** in your case and select additional users or admins who can access all information.

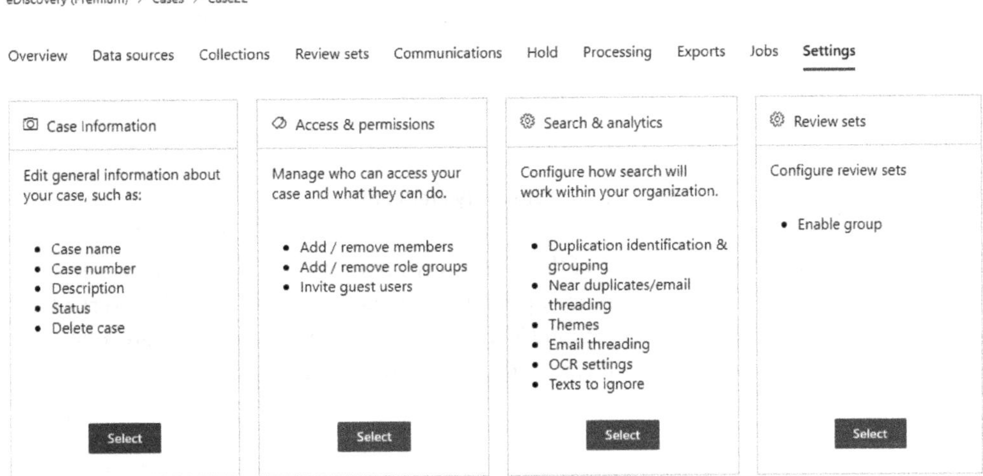

Figure 11.30 – Define access and permissions for a new case

Creating an eDiscovery Premium case is the next step in unlocking the advanced capabilities of Microsoft Purview for managing comprehensive eDiscovery requirements. Let's explore how to initiate and configure eDiscovery Premium cases, highlighting the key distinctions when compared to the **Standard** option.

Creating and configuring eDiscovery premium cases

Create a new eDiscovery Premium case with access to Microsoft Purview Admin Center. Begin by logging into Microsoft Purview Admin Center using the administrative credentials with the necessary permissions for creating and managing eDiscovery Premium cases:

- **Navigate to eDiscovery Premium**: Within the Admin Center, locate and select the eDiscovery Premium section. This is where you'll kickstart the process of setting up and configuring Premium eDiscovery cases.
- **Create a new eDiscovery Premium case**: Look for the option to create a new eDiscovery Premium case. This involves providing essential case details, such as the case name, description, and any pertinent information relevant to the case's context. Clear documentation is key for a well-organized case.

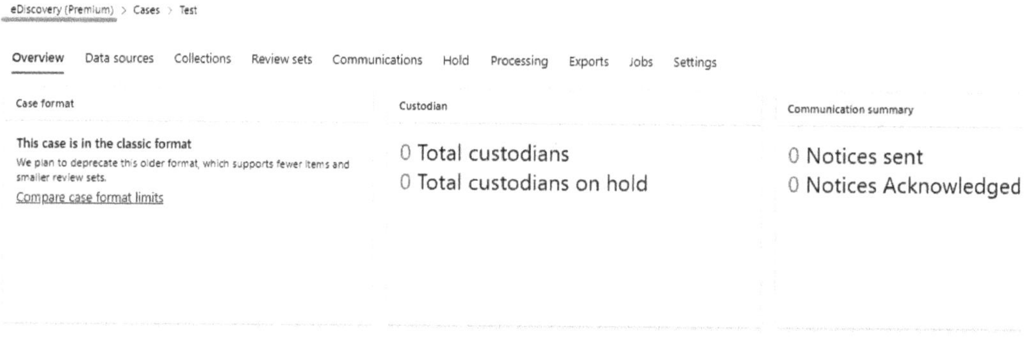

Figure 11.31 – eDiscovery Premium

- **Define case scope**: Specify the scope of the eDiscovery Premium case. This includes selecting the data sources and locations to be encompassed within the case. Premium eDiscovery often covers a broader range of sources, including Microsoft 365 services (Exchange, SharePoint, and OneDrive), as well as the ability to integrate data from non-Microsoft sources.

- Open a **New Case** in eDiscovery Premium and select **Data sources** and define new **Data sources**:

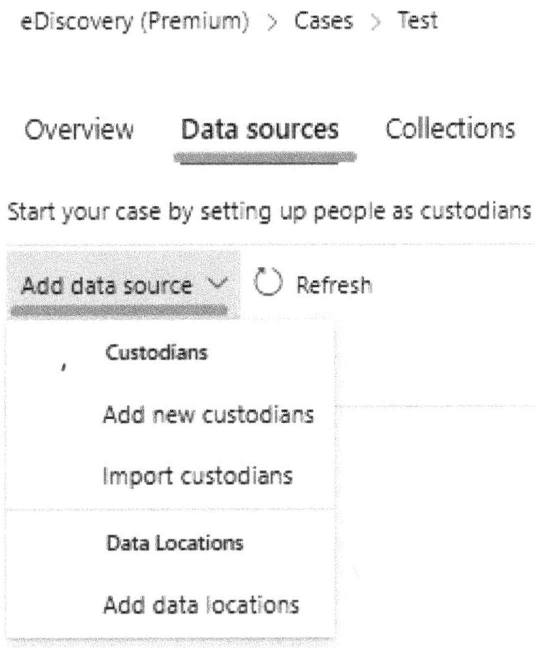

Figure 11.32 – Add data source

- **Set legal holds**: Just like with the Standard cases, implement legal holds on the selected data sources within the Premium case. Legal holds serve the crucial purpose of preserving data integrity throughout the eDiscovery process. Ensure that you're well-versed in the specific legal requirements and parameters of your case to set holds accurately.
- **Advanced search capabilities**: One of the key distinctions in eDiscovery Premium is the availability of advanced search capabilities. Configure search criteria that align with your investigative objectives, which can include intricate search terms, conditions, and filtering options. These advanced features can help streamline the search process and reduce the volume of data to be reviewed.
- **Review and tagging workflows**: Implement workflows for the review and tagging of data. Premium eDiscovery facilitates more sophisticated review processes, enabling users to efficiently categorize and mark data for further action.
- **Data export procedures**: Set up procedures to export data for legal review and production, such as the Standard option. Specify the format, delivery method, and intended recipients for the exported data.

- **Monitoring and reporting**: Leverage robust monitoring and reporting mechanisms to stay informed about the status and progress of your eDiscovery Premium case. These tools are indispensable for maintaining transparency and compliance with legal and regulatory standards.
- **Configure settings**: There are more options in eDiscovery Premium, as you can see in the following screenshot:

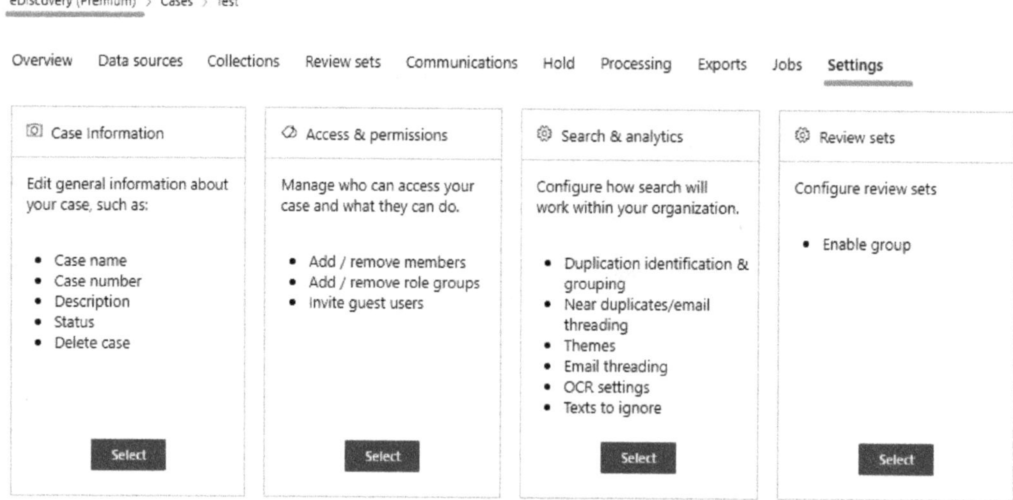

Figure 11.33 – Settings in eDiscovery Premium

By following these steps, your organization can fully harness the advanced capabilities of **eDiscovery Premium** cases, efficiently manage complex investigations, and ensure alignment with legal and regulatory requirements. The ability to integrate a broader range of data sources, coupled with advanced search and review functionalities, makes eDiscovery Premium a powerful tool for addressing intricate eDiscovery demands.

Auditing and alerts

Microsoft Purview's extensive set of auditing and alerting capabilities has been meticulously designed to equip organizations with the essential tools required for the proficient management of logs, vigilant tracking of data access, and swift response to security incidents. These capabilities are of paramount importance in upholding the integrity of data, ensuring compliance with regulatory standards, and establishing a formidable defense against potential security threats.

In this overview, we will take on a deeper exploration of these critical features and delve into the best practices that govern the domains of auditing and alerting within the Microsoft Purview ecosystem. Auditing within Microsoft Purview is grounded in its meticulous Audit Logs. These logs are digital records that capture a comprehensive spectrum of user activities across the platform's multifaceted services. Whether it's interactions with SharePoint, OneDrive, Exchange, or other services, these logs serve as the vigilant guardians of data access and utilization. Their comprehensive data trail is indispensable for gaining insights into the who, what, and when of data interactions.

Central to this auditing framework is the Security and Compliance Center, a user-friendly interface that empowers administrators to configure audit policies, scrutinize audit reports, and establish timely alerts for specific events. The Center acts as the nucleus from which organizations derive both information and actionable insights, ensuring proactive responses to critical activities within their environment.

To manage the substantial data generated through auditing effectively, Microsoft Purview has introduced **data retention policies**. These policies enable organizations to stipulate the duration for which audit logs should be preserved. This capability is pivotal in maintaining compliance with regulatory retention requirements and supporting in-depth forensic investigations. Augmenting the auditing toolkit is the integration of **advanced threat protection** features. These encompass threat intelligence and advanced security management, elevating the effectiveness of auditing by identifying, pre-empting, and effectively mitigating security threats and vulnerabilities.

Before starting with audits, Administrators must have proper permission. To access audits and search through logs, these must be assigned to at least one of the following audit-related role groups:

- Audit Manager
- Audit Reader

Audit portal can be accessed in the following way:

1. Log onto the Microsoft Purview portal and select **Audit**:

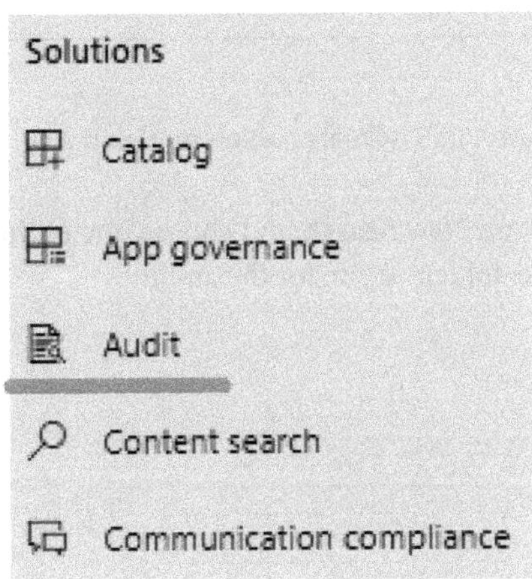

Figure 11.34 – Audit portal

2. Click on **Audit retention policies** and create a policy:

New audit retention policy

Create a policy to retain audit logs for up to ten years based on the Microsoft 365 service where the activities occur, specific activities in the selected services, and the user who performs an activity. Learn more

Policy name *

Enter a name

Description

Enter a description

Please choose users or record types to apply this policy to. *

Users

Search

Record type

Select record types

Duration *

Choose how long to retain logs that match this policy's conditions before they're automatically deleted. Learn more about licensing

Select duration

Priority *

Enter a number

Figure 11.35 – Create audit retention policy

3. For audit and search, click on **New Search** and choose one of the predefined reports. Define the time, users, groups, file, folder, or site for the audit:

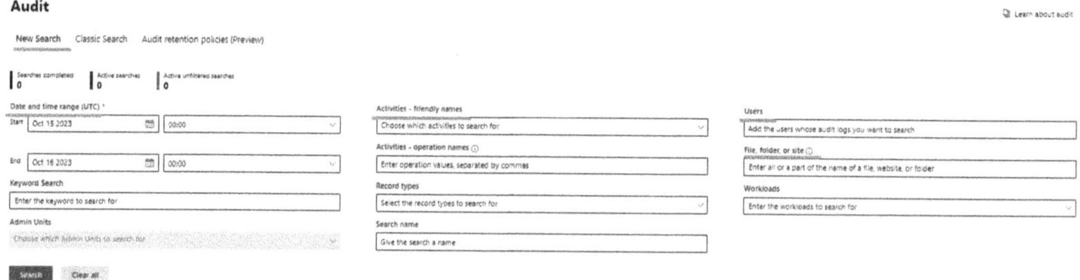

Figure 11.36 – New search in audit

Microsoft Purview's alerting capabilities are designed to facilitate prompt responses to significant events within the platform. Alert policies can be configured to cater to the organization's unique security and compliance needs. Rather than a *one-size-fits-all* approach, these policies can be finely tuned to ensure that the right individuals are promptly notified of critical occurrences.

Real-time alerts are a notable component of this framework. They can be triggered by critical events, such as, unauthorized access attempts, potential data breaches, or suspicious activities. The alerts can be delivered through various channels, including email and SMS, and can also be seamlessly integrated with other communication and incident response tools.

Moreover, these alerting capabilities extend beyond mere notifications. They facilitate incident response by enabling automated actions in response to alerts. For instance, in the event of a compromised account, automated responses can include temporarily blocking access, initiating investigations, and triggering predefined workflows.

In conclusion, Microsoft Purview's auditing and alerting capabilities form a robust and sophisticated framework that empowers organizations to take charge of their data security, compliance, and incident response. Through meticulous auditing and proactive alerting, organizations can navigate the complexities of modern data management with confidence and ensure they are well-equipped to face the ever-evolving landscape of potential threats and regulatory standards.

Summary

In summary, getting a handle on the ins and outs of auditing and records lifecycle management in the Microsoft 365 landscape is a critical need for organizations aiming to successfully navigate the intricacies of data governance and compliance.

Think of auditing as the supreme watchman, constantly keeping tabs on data-related activities to maintain data security and integrity. It offers a window into who's interacting with the data, what they're up to, and when these actions take place.

Record lifecycle management, on the other hand, assumes the role of a trusted custodian for an organization's regulatory, legal, and mission-critical records. It not only helps in meeting legal requirements and showcasing regulatory compliance but also streamlines the process of tidying up data that have served their purpose, enhancing operational efficiency along the way.

Arming yourself with these fundamental concepts empowers organizations to establish robust data governance, ensuring the safety of sensitive information. It also equips them to confidently tackle the ever-evolving challenges that come with data management in the digital age. This knowledge serves as the cornerstone for building trust, achieving compliance, and fostering operational excellence in a data landscape that is in a constant state of change.

We would like to thank you for reading all the chapters—We hope you did not skip any of the content ;-) This book provided an overview of the security, compliance, and governance features and capabilities of Microsoft 365 and covered numerous topics such as threat protection, information protection, data governance, compliance management, and security management. This book also explained how to get started with Microsoft Defender products, Microsoft 365 Security features, vulnerability management, eDiscovery, Purview solutions, and many more.

While the topics of Microsoft 365 security, governance, and compliance embrace multiple products and features, including them at the number, scope, and depth that we wanted simply was not possible for various reasons. The book would have had too many pages, and it would have taken too long to finish, and in this fast-paced, rapidly evolving, and changing information technology era, we emphasized and prioritized you—our esteemed readers and professionals—and strived to finalize the book as fast as possible, knowing you will need it to start embracing and learning about Microsoft 365 as fast as possible.

Security, compliance, and governance are essential aspects of any organization's digital transformation journey. Microsoft 365 offers a comprehensive and integrated solution that helps you protect your data, devices, and users from various threats and risks while also meeting your regulatory and legal obligations. Microsoft 365 enables you to leverage the power of the cloud, artificial intelligence, and automation to simplify and streamline your security and compliance processes and to gain insights and visibility into your security and compliance status. By adopting Microsoft 365, you can enhance your security, compliance, and governance capabilities and achieve more with less.

Index

A

C

D

E

N

O

P

Q

R

S

T

U

W

packtpub.com

Subscribe to our online digital library for full access to over 7,000 books and videos, as well as industry leading tools to help you plan your personal development and advance your career. For more information, please visit our website.

Why subscribe?

- Spend less time learning and more time coding with practical eBooks and Videos from over 4,000 industry professionals
- Improve your learning with Skill Plans built especially for you
- Get a free eBook or video every month
- Fully searchable for easy access to vital information
- Copy and paste, print, and bookmark content

Did you know that Packt offers eBook versions of every book published, with PDF and ePub files available? You can upgrade to the eBook version at packtpub.com and as a print book customer, you are entitled to a discount on the eBook copy. Get in touch with us at customercare@packtpub.com for more details.

At www.packtpub.com, you can also read a collection of free technical articles, sign up for a range of free newsletters, and receive exclusive discounts and offers on Packt books and eBooks.

Other Books You May Enjoy

If you enjoyed this book, you may be interested in these other books by Packt:

Microsoft Intune Cookbook

Andrew Taylor

ISBN: 9781805126546

- Set up your Intune tenant and associated platform connections
- Create and deploy device policies to your organization's devices
- Find out how to package and deploy your applications
- Explore different ways to monitor and report on your environment
- Leverage PowerShell to automate your daily tasks
- Understand the underlying workings of the Microsoft Graph platform and how it interacts with Intune

Mastering Microsoft 365 Defender

Ru Campbell, Viktor Hedberg

ISBN: 9781803241708

- Understand the Threat Landscape for enterprises
- Effectively implement end-point security
- Manage identity and access management using Microsoft 365 defender
- Protect the productivity suite with Microsoft Defender for Office 365
- Hunting for threats using Microsoft 365 Defender

Packt is searching for authors like you

If you're interested in becoming an author for Packt, please visit `authors.packtpub.com` and apply today. We have worked with thousands of developers and tech professionals, just like you, to help them share their insight with the global tech community. You can make a general application, apply for a specific hot topic that we are recruiting an author for, or submit your own idea.

Share Your Thoughts

Now you've finished *Microsoft 365 Security and Compliance for Administrators*, we'd love to hear your thoughts! Scan the QR code below to go straight to the Amazon review page for this book and share your feedback or leave a review on the site that you purchased it from.

`https://packt.link/r/1837638373`

Your review is important to us and the tech community and will help us make sure we're delivering excellent quality content.

Download a free PDF copy of this book

Thanks for purchasing this book!

Do you like to read on the go but are unable to carry your print books everywhere?

Is your eBook purchase not compatible with the device of your choice?

Don't worry, now with every Packt book you get a DRM-free PDF version of that book at no cost.

Read anywhere, any place, on any device. Search, copy, and paste code from your favorite technical books directly into your application.

The perks don't stop there, you can get exclusive access to discounts, newsletters, and great free content in your inbox daily

Follow these simple steps to get the benefits:

1. Scan the QR code or visit the link below

`https://packt.link/free-ebook/9781837638376`

2. Submit your proof of purchase
3. That's it! We'll send your free PDF and other benefits to your email directly

www.ingramcontent.com/pod-product-compliance
Lightning Source LLC
Chambersburg PA
CBHW081038220326
41598CB00038B/6911